Hands-On Application Development with PyCharm

Accelerate your Python applications using practical coding techniques in PyCharm

Quan Nguyen

BIRMINGHAM - MUMBAI

Hands-On Application Development with PyCharm

Copyright © 2019 Packt Publishing

All rights reserved. No part of this book may be reproduced, stored in a retrieval system, or transmitted in any form or by any means, without the prior written permission of the publisher, except in the case of brief quotations embedded in critical articles or reviews.

Every effort has been made in the preparation of this book to ensure the accuracy of the information presented. However, the information contained in this book is sold without warranty, either express or implied. Neither the author, nor Packt Publishing or its dealers and distributors, will be held liable for any damages caused or alleged to have been caused directly or indirectly by this book.

Packt Publishing has endeavored to provide trademark information about all of the companies and products mentioned in this book by the appropriate use of capitals. However, Packt Publishing cannot guarantee the accuracy of this information.

Commissioning Editor: Pavan Ramchandani
Acquisition Editor: Alok Dhuri
Content Development Editor: Ruvika Rao
Technical Editor: Pradeep Sahu
Copy Editor: Safis Editing
Language Support Editor: Storm Mann
Project Coordinator: Prajakta Naik
Proofreader: Safis Editing
Indexer: Rekha Nair
Production Designer: Alishon Mendonca

First published: September 2019

Production reference: 1270919

Published by Packt Publishing Ltd.
Livery Place
35 Livery Street
Birmingham
B3 2PB, UK.

ISBN 978-1-78934-826-2

www.packtpub.com

To my two great teachers in life: my mother, Chi Lan, and father, Bang.

In memory of my grandmother and my two dear grandfathers.

– Quan Nguyen

Packt.com

Subscribe to our online digital library for full access to over 7,000 books and videos, as well as industry leading tools to help you plan your personal development and advance your career. For more information, please visit our website.

Why subscribe?

- Spend less time learning and more time coding with practical eBooks and Videos from over 4,000 industry professionals

- Improve your learning with Skill Plans built especially for you

- Get a free eBook or video every month

- Fully searchable for easy access to vital information

- Copy and paste, print, and bookmark content

Did you know that Packt offers eBook versions of every book published, with PDF and ePub files available? You can upgrade to the eBook version at www.packt.com and as a print book customer, you are entitled to a discount on the eBook copy. Get in touch with us at customercare@packtpub.com for more details.

At www.packt.com, you can also read a collection of free technical articles, sign up for a range of free newsletters, and receive exclusive discounts and offers on Packt books and eBooks.

Contributors

About the author

Quan Nguyen is a data scientist and Python enthusiast. He has a dual degree in mathematics and computer science, with a minor in philosophy, from DePauw University. Quan is interested in scientific computing and machine learning and enjoys incorporating technology automation into everyday tasks through programming.

Quan's passion for Python has led him to be heavily involved in the Python community. He started as a primary contributor to the book *Python for Scientists and Engineers* and various open source projects on GitHub. Quan is also a writer for the Python Software Foundation and a content contributor for DataScience.com. He is currently pursuing a Ph.D. in computer science at Washington University in St. Louis.

> *I'd like to, first and foremost, thank my parents for their incredible support throughout the process of writing this book. None of this would have been possible without their help and encouragement. Also, a big thanks to the team at Packt: Ruvika and Storm, who offered great insights that drastically improved the quality of this text; my reviewers for their excellent comments; and all others who helped to make this work possible.*

About the reviewers

Luis Felipe Vera was born and raised in Caracas, Venezuela, where he received a degree in computer science from the Open National University in 2000. Subsequently, Luis Felipe completed a telecommunications specialization at Clodosbaldo Russian University and France Telecom in 2004 in Bordeaux, France.

Luis Felipe is the cousin of Blanca Vera Azaf. He is the creator of projects and applications with real-time capabilities in Django. Luis Felipe lives in Miami, Florida, with his wife, Susy, and their daughter and son, Gaby and Andres.

Dr. Gowrishankar S. is currently working as an Associate Professor in the Department of Computer Science and Engineering at Dr. Ambedkar Institute of Technology, Bengaluru, India. He earned his Ph.D. in engineering from Jadavpur University, Kolkata, India, in 2010, and an MTech in software engineering and a BE in computer science and engineering from Visvesvaraya Technological University (VTU), Belagavi, India, in 2005 and 2003, respectively. His current research interests are mainly focused on data science, including its technical aspects as well as its applications and implications. Specifically, he is interested in the application of machine learning, data mining, and big data analytics in healthcare. His Twitter handle is `@g_s_nath`.

Packt is searching for authors like you

If you're interested in becoming an author for Packt, please visit `authors.packtpub.com` and apply today. We have worked with thousands of developers and tech professionals, just like you, to help them share their insight with the global tech community. You can make a general application, apply for a specific hot topic that we are recruiting an author for, or submit your own idea.

Table of Contents

Preface — 1

Section 1: The Basics of PyCharm

Chapter 1: Introduction to PyCharm - the Most Popular IDE for Python — 9
  The background of PyCharm — 10
    The recent rise of Python — 10
    The philosophy of IDEs — 13
    PyCharm as a Python IDE — 14
  PyCharm – an essential part of the Python community — 17
  Differentiating PyCharm from other editors/IDEs — 17
  Understanding the Professional and Community editions — 19
    Prices and licensing — 19
    Further support in the Professional Edition — 21
    Choosing a PyCharm edition that fits your profession — 22
  Summary — 23
  Questions — 24
  Further reading — 24

Chapter 2: Installing and Configuring PyCharm — 27
  Technical requirements — 28
  Downloading, installing, and registration — 28
    System requirements — 28
    Downloading — 28
    Installing — 30
    License activation — 31
  Setting up PyCharm — 33
    General preferences — 34
      What is included in the settings — 35
      How to do it in PyCharm — 35
    Editor — 36
      What is included in the editor — 36
      How to do it in PyCharm — 38
    Keymap — 39
      The background of keymap — 39
      How to do it in PyCharm — 40
    Shortcut customizations — 41
  Getting started with PyCharm projects — 45
    Creating a project — 46
    Interacting with a PyCharm project — 48

Getting the source code from GitHub	51
Summary	52
Questions	53
Further reading	53

Section 2: Improving Your Productivity

Chapter 3: Customizing Interpreters and Virtual Environments	57
Technical requirements	58
Customizing the PyCharm workspace	58
Inside a project window	58
Navigating within a project	62
Panels in a project window	63
Installing packages	67
Moving panels within a project window	69
Creating a PyCharm project – revisited	72
Choosing a project type	72
Project-specific boilerplate code	74
Considerations about Community PyCharm	76
Virtual environments and interpreters	76
Understanding the concepts	76
Python interpreters	77
Virtual environments in Python	77
Virtual environments and interpreters together	78
Managing virtual environments and interpreters in PyCharm	80
Configuring the interpreter for a created project	83
Why does it matter?	83
Options in PyCharm	85
Importing an external project into PyCharm	86
Summary	89
Questions	90
Further reading	91
Chapter 4: Editing and Formatting with Ease in PyCharm	93
Technical requirements	93
Code inspection	94
Specifics of the code analyzer	94
Code inspection in a PyCharm project	94
Dead code	96
Unused declarations	96
Unresolved references	97
PEP 8 style suggestions	97
Customizable code completion support	99
The case for code completion support	100
How is code completion different in PyCharm?	102
Basics versus smart code completion	102

[ii]

Postfix code completion	105
Hippie completion	107
Intentions	108
Customizing your code completion engine	111
Match case	113
Sorting suggestions alphabetically	113
Showing the documentation popup in [...] ms	114
Parameter information	114
Intentions	115
Collecting runtime types	116
Troubleshooting	118
Indexing process	118
Power save mode	118
Out-of-scope files	119
Refactoring	**119**
What is refactoring?	120
Refactoring in PyCharm	123
Renaming	124
Inline variable	127
Extracting methods	128
Conversion between method and function	131
Exporting a function to another file	132
A dynamic approach to documentation	**134**
Docstrings – documentation for Python	134
Creating documentation	134
Viewing documentation	138
Quick Documentation	138
Quick Definition	139
Summary	**140**
Questions	**140**
Further reading	**140**
Chapter 5: Version Control with Git in PyCharm	**143**
Technical requirements	**144**
Version control and Git essentials	**144**
What does version control mean?	144
Situations that require version control	145
Git and GitHub	**146**
Downloading Git and registering for GitHub	146
Setting up a repository	147
Add, commit, and push	147
Fork, clone, and pull requests	148
Branching and merging	151
Ignoring files	151
Version control in PyCharm	**152**
Setting up a local repository	153
The Version Control panel	153

Table of Contents

Add, commit, and push	154
Branching and merging	158
Ignoring files	159
Version control diagrams	159
Summary	**161**
Questions	**162**
Further reading	**162**
Chapter 6: Seamless Testing, Debugging, and Profiling	**163**
Technical requirements	**163**
Testing	**164**
Unit testing fundamentals	164
Unit testing in Python	165
Unit testing in PyCharm	167
PyCharm's run arrows	167
The Run panel in the context of unit testing	169
Creating unit tests with PyCharm	172
Tests for the Counter class	175
Debugging	**176**
Debugging fundamentals	176
Debugging in PyCharm	177
Starting a debugging session and the Debug panel	178
Placing breakpoints	181
Stepping functionalities	184
Watches	186
Evaluating expressions at all times	188
Profiling	**189**
Profiling fundamentals	189
Profiling in PyCharm	190
Summary	**194**
Questions	**195**
Further reading	**195**

Section 3: Web Development in PyCharm

Chapter 7: Web Development with JavaScript, HTML, and CSS	**199**
Technical requirements	**199**
Introduction to JavaScript, HTML, and CSS	**200**
Understanding the importance of HTML and CSS	200
Writing our code with HTML	200
Writing our code with CSS	202
Understanding the importance of JavaScript	203
Implementing web pages in PyCharm	**205**
Using HTML and CSS in PyCharm	205
Creating new HTML files	206
Including external files in HTML code	207
Viewing documentation	208

[iv]

Emmet	209
Viewing HTML output in browsers	210
Extracting HTML source code in PyCharm	211
Using JavaScript in PyCharm	212
Choosing the version for JavaScript	213
Hints about parameters	213
Debugging the code	214
Live editing	216
Specifying a framework for new applications	218
Summary	219
Questions	219
Further reading	220
Chapter 8: Integrating Django in PyCharm	221
Technical requirements	221
An overview of Django	222
Django and the idea of web frameworks	222
What makes Django special?	223
Django models	223
Admin access in Django	224
Django templates	225
Jinja	225
Django versus Flask	227
Django in PyCharm	228
Starting a Django project	228
Structure of a Django project	230
Initial configurations	231
Running manage.py and launching the server	232
Creating Django models	234
Making migrations	236
The admin interface	238
Creating a superuser and logging in	239
Connecting the admin interface to models	240
Creating Django views	244
Customizing the run/debug configuration	246
Making templates	247
Summary	250
Questions	250
Further reading	251
Chapter 9: Understanding Database Management with PyCharm	253
Technical requirements	254
Connecting to a data source	254
Working with a database in PyCharm	260
Working with SQL	260
SQL fundamentals	260
Using SQL in PyCharm	261

[v]

The PyCharm table view	264
Comparing and exporting query output	266
Diagrams for databases	268
Relational database	268
Diagrams for database objects	269
Diagrams for queries	272
Summary	272
Questions	273
Further reading	273
Chapter 10: Building a Web Application in PyCharm	**275**
Technical requirements	275
Starting a web project in PyCharm	276
Creating a Django project	276
Creating a Django application and models	278
Using the admin interface	280
Working with the Database panel	284
Making queries via Python code	286
Creating Django's list views	287
Creating Django's detail views	294
Forms and emails	297
Creating the interface for the share feature	297
Configuring Django emails	302
Deploying your web project	304
Hosting services	304
Amazon Web Services	304
Google Cloud	304
DigitalOcean	305
Heroku	305
Production-specific settings	306
Summary	307
Questions	308
Further reading	308

Section 4: Data Science with PyCharm

Chapter 11: Turning on Scientific Mode	**313**
Technical requirements	313
Starting a scientific project in PyCharm	314
Creating a scientific project in PyCharm	314
Setting up a scientific project	316
The README.md file	316
Installing packages	318
Running the code	318
Toggling Scientific Mode	320

Understanding the advanced features of PyCharm's scientific projects	322
The documentation viewer	322
Using code cells in PyCharm	323
Implementing PyCharm code cells	323
Working with CSV data	327
Using the CSV plugin	328
Summary	329
Questions	330
Further reading	330
Chapter 12: Dynamic Data Viewing with SciView and Jupyter	331
Technical requirements	332
Data viewing made easy with PyCharm's SciView	332
Viewing and working with plots	333
Viewing and working with data	335
Understanding IPython and magic commands	341
Installing and setting up IPython	341
Introducing IPython magic commands	342
Leveraging Jupyter notebooks	345
Understanding Jupyter basics	347
The idea of iterative development	347
Editing Jupyter notebooks	348
Jupyter notebooks in PyCharm	355
Summary	358
Questions	359
Further reading	359
Chapter 13: Building a Data Pipeline in PyCharm	361
Technical requirements	362
Working with datasets	362
Starting with a question	362
Collecting data	366
Version control for datasets	367
Data cleaning and pre-processing	368
Reading in dataset	369
Data cleaning	372
One-hot encoding	375
Problem-specific techniques	378
Saving and viewing processed data	385
Data analysis and insights	386
Starting the notebook and reading in data	386
Using charts and graphs	387
Machine-learning-based insights	392
Scripts versus notebooks in data science	396

Summary	397
Questions	397
Further reading	398

Section 5: Plugins and Conclusion

Chapter 14: More Possibilities with PyCharm Plugins	401
Technical requirements	402
Exploring PyCharm plugins	402
Opening the plugin window	402
Downloading and installing a plugin	405
Updating and removing plugins	408
Best plugins to use for your PyCharm projects	409
Using Database Navigator	409
Using LiveEdit	410
Using the CSV Plugin	411
Using Markdown	412
Using String Manipulation	413
Advanced plugin-related options	414
Required plugins	414
Installing plugins from disk	416
Developing custom plugins	417
Summary	418
Questions	419
Further reading	419
Chapter 15: Future Developments	421
Technical requirements	421
Miscellaneous topics in PyCharm	421
Using remote Python interpreters	422
Using macros	429
File watchers	433
Taking a step back	435
Improving your productivity	436
Web development with PyCharm	437
Data science with PyCharm	438
Moving forward with PyCharm	439
Using official documentation	439
Future updates and releases	440
PyCharm – the Educational Edition	442
Troubleshooting at a high level	443
Summary	444
Questions	445
Further reading	445
Assessments	447

Other Books You May Enjoy 465

Index 469

Preface

This book is divided into five long sections, each covering a fundamental idea about the usage of PyCharm. In the first section, a basic introduction to PyCharm is presented. The section addresses a number of notable differences between PyCharm and other common Python editors or IDEs, comparisons between the Professional and the Community versions of PyCharm, and a step-by-step guide on how to download, register, and set up your very own PyCharm distribution on a system.

Before we turn our attention to the specifics of the PyCharm software itself, let's first consider the organization of the book. Being a comprehensive guide to a hands-on, flexible understanding of how to use PyCharm in various situations, this book contains a wide range of topics regarding PyCharm. While working on a project, most of the time, you might only be interested in a specific topic or a particular functionality of PyCharm; you are most likely not going to go through the complete book to teach yourself all the features of PyCharm (however, you are more than welcome to do so!).

Who this book is for

Any beginner or expert user of the Python programming language looking to improve their productivity via one of the best IDEs for Python can greatly benefit from *Hands-On Application Development with PyCharm*. Throughout this book, a basic knowledge of Python programming is assumed, together with a beginner's understanding of popular applications of Python such as software engineering, data science, and web development.

What this book covers

Here, we will go through the structure of the book and examine which specific topics are covered and where. After this, feel free to jump around the book as you look for specific features or use cases of PyCharm.

Chapter 1, *Introduction to PyCharm - the Most Popular IDE for Python*, introduces the general idea of an **Integrated Development Environment** (**IDE**) and PyCharm's place among the rest of the IDEs for the Python language. This chapter also distinguishes between the two editions of PyCharm: the Community Edition and the Professional Edition.

Preface

Chapter 2, *Installing and Configuring PyCharm*, walks you through the process of downloading, installing, and registering your PyCharm software. Afterward, a brief discussion regarding how to customize the general configurations (including the theme, editor, and shortcuts) in PyCharm is included.

Chapter 3, *Customizing Interpreters and Virtual Environments*, discusses the process of managing and customizing your PyCharm workspace. This includes how to arrange a project window as well as choosing Python interpreters and virtual environments.

Chapter 4, *Editing and Formatting with Ease in PyCharm*, offers a detailed view of how PyCharm supports the process of developing Python applications. Specifically, we will look at the features in PyCharm that facilitate important tasks such as code inspection, code completion, refactoring, and documentation.

Chapter 5, *Version Control with Git in PyCharm*, includes a theoretical discussion about what version control is and why it is important. A hands-on tutorial on how to facilitate version control with Git in PyCharm is subsequently included, covering concepts such as adding, committing, pushing, branching, and merging.

Chapter 6, *Seamless Testing, Debugging, and Profiling*, focuses on the use of PyCharm to streamline important, yet often overlooked, processes in programming such as testing, debugging, and profiling. You will gain a theoretical understanding of what these processes are as well as hands-on knowledge of the features in PyCharm that support them.

Chapter 7, *Web Development with JavaScript, HTML, and CSS*, starts our discussion on PyCharm in the context of web applications. Here, we are concerned with the general idea behind the web development trio languages: JavaScript, HTML, and CSS. We will explore how these languages are supported in a PyCharm environment.

Chapter 8, *Integrating Django in PyCharm*, introduces Django, the premier web development framework in Python. This chapter discusses what the Django framework is intended to do while also explaining a number of its most important features in the context of a web application.

Chapter 9, *Understanding Database Management with PyCharm*, incorporates the process of database management into the current discussion. Specifically, we will see how PyCharm assists its users during the process of working with database sources and interacting with the data included in them.

Chapter 10, *Building a Web Application in PyCharm*, serves as the conclusion of the topic of web development with PyCharm. By walking through a hands-on example of developing a library application, we will combine everything we have learned so far on the topic, while also introducing a few more new Django-related concepts.

Chapter 11, *Turning on Scientific Mode*, introduces the topic of data science and scientific computing with PyCharm. By considering a number of central features that can improve our productivity when viewing and working with data, we will see the power and flexibility that PyCharm offers to its data scientist users.

Chapter 12, *Dynamic Data Viewing with SciView and Jupyter*, focuses on two of the most important features PyCharm has to offer in the context of data-related projects: the SciView panel and support for Jupyter notebooks. While some programmers might assume that we will lose the ability to work with Jupyter when using an IDE, it is not the case with PyCharm, as we will see in this chapter.

Chapter 13, *Building a Data Pipeline in PyCharm*, plays a conclusory role for the topic of data science. Here, we will use our knowledge from the last few chapters to explore a real-life dataset, thus gaining hands-on experience of building a data pipeline, which is one of the most important jobs of data scientists in the industry.

Chapter 14, *More Possibilities with PyCharm Plugins*, discusses in detail and goes through some of the most popular plugins for PyCharm. What we can get out of PyCharm does not necessarily end with its built-in features; some of the time, we are able to leverage external plugins that we can add on to our current PyCharm software.

Chapter 15, *Future Developments*, concludes the book by introducing a number of miscellaneous features in PyCharm as well as a general discussion regarding how Python programmers should use PyCharm.

To get the most out of this book

- Readers of this book should be familiar with the general syntax and practices found in Python programming, such as using variables, functions, and importing packages.
- An up-to-date version of Python is required before installing PyCharm. Python 3.6 and 3.7 were the current versions at the time of writing. You are also encouraged to have a distribution of Anaconda installed.
- A good internet connection is required for various parts of this book, where external tools and libraries are downloaded and used.

Preface

Download the example code files

You can download the example code files for this book from your account at www.packt.com. If you purchased this book elsewhere, you can visit www.packt.com/support and register to have the files emailed directly to you.

You can download the code files by following these steps:

1. Log in or register at www.packt.com.
2. Select the **SUPPORT** tab.
3. Click on **Code Downloads & Errata**.
4. Enter the name of the book in the **Search** box and follow the onscreen instructions.

Once the file is downloaded, please make sure that you unzip or extract the folder using the latest version of:

- WinRAR/7-Zip for Windows
- Zipeg/iZip/UnRarX for Mac
- 7-Zip/PeaZip for Linux

The code bundle for the book is also hosted on GitHub at https://github.com/PacktPublishing/Hands-on-Application-Development-with-PyCharm. In case there's an update to the code, it will be updated on the existing GitHub repository.

We also have other code bundles from our rich catalog of books and videos available at https://github.com/PacktPublishing/. Check them out!

Download the color images

We also provide a PDF file that has color images of the screenshots/diagrams used in this book. You can download it here: https://static.packt-cdn.com/downloads/9781789348262_ColorImages.pdf.

Code in Action

To see the Code in Action please visit the following link: http://bit.ly/2no4gi6.

Preface

Conventions used

There are a number of text conventions used throughout this book.

`CodeInText`: Indicates code words in text, database table names, folder names, filenames, file extensions, pathnames, dummy URLs, user input, and Twitter handles. Here is an example: "To follow this example, import the `Chapter04/Inspection` project into your workspace and open the `main.py` file, or copy and paste the following code into a PyCharm project."

A block of code is set as follows:

```
def main():
    print(math.sqrt(4))

if __name__ == '__main__':
    main()
```

When we wish to draw your attention to a particular part of a code block, the relevant lines or items are set in bold:

```
def distance(self, p):
    diff = self - p
    distance = sqrt(diff.x**2 + diff.y**2)
    return distance
```

Any command-line input or output is written as follows:

```
python manage.py runserver
```

Bold: Indicates a new term, an important word, or words that you see on screen. For example, words in menus or dialog boxes appear in the text like this. Here is an example: "PyCharm also provides a customized view that optimally organizes workspaces in a scientific project called the **SciView**."

Warnings or important notes appear like this.

Tips and tricks appear like this.

[5]

Preface

Get in touch

Feedback from our readers is always welcome.

General feedback: If you have questions about any aspect of this book, mention the book title in the subject of your message and email us at `customercare@packtpub.com`.

Errata: Although we have taken every care to ensure the accuracy of our content, mistakes do happen. If you have found a mistake in this book, we would be grateful if you would report this to us. Please visit `www.packt.com/submit-errata`, selecting your book, clicking on the Errata Submission Form link, and entering the details.

Piracy: If you come across any illegal copies of our works in any form on the internet, we would be grateful if you would provide us with the location address or website name. Please contact us at `copyright@packt.com` with a link to the material.

If you are interested in becoming an author: If there is a topic that you have expertise in and you are interested in either writing or contributing to a book, please visit `authors.packtpub.com`.

Reviews

Please leave a review. Once you have read and used this book, why not leave a review on the site that you purchased it from? Potential readers can then see and use your unbiased opinion to make purchase decisions, we at Packt can understand what you think about our products, and our authors can see your feedback on their book. Thank you!

For more information about Packt, please visit `packt.com`.

Section 1: The Basics of PyCharm

This section includes the first two chapters of this book. Mainly concerned with introducing readers to the idea of an **Integrated Development Environment (IDE)** as well as the details of PyCharm, this section will discuss various comparisons between PyCharm itself and other notable editors/IDEs in the Python community, in combination with the differences between the two versions of PyCharm available for download.

The first chapter will not go into any technical details of using PyCharm. Instead, we will analyze the purpose of using an IDE for programming projects and who (in terms of the level of competence, familiarity with Python, and so on) will benefit the most from using an IDE in general and using PyCharm specifically. The case will be made for choosing to use PyCharm over other editors and IDEs for your Python projects (given that some pre-conditions are satisfied).

The second chapter will then lay out a step-by-step guide that walks you through the process of downloading, registering, and setting up your PyCharm environment, which will put you in the optimal position to start any Python project with the full support of PyCharm.

This section includes the following chapters:

- `Chapter 1`, *Introduction to PyCharm – the Most Popular IDE for Python*
- `Chapter 2`, *Installing and Configuring PyCharm*

Introduction to PyCharm - the Most Popular IDE for Python

Welcome to *Hands-On Application Development with PyCharm*, and congratulations on taking the first step in exploring the powerful and dynamic functionalities that the most popular Python IDE, PyCharm, provides. Throughout this book, we will be familiarizing ourselves with the general interface of PyCharm, various customizations of PyCharm's functionalities to best support different types of projects, and options to integrate additional features into a base Python project.

This chapter first talks about the specifics of IDEs in programming and an overview of what PyCharm is and what its general options provide. We will then discuss the usage of PyCharm among the Python community and outline several reasons for PyCharm's popularity in the community. This discussion will help us focus on why PyCharm is such a great tool for Python programmers.

We will also be making comprehensive comparisons between PyCharm and other popular Python editors/IDEs, as well as between the paid Professional Edition and the free Community Edition of PyCharm. Any Python programmer is undoubtedly familiar with a number of different Python development tools, so these comparisons will offer a way for you to decide which edition of PyCharm is the right tool for you.

The following topics will be covered in this chapter:

- The purpose of PyCharm as a Python IDE and some notable details on its developing company, JetBrains
- The usage of PyCharm within the community and a breakdown of which professions tend to utilize PyCharm the most

- A comprehensive outline regarding the advantages and disadvantages of using PyCharm, in comparison to other Python editors/IDEs
- The differences between the Professional and the Community editions of PyCharm and the additional functionalities that the paid edition offers

On the other hand, if you have already decided that PyCharm is the Python IDE for you, feel free to jump to `Chapter 2`, *Installing and Configuring PyCharm*, to go through the installation and registration process. If you have already downloaded and successfully set up PyCharm on your system, you might want to begin at the second section of the book, starting from `Chapter 3`, *Customizing Interpreters and Virtual Environments*.

The background of PyCharm

Let's begin by discussing the topic of the book—PyCharm. First, we will discuss the Python language as it is the only reason why you would choose to use PyCharm in the first place. After this, it is important to start the conversation about PyCharm by pointing out the fact that there are considerable discussions surrounding the question of whether it is appropriate to use an IDE for Python programming.

Unlike many other programming languages, Python (as you already know) can be edited using just a simple text editor, due to the simplicity and readability of the code. You can then instruct a Python interpreter to execute a text file containing Python code and a Python program is thus complete.

Why would we want to use a heavy and complex IDE for Python to achieve the same result? In the following subsections, we will address this question by learning more about the idea of an IDE for Python and what specific problems PyCharm can help to solve.

The recent rise of Python

Python is one of the most popular programming languages out there (if not the most) by many standards and for good reasons. The user-friendliness, readability, and simple syntax of Python make it, arguably, the most accessible programming language. This is also why most colleges all over the world are redesigning their entry computer science courses to have Python as the main programming language.

The ease of learning the language leads to one of the most important factors regarding Python, which is its support community. If you are a beginner programmer, you are more likely to start out with Python, and then you will more likely make it your main programming language.

To understand how quick and efficient development in Python is, especially in comparison to other programming languages, we can turn to the creator of Python, Guido van Rossum, and see what he has to say. In a paper for the *OMG-DARPA-MCC Workshop on Compositional Software Architecture*, Guido van Rossum states that development in Python is estimated to be 3-5 times faster than that in Java, and 5-10 times faster than that in C/C++. Keeping this difference in mind, we can easily understand why Python is being used so ubiquitously.

You can find Guido van Rossum's complete essay here: `http://www.python.org/doc/essays/omg-darpa-mcc-position/`.

Obviously, the comparison between Python and Java or C/C++ is a weak one, since these languages are designed and used for different applications. However, it goes without saying that Python is relatively easier to write and develop programs with than the others, given its simple syntax.

All of these factors (and undoubtedly others) have resulted in a community that keeps growing stronger every day, taking in developers from all areas and of different backgrounds. Python libraries and packages are also being developed and released regularly, supporting a wide range of development tasks such as software engineering, video game development, web development, and scientific computing.

If you are a Python user, you are also likely to have noticed a sudden increase in Python usage in recent years. This is due to a new wave of data scientists and machine learning engineers who have recognized the advantages offered by Python over the long dominator of the field, R. In short, the Python community is growing like never before.

With numerous libraries and tools available, Python is seen as enticing by new programmers and developers who are looking for simpler ways to do various tasks, and thus, it generates more audience. I call this *the cycle of Python*, where its convenience attracts developers to use it for work, which in turn makes Python even more popular and easy to use. In fact, Codecademy (the premier online platform that offers interacting coding classes) noted recently that Python is the most popular language among their learners, and titled it *The Programming Language of the Year* (more details can be found here: `http://news.codecademy.com/why-learn-python/`).

Introduction to PyCharm - the Most Popular IDE for Python

The following chart also illustrates the growth of Python in recent years, in comparison to other popular languages (based on activities on Stack Overflow):

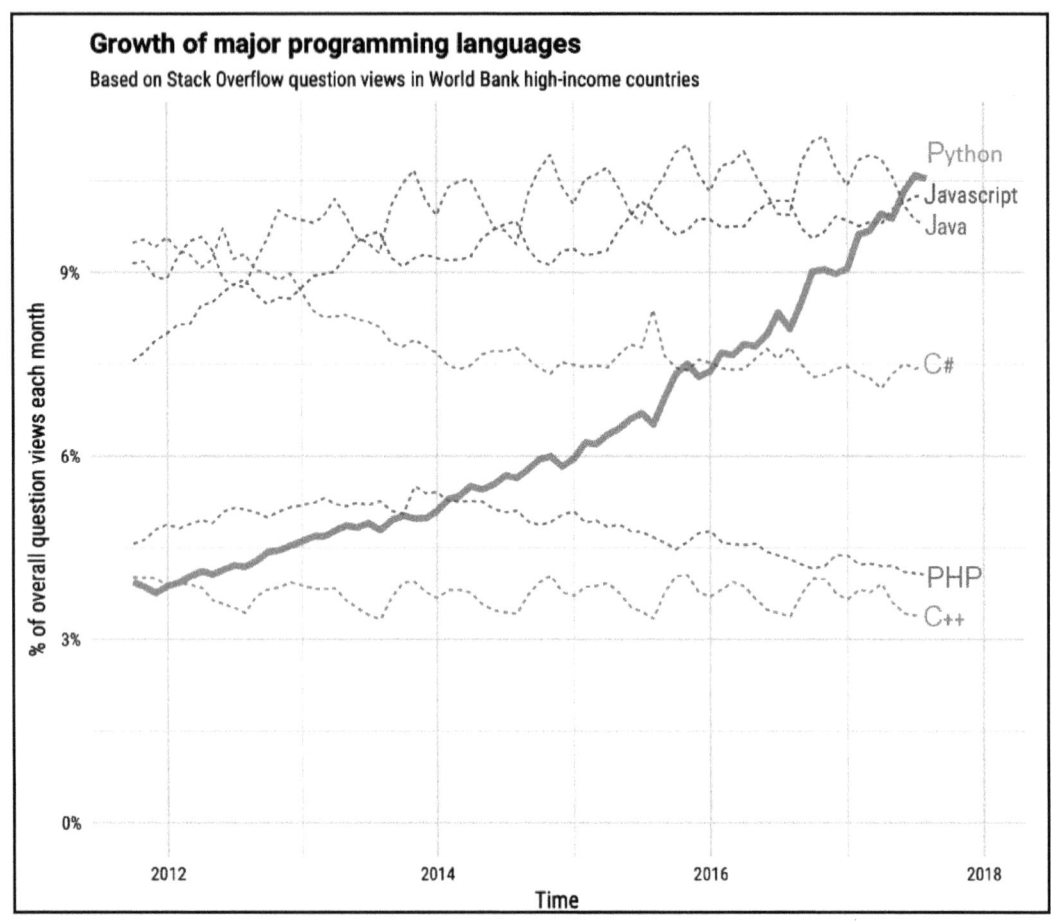

With the rise of Python observable, as stated previously, various development environments have been developed and enhanced to support its growing user community.

In the following sections, we will learn more about the background of one of these development environments, and the topic of our book—PyCharm—and why it has proven itself to be a top contender in competition with other environments.

The philosophy of IDEs

A good development environment is the first step to better productivity, and Python programming is no exception. While a beginner might be better equipped with a minimal, unintegrated environment such as Python IDLE (which comes with any Python distribution), Notepad++, Emacs, or Vim, once you have become sufficiently familiar with Python, you will undoubtedly benefit from the design and support of a good IDE.

First, let's define some terms. In the context of development environments (meaning how a programmer writes their code and develops projects), an editor typically indicates a simple, minimal text editor without any additional highlighting or aligning functionalities; on the other hand, an IDE is special software that provides such features. An intuitive comparison that I'd like to make is when we draw a parallel between programming and word processing. An editor would be a simple notepad, while an IDE would be Microsoft Word, Google Docs, or similar multi-function word processors. An IDE can have various features integrated, including syntax highlighting, automatic indention, debugging tools, and so on.

As mentioned previously, the development of some programming languages does rely heavily on the use of an IDE. This is especially true for languages where there is a considerable amount of what is generally known as boilerplate code, which is necessary for the whole program itself but does not add further logic to the program instructions. Boilerplate code is typically part of the syntax of the given programming language and is always present, regardless of what the program is designed to do.

It is in these boilerplate-code-heavy programming languages that an IDE becomes convenient, or even essential. IDEs help generate boilerplate code and appropriately place it around the core instructions that the programmer wrote, saving their time and helping them focus on the development process. This is, however, not the case for Python, a language that requires minimal boilerplate code and focuses on the actual logic of the program. In other words, once you have finished the general instructions of your Python program, it is most likely ready to be executed by a Python interpreter.

How, then, can a Python developer benefit from using an IDE? Writing Python code can be done in a sufficient way using a simple text editor, but there are other aspects of Python aside from writing code such as testing/debugging, version control, the management of environments and packages, and so on that can be boiler-plate-heavy and not quite straightforward. It is during these somewhat grinding tasks that a Python IDE can shine by streamlining them and helping developers focus on the development process.

Introduction to PyCharm - the Most Popular IDE for Python

With that said, it is not always recommended for a Python developer to use an IDE in their projects. Some have argued that relying on an IDE too much can make programmers forget, or altogether prevent them from learning, the core principles and syntax of a given programming language. Say you are asked to write a class in Python with various functionalities and methods. This is a great opportunity to take advantage of an IDE since you can import the general structure of a skeleton Python class with a single command in PyCharm (or in other IDEs). The only part left is to edit the inserted code with custom instructions according to our purposes. Throughout this process, the programmer does not need to remember, or even learn in the first place, the structure of a Python class and the syntax involved.

As such, there is a certain degree of trade-off being made when choosing to use an IDE to program, even in Python. However, you cannot argue with the fact that using a good IDE can truly improve your programming productivity, and if it enhances yours, you have every reason to use one. In general, a good strategy is to start off using a simple editor to familiarize yourself with the language and its core syntax structure. Once a good understanding of the language has been gained, you can then explore advanced functionalities that an IDE provides to see if they will be able to make you more productive. Being familiar with a text editor can also help you learn how to use an IDE faster, so that is more reason to employ this strategy.

PyCharm as a Python IDE

We have discussed the fact that an IDE for Python programming can be a solution to your productivity problem, given that you already have a solid familiarity and understanding of the language. Let's now turn our attention to PyCharm itself to see why it is a good IDE for us to learn to use.

Written in Java and Python, PyCharm was first introduced to the Python community in 2010, when the beta version was available for download. In 2013, the open source distribution of the software (called the Community Edition), which is free to download and use, was released. According to the developer, JetBrains, PyCharm operates on the following two core principles:

- **Improving productivity**: This is undoubtedly the most important feature of any good IDE. Again, PyCharm takes away most of the repetitive, uncreative aspects of Python programming, especially in large projects, helping programmers stay focused on the core development portion.

- **Real-time assistance**: It is no fun to complete a large project and realize afterward that there are inconsistencies and errors spreading all over the project code. PyCharm looks to address this problem by having an intelligent assisting feature that focuses on code completion, real-time checking logic for errors, PEP 8 code styles, and corresponding quick fixes, among other important functionalities.

From these two core principles, PyCharm also includes a number of higher-level features that help facilitate these principles. They are as follows:

- **Intelligent coding assistance**: As described previously, this real-time support system offers code-completion options, syntax and error analyses, as well as automated ways to refactor your code (which we will discuss further in `Chapter 4`, *Editing and Formatting with Ease in PyCharm*, in the *Refactoring* section). The smart search option also allows you to navigate through large projects seamlessly.
- **Streamlined programmer tools**: Again, programming is only a part of the actual development process; most of the time, programmers have to spend their time debugging, testing, and profiling their code, as well as managing the databases and packages necessary for their projects. With a straightforward GUI, PyCharm provides a way to achieve all of this in a way that is consistent, unified, and painless.
- **Web development options**: As a result of the fast-growing nature of Python, web development is becoming more and more common in the community. This is why PyCharm places an emphasis on good support systems for web development projects, specifically, various Python web development frameworks (Django, web2py, and Flask), as well as other major elements such as JavaScript, CoffeeScript, TypeScript, HTML, CSS, AngularJS, and Node.js. As mentioned previously, we will look at more details on the integration of these web development tools in PyCharm in section three of the book, starting from `Chapter 7`, *Web Development with JavaScript, HTML, and CSS*.

Introduction to PyCharm - the Most Popular IDE for Python

- **Scientific computing support**: The growth of the data science field has played an important role in the growth of Python itself, and Python is now the most common programming tool used in scientific projects (even more common than R). Notable functionalities included in PyCharm that facilitate scientific computing are the integration of IPython notebooks and an interactive console. The support for scientific computing in PyCharm is detailed in section four of the book, starting from Chapter 11, *Turning On Scientific Mode*. PyCharm also provides a customized view that optimally organizes workspaces in a scientific project called the **SciView**, which is shown in the following screenshot:

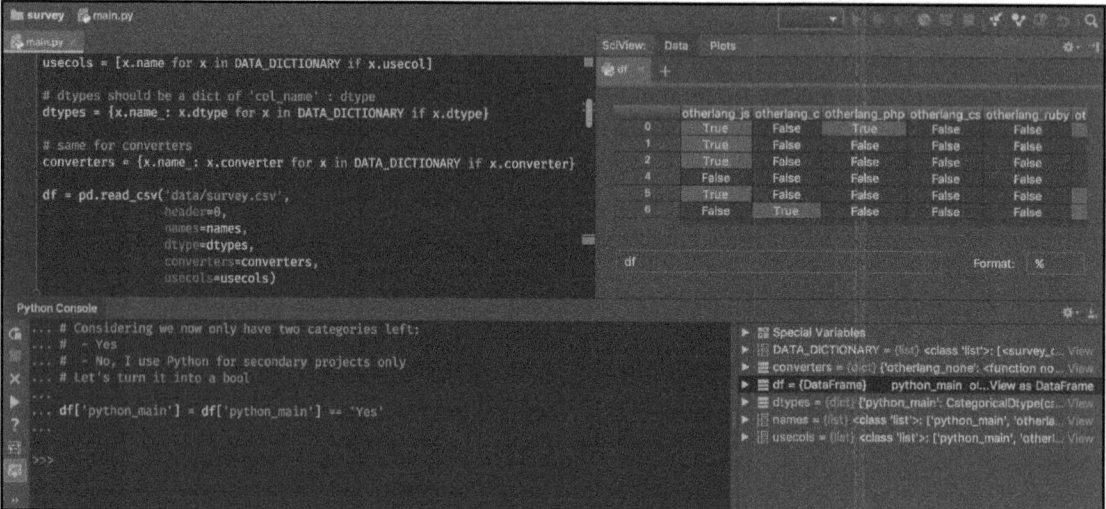

- **Visual debugging**: Two extreme stances that we programmers typically take in the topic of debugging in Python are: using print statements, which might prove to be too simple and limited in terms of expressing the changes taking place during the execution of a program, and using Python debuggers such as the pdb module, which can be too intimidating, and therefore inaccessible, for beginners. PyCharm offers its own solution to the debugging task—a GUI that visualizes different steps in the debugging process. In addition to being faster than pdb or any other current Python debugger, PyCharm's debugger allows us to view and customize changes in variables via watches and breakpoints.

Keeping the fundamentals of PyCharm's features and functionalities in mind, let's discuss the prevalence of the software in the Python community and see how its use is distributed across different professions.

PyCharm – an essential part of the Python community

In 2017, the Python Developers Survey (conducted by the Python Software Foundation and JetBrains) found that PyCharm is indeed the most popular development tool among all Python programmers in terms of editors and IDEs.

You can have a look at this survey here: https://www.jetbrains.com/research/python-developers-survey-2017/.

As observed from the **Editors and IDEs** section in the survey, both editions of PyCharm top the result poll for the question—*what is the main editor you use for your current Python development?* The results of the survey outlined that 17% of all developers used the Professional Edition and 15% used the Community Edition.

As we mentioned earlier, two of the largest subgroups in the Python community are web developers and scientific programmers. If we looked at editor/IDE use in these subgroups, we would see that the two editions of PyCharm are still the most dominant Python development environment; 30% of web developers use Professional PyCharm and 17% of scientists use Community PyCharm.

It is notable that, according to the results of the survey, other widely used editors/IDEs for Python programming are Sublime, Vim, IDLE, Atom, and Visual Studio Code. These are all viable development tools for Python programming but they might still fall short in comparison to PyCharm in a number of respects.

In the next section, we will look at a number of core differences between PyCharm and these popular editors/IDEs, and why they help PyCharm emerge as the most widely used.

Differentiating PyCharm from other editors/IDEs

We laid out several features of PyCharm in earlier sections, but it might be beneficial to repeat some of them here in comparison to other editors and IDEs in order to truly highlight the differences among them. We will start by looking at PyCharm and another powerful Python IDE (Spyder) side by side, since they generally set out to solve the same set of problems, and therefore, hold significant similarities.

In general, Spyder, like many other editors and IDEs, is a lightweight development environment. This results in less memory space, fewer system resources, and better speed in starting the software. PyCharm, on the other hand, comes as a fully supported IDE with a large set of functionalities, which will be heavier in storage and slower in execution.

In terms of support, Spyder has a simpler UI (which resembles that of MATLAB's). This can be beneficial for beginner programmers as well as people transitioning from MATLAB to Python. As for PyCharm, a comprehensive interface with different options for customization can be intimidating for unfamiliar programmers, but it can greatly improve productivity, as we have discussed and will learn first-hand in the second part of the book (`Chapters 3`, *Customizing Interpreters and Virtual Environments*, to `Chapter 6`, *Seamless Testing, Debugging, and Profiling*). However, since they are produced by the same company, users of IntelliJ IDEA specifically will also have no problem switching to PyCharm.

One previously notable way in which Spyder was superior to PyCharm was the support it offered for scientific computing, (**Spyder** short for **Scientific Python Development Environment**). The most commonly used support in Spyder is most likely the **Variable explorer** feature, where we have the option to inspect the value of the variables included in our program. The following screenshot demonstrates this **Variable explorer** feature of Spyder (please refer to this URL for more information: `https://www.marsja.se/wp-content/uploads/2016/01/Spyder_variable_explorer.png`):

However, this superiority Spyder had over PyCharm was only applicable until recently. PyCharm has been making some substantial improvements to its own support for scientific computing, and now it has deservedly become a serious contender to be the best scientific programming tool in Python with SciView and its other functionalities. If there is a good time to start using PyCharm for your scientific projects, then it is now!

One major difference between PyCharm and any other editor/IDE is, of course, the extensive support for complex aspects of programming from PyCharm such as version control with Git, testing and debugging, profiling, and so on. Again, the general strategy when it comes to these tasks is to first understand the foundational idea of each task and know how to do it manually before using PyCharm to automate and streamline that process. At that point, after using these support features, you will be able to appreciate the time and effort you are saving with the help of PyCharm.

Let's now take a step back and look at other editors and IDEs as well. Compared to other popular IDEs such as Visual Studio Code with the **PTVS** plugin (short for **Python Tools for Visual Studio**) or Eclipse with the PyDev plugin, PyCharm is better supported in terms of debugging and testing, web development frameworks, Jupyter Notebook and Anaconda, the real-time analysis of code, and refactoring options.

Chapter 1

Another factor that convinces Python programmers to choose PyCharm over Visual Studio Code is its support for emulating Vim, the famous Unix text editor. Specifically, PyCharm offers a plugin that simulates the complete experience of using Vim for hardcore users. For anyone who is looking to leverage PyCharm's powerful features but still wants to keep the old Vim key bindings and interface, they can find the optimal solution with PyCharm.

A more comprehensive comparison can be found in this report (compiled by JetBrains themselves): http://resources.jetbrains.com/storage/products/pycharm/docs/Comparisons_PyCharm.pdf. Additionally, to look at different support features between most (if not all) Python editors and IDEs, you can head to this Wikipedia page: http://en.wikipedia.org/wiki/Comparison_of_integrated_development_environments#Python.

Overall, the discussed features offered by PyCharm help it stand out from its competitors. While it is true that PyCharm will take up more memory space and appear uninviting to new programmers of the Python community, once you have mastered the general fundamentals of Python programming and familiarized yourself with different best practices, PyCharm will boost your productivity to another level.

I hope at this point you are somewhat convinced that PyCharm is a good IDE for Python programming. However, before heading to the website to download it, another topic that we need to discuss is the edition of PyCharm we will be using.

Understanding the Professional and Community editions

In this section, I will outline a number of the biggest differences between the two editions of PyCharm that are currently available and discuss the benefits of each edition with regard to different Python programmer subgroups.

Prices and licensing

Before you ask, yes, there are two editions of PyCharm—a free and a paid edition. The Community Edition is entirely free to download; in fact, as mentioned, JetBrains actually made the source code of the Community Edition available on GitHub in 2013.

Introduction to PyCharm - the Most Popular IDE for Python

 You can find its GitHub page at `http://github.com/JetBrains/intellij-community/tree/master/python`.

The Professional Edition, on the other hand, has to be purchased; a license is then provided to you so that you can actually use it.

The Professional Edition can be purchased at $89.00 for the first year, with that price decreasing in the following years. However, there are ways that you can qualify for a discount, or a free license, for the Professional Edition:

- If you are a student, a teacher, or otherwise work in an educational setting, you are eligible for free licensing to install PyCharm (in fact, all JetBrains tools) on your system. This applies to faculty and staff of training courses, coding schools, boot camps, and developer recognition programs (for example, active Microsoft Most Valuable Professionals, ASPInsiders, Java Champions, Google Developers Experts, and so on).

 Head to this website to find out more information and register for a free license: `http://www.jetbrains.com/student/` (be sure to use your organization-domain email while registering).

- If you are working on an open source project, chances are you also qualify for a free distribution of PyCharm, Professional Edition. There are, however, several conditions regarding your open source project that need to be met.

 Go to this website to read about these conditions and register for a license if your project meets all of them: `http://www.jetbrains.com/buy/opensource/`.

- Former students, start-up employees, and non-profit organization members are also eligible for various forms of discount when purchasing the Professional Edition.

In the following subsection, we will be going into details regarding the additional features that the Professional Edition includes but the Community Edition does not.

Further support in the Professional Edition

In terms of the actual software differences between the two editions of PyCharm, all functionalities available in the Community Edition are included in the Professional Edition. Simply put, functionalities in the Community Edition are a subset of those in the Professional Edition.

Firstly, all the core functionalities of the GUI that puts PyCharm ahead of the competition of other editors/IDEs are fortunately available in both editions. These include the real-time code analyzer, graphical debugging features, refactoring and testing, version control, the management of packages, and virtual environments. The following screenshot shows the intelligent code analyzer (which, again, is available in both editions of PyCharm) performing a code-completion task:

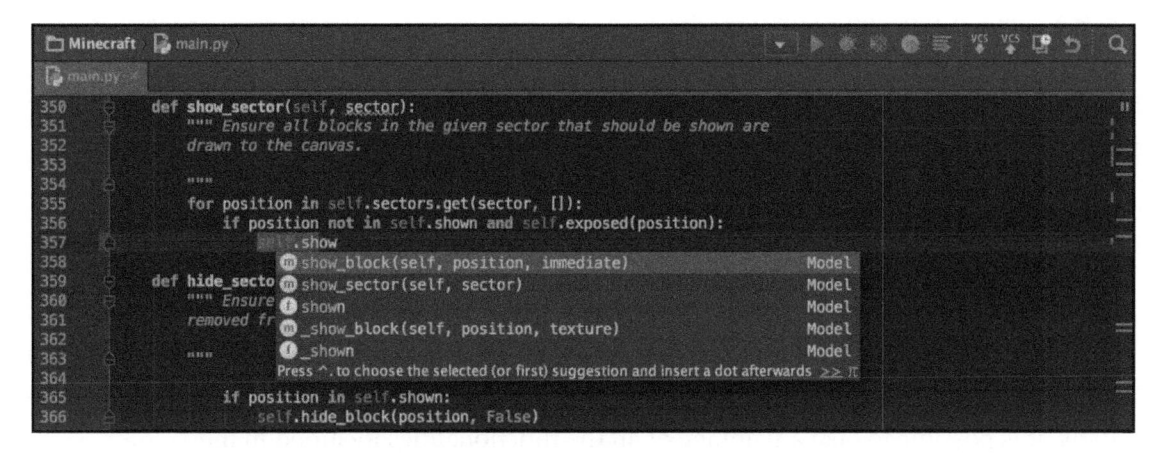

Specifically, this analyzer looks at what you are typing in real time and displays a list of possible ways to complete that line of code. This can be a function/method call (similar to the previous example), variable names, or a specific syntax. This feature allows us to write code in a faster and more accurate way.

On the other hand, almost all support for web development and scientific computing projects is only included in the Professional Edition. Web development tools such as JavaScript (and its debugger) or CoffeeScript, along with Python web frameworks such as Django, Flask, and web2py are not handled by the Community Edition. In a similar manner, features that facilitate scientific computing (most notably the SciView, a variable viewer for Pandas and NumPy data structures) can only be found in the Professional Edition.

In terms of the materials covered in this book, some sections and chapters will focus on a number of features that are exclusive to the Professional Edition. Note that these chapters do not discuss *only* exclusive features, as there are still features available in both editions that are worth considering. For example, in section four of the book (where we focus on data science tools), the scientific mode of PyCharm and the SciView are only included in the Professional Edition, but the integration of IPython and Jupyter Notebook is applicable to both editions. In short, whichever edition you are using, it might be beneficial for you to go through all the topics that you are interested in, even if they are not supported by your Community Edition.

> Additionally, a complete comparison matrix between the Community Edition and the Professional Edition of PyCharm (compiled by JetBrains) can be found on this site: `http://www.jetbrains.com/pycharm/features/editions_comparison_matrix.html`.

Choosing a PyCharm edition that fits your profession

So which edition of PyCharm should you choose? You may have figured out by now whether you should purchase the Professional Edition (given that you do not already have it), or simply use the free Community Edition. This will mainly depend on your own Python projects and what functionalities those projects need.

Firstly, it is possible to take advantage of all the functionalities included in the Community edition of PyCharm, whatever your profession is and whatever your project's focus is on. After all, every project can benefit from the intelligent coding assisting features and various other support features in Community PyCharm.

So, whether you are a software engineer, web developer, or data scientist, Community PyCharm will undoubtedly improve your overall productivity anyway, especially if you are working on a significantly large project.

It is important to note that, if you are working on a complex web development project that involves JavaScript, it is highly recommended that you use the Professional edition. Not only does Professional PyCharm have a powerful editing environment for JavaScript and other popular web languages, but it also offers a dedicated debugger for JavaScript, which will undoubtedly prove to be useful in your advanced web project.

Additionally, if your web applications interact with a database in a complicated manner, Professional PyCharm can help you simplify the process with the integration of various features and the visualization of data relationships in databases.

For example, say you'd like to add some data to a project by connecting to an SQLite database; you can do that in a fairly straightforward way in Professional PyCharm, as illustrated in the following screenshot:

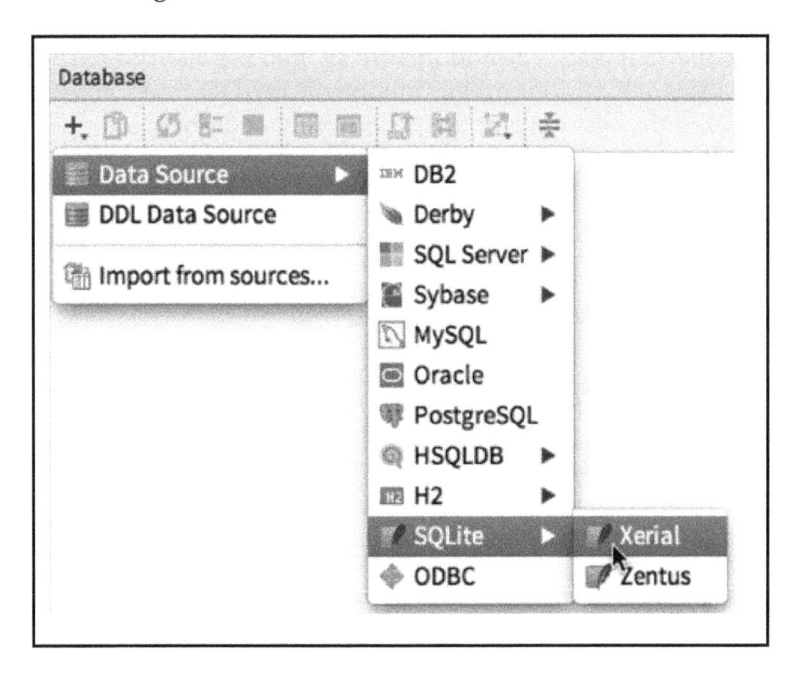

By the same token, if you are a data scientist working with a fairly complex stack, specifically, if your projects interact with a database, it might be beneficial to take advantage of the features of the Professional Edition. The integration of IPython and Jupyter Notebook might also be a great addition to your data science workflow, but these are web-based tools that are already well-supported by web browsers such as Google Chrome. Furthermore, if your whole pipeline is designed to revolve around the web-based interface of the software, it might be worth continuing using the bare-bones Jupyter platform without PyCharm's support.

Overall, the development work you do will dictate whether it is worth it for you to purchase the Professional Edition of PyCharm or not. A good strategy is to take advantage of the free 30-day trial of the Professional Edition to see if an upgrade from the Community Edition is worth purchasing.

Summary

In this chapter, we introduced the Python language itself, as well as the background behind Python IDEs in general, and specifically, PyCharm.

We also discussed the usability of PyCharm for Python programmers. Specifically, to be able to take full advantage of all the features and functionalities that PyCharm offers without becoming too dependent on the IDE, a programmer should first master the fundamentals of the Python language and its core syntax. We also looked at comparisons between PyCharm itself and various other Python editors/IDEs and the reason why PyCharm is considered the best development environment of them all.

Finally, we compared the two editions of PyCharm that are available for download: the paid Professional Edition and the free Community Edition. If you are working with large, complex projects with many moving parts (including database management, web development languages, and view-ability in scientific reports), then you will most likely benefit from using the Professional Edition.

In the next chapter, you will learn how to download PyCharm, set it up on your system, and configure its environment for your Python projects. This will serve as the first step in getting started with PyCharm, after which, we will start discussing the specific features PyCharm offers that this book covers.

Questions

1. Programmers typically develop their code with an editor or an IDE. What is the difference between the two, and which one is PyCharm?
2. Why do some think that an IDE for Python development might be inappropriate or unnecessary?
3. What is the recommended strategy for using an IDE for Python development?
4. What are some key features of PyCharm? Of those features, which give PyCharm an edge over other editors/IDEs?
5. What are the two editions of PyCharm? What are the key differences between them?
6. Who should use the Community Edition of PyCharm? Who should use the Professional Edition of PyCharm?

Further reading

For more information, you can refer to the following literature:

- *PyCharm, The Python IDE for Professional Developers*, JetBrains s.r.o. (https://www.jetbrains.com/pycharm/)
- *Text Editors vs IDEs for Python development: Selecting the Right Tool*, by Jason Fruit, (https://www.pythoncentral.io/text-editors-vs-ides-for-python-development-selecting-the-right-tool/)
- *Mastering PyCharm*, Quazi Nafiul Islam, by Packt Publishing (https://www.packtpub.com/in/web-development/mastering-pycharm)
- *Python Developers Survey 2017 Results*, JetBrains s.r.o. (https://www.jetbrains.com/research/python-developers-survey-2017/)
- *How does PyCharm match up against competing tools?*, JetBrains s.r.o. (https://resources.jetbrains.com/storage/products/pycharm/docs/Comparisons_PyCharm.pdf)

2
Installing and Configuring PyCharm

In the previous chapter, we looked at the most popular features of PyCharm and considered some of the reasons why a programmer may find using PyCharm useful and productive. This chapter, in turn, provides a step-by-step walk through of the installation of PyCharm on a computer system, including the process of registering for a license for the Professional edition.

As PyCharm is a highly customizable tool, a considerable amount of initial configuration is typically necessary, which this chapter will tell you about in detail. Productivity-related customizations such as keymap and shortcuts will also be discussed. Finally, we will talk about the process of downloading the code that is used as examples in various chapters of this book.

The following topics will be covered in this chapter:

- Downloading, installing, and configuring PyCharm in a computer system
- Customizing projects, keymap, and shortcuts within PyCharm
- Downloading the code repository used in this book from GitHub

Installing and Configuring PyCharm

Technical requirements

A computer system with access to the internet is all you will need to complete this chapter.

Downloading, installing, and registration

Let's start with a disclaimer—this section is solely concerned with the process of downloading and registering the PyCharm software in a computer system. If you have successfully installed and set up PyCharm on your computer already, feel free to jump to the next section, where we will be discussing some initial configuration for PyCharm.

System requirements

Before we walk through the process of installing PyCharm, we need to make sure that our system has the requirements to install and run the software. You can find the complete list of these requirements online, but the most noteworthy ones are as follows:

- We must have at least 4 GB of RAM (8 GB recommended)
- We must have at least 1.5 GB of disk space and 1 GB for caches
- We must have Python 2.7 or Python 3.5 (or newer) already installed

After making sure that our system satisfies all of these requirements, let's move on to the actual downloading process.

Downloading

The process of downloading PyCharm is similar to that of any computer software—after all, PyCharm is a piece of computer software. Let's get started:

1. First, head to JetBrains' website, where we can download PyCharm (http://www.jetbrains.com/pycharm/download/). The display will look similar to the following screenshot:

Chapter 2

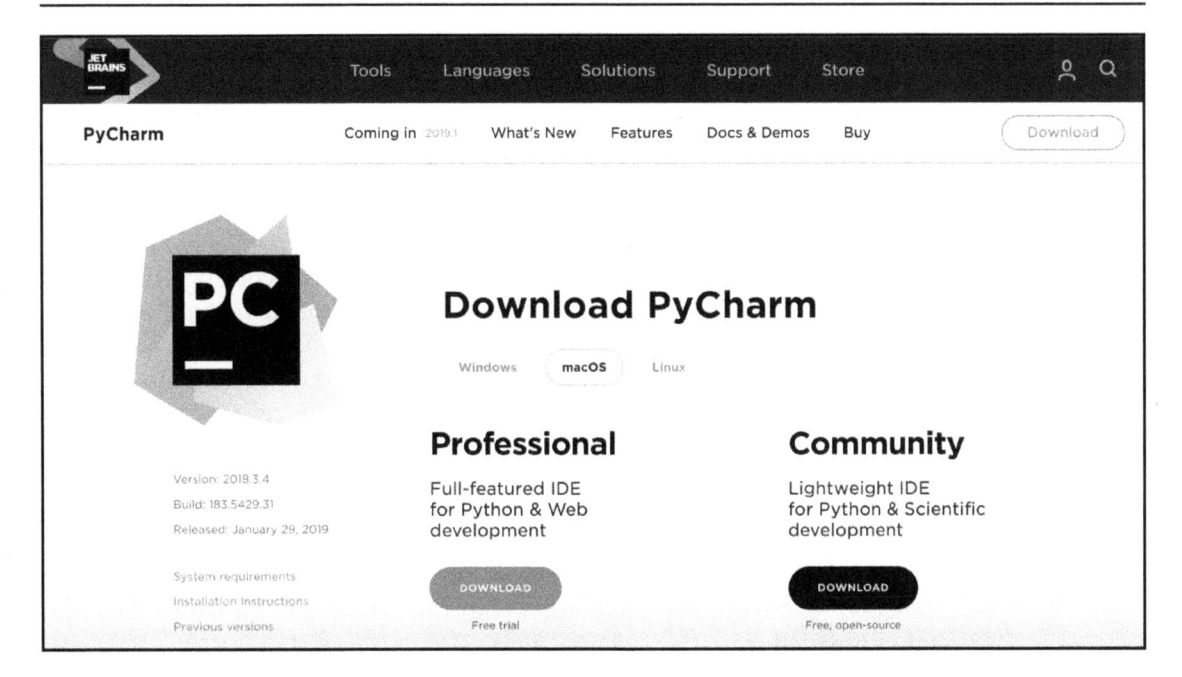

Downloading PyCharm

2. Notice the different options for operating systems below the **Download PyCharm** line. When you visit the site, the code on the site will detect the operating system you are using, and the default option should correspond to that operating system (my laptop is a MacBook, so the default option is macOS).
3. With your correct system option selected, click on either of the **DOWNLOAD** buttons.

> If you were to download the Professional edition, you would automatically enter a 30-day free trial period, during which you can take full advantage of the powerful features that the Professional edition exclusively includes. After this period, you have to either purchase a license for the Professional edition or stop using it altogether. If you are only downloading the Community edition, you will be all set to use PyCharm right after installation.

The previous chapter covers extensive comparisons between the two editions of PyCharm, and how to decide whether the paid Professional edition would help you better than the free Community edition. Head to the *Choosing a PyCharm edition that fits your profession* section of `Chapter 1`, *Introduction to PyCharm - The Most Popular IDE for Python*, for more details.

Additionally, if you are not sure whether you qualify for the free license for the Professional edition of PyCharm (for being a student/teacher, working on an open-source project, and so on), also head to `Chapter 1`, *Introduction to PyCharm - The Most Popular IDE for Python*, to find out. A large number of developers fail to realize that they do qualify for the Professional edition, and therefore miss the opportunity to take advantage of the full combination of features that PyCharm offers.

4. Either way, as you click on one of the two **DOWNLOAD** buttons, the download process will start within your browser. It might take a while for the download to complete (especially if you are downloading the Professional edition).
5. When the download has completed, open your file explorer in the folder that the file was downloaded to.

Now, let's move to the next subsection to begin the installation process.

Installing

Again, installing PyCharm is similar to installing any other software. Run the downloaded file to start the installation. As usual, there will be a number of different windows displaying different configuration options while you install PyCharm on your system.

> Additionally, even after the installation process, you will always have the option to change these settings later on if you so choose.

Leaving all the default options intact and simply clicking through the windows is typically the general strategy:

1. If you are using macOS, you will need to drag the PyCharm icon to the `Applications` folder to begin the installation process
2. One additional thing to note is—especially if you have used PyCharm before—that programmers used to be required to download and install Java separately in order to run PyCharm (since PyCharm is written, partly, in Java)
3. Now, if you have installed the **Java Runtime Environment** (**JRE**) bundle during the installation of PyCharm, which is one of the default options, then PyCharm will be ready to execute upon successful installation—there is no need to download and install Java separately
4. If everything runs successfully, upon opening, PyCharm will display its welcome window

And that is it! You have successfully installed PyCharm, the best Python IDE at the time of writing.

Note that, if you are installing the Professional edition, PyCharm will now ask you for your license if you are not using it during a 30-day free trial. If you do have a license, head to the next subsection to see how to activate it.

Otherwise, while any powerful features and functionalities of PyCharm are waiting to be explored, we need to properly set up the general settings and configurations for PyCharm. Simply skip the next subsection where the license activation process for the Professional edition is discussed, and jump to the *Setting up PyCharm* section, to continue our discussion.

License activation

In this subsection, we will discuss the process of registering and activating the license for a Professional edition of your PyCharm distribution. If you are using Community PyCharm, you should go ahead and skip to the next section. Overall, this procedure is fairly simple, and most of the information you need will have been generated when you purchased/applied for a license.

Installing and Configuring PyCharm

Given that you have already purchased/applied for a Professional PyCharm license, there are three main ways to activate it, all of which happen after you have successfully downloaded and installed Professional PyCharm. Let's get started:

1. Open the program, and it will display a prompt asking for your license information. The prompt will look similar to the following screenshot:

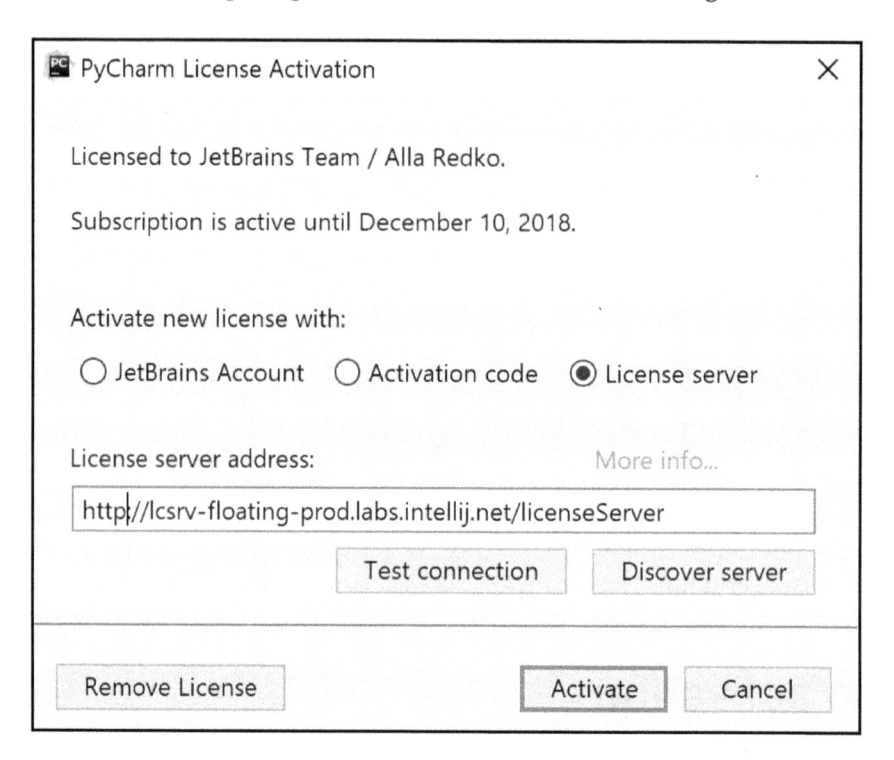

PyCharm license activation

Notice the options following the **Activate your license with** prompt: **Activation code**, **License server**, and **JetBrains Account**. They are the available methods to activate your license. Here, you can choose to use one of the following:

> - Your JetBrains account information, which is used to simply log you in to the JetBrains server and verify your license.
> - Your activation code, which was generated during the purchase. For your reference, at the time of writing, a PyCharm license ID (also known as an activation code) is a string of 10 characters. Each is either a digit or a capitalized letter.
> - A JetBrains license server, which is used to manage licenses for JetBrains products within a company. Most of the time, you will use one of the other two methods to activate your license, so I will not be discussing this method here.

2. Make sure that you select the appropriate method in the prompt before entering the corresponding information.
3. Click **Activate** when all the required information has been entered. If all runs successfully, you are now ready to use the powerful, fully-supported Professional edition of PyCharm.

> To learn more about this license activation process, you can head to `http://www.jetbrains.com/help/pycharm/license-activation-dialog.html`.

We have covered the process of downloading and installing PyCharm. In the next section, we will be looking at various options in terms of setting up and customizing our PyCharm software.

Setting up PyCharm

With PyCharm's powerful functionalities at our disposal, we might be tempted to jump right in and work on our Python projects. However, it can be more beneficial for us to work on some initial settings and configurations before interacting with an actual Python project.

After all, with your development environment set up and optimized to your preferences, you will be set on the right track with PyCharm.

Installing and Configuring PyCharm

General preferences

Within the welcome window of PyCharm, you will notice a dropdown named **Configure** in the bottom right-hand corner. With this dropdown, you can manage several general options regarding your PyCharm software, such as checking for updates or managing your license. However, we will be focusing on configuring the settings for PyCharm first, which corresponds to the **Preferences** option, as indicated in the following screenshot:

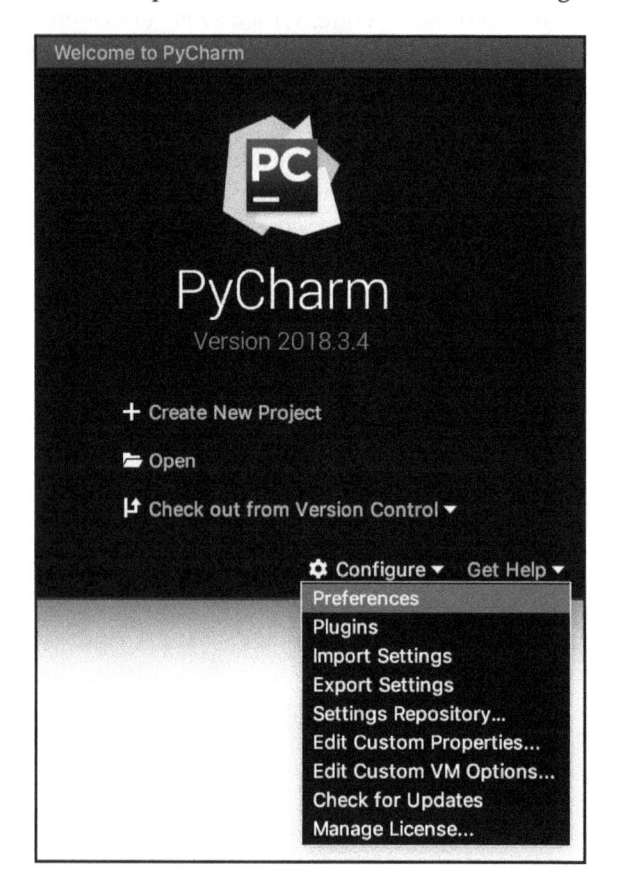

Configure option in PyCharm

It is important to note that if you are using an operating system that is not macOS, you might see a slightly different interface. For example, **Configure** in the Windows version of PyCharm will be named **Settings**. Throughout this book, I will be showing screenshots from examples on my macOS system, but the navigation and functionalities should not differ too much if you are running a different operating system.

What is included in the settings

This option will take us to the settings of PyCharm, where you can adjust various options to your liking, such as PyCharm's appearance and organization, Python editor font and formatting, and interpreters for your projects.

For example, the theme of his or her development environment is something that a programmer considers seriously. I have personally chosen the theme for my PyCharm to be **High contrast**; the high contrast theme specifically focuses on readability—not just for the code in the editor, but for all windows in general. It is my personal favorite theme, and the screenshots on my PyCharm throughout this book will be in this theme.

Another useful option you can take advantage of is **System Settings**, where you can customize the general behavior of PyCharm when starting/closing it or when a new project is open (note that we will also talk about projects in more detail later on in this chapter). For example, I always have my PyCharm resume the project that I last worked on whenever I launch the software, and a new PyCharm project is always open in a new window.

How to do it in PyCharm

In the settings window, select the **Appearance & Behavior** | **Appearance** tab on the left-hand side section. As we can see in the following screenshot, other than **High contrast**, you can choose your theme to be either **Light** or **Darcula**—whichever fits your preferences the best:

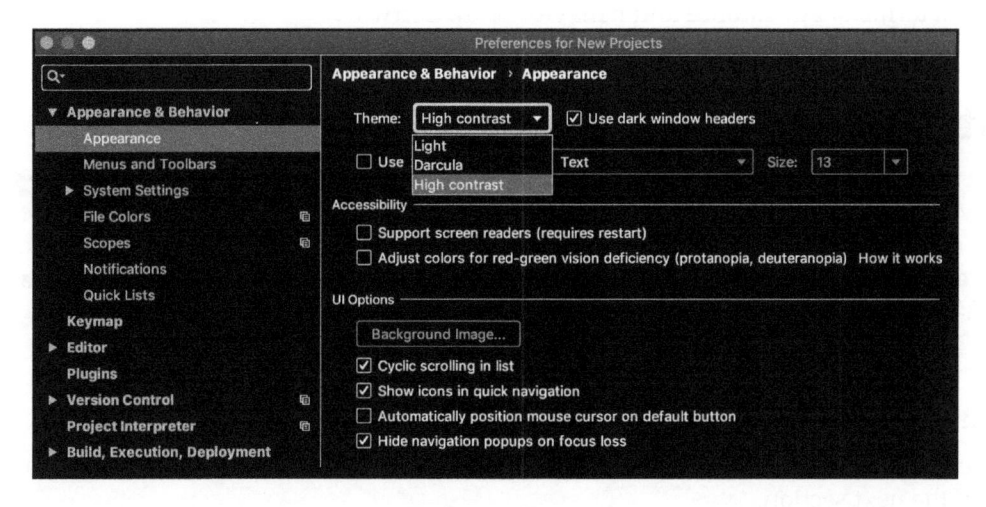

Choosing a theme for your PyCharm

Installing and Configuring PyCharm

Still in the **Appearance & Behavior** tab, go to **System Settings** to customize the general behavior of your PyCharm. Your window should look similar to the following screenshot:

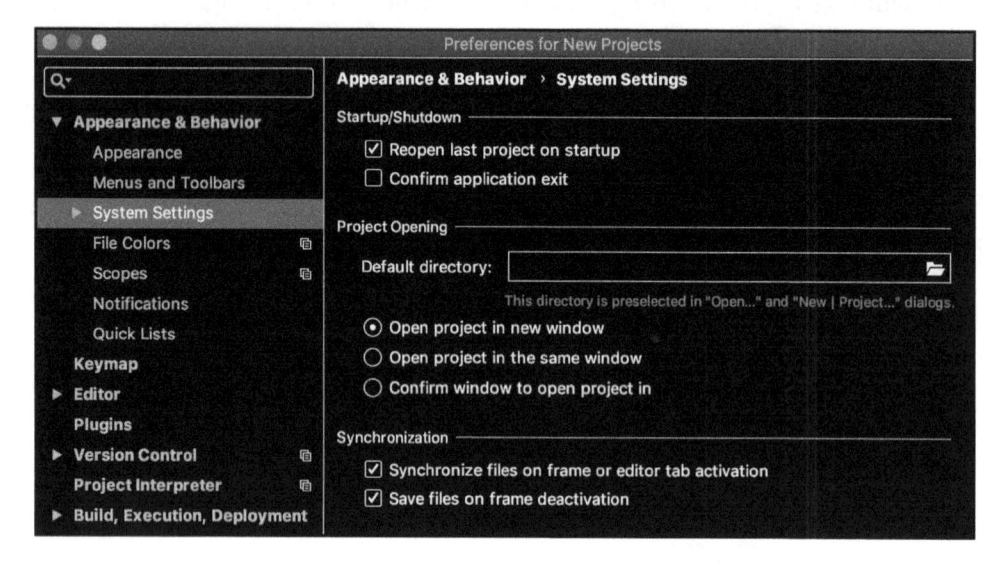

Starting/closing behaviors

Needless to say, there are numerous other options in this section that you can take advantage of if you want to fully customize the appearance of your PyCharm software. Don't be afraid to try combinations of different settings to find your favorite configuration, at least in terms of appearance and behavior of the software.

Editor

Notice that settings in the general appearance section apply for all PyCharm windows. However, you can have additional settings for the editor window (the window where you edit your code, and therefore arguably the most important window). These settings for the editor are applied separately from the general settings and are located in the **Editor** tab on the left-hand side.

What is included in the editor

First, let's consider what options are available in this tab before learning how to customize them in the next section.

In the setting options for the editor, you can choose the font (and the size and line spacing) of your code. Most programmers are particular about the font of their code, so you will appreciate these settings if you are one of them.

As we mentioned previously, it is also possible to change the theme of the editor, independently from the general theme of PyCharm, which we have learned to set in the previous subsection. You can also choose the theme (or, to be more exact, the scheme) of your PyCharm editor. As an example, my personal scheme is **Monokai** (which is the default color scheme of Sublime, so Sublime users migrating to PyCharm might appreciate this option).

The next setting of interest to editors is in the line wrapping section (using **Editor | Code Style | Python | Wrapping and Braces**), which is used to specify how long a line of code in your editor should be. Following the current style guide for Python code, PEP 8, the maximum length of a line in a Python file should be 79 characters, so I typically set the entry in this setting to 79.

By specifying this, PyCharm will then display a vertical line at the 79th column, indicating a point where the programmer should break his or her line of code, which is about to become too long, into multiple lines. Users of other Python editors should already be familiar with this visual guide functionality. The following is a screenshot of a Sublime window:

Line length visual guide in Sublime

Installing and Configuring PyCharm

How to do it in PyCharm

In the **Editor** | **Font** tab, you can customize the font of your code, as shown in the following screenshot. Notice that a preview of some code with the current font settings applied is available in the lower portion of the window:

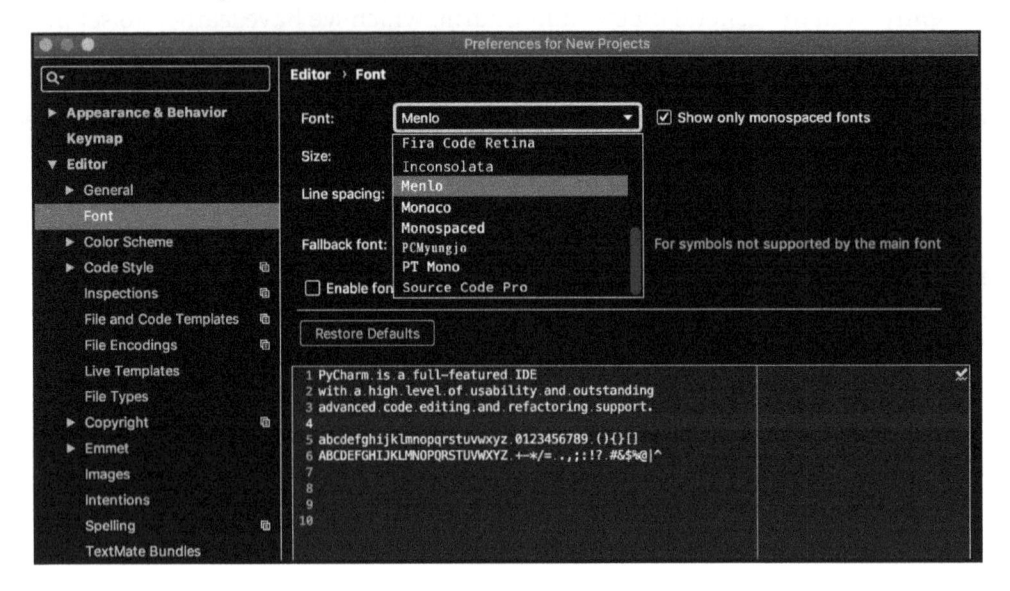

Editor font settings

To change the theme of the editor, independently from the general theme of PyCharm, use the option called **Color Scheme**, which is the sub-tab in the **Editor** tab directly below **Font**, which is what we were looking at in the preceding screenshot.

Note that you will not be able to see the changes you have made right now, as we are not working with the editor yet. We will, however, see these effects as we start working with projects (and then you can further adjust these settings if those effects are not to your liking).

To customize line-wrapping settings, use the **Editor** | **Code Style** tab. As we mentioned previously, the general convention is to have a visual guide after 79 columns, as shown in the following screenshot:

Chapter 2

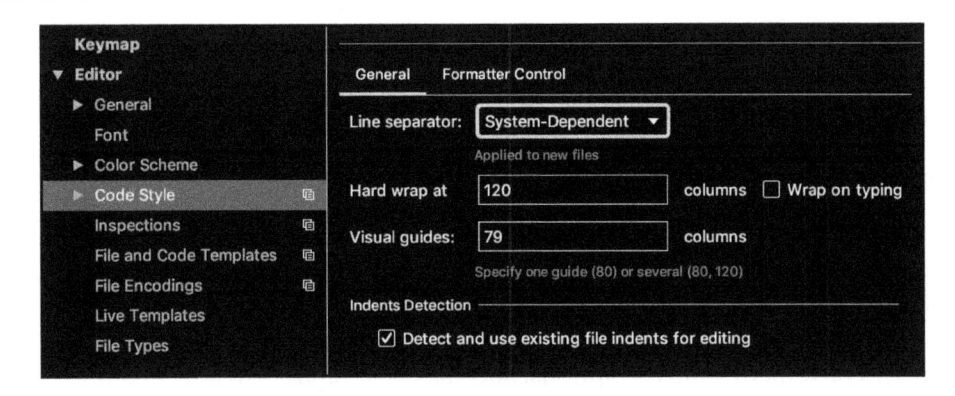

Line wrapping

You can also set the entry at **Hard wrap at** to 79 to forcibly wrap a line of code if it exceeds the recommended 79-character limit. All in all, these features will make sure that your code is following the standard Python style guidelines in terms of line length.

Keymap

You might have noticed that, on the left-hand side navigation in the settings, we have skipped over the **Keymap** tab, going from **Appearance & Behavior** to **Editor**. This is because keymap is arguably the most technical functionality out of the three, and so it is worth saving it for last in our discussion on the topic of setting up PyCharm.

The background of keymap

Keymap, in the most general sense, is the way a computer system defines the mappings of keys—this includes both keyboard keys and buttons from other external hardware such as a mouse. The simplest example for different keymaps is when a left-handed person changes his or her mouse button mapping so that the right button of the mouse is the primary button. In this case, the change in the keymap is simply a switch between the two mouse buttons.

Another example of a keymap is using a Windows keyboard with a macOS system, or vice versa. Even though most of the keyboards of the two systems are the same, there are a number of differences—the ⌥ option key or the ⌘ command key on macOS keyboards, and the *Alt* key and the key with the Windows logo on Windows keyboards. If you are connecting a keyboard intended for one system to another, some mapping to ensure that the keys are unique to the intended system would have to be applied.

[39]

Installing and Configuring PyCharm

Generally, in the context of text editors and **integrated development environments** (**IDEs**), we can use this term to indicate both the mappings of keys and keyboard shortcuts. As a programmer, it's likely that you are more than familiar with keyboard shortcuts, some of the most common of which are *Ctrl/command* + *C* for copying, *Ctrl/command* + *A* for selecting all the elements in a page, and so on.

Editors and IDEs have their own version of keymap. For example, if you are an Emacs user, you are likely to be aware of Emac's unique shortcut to save and exit out of editing, C-x C-c, or the C-w C-y shortcuts to cut and paste, respectively. Eclipse, on the other hand, uses the common *Ctrl/command* + *X*, *Ctrl/command* + *V* for cutting and pasting. Eclipse, however, also has other convenient shortcut options, such as *Ctrl* + *Shift* + */* to add a comment block, or *Ctrl* + *F7* and *Ctrl* + *Shift* + *F7* to move between views.

All of this is to say that there is significant variation among keymaps of different development environments, and programmers understandably get mixed up with keymap options while using more than one environment.

How to do it in PyCharm

Let's turn our attention back to PyCharm and see what keymap options it offers in the **Keymap** tab in settings. First of all, we notice that we can choose from a wide range of options regarding which keymap PyCharm should apply to our development environment by using the **Keymap** dropdown menu at the top of the window, as shown in the following screenshot:

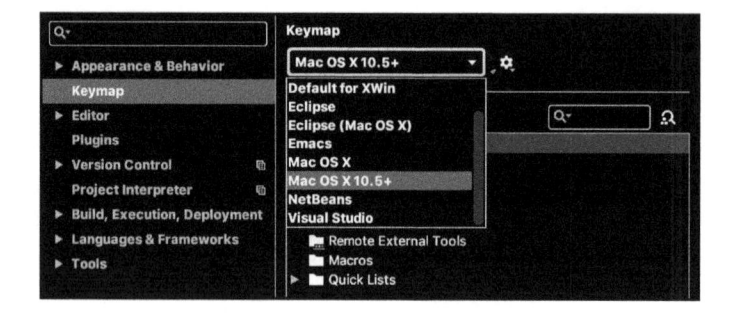

Choosing a keymap

Multiple options are available, including the aforementioned Eclipse and Emacs. This means that if you are transitioning from, say, Eclipse (or Emacs, or Visual Studio) to PyCharm and do not want to forgo the keymap and shortcuts you have learned about while using the previous editor/IDE, you can simply apply that keymap here and continue to utilize the keymap and shortcuts when using your PyCharm.

Shortcuts are incredibly important to programmers, and this feature in PyCharm looks to support the ease in using them. This will also help us avoid the confusion that might result from using multiple keymaps at the same time, which we described previously.

In the following subsection, we will learn more about the options that are available in PyCharm when it comes to using shortcuts.

Shortcut customizations

PyCharm also gives you the power to find, edit, and customize your own shortcuts. This means that not only can you preserve the shortcuts you have mastered in other environments, but you can also extend that set of shortcuts to perform other tasks that you couldn't before.

To see this functionality in action, move to the lower section of the current **Keymap** tab and inspect one of the lists that's available. For example, the following screenshot was taken when I opened the first list, **Editor Actions**:

Inspecting shortcuts

Installing and Configuring PyCharm

This list contains available actions and tasks that you can add or customize your own shortcuts for; they are ordered alphabetically, so you can look for a specific action that way. Let's consider some examples. For the **Delete Line** action (which will delete the whole line of code that the caret is currently at), we can see that it is associated with the shortcut ⌘⌫ (command + delete) in macOS.

Say, for some reason, you would like to unhook this link so that every time you enter the shortcut, the current line isn't deleted. We can do this simply by right-clicking on the **Delete Line** action (or any action you'd like to avoid) and choosing **Remove ...** to unhook that shortcut.

Additionally, you can always come back to this setting and rehook the action to the shortcut, if you ever find that you'd like to keep the shortcut after all. And for that matter, you can also add your own key combination for the shortcut, including keys on the mouse.

You will also see that, in our list of actions available for shortcuts, some are not yet associated with any shortcut (for example, **Move Caret Backward a Paragraph** or **Decrease Font Size** in the preceding screenshot). By right-clicking on these options and attributing different key combinations to them using **Add Keyboard Shortcut** or **Add Mouse Shortcut**, you can also create your own shortcuts for any tasks you find convenient.

This customization is illustrated as follows:

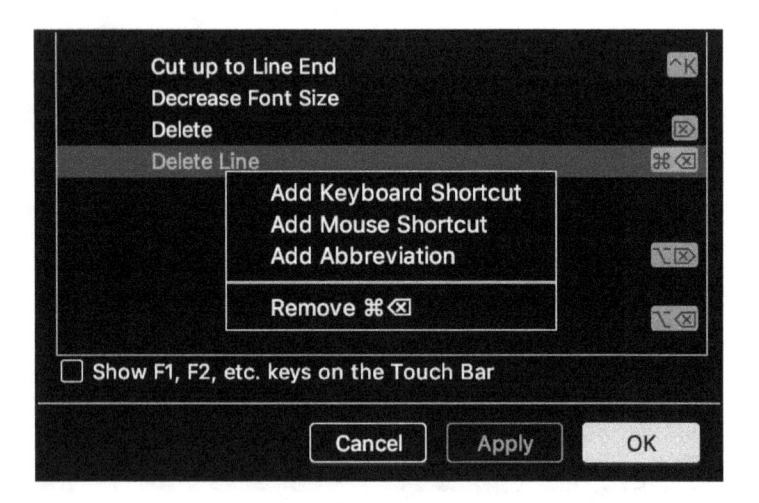

Customizing a shortcut

[42]

On the topic of shortcuts, PyCharm offers unique functionality that maximizes your productivity in this area.

Say you are listening to a talk or watching a presentation from another developer. This developer has their PyCharm environment open to show their project and illustrate some real-time coding. As they code, they use various shortcuts that prove to be extremely convenient and make their editing much faster. Say one of the shortcuts you see them utilize moves the caret to the end of a code block and selects the line that it passes through—you can find out which shortcut they used by searching for it in the PyCharm search bar.

In the following screenshot, I typed in `move caret block` (separate, independent keywords—similar to googling—as opposed to an actual phrase) to narrow down the list of actions returned by PyCharm, and was able to find that the action name was technically **Move Caret to Code Block End with Selection**, and that the shortcut for that task (on a macOS system) is ⌥ ⇧ ⌘] (or *option + Shift + command +]*):

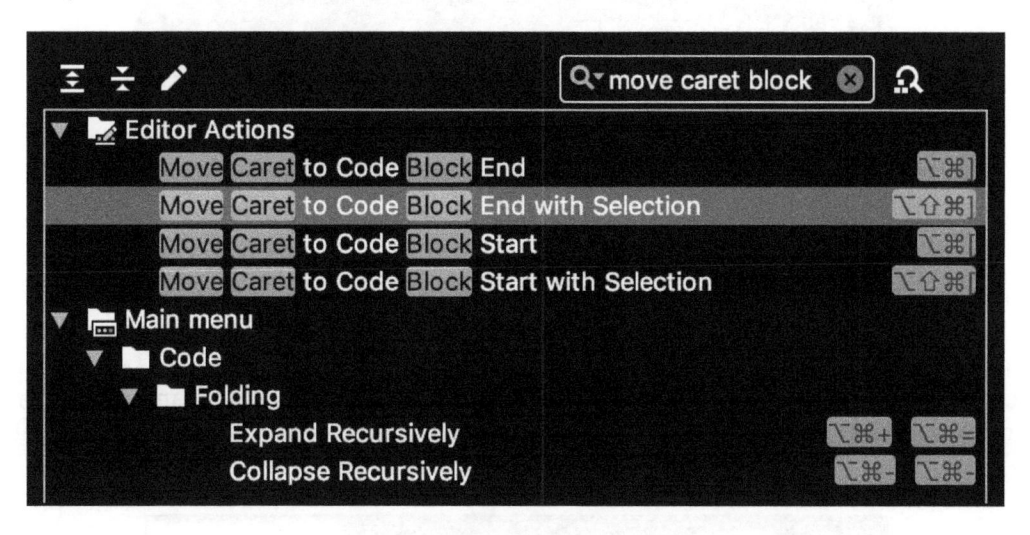

Searching for shortcuts

We can see that the search bar can not only find the shortcut command for a particular given task but that it also gives us the exact name for the task. It is important to note that this search functionality is not only limited to finding shortcut actions. In fact, users can use it to find files, settings, and even classes and objects within Python code. This is why this functionality is called **Search Everywhere**, and it is one of the many powerful features that set PyCharm apart from other editors/IDEs.

Installing and Configuring PyCharm

We have seen that PyCharm allows you to find the shortcut for a particular action using its search functionality, which is widely used by programmers to find and customize their shortcuts in PyCharm. However, PyCharm also provides a reverse search functionality that most users typically do not take advantage of. Specifically, the functionality is called **Find Actions by Shortcut**, and is invoked when the button right next to the search bar that we have been considering is clicked, as shown in the following screenshot:

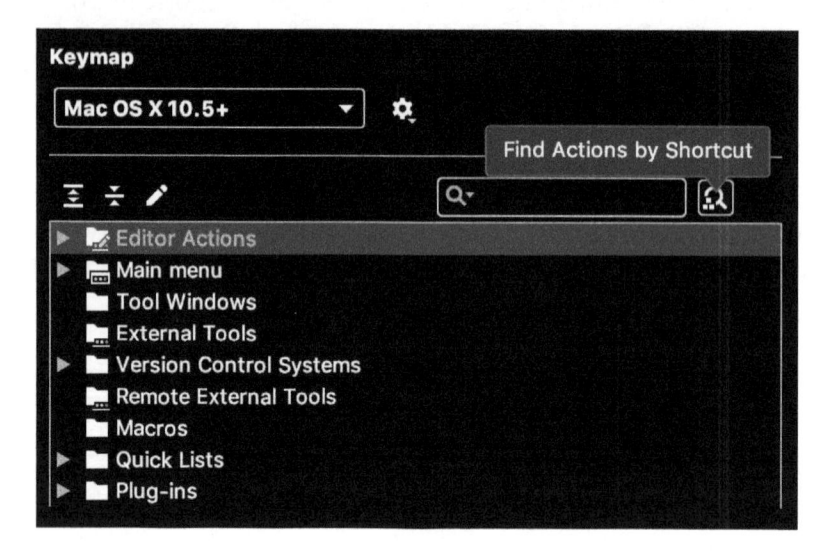

Find Actions by Shortcut button

When using this search, you can enter in a key combination, and PyCharm will tell you which, if any, action is associated with that keyboard shortcut. For example, if I wanted to find out what the combination of *command* + *home* on a macOS keymap does, I can use this search to find out that the **Move Caret to Text Start** action (which, as its name suggests, will move the caret to the beginning of the file currently opened in the editor) is associated with the shortcut. The following screenshot illustrates this process:

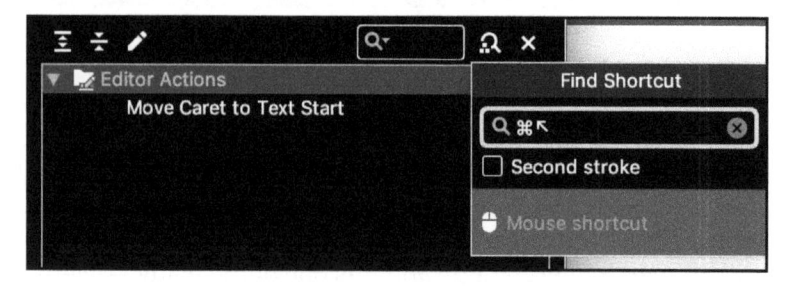

Finding a particular action using its shortcut

[44]

Chapter 2

It is important to note that, at the time of writing, this **Find Actions by Shortcut** functionality is only available within the **Keymap** settings tab.

In this section, we have looked at various options regarding how to customize our PyCharm workspace, including themes for both the PyCharm interface and the editor within, as well as keymap and shortcut options. However, these are more general settings regarding the overall usage of PyCharm that you yourself can explore.

In the next section, we will be discussing the customizations at the project level and learn about more settings and features in PyCharm.

Getting started with PyCharm projects

So far, we have only looked at the settings of PyCharm. In this section, we will go beyond the welcome window and settings tabs to create a new PyCharm project from scratch. To create a new Python project within PyCharm, simply choose the corresponding option in the welcome window, as shown here:

Creating a new project

[45]

Installing and Configuring PyCharm

After choosing this option, the process of creating a PyCharm project will start. This process consists of multiple distinct steps, each of which specifies important customizations for the project we are creating.

Additionally, note that all the code and project structures that have been generated during the discussions in this book can be found in this book's GitHub repository at `github.com/PacktPublishing/Hands-on-Application-Development-with-PyCharm`.

It is encouraged that you follow along with the discussions and create the projects within your own PyCharm, but if you wish to use the source code as a reference, you are welcome to do so. In fact, if you successfully download the source code from GitHub, you can then import it into PyCharm as an actual project. More details on the GitHub repository can be found in the *Getting the source code from GitHub* section of this chapter.

Creating a project

Getting back to the process of creating a PyCharm project from scratch, let's get started:

1. After choosing the **Create New Project** option in the welcome window, you will be prompted to select the type of project you'd like to create. This step is used to specify which general project you are working on, where you'd like to store the project, and which interpreter/environment to use. The prompt in which you can select your project type is as follows:

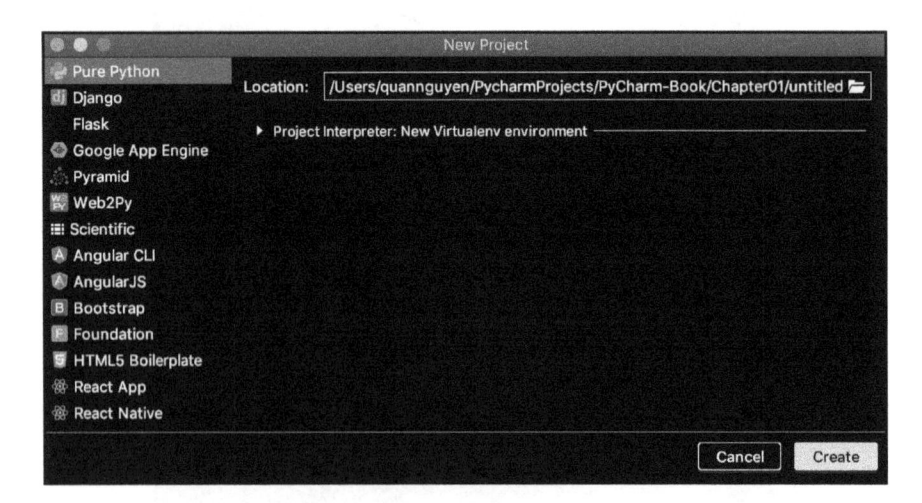

Creating a PyCharm project

> **TIP**
> If you are using the Community edition, you will not see the left-hand side of the window that's shown in the preceding screenshot. Don't panic, as that feature is used to create boilerplate files for specific types of Python projects (such as Django or Flask), which can also be generated manually without any difficulty in the Community edition anyway.
> Furthermore, in this section, we are creating a **Pure Python** project, which can be done using Community PyCharm. If you are a Professional PyCharm user, also ignore the left panel for now.

2. As such, go ahead and choose a name for your PyCharm project by changing `untitled` to whatever name you wish in the **Location** prompt. As suggested by its name, this option also allows you to specify the location of your project. In the following screenshot, I am naming this project `FirstProject`:

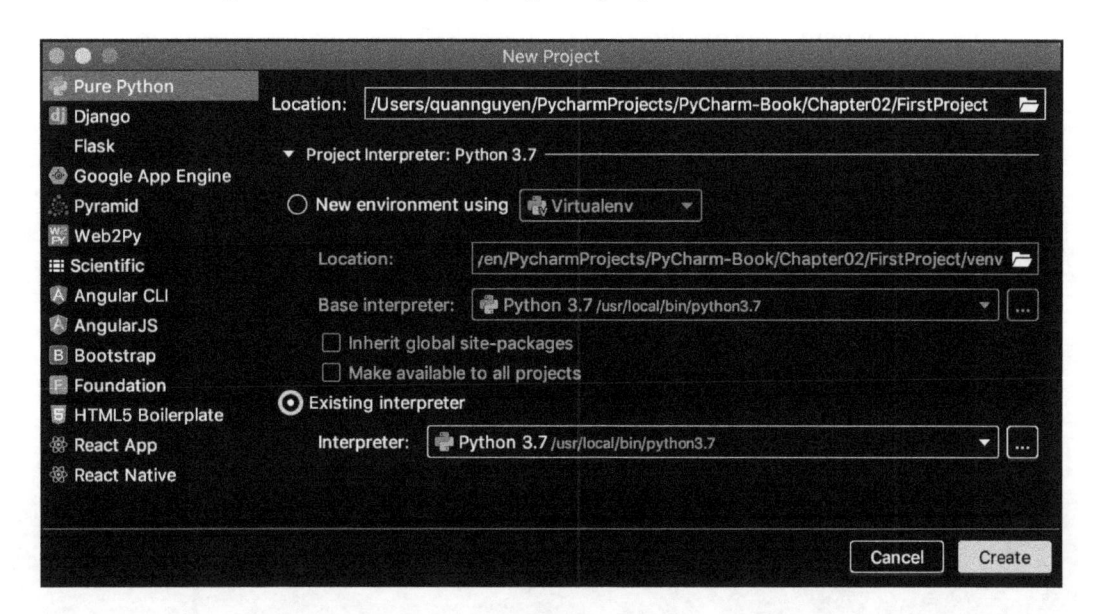

Project specifications

3. Also notice that, once you click on the **Project Interpreter** prompt in the middle of the window, PyCharm will expand that section out, as shown in the preceding screenshot. Here, you can specify which interpreter PyCharm should use to execute the code in the project you are creating. You can see that I am choosing the option to use my global Python interpreter (stored in `/usr/local/bin/python3.7` by default in macOS; yours might be different) by selecting the **Existing interpreter** option.

Installing and Configuring PyCharm

The default option is to create a completely new virtual environment for your Python project. We will look into the specification of virtual environments and interpreters later in the next chapter, in the *Virtual environments and interpreters* section. For now, simply choose your own global Python interpreter for this project we are creating

Now, since we've created a project, let's see how we can work with it within PyCharm.

Interacting with a PyCharm project

Still following the example from the previous subsection, we will be looking into how to finally create and interact with a PyCharm project. Let's get started:

1. Click the **Create** button to finalize the process. PyCharm will take you to another window where your newly created project is. The following screenshot shows what I obtained from my PyCharm:

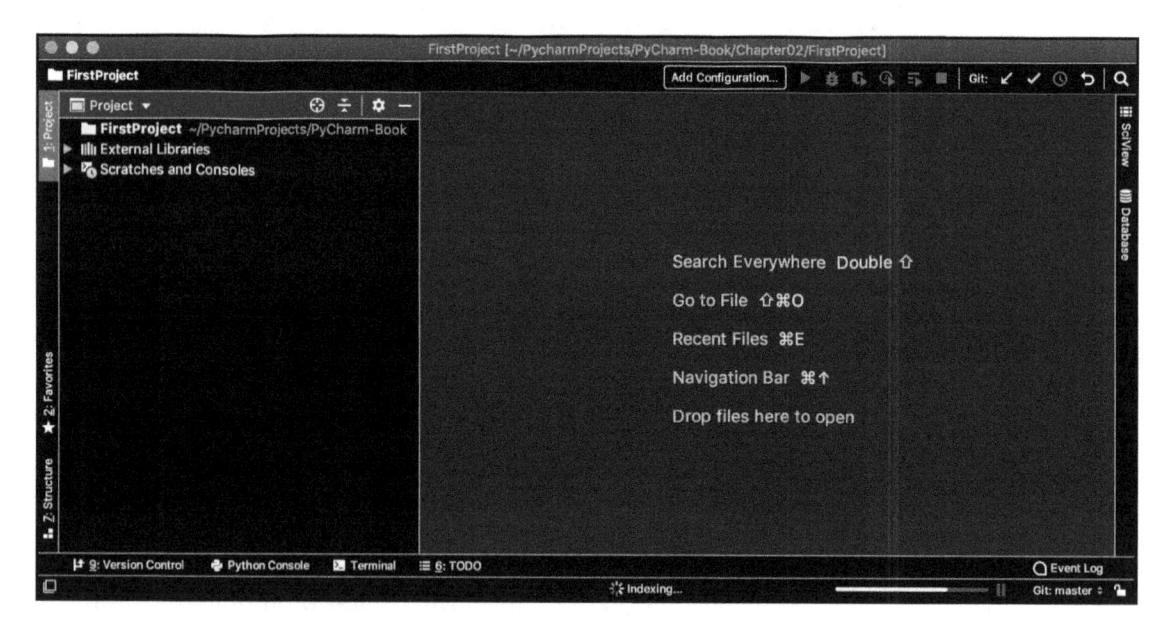

A new project in PyCharm

> Notice that, aside from the directory folder in the left-hand panel, there is not much for us to interact with here since there are no files in our project currently.

3. To add a new file to our project, right-click on the project in the left panel and choose **New** | **Python File**. You will notice that there are quite a number of other file types that you can create. For our purposes, we will choose the **Python File** option for now.
4. A prompt will pop up, asking for the name of this Python file, as shown here:

Naming a new file

5. Here, I'm using `test.py` to name my file. Notice that we do not actually have to put in the `.py` file extension while naming the file since we have already specified that it is a Python file. Click **OK** to generate this file.
6. After clicking **OK**, PyCharm might ask you whether you want to add this newly created file to Git or not. Git is the version control manager that's integrated with PyCharm so that we can use it within our PyCharm projects. We will go into further details regarding version control with Git in `Chapter 5`, *Version Control with Git in PyCharm*; for now, simply choose not to do this in the prompt.
7. We will see that our `test.py` file has been successfully created and is now opened in the editor. As per tradition, we will print out a `Hello, World!` message in this Python file. Input the following into your own `test.py` file:

```
if __name__ == '__main__':
    print('Hello, World!')
```

8. To run our first program in PyCharm, we have several options. First, we can go to the **Run** tab at the top and choose the second **Run** option (instead of the first **Run**), as shown here:

Installing and Configuring PyCharm

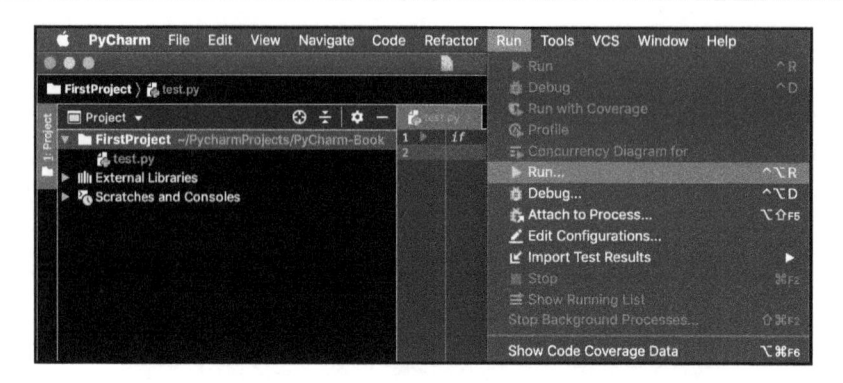

Running a PyCharm file

9. Another prompt will appear after this; choose `test` (or the name you use for your file) to run our program. Here, we will see a panel appear in our PyCharm window (most likely at the bottom), printing out the output of our program, `Hello, World!`. This is the **Run** panel of PyCharm, which displays various information regarding the Python program we just ran. For example, the information I have in my **Run** panel is the following (which includes the location of the Python file and the exit status, in addition to any printed output):

```
/usr/local/bin/python3.7 /Users/quannguyen/PycharmProjects/PyCharm-
Book/Chapter02/FirstProject/test.py
Hello, World!

Process finished with exit code 0
```

That is how you run a Python program in PyCharm. Additionally, you may also notice, to the left of the **Run** panel, that there is a green run button, as indicated in the following screenshot:

Rerunning a Python file

[50]

You can click on this button (or use its shortcut–⌘ R in the case of macOS – when the cursor is in the **Run** panel) to execute the file again. Specifically, this functionality reruns the last file executed, so you can use it to run a file multiple times in a row. However, this is not possible when you are switching between executing multiple files.

Another way to run a Python file is by using the **Run context configuration** action, which can be invoked when your cursor is on the line of the file you'd like to run (in the editor).

This action has the default shortcut of ^ ⇧ R (*Ctrl* + *Shift* + *R*) for macOS, and *Ctrl* + *Shift* + *F10* for Windows, and can, again, be changed using the **Keymap** settings that we discussed previously. Move your cursor to `test.py` in your editor and try the shortcut to run the file.

With the functionalities that we have discussed, it is possible to begin developing Python projects in PyCharm—we can now create a new blank project, create Python files, and run them. However, we are merely scratching the surface of what PyCharm can do, and future chapters of this book will go into more detail regarding various aspects of using PyCharm.

For example, immediately after this chapter, we will learn more about other types of PyCharm project, as well as the management of virtual environments and interpreters, both of which topics we have skipped over in this chapter. However, before we move any further, let's begin the process of downloading the code examples that will be used in this book from GitHub.

Getting the source code from GitHub

As we mentioned previously, while we will be working through all the code examples in this book step by step, you may also take advantage of the code repository of this book, which is stored on GitHub.

Generally, you should follow the discussions in individual chapters and edit your projects as you go to get a full understanding of the materials. With that being said, you can potentially point your PyCharm to the completed projects in the repository to import them into your workspace. We will see how to do this (importing an existing project into PyCharm) in the next chapter, though you should only do this if you have sufficiently familiarized yourself with the materials for a given project.

Installing and Configuring PyCharm

Now, let's get back to downloading the repository from GitHub:

1. First, visit `github.com/PacktPublishing/Hands-on-Application-Development-with-PyCharm`. To download the repository, simply click on the **Clone or download** button in the top right corner of your web browser window. Choose the **Download ZIP** option to download the compressed repository to your computer. The download prompt should be similar to the following screenshot:

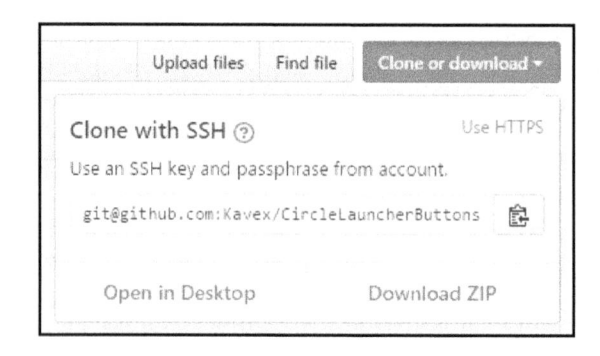

Downloading the code repository from GitHub

2. Find the downloaded file in your computer and uncompress it to generate the folder that contains all our code. The folder should have the name `Hands-on-Application-Development-with-PyCharm-master`.

Separate subfolders titled `ChapterXX` are inside this folder, where XX indicates the chapter number that uses the code in that subfolder. For example, the `Chapter03` folder contains the code examples we will cover in Chapter 3, *Customizing Interpreters and Virtual Environments*. There are varying folder directory structures (for different PyCharm projects) in these subfolders; we will learn about which subfolder to look at as we move through this book.

Summary

In this chapter, we have discussed the process of downloading, installing, and setting up PyCharm in our computer system (including how to register a license if we are using the Professional edition). We have seen a subset of the features and functionalities PyCharm offers when it comes to customizing our workspace, including the theme for our PyCharm, as well as the customizations for keymaps and shortcuts. Overall, PyCharm gives you total control over customizing various mechanisms, making it a dynamic and flexible development environment.

We have also learned how to create a minimal Python project, create Python files, and execute programs in Python. This officially concludes the first part of this book, where we consider the basics of PyCharm. Again, the information you have learned about here will help you navigate through simple usage of PyCharm, but there is so much more to PyCharm than a simple editor with convenient shortcuts. Other parts in this book will expand on this foundation, and discuss multiple specific situations when using PyCharm.

Specifically, multiple mentions throughout this chapter of the different options PyCharm offers in this process, such as the choice in project type, interpreter, virtual environment, and so on, will be fully addressed in the next chapter, where we will look into these options in more details.

Questions

1. What are the editions of PyCharm that are available for download?
2. How can we activate a license for the Professional edition of PyCharm?
3. How can we change the general theme of PyCharm and the theme of its editor?
4. What is a keymap, and why is it important in the context of development environments?
5. How can we search for a specific shortcut within PyCharm using the name for the corresponding action? Can we do the reverse and search using a particular shortcut?
6. How can we create a minimal Python project, add Python files to that project, and execute them in PyCharm?

Further reading

For more information, you can refer to the following links:

- *Install PyCharm and Anaconda (Windows/Mac/Ubuntu)*, by Michael Galarnyk, Medium (https://medium.com/@GalarnykMichael/setting-up-pycharm-with-anaconda-plus-installing-packages-windows-mac-db2b158bd8c)
- *Mastering PyCharm*, Quazi Nafiul Islam, by Packt Publishing (https://www.packtpub.com/web-development/mastering-pycharm)
- *Modern Python Development With PyCharm*, by Pedro Kroger (https://pedrokroger.net/pycharm-book/)

Section 2: Improving Your Productivity

This section starts with Chapter 3, *Customizing Interpreters and Virtual Environments*. In this section, we will be discussing the features and functionalities of PyCharm that make it one of the best, and definitely the most popular, development environments for Python programming. From intelligent coding assistance to syntax highlighting and suggestions, PyCharm offers a convenient way of following best programming practices in real time as you work on your projects. Furthermore, the tedious management tasks of organizing packages, interpreters, and virtual environments are also taken care of in a straightforward manner.

Python development (or developing in any programming language, for that matter) does not only involve writing code; it also consists of testing, debugging, and profiling—important procedures in programming that are often overlooked. However, given the complexity of these tasks and the deep understanding of software development they require, many are intimidated by them and consequently tend not to be concerned with them in their projects. PyCharm looks to resolve this situation by providing intuitive, graphical methods for carrying out these tasks, and that is what we will also be discussing in this section.

Section 2: Improving Your Productivity

The following screenshot includes an instance in which the graphical debugger in PyCharm is used:

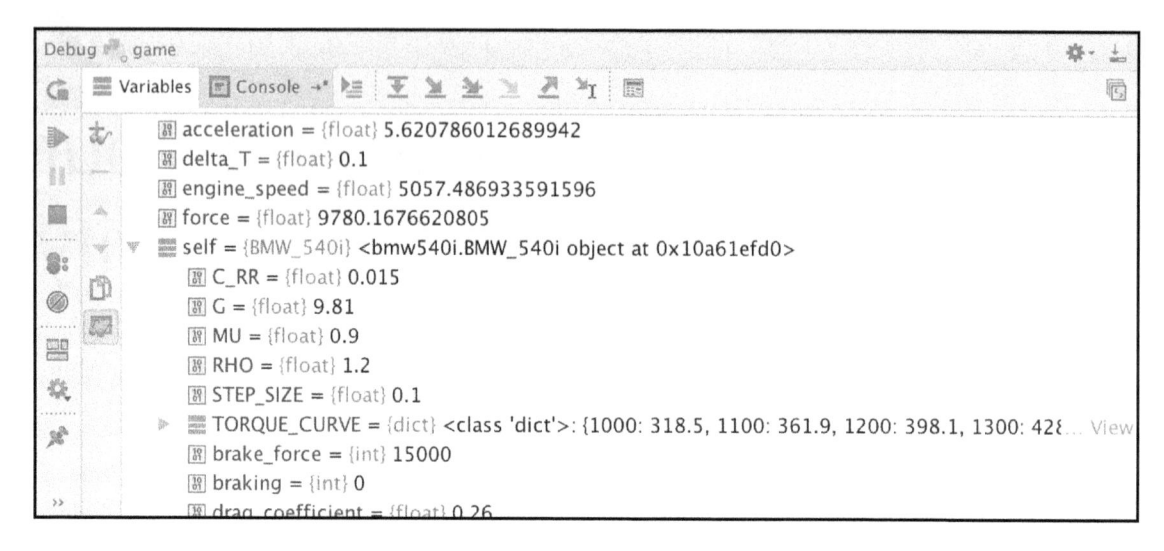

```
Debug  game
   Variables   Console
      acceleration = {float} 5.620786012689942
      delta_T = {float} 0.1
      engine_speed = {float} 5057.486933591596
      force = {float} 9780.1676620805
      self = {BMW_540i} <bmw540i.BMW_540i object at 0x10a61efd0>
         C_RR = {float} 0.015
         G = {float} 9.81
         MU = {float} 0.9
         RHO = {float} 1.2
         STEP_SIZE = {float} 0.1
         TORQUE_CURVE = {dict} <class 'dict'>: {1000: 318.5, 1100: 361.9, 1200: 398.1, 1300: 428... View
         brake_force = {int} 15000
         braking = {int} 0
         drag_coefficient = {float} 0.26
```

Example of visually debugging in PyCharm

This section includes the following chapters:

- Chapter 3, *Customizing Interpreters and Virtual Environments*
- Chapter 4, *Editing and Formatting with Ease in PyCharm*
- Chapter 5, *Version Control with Git in PyCharm*
- Chapter 6, *Seamless Testing, Debugging, and Profiling*

[56]

3
Customizing Interpreters and Virtual Environments

This is the first chapter of the second section of this book, where we will focus on the options and features in PyCharm that look to improve our productivity. In the previous chapter, we started discussing the process of creating Python projects in PyCharm and how to navigate through options to create and run Python files in a project window. This chapter picks up from where we left off, and will go through the other options provided by PyCharm so that we can customize our workspace, specifically to add in panels and tools to improve our productivity.

This chapter will also lay out a detailed guide regarding different types of projects that can be created in PyCharm. Next, we will discuss the management of Python interpreters and virtual environments between different projects, and how PyCharm makes it dynamic and convenient. Finally, we will learn how to import an external project into our PyCharm workspace.

The following topics will be covered in this chapter:

- The different options regarding the customization and organization of your PyCharm project workspace
- The variety of project types PyCharm offers and how different project types affect the boilerplate code that's generated automatically by PyCharm
- The concept of an interpreter and how to switch back and forth between different Python interpreters within a PyCharm project
- The concept of a virtual environment and its management in PyCharm

Technical requirements

The following is a list of prerequisites for this chapter:

- Ensure that you have both Python 3.6+ and PyCharm installed on your computer
- Download the GitHub repository at `https://github.com/PacktPublishing/Hands-on-Application-Development-with-PyCharm`
- Have the `matplotlib` package installed for your Python interpreter
- In this chapter, we will be working with the subfolder named `Chapter03` in the downloaded code repository

Customizing the PyCharm workspace

At the end of the previous chapter, we created a new Pure Python project in PyCharm (named `FirstProject`) and wrote a quick program to print out a **Hello, World!** message. If you still have your PyCharm window option in that project open from the previous chapter, great! Otherwise, start your PyCharm up and navigate to that project.

In this section, we will consider a number of important features in PyCharm that allow us to fully customize our workspace and create the most optimal organization and navigation for our projects. First, we will be looking at various components in our current project window that we did not consider in the previous chapter.

Inside a project window

As a reference, the window we are working with should look similar to the following:

Chapter 3

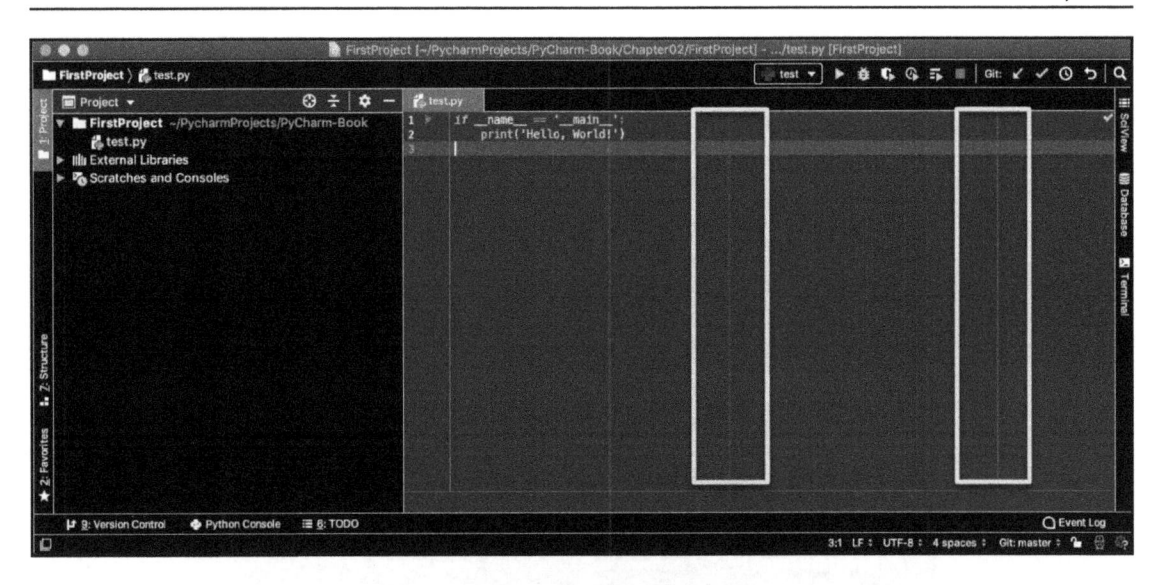

Sample PyCharm project window

Again, we have already seen this window in the previous chapter, but it is worth going over it again. First, we can see that this window consists of two big sections—the directory tree on the left-hand panel and the editor right next to it on the right (which only contains a simple program printing out **Hello, World!**).

You may notice that the general high contrast theme that we have picked for our PyCharm is applied in the directory tree panel and other PyCharm windows, while the theme we have picked for our editor is also appropriately applied (specifically, if you are a Sublime user, you will see that our editor now has the default theme of Sublime).

Another important component in a PyCharm project window is the visual guide for line wrapping (the two lines highlighted by green boxes). In Chapter 2, *Installing and Configuring PyCharm*, we discussed that, according to the official Python style guide PEP, a line of Python code should be at most 79 characters long, and therefore specified that there should be a vertical line in our editor to indicate the end of the 79th column of text, which is the vertical line on the left (the second one on the right is simply another visual guide at the 120th column). Again, this feature is rather useful as most programmers tend to forget about this constraint for the maximum length of a line of code while working on a project.

Customizing Interpreters and Virtual Environments

One final element that's worth noting in a PyCharm project window is the button for the search everywhere functionality, located in the top right corner of the window in the magnifying glass icon. As we mentioned in the previous chapter, search everywhere can be used to search for settings, shortcuts, official documentation, and even classes and objects in our own code. Now, you can use it inside a PyCharm project so that you can dynamically look things up as you are working on your project.

Additionally, there are various miscellaneous components in a PyCharm project window that you should be aware of. First is the `Scratches and Consoles` section within the directory tree panel on the left-hand side of our window:

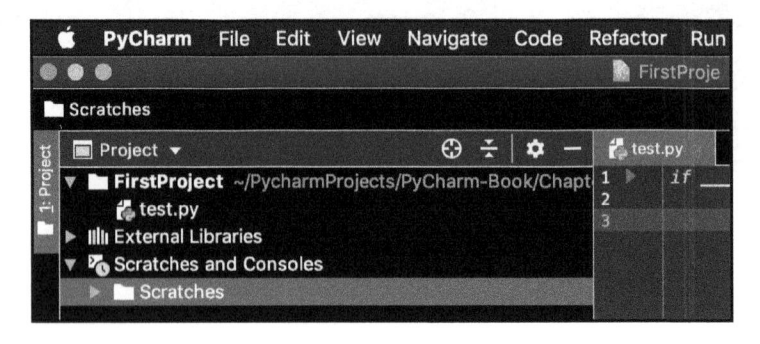

Scratches folder in PyCharm

According to the official documentation from JetBrains, scratch files are fully functional Python scripts that can run independently from other files in the project you are working on. Creating a scratch file can be done in a similar way to what we did to create a new Python file in the previous chapter—right-click on the project folder in the left-hand side panel and choose **New | New Scratch File**, after which you will be prompted to choose the language of the file.

All created scratch files are stored in the `Scratches and Consoles` directory in the preceding screenshot. Technically speaking, scratch files are not a part of any PyCharm project, but they can be accessed in all projects (and not just in the project that you create the scratch files in). This option is quite useful in situations where you are working on a specific project and then you come up with a new idea for another project that you want to save and use for later.

The last minor detail regarding the PyCharm project window is actually quite common and unfortunately often leads to confusion and frustration on the programmer's part. After you have completely closed all PyCharm windows and exited the program, the next time you run PyCharm again and access a specific project, you will most likely see a progress bar near the bottom right corner of the project window, similar to the highlighted portion in the following screenshot:

Progress bar upon startup

This progress bar denotes the indexing process where PyCharm scans through files and documents in your current project to support important functionalities such as search, syntax highlighting, and code completion. This process is to be done every time a project is started or when a new package is installed—basically, when a new file is added to your project. The progress bar we can see here is sometimes replaced by a message saying *X processes running* if there is more than one background indexing task running.

The problem we mentioned that often causes confusion from PyCharm users is that when this indexing process is still running, a number of options in PyCharm (understandably) are not available for use. For example, to create an entirely new project when you are already in a project window, you can go to **File** | **New Project**, and the process of creating a PyCharm project that we discussed in the previous chapter will start. However, if there is still an indexing task running in the background of your PyCharm, that option will appear as though it is disabled, as shown in the following screenshot:

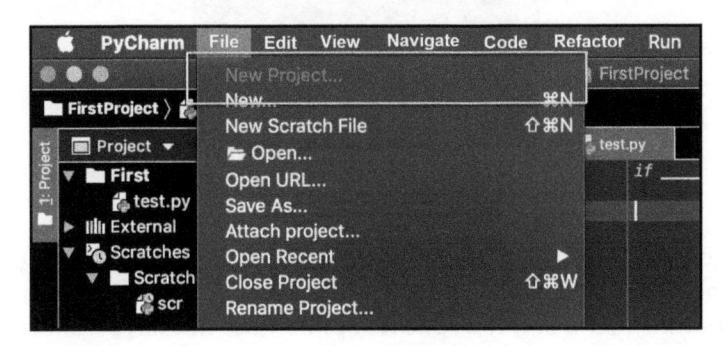

Disabled options when indexing

The lesson to be learned here is that, while working with PyCharm (especially when something is just added to your current project), some features might not be functional. Most of the time, this will not be the case as soon as the indexing process completes. As such, if you realize that something is not working in PyCharm, check to see if there is a background task running or not before panicking and reporting that as an error.

We have identified and discussed some of the most important elements in a PyCharm project window. In the next subsection, we will consider navigating from a PyCharm project to various other windows.

Navigating within a project

With the search everywhere functionality, you can potentially search for and customize various features and settings within PyCharm. This way, you can dynamically make changes to the settings inside a project window. With that said, while working on a specific project, you may still want to directly open the **Preferences** window (the one we worked with in the previous chapter) to go through specific settings yourself, as opposed to searching for a specific one.

In that case, you can do this by going to **PyCharm** | **Preferences** (in macOS) or **File** | **Settings** (in Windows or Linux). Also, notice the shortcut associated with the option when you choose it. For example, the shortcut to open **Preferences** in macOS is ⌘, while it is *Ctrl + Alt + S* in Windows:

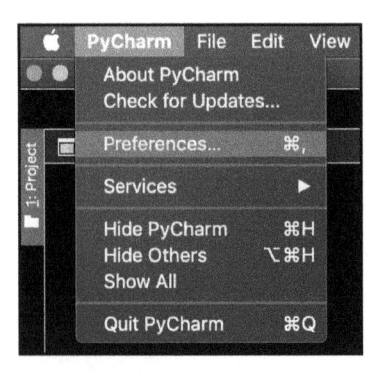

Opening Preferences in PyCharm

It is generally a good idea to take note of the shortcuts associated with actions and tasks that you commonly use; using shortcuts, as we know, can be much faster and more efficient than choosing from the menu bar. If a specific option does not have a shortcut assigned to it yet, remember that you can attribute your own custom shortcut to it.

Again, PyCharm offers extensive flexibility in terms of customizing your working environment, and this is an example of that.

In the same **File** tab (as well as in other tabs), there are also various useful options that you might want to take advantage of regularly, including the following:

- **Close Project**: Personally, I often use this command to exit out of the current project window and go back to the initial welcome window whenever I've finished working on a project
- **File | Open Recent**: This, on the other hand, allows you to quickly switch to another project that you have recently worked on
- **Edit | Macros** (which we will discuss in detail later on): This provides a way to record and replay specific sequences of actions within PyCharm, with the goal of automating repetitive and tedious processes

In general, I recommend going through all the available options and actions in different tabs to narrow down those that you anticipate using often and take note of them. Again, if there is a specific action you will use regularly that does not have a shortcut combination attributed to it, you can add in your own custom shortcut in PyCharm's settings window.

Panels in a project window

Go to **View | Tool Windows** and take a look at the available options, as shown in the following screenshot:

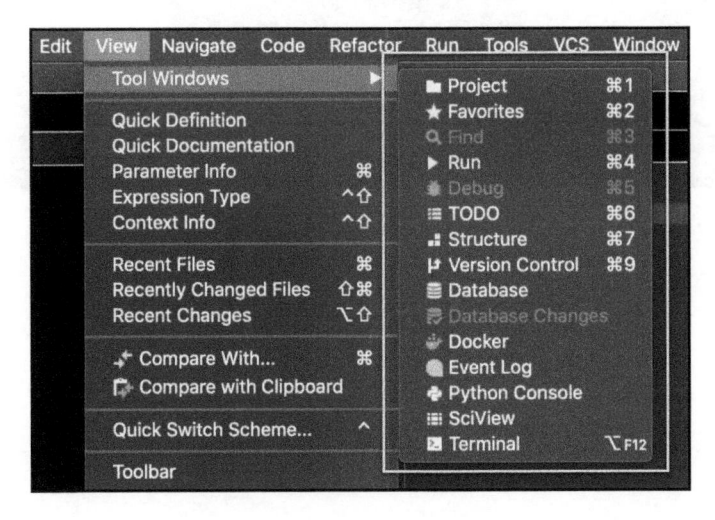

PyCharm tool windows

Customizing Interpreters and Virtual Environments

These tool windows are what I'd like to call panels, which can be displayed and dynamically arranged within a project window.

If you have used a text editor to write Python code, think about the process of running a Python program—you would (typically) edit the code using the editing software, then open a Terminal and run a Python command to execute the Python script. Here, in PyCharm, you can have a **Terminal** panel in the same window as your editor (notice the last option in the preceding screenshot).

This is only one of the potential panels that you can include in your PyCharm workspace; we will see that this ability to organize our PyCharm panels will greatly improve our productivity as programmers. For example, the following screenshot is my PyCharm workspace for the project named `FirstProject`, which we have been considering so far:

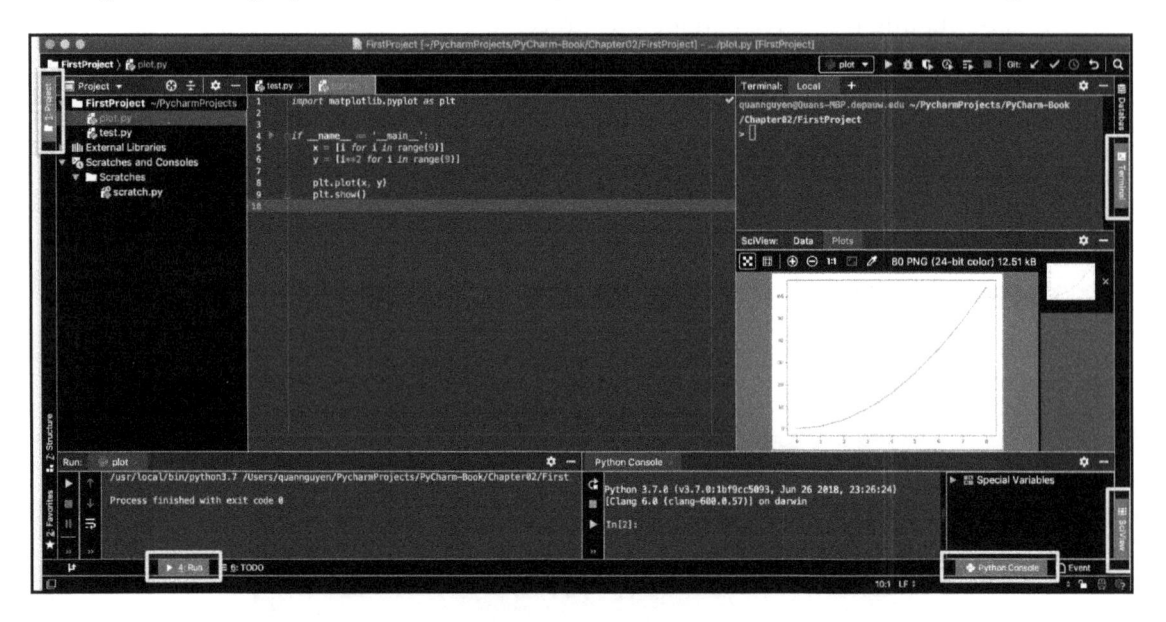

Project window with various panels

[64]

There are many elements going on in this window, so let's break it down together:

- The left-hand side panel is still the familiar directory tree, as well as the editor in the middle of the window (which now contains a new Python script named `plot.py`—don't worry about that for now).
- We have a **Terminal** panel in the top right corner and directly below it is the panel that contains all the visualizations that are produced by the code in our project.
- Turning our attention to the bottom left corner, we can see the **Run** panel, which we know displays relevant information and the printed output of the Python program we most recently ran (in this case, it is the `plot.py` file).
- Finally, in the bottom-middle section of the window, we have another panel for a Python console. In case you are not familiar with the concept, a Python console is essential what you have when you type in `python` or `python3` in the Terminal of a system that has Python (specifically Python 3) installed. You can type in individual Python code and run it immediately. This is specifically helpful for testing quick syntax, methods, or functions.

You may also notice the tags that are correspondingly associated with the panels that we just described, which are highlighted in green boxes in the preceding screenshot. For example, the tag in the top left corner says **Project**, which corresponds to the directory tree panel in the same area of our project window. The same goes for the **Terminal**, **SciView**, **Run**, and **Python Console** tags. If a specific panel is active (displayed in the **Project** window), its corresponding tag will have a background color of deep blue (see the preceding screenshot).

Let's take a moment to discuss the functionality of some noteworthy panels. Note that some of these panels are available to be displayed via **View** | **Tool Windows**, while others will dynamically appear when the corresponding command is run:

- The **Project** panel displays the directory tree for your project so that you can expand and inspect the structure of your current project.
- The **Run** panel, as we have seen, displays runtime information and printed output of a recently executed Python script.

- The **Debug** panel, as the name suggests, is used during the debugging process with the graphical debugger in PyCharm.
- The **TODO** panel lists out all the locations in your project that contains a line that starts with `# TODO: ...` (which, as you probably already know, is a conventional way to denote to-do tasks while programming). The data that's displayed in this panel is compiled from indexing processes and is quite useful when working on a large project.
- The **Terminal** panel is simply a way to directly interact with your Terminal within PyCharm. One important thing to note regarding the **Terminal** panel is that, if the current project has a virtual environment, the profile that's used in the **Terminal** panel will automatically be associated with that virtual environment. This means you won't have to manually activate the virtual environment when working with the Terminal.
- The **SciView** panel (not available in the Community edition of PyCharm) automatically displays relevant information in a scientific computing project. This includes any important data being used and, as we have seen, displayed visualizations from our programs. As we mentioned in Chapter 1, *Introduction to PyCharm – the Most Popular IDE for Python*, we have an entire section of this book dedicated to scientific computing and data science work in PyCharm, where we will look at the **SciView** functionality in more depth.

There are, of course, other panels that might be useful in your PyCharm projects as well. For now, we will move on with our discussion. Now, let's create the `plot.py` file in our project:

1. First, create a new Python file inside our current `FirstProject` project named `plot.py` and enter the following code (which roughly visualizes the graph of the $f(x) = x^2, 1 \leq x \leq 9$ function):

    ```
    import matplotlib.pyplot as plt


    if __name__ == '__main__':
        x = [i for i in range(9)]
        y = [i**2 for i in range(9)]

        plt.plot(x, y)
        plt.show()
    ```

> Note that you can also import the source code from GitHub into your PyCharm so that you don't have to input the code yourself. In the *Importing an external project into PyCharm* section of this chapter, we will discuss the process of importing an external project into our own PyCharm.

2. Getting back to our discussion, let's try to run the script we just entered. But, before we can do that, we have to install the `matplotlib` library, which is the visualization package that we import and utilize in the script.

If you already have `matplotlib` installed on your computer, simply skim through the following section.

Installing packages

To install a package using PyCharm, you can use either of the following methods:

- Graphical installer
- Type in Terminal commands

The first option, which utilizes the graphical installer, is as follows:

1. First, open PyCharm's settings, again, by going to **PyCharm | Preferences** (in macOS) or **File | Settings** (in Windows or Linux).
2. Then, go to **Project: FirstProject** (or the name of your project) and choose **Project Interpreter**. Here, you will see a window displaying all the libraries and packages that have been installed for your project (or more specifically, your current interpreter).

3. To install/uninstall another package in/from our project, click on the **+/-** button located in the bottom left corner of the middle section of the window, as shown here:

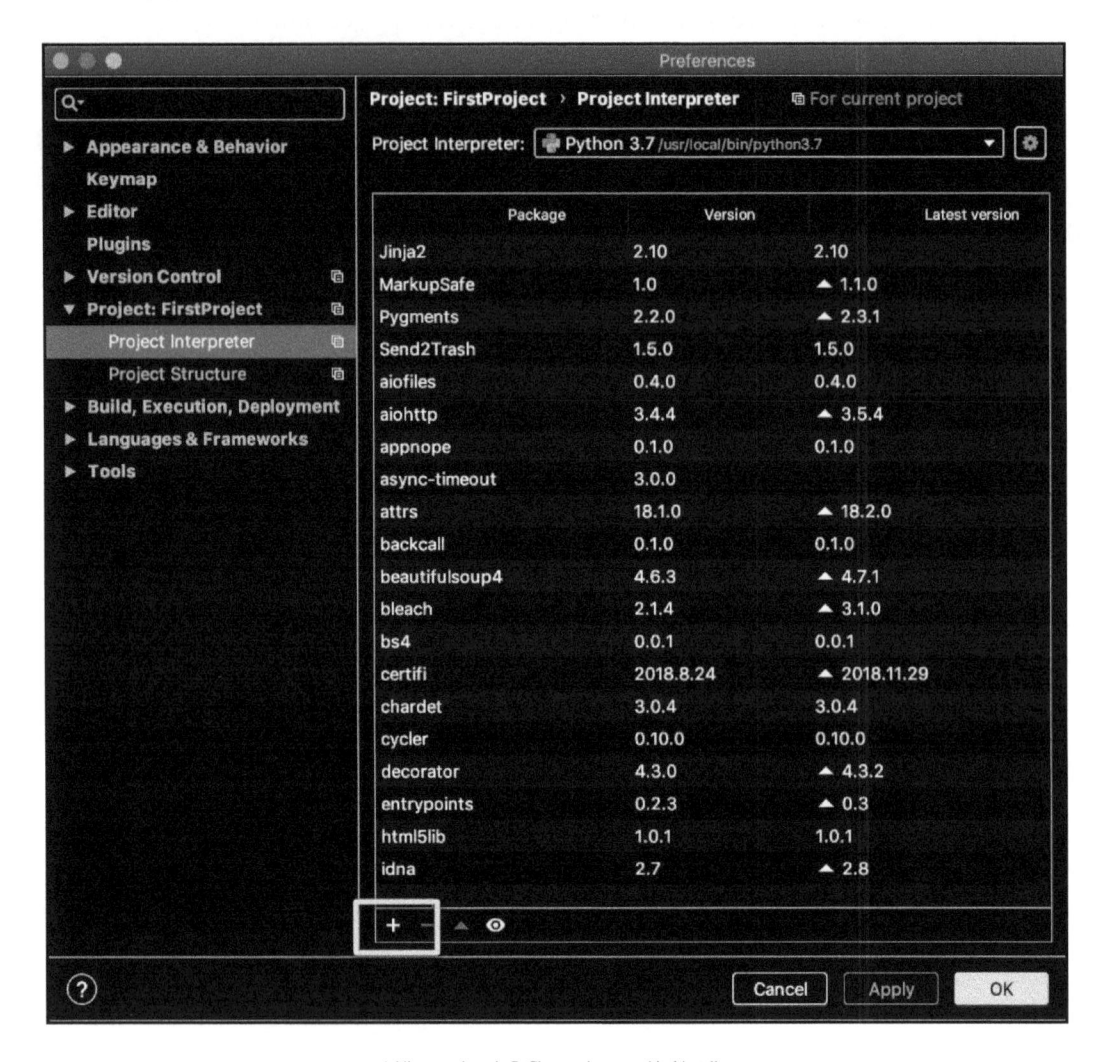

Adding a package in PyCharm using a graphical installer

4. Then, you will be taken to another window with a comprehensive list of Python packages available for installation.
5. Scroll to the `matplotlib` option and click on the **Install Package** button in the bottom left corner.

6. After this, our project will install `matplotlib` and we will be able to use it in our Python code.

> Aside from this method of downloading Python packages via a graphical installer, most of you might agree that the faster way to do this is to run a `pip install` command in the Terminal. So, if you are comfortable working with a Terminal, simply run the following command into the **Terminal** panel (after opening it by selecting **View** | **Tool Windows** | **Terminal**): `pip install matplotlib`.

Whichever method you choose to download and install `matplotlib`, after the installation process, you should now be able to run the `plot.py` script. After doing so, you will see two of the panels we discuss earlier pop up, displaying the output visualization that our program created:

- The **Run** panel (which we already saw in the previous chapter)
- The **SciView** panel

For the rest of the panels, again, simply go to **View** | **Tool Windows** and select the options that correspond to the panels we want (that is, **Python Console** and **Terminal**) to activate them in our project window.

> We can also deactivate a panel (and also reactivate it) by clicking on its tag.

Here, we have learned about the different panels that can be activated and displayed within PyCharm. Next, we will see how we can rearrange the panels in a project in a dynamic way.

Moving panels within a project window

Additionally, you will see that, as you select a specific panel to pop up, it will be located at various places in our project window, either along the side edges or at the bottom section. Now, PyCharm provides the ability to dynamically reorganize these panels to be in an optimal arrangement for our workspace. Specifically, we can move a panel to another region in the project window by dragging and dropping its corresponding tag along the side and bottom edges of the project window.

Customizing Interpreters and Virtual Environments

For example, in the preceding screenshot, my **Run** panel was originally in the bottom left corner. Now, I can drag its tag (highlighted in the green box in the following screenshot) as follows:

Dragging the Run tag

Now, I will drop it to the bottom area of the left edge of the project window, and the whole panel will be moved to the corresponding area. After this process, the **Run** panel is now located in the middle area of the left-hand side of the project window, as follows:

Dropping the Run along the left edge of the window

As we mentioned previously, you can drag and drop a panel tag along the left, right, and bottom edges of the project window. Specifically, there are six sections in total to which you can drag and drop a panel tag, as follows:

- **Top of the left edge**: To display a panel in the top left corner. For example, my directory tree.
- **Bottom of the left edge**: To display a panel in the middle of the left section of the window.
- **Left of the bottom edge**: To display a panel in the bottom left corner.
- **Right of the bottom edge**: To display a panel in the bottom right corner.
- **Top of the right edge**: To display a panel in the top right corner.
- **Bottom of the right edge**: To display a panel in the middle of the right section of the window.

So, to create the specific arrangement in the previous screenshot of my project window, you can move the following tags:

- The **Project** tag to the top of the left edge
- The **Run** tag to the left of the bottom edge
- The **Python Console** tag to the right of the bottom edge
- The **Terminal** tag to the top of the right edge
- The **SciView** tag to the bottom of the right edge

However, keep in mind that this is my own custom arrangement. It is possible for you to not only have a different arrangement, but also a different set of panels than what I have. Depending on your projects, you might have different arrangements for different projects as well.

For example, you might want the **Database** panel rather than the **SciView** panel while working with databases, or you might want to include the **Version Control** panel when working with Git. I would suggest taking some time to try different panel combinations to see what works and don't be afraid to switch things up when you realize that the current organization is not optimal. All of this dynamic organization is possible in PyCharm.

The organization of panels in a PyCharm project window concludes our discussion on the topic of customizing our PyCharm project workspace. In the next section, we will take a step back and discuss the different options that are available for project types in PyCharm.

Customizing Interpreters and Virtual Environments

Creating a PyCharm project – revisited

A specific type of PyCharm project can be selected during the process of creating that project. In this section, we will be discussing that process again and looking at the options that we did not consider in the previous chapter regarding PyCharm project types. Let's walk through the process of creating a new project in PyCharm again.

In the previous chapter, we saw that, after choosing the **Create New Project** option in the welcome window, we will be prompted to select the type of project we'd like to create. However, if you are already in a project (like we are now) and need to create a new project, you can go to **File** | **New Project** to achieve the same result as well. Let's choose this option.

Additionally, it is important to reiterate that this option might not be available until the indexing process is completed, in which case you should wait for the processes (indicated in the bottom right-hand corner of your PyCharm window) to finish.

Choosing a project type

As we select the option to create a new project, we will be taken to a configuration window. This window is used to specify which general project you are working on, where you'd like to store the project, and which interpreter/environment to use. The prompt in which you can select your project type is as follows:

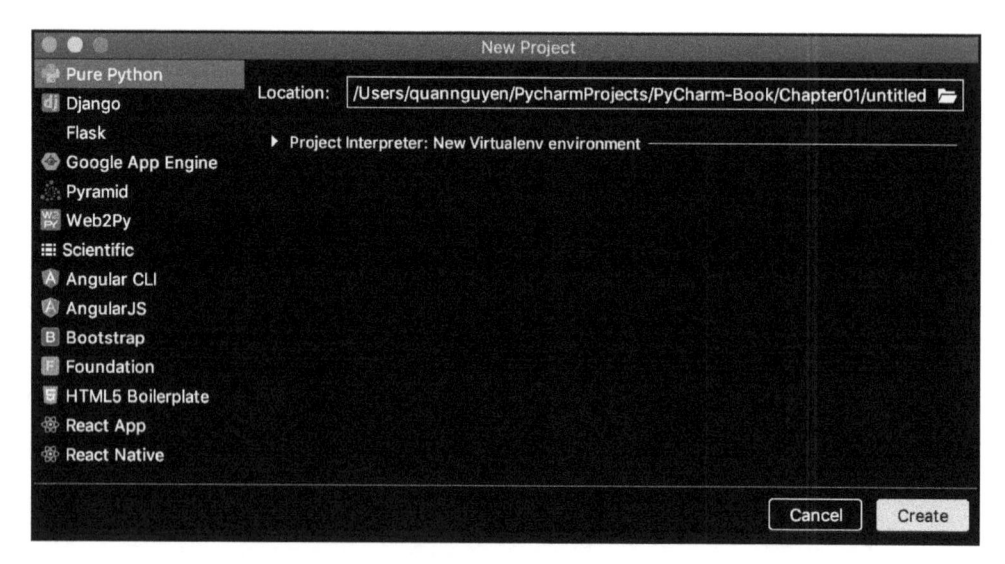

Choosing a PyCharm project type

[72]

Chapter 3

If you are using the Community edition, you will not see the left-hand side of the window. Don't panic, as that section is only used to create boilerplate files for specific types of Python projects, which can also be generated manually without any difficulty in the Community edition anyway.

This section will not be irrelevant to users of the Community edition either, as we will also be discussing the options of specifying the location and the interpreter for your projects, which are available in both editions, so be sure to stick around and not skip to the next section!

With that said, let's consider the left-hand side of the window for now. From this section, we can see all the available options for the type of a PyCharm project—pure, minimal Python, **Django** or **Flask** for web development, **Google App Engine**, and so on. If you do not select the first option, **Pure Python**, then various base files with boilerplate code are generated in a way that corresponds to the type of project that you select.

To see this generation of boilerplate code in action, go ahead and choose, for example, **Django** as the project type in the left-hand panel (if you are using the Professional edition). In the **Location** prompt (which is at the top of the main panel), simply choose a convenient location for this project in your system. The more important option is the specification of the project interpreter, which can be achieved in the section directly below the **Location** prompt.

The default option for the project interpreter is to create a new virtual environment altogether, which is also a general good practice in Python development. If you click on the section to expand it, you will see the following:

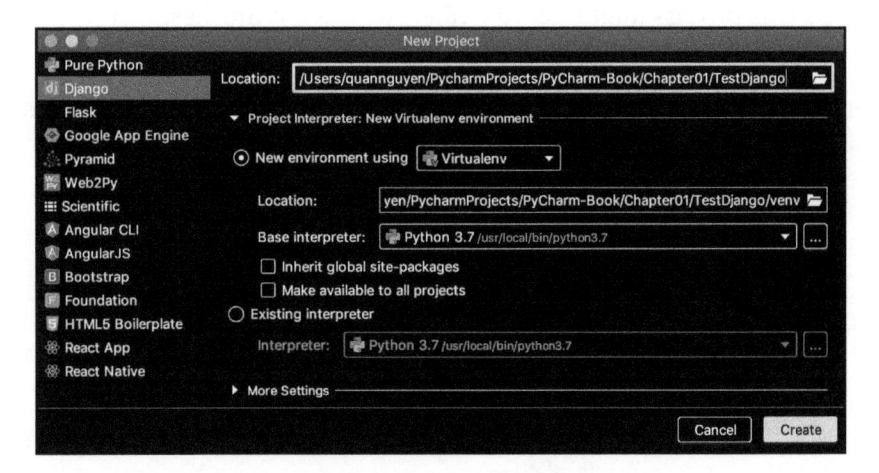

Selecting the project's location and interpreter

[73]

Customizing Interpreters and Virtual Environments

Here, you can also see various options regarding the creation of the virtual environment. If you are not familiar with the concepts of the virtual environment and interpreter, we will be discussing them, along with the options to manage them in PyCharm projects, in the next section.

For now, go ahead and proceed with our new project creation. Here, I am creating a new **Django** project called `TestDjango` (note that you can specify the location of the project as you type in the project name). This project is to have a new environment created using **Virtualenv** in the project folder itself. Again, if you are using the Community edition of PyCharm, ignore the option to specify the project type.

In the section directly below **Project Interpreter**, we will see **More Settings**. Expand it, and you will see that this section contains various Django-related configuration options such as the template language (**Django** or Jinja2), the name of the templates folder, the optional name for the application, as well as whether PyCharm should enable the **Django admin** option or not.

Don't change any of these settings for now; if you are interested in leveraging PyCharm's power to improve your Django projects, an entire part of our book dedicated to Django can be found later. Let's continue.

Project-specific boilerplate code

Next, click on the **Create** button in the bottom right corner of the window. PyCharm will generate a folder in the location you specify with all the skeleton files and code for your specific project. This process might take a while, but when it finishes, you will see a PyCharm window that contains your project.

The following window is what my PyCharm displayed when the creation process finished:

Chapter 3

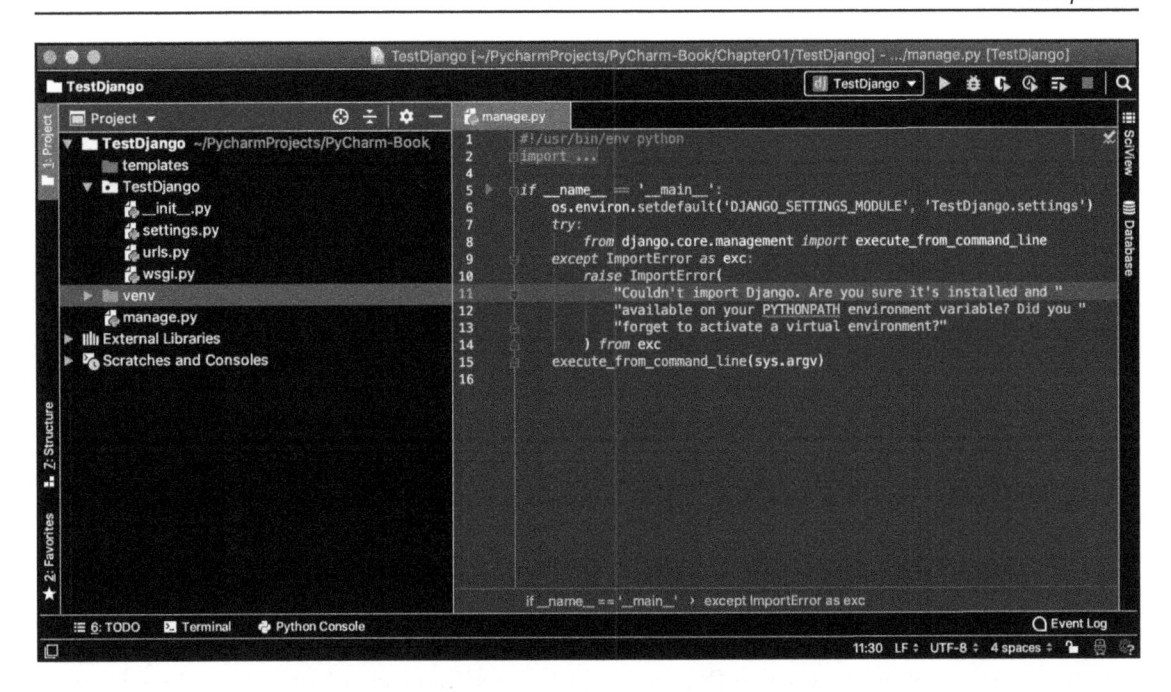

Django project created in PyCharm

If you are familiar with the Django web development framework, you will find that the `manage.py` file (which is currently being opened in the editor in the preceding screenshot) is one of the essential parts of a Django project. Turning our attention to the left-hand side panel (which is our project directory), we will also see other typical Django folders and files such as `settings.py` and `urls.py` in the `TestDjango` subfolder as well as the `templates` subfolder.

So, if you were to work on a new Django project from scratch and used PyCharm as your development environment, you could potentially start working on the actual functionalities and features of your web project, as opposed to having to spend time creating boilerplate code and files. In *Chapter 1, Introduction to PyCharm - the Most Popular IDE for Python*, we discussed that the generation of boilerplate code is one of the main responsibilities of an IDE, and we are seeing that (Professional) PyCharm excels in this matter.

Considerations about Community PyCharm

Comparing this project and the minimal project we created in the previous chapter, FirstProject, we can see that no boilerplate code is generated in a **Pure Python** project. Since users of the Community edition of PyCharm only have the option to create **Pure Python** projects, they will have to start from scratch while working on a Django project. However, as Django developers know, a small set of simple Django commands can also achieve the same result and generate the appropriate boilerplate code and structure of the directory tree for us.

So, in the end, the Professional edition of PyCharm might allow you to skip a particular set of steps in the process of setting up a specific Python project, but these steps can also be accomplished easily and independently of PyCharm. However, this is not to say that it is better to forgo PyCharm altogether if you are using its Community edition. On the contrary, we have seen various forms of customization and flexibility that both editions of PyCharm offer, specifically when it comes to organizing our workspace, in this chapter. We will see a similar trend in future chapters as well.

On another note, if you are using the Professional edition, aside from a Django project, you can choose to create other types of Python project, as we have seen from the options in the preceding screenshot (for example, Google App Engine, Angular, or even React applications). We will go into more detail regarding two types of Python project—Django projects and Scientific projects—later on in this book, but feel free to explore other project types that you are interested in.

Virtual environments and interpreters

In the previous sections, we talked about the different types of projects you can create with PyCharm and skipped through the discussion of choosing the appropriate virtual environments and interpreters for your projects. In this section, we will have that discussion, and see how the management of virtual environments and Python interpreters within PyCharm projects tie into all that we have learned.

Understanding the concepts

While you might already be familiar with virtual environments and Python interpreters, it is worth going into the concepts so that we can get our terminologies straight. There will be no confusion from here on out, especially since some of the terminologies tend to be utilized interchangeably by various user groups.

Python interpreters

First of all, when you download Python to your system, you are specifically downloading a Python interpreter. As the term suggests, it is a program that can take in Python code, interpret it, and translate that code into lower-level machine language, thus executing the Python program. If you have both Python 2.7 and Python 3.6 on your computer, for example, this means that you have two different and separate Python interpreters—in essence, you have two ways to interpret a specific Python program.

Virtual environments in Python

To understand what a Python virtual environment is and why we need it, imagine a scenario where you are working on two separate projects—a large-scale project at work with multiple other employees, and a small, independent side project at home. These projects are stored on your computer, utilize the same Python interpreter, and are in the same environment.

Additionally, we have briefly discussed the fact that Python libraries support almost all possible computing subfields and topics. So, if you are working on a project with enough complexity, chances are there is a library out there that can assist you efficiently. It is, therefore, very likely that you use external libraries and packages. This is also due to the idea to avoid reinventing the wheel in programming: if someone has already invented a tool to address a problem with considerable success, you should (in most cases) take advantage of that tool.

In short, when you are working on a Python project, you are most likely (and should be) using external libraries and packages in that project. Getting back to the two projects in our imaginary scenario, say both projects make use of the `requests` module (a Python library providing simple methods to make HTTP requests) and an update to the module with major improvements has just been released. As a responsible programmer who keeps themselves up to date with the current technology, you plan to apply this update to your two projects.

A problem arises when you realize that the API of the `requests` module changes during this update and that it will require a code revision every time your code uses the `requests` module. This is not ideal for either project, but it is manageable for the second, which is smaller in scale and, after all, a personal side project. Your first project, on the other hand, would need to be completely rewritten if the update is to be applied. This is obviously not desirable, given the fact that it is a work project with multiple people contributing to it.

Customizing Interpreters and Virtual Environments

You might think you could simply not update the `requests` module at all so that you wouldn't have to fix the syntax in either project. However, the updated API would actually help your second and personal project significantly, so you would like to somehow apply the update only to the second project. Here is where the concept of virtual environments comes in. In this scenario, we need a way to separate the two projects in the sense that an update to a library in one project would not affect the same library in the other.

Virtual environments, in essence, are independent, isolated environments that manage their own libraries and packages. This means that when a project changes specific things in a library, other projects will not be affected. As such, it is also a great way to organize and compartmentalize your Python projects.

In terms of the actual process of creating virtual environments for your Python projects, there are a number of tools available in Python—Virtualenv, Pipenv, and Conda. All three of them are virtual environment and package managers that offer various levels of functionality and control.

> If you work with the Anaconda platform, you have likely used Conda as your virtual environment manager already.

All in all, each of these is widely used by Python programmers, but usage commands and details differ widely among the three tools. Luckily, PyCharm provides the option to utilize all of them in the process of creating a virtual environment, and, as we will see later, all the commands to set up, activate, and deactivate a specific virtual environment are all taken care of by PyCharm.

Virtual environments and interpreters together

Interpreters and virtual environments are actually two interconnected concepts in Python. Intuitively, since Python virtual environments specify separate and isolated workspaces, they should also have separate interpreters as well. In the same lines as the preceding scenario, we can image situations where we have some projects in Python 2 and others in Python 3. In this case, having separate interpreters for different projects is a good thing to have.

The following illustration is an example of the separation of library and package dependencies among different Python projects on the same system:

Chapter 3

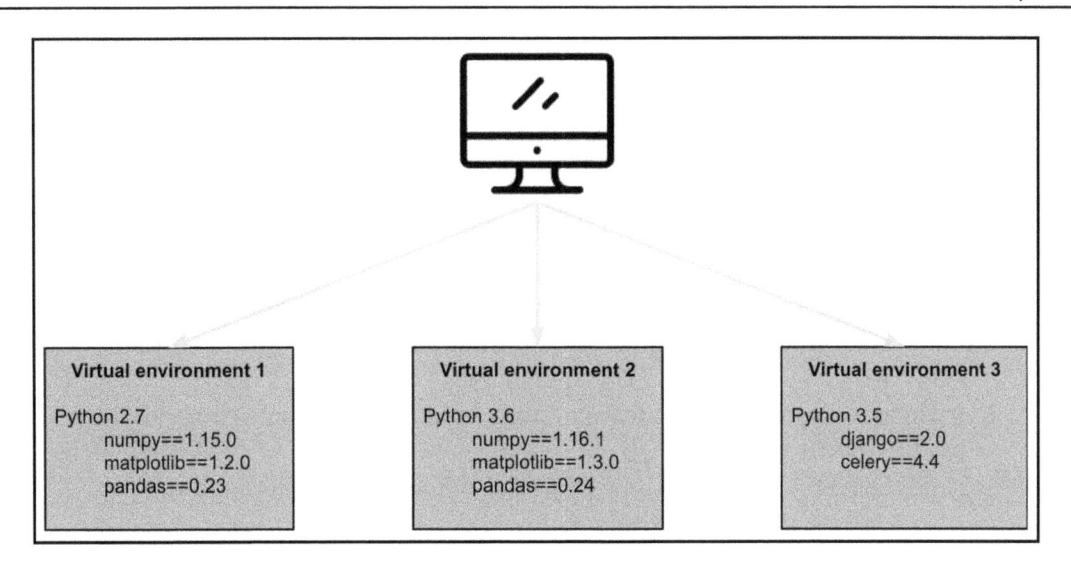

Example of virtual environments

Specifically, we have three different Python projects in total, encapsulated in three separate virtual environments:

- The first and second projects are related to scientific computing, taking advantage of the same set of scientific modules such as `numpy`, `matplotlib`, and `pandas`. Though having the same libraries and packages, the two projects have different Python interpreters (2.7 and 3.6), and the versions of the packages are also different among them. Again, this means that a package update in one project would not affect the functionality of the other.
- Looking at the third environment, which is a web development project with Django and Celery, we can see it uses a completely different set of external libraries and packages. Since the third project does not, and should not, need the scientific computing packages that are used by the other projects—and the same goes for those projects and the web development packages used by the third project—having separate virtual environments is specifically beneficial.

However, you might be tempted to think that an interpreter is a part of a virtual environment; that is, virtual environments manage not only packages but Python interpreters themselves. This is not correct—each virtual environment can potentially utilize multiple interpreters, and each interpreter can also be used in multiple virtual environments. In the next section, we will see that we can switch between interpreters and virtual environments independently.

Customizing Interpreters and Virtual Environments

Managing virtual environments and interpreters in PyCharm

In this section, we will see what options there are in terms of managing virtual environments and interpreters that PyCharm provides. To do this, we will create another PyCharm project:

1. If you are still in the `TestDjango` project, go ahead and select **File** > **New Project**; if you are at the PyCharm welcome window, simply choose **Create New Project**.
2. In the next window, we will see various options for the new project, which we briefly looked at earlier.
3. Here, I am specifying this new project as a **Scientific** project and naming it `TestScientific`, as shown here:

> If you are using the Professional edition, feel free to select whichever project type you are interested in so that you will be able to see what project-specific boilerplate code will be generated afterward.

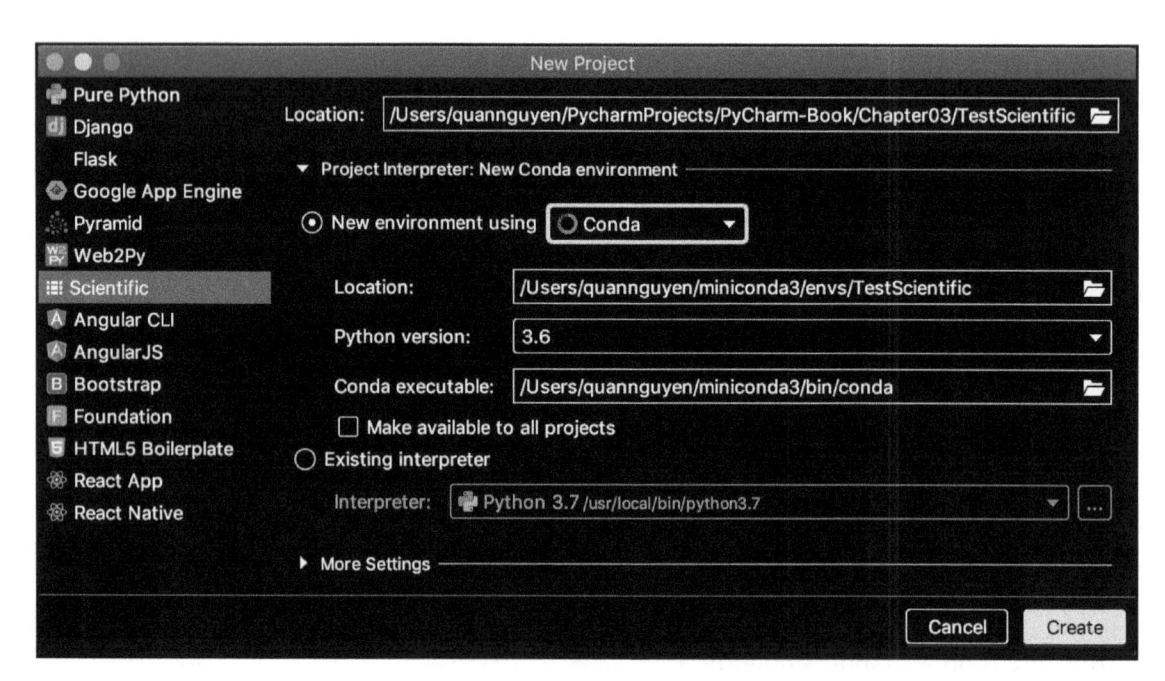

Using Conda to create a virtual environment

[80]

4. Expand the **Project Interpreter** option to set the specifics of the virtual environment for our new project. For the sake of a complete comparison, I am selecting the new environment to be created by Conda, and its own interpreter will be Python 3.6. There is also an option for **Pipenv**; feel free to try this as well if it interests you more.

If you are a Conda user, you will see that the location of the environment folder is appropriately stored in my Miniconda directory, as opposed to the same folder as the project, like in virtual environments created by Virtualenv, which we saw earlier with `TestDjango`. These are simply different practices between Conda and VirtualEnv, and PyCharm does a good job of preserving them. So, there is a technical consistency between creating a virtual environment on your own and doing it using PyCharm, regardless of what virtual environment tool you are using.

> Note that there is an option at the bottom of the **Project Interpreter** section named **Existing interpreter**, which we used to create our first project in the previous chapter. As the name suggests, by selecting this option, we will not have PyCharm create a new virtual environment for the current project, and it will utilize an existing interpreter. However, as long as a new virtual environment is to be created, that environment will have its own Python interpreter (in our current example, it is a Python 3.6 interpreter).

5. Go ahead and click **Create**. After around 10 seconds, you will be taken to the window of the newly created project. If you are a user of the Professional edition and chose a specific type for this current project, you can take a moment to inspect the boilerplate code that was generated automatically by PyCharm. However, we should also consider the virtual environment and interpreter of this project.

Customizing Interpreters and Virtual Environments

6. Open the **Python Console** panel, which is typically a default part of the project window. Alternatively, you can open it up by going to **View** | **Tool Windows** | **Python Console**. The information that's displayed in this panel tells us which interpreter our current project is using. For example, the following screenshot shows the information that's given in my **Python Console** panel:

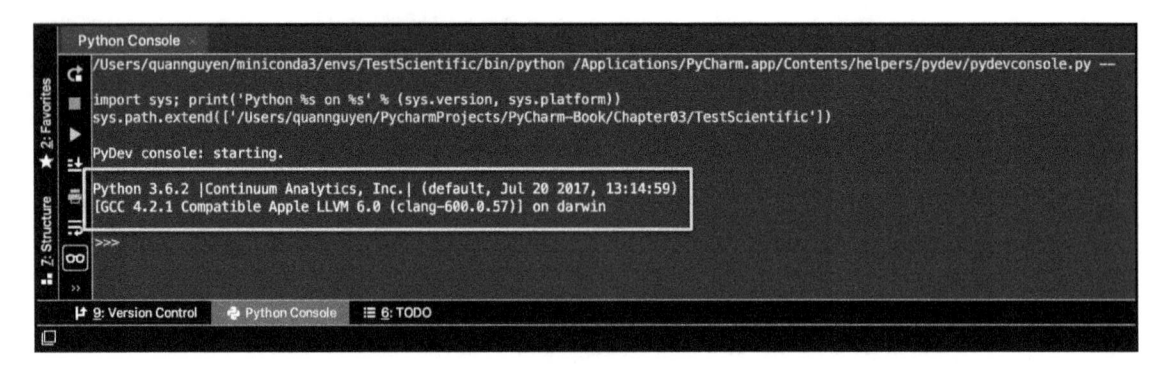

Interpreter information in the Python Console panel

The section that's highlighted by the green box shows us that we are using a Python 3.6.2 interpreter, which corresponds to the options that we chose while creating this project earlier.

As another way to check which Python interpreter you are using, you can take advantage of the `which` command in the Terminal/command line. The following is the output I received when I typed in `which python` (used to determine the path to the current Python interpreter) and `which conda` (used to determine the path to my Conda root folder):

```
> which python
/Users/quannguyen/miniconda3/bin/python
> which conda
/Users/quannguyen/miniconda3/bin/conda
```

Since we used Conda to create this current virtual environment, the corresponding Python interpreter is appropriately stored with, and managed by, Conda. Again, this is a consistent way of having virtual environments created by different tools that PyCharm offers.

I personally like to use Virtualenv to create the virtual environments for my PyCharm projects, simply because that is the tool I used before PyCharm. So, from now on, the example projects that are used in this book will have their respective virtual environments created via Virtualenv.

With that said, I suggest that you also keep using your go-to virtual environment tool, as you yourself know best about the specifics of that tool. Furthermore, we have seen that whichever option we choose in PyCharm to create a virtual environment, the subsequent details of managing that environment remain consistent.

Configuring the interpreter for a created project

As we mentioned earlier, in a virtual environment, a Python interpreter, though considerably connected with that environment, is technically not a part of it. This means that a project can utilize multiple interpreters for its code.

We have already seen that a new interpreter will be created along with a virtual environment when we create a new project in PyCharm. In this section, we will learn how to change the interpreter of a PyCharm project after it has been created.

Why does it matter?

It is worth discussing the reason why we might want to point to a project that has already been created for a specific Python interpreter. After all, that project already has its own interpreter, and shouldn't all the elements regarding the interpretation and execution of code in a project be bound in its corresponding virtual environment (like the case we have made for the general use of virtual environments)?

As it turns out, it is beneficial to be able to share an interpreter across multiple projects, especially in transitional situations. Say you are working on a large project using Python 2.7 and are thinking of updating your interpreter to Python 3.6. However, you are not sure if, for example, all your print statements or numerical divisions will work as intended after the update. In this case, you could simply point your project to a Python 3.6 interpreter and try executing your code. Any warnings and errors you receive during that execution will help you decide whether the update is feasible.

In some other situations, your computer platform might dictate what Python interpreter is appropriate. For example, a specific version of the computer vision library, OpenCV, may only support Python 3.5 on macOS but can support Python 3.6 on Linux and Windows (this is simply an example, but there are similar problems when you work with OpenCV in Python). So if you are working on a project using OpenCV on multiple platforms at the same time (maybe at work and at home), you will find the ability to switch to the interpreter of each of your projects incredibly helpful.

Customizing Interpreters and Virtual Environments

All in all, PyCharm gives us the freedom to switch between different interpreters across multiple projects. While it is important to keep specific goals in mind while starting a new project, we shouldn't be afraid to be flexible and change things up as the project moves forward. This is certainly the case for the usage of the interpreter in a PyCharm project.

Now, you may remember from the diagram for the example of three separate projects (two scientific projects and one web project) we used earlier that the interpreters were drawn to be a part of their respective virtual environment. But now, we need to revise that diagram so that it reflects our ability to dynamically configure the interpreter of PyCharm projects, as follows:

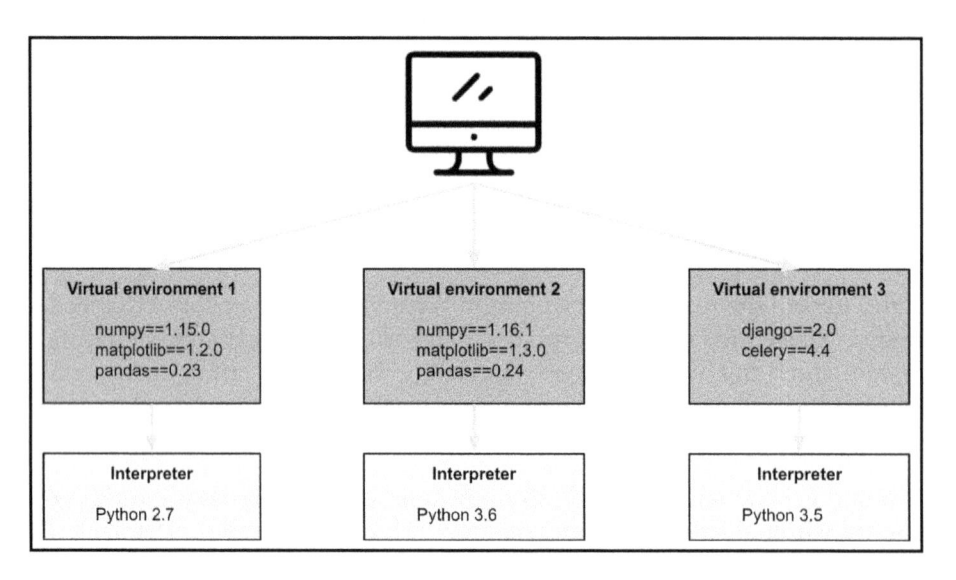

Virtual environments and interpreters

Each of our projects is associated with its corresponding interpreter, as we saw earlier, but the interpreters are not a part of their respective virtual environments anymore. In fact, we can point a project to a different interpreter. For example, the first two projects can potentially utilize the second interpreter (Python 3.6), or all three projects can share the third (Python 3.5), given that all the dependencies are met.

Options in PyCharm

Now, let's see how we can do this in PyCharm. Navigate to the project we just created (`TestScientific`) if you are not already there. Again, the interpreter that's currently being used for this project should be Python 3.6, and created using Conda:

1. We will open the settings and go to **Project: TestScientific | Project Interpreter**, which we already saw when we learned how to install external libraries and packages for our projects.
2. Now, click on the dropdown button in the **Project Interpreter** prompt in the upper section of the window and select **Show All...**, as follows. This will show us all the Python interpreters that are available on our system:

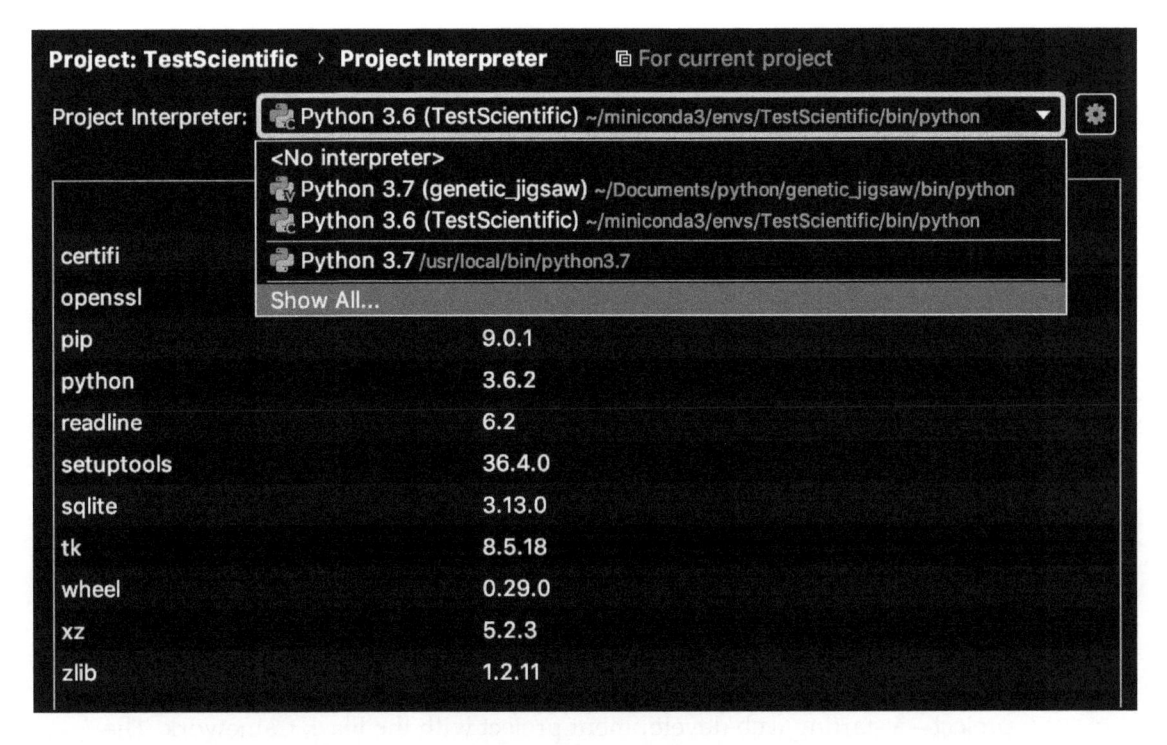

Showing the available interpreters in PyCharm

3. From here, you will be able to select one of the interpreters that's available to be used by PyCharm projects. As an example, I will choose the Python 3.7 interpreter that was created for the `TestDjango` project earlier.
4. Click **OK** and **Apply** to point our current project to that specific interpreter. For this change to take full effect, we need to relaunch PyCharm.
5. After reopening the PyCharm project, you will notice, in the **Python Console** and **Terminal** (using the `which python` command again), that our interpreter has indeed been changed.

That is how you select and change the interpreter for your PyCharm projects, even after they have already been created. In the next section, we will look into the process of importing external projects into PyCharm.

Importing an external project into PyCharm

We have seen how the management of project types, virtual environments, and interpreters is done in PyCharm. In this final section, we will discuss the process of importing an existing project, previously external to PyCharm, into our workspace. This option is considerably useful, especially when you are working on collaborative projects that are cross-platform and cross-system. For example, you can import the source code of this book into your own PyCharm so that you don't have to manually enter the code yourself while following the examples in later chapters.

We will take a hands-on approach and try to import a small project that I previously prepared that's included in the GitHub repository for this book. Specifically, if you have already downloaded and unzipped the repository on your computer, the project we are trying to import into PyCharm is included in `Chapter03/TestImport`. To do this, we need to follow these steps:

1. Go to **File** | **Open...** (or choose **Open** in the welcome window), navigate to that folder, and choose **Open**.
2. A PyCharm project window will open. Inside, you will see the content of this project—a starting web development project with the Flask framework. The following is a screenshot of this project window, showing the `main.py` file in the editor:

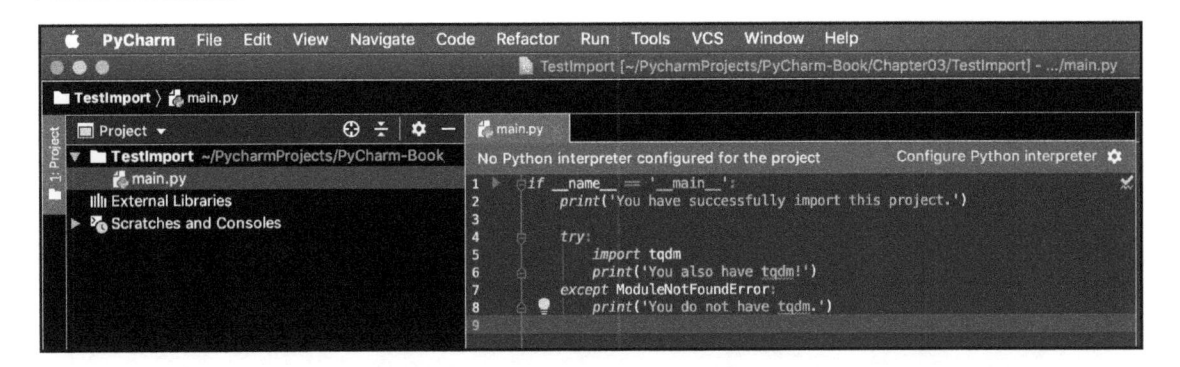

Importing an external project into PyCharm

3. In the preceding screenshot, you may have noticed—and potentially in your window as well—that there is a warning message above our editor that says **No Python interpreter configured for the project**. This should be expected since as we are importing an external project that has never been read by our PyCharm software before, so it won't know the specifics regarding the interpreter (and virtual environment) of the project.

Looping back to what we discussed previously, when a project is being worked on cross-platform, it is good practice to maintain separate virtual environments and interpreters in the different platforms. In other words, since different platforms may require different combinations of interpreters and libraries or packages, developers should only exchange and collaborate on the actual source code of the project, not including interpreters, virtual environments, or library dependencies.

If we look at the **Python Console** of the `TestImport` project we just imported into PyCharm, we will see that the global Python interpreter is being used, which supports the fact that PyCharm does not know which interpreter is appropriate for this specific external project.

4. To select an interpreter, simply click on the text **Configure Python interpreter** (or open the settings and go to **Project Interpreter**). You will be taken to the interpreter-selecting window that we examined earlier. In my case, I will select my global Python interpreter for simplicity's sake.

5. After choosing an interpreter for the project, another warning will potentially pop up, saying that the package and library requirements for this project are not being met:

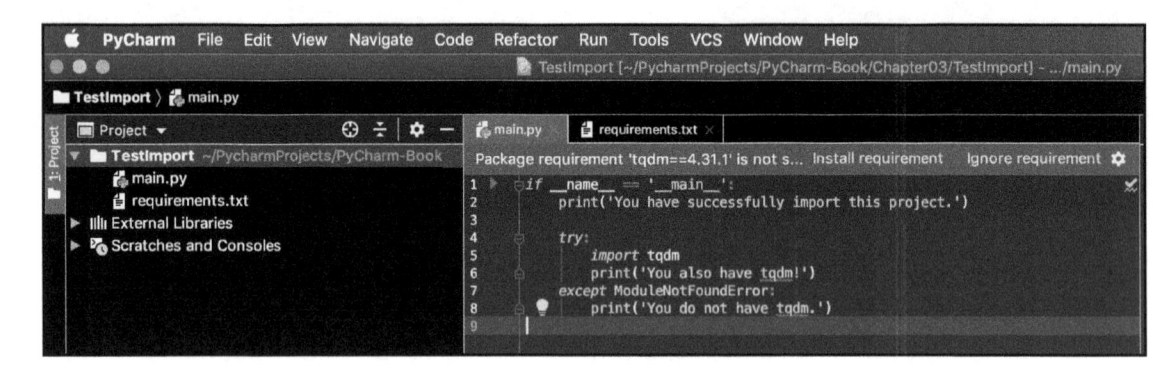

Unsatisfied package requirements in imported projects

6. Specifically, the `tqdm` module (that I arbitrarily chose to use as an example), which is being used in `main.py` and specified in `requirements.txt`, is not available for the Python interpreter I selected. If you don't have the `tqdm` module installed on your system, you will receive this warning as well. If you run the script, the execution will fail inside the try block in the code, and you will receive the following output:

```
You have successfully imported this project.
You do not have tqdm.
```

7. Going back to the warning message, you can select the **Install requirement** option and PyCharm will automatically download and install all the unsatisfied packages for you.
8. After the installation process has completed, rerunning the Python script again will give us a different output:

```
You have successfully imported this project.
You also have tqdm!
```

The reason PyCharm was able to detect the unsatisfied package requirement for `tqdm` is not because it analyzed the line of code where we import the package, but because we have the `requirements.txt` file in our project, which specifies that the dependency for this project is `tqdm` version 4.31.1.

As you already know, having a `requirements.txt` file that lists all the external libraries and packages a project requires is good practice in Python development that you should always follow, especially when working cross-platform. Our experiment just now has shown us that when we import a Python project with an appropriate `requirements.txt` file, PyCharm will assist us in the process of downloading and importing all the unmet dependency requirements.

> For your reference, a quick command to generate the appropriate `requirements.txt` file for your project is `pip freeze > requirements.txt`, which should be run in your Terminal. The `pip freeze` command lists all the external libraries and packages that your Python interpreter has, and the second part of the command will transfer the output data into a `requirements.txt` file.
>
> Every time you'd like to transfer a project outside of your system and import it into PyCharm in another system, run this command and include `requirements.txt` in your project for a smooth transition, which will be assisted by PyCharm.

Notice that the combined usage of virtual environments and the `requirements.txt` file is common with Virtualenv. If the project you are importing uses Pipenv and `Pipfile` files as the virtual environment manager, PyCharm also offers the same functionalities to help you import your dependencies with one click.

Overall, we have learned how to import external projects into PyCharm. Moving forward with this book, you can go through this process again to import code examples from this book's GitHub repository into your own PyCharm while following the discussions in this book.

Summary

In this chapter, we have considered the ability to work with multiple types of Python projects, virtual environments, and interpreters in PyCharm. Overall, PyCharm provides a wide range of options so that users are able to customize their projects, and they can do it in a dynamic way, even after a project has already been created.

In the Professional edition of PyCharm, you can have specific types of Python projects created, such as Django/Flask web development projects or scientific computing projects. This option will populate the new project with various boilerplate code and a directory structure that follows the convention of the corresponding project type. For example, a new Django project will have a `templates` folder and a `manage.py` file, while a scientific computing project will have commonly used folders such as `data`, `models`, and `notebooks`.

It is important to note that, while this functionality of generating boilerplate code allows users to save a significant amount of time when a new project is created, the whole process can be done manually in the Community edition.

We have also looked at how to create and customize a virtual environment and a Python interpreter for a PyCharm project. PyCharm's dynamic nature is demonstrated with the ability to switch the interpreter for a project freely, even after the project has already been associated with an interpreter of its own. This allows for easy and intuitive dependency-based testing processes in Python development.

Finally, we have seen how to import an external project into our PyCharm workspace and install all of its package and library requirements using the `requirements.txt` file. PyCharm actively combs through this file and looks for any unmet requirements in the current interpreter, effectively taking the pain of installing project dependencies away from the developer.

As you have probably noticed, the first few chapters have concerned themselves with setting up various aspects of the usage of PyCharm in order to create an optimal workspace for our projects.

In the next chapter, we will go into details about the assistance PyCharm provides when it actually comes to programming and writing code. Specifically, we will consider PyCharm's real-time smart coding assistance, together with the refactoring and documentation processes and how PyCharm streamlines them.

Questions

1. What types of panels (or window tools) are available in a PyCharm project window? How can we arrange the panels to our liking in a PyCharm project window?
2. A progress bar typically appears when we open a Python project in PyCharm. What does the bar indicate? What problem arises for some PyCharm functionalities when the progress bar is still running?

3. What types of projects are available during the creation of a PyCharm project? Are they available in both editions of PyCharm?
4. What is the difference between a **Pure Python** project and other types of PyCharm project? Does this difference matter in the long run?
5. What is a Python interpreter? What is a Python virtual environment? Are Python interpreters dependent on virtual environments? Is the reverse true?
6. What methods of creating a virtual environment are available during the creation of a PyCharm project? Are there any differences in usage within PyCharm after the virtual environment is created among these methods?
7. How can we choose to use another project interpreter that is different from the one we created and associated with the project? What is the benefit of being able to do this?
8. How can we import an external project into PyCharm? What is the role of `requirements.txt` in this process?

Further reading

For more information, you can refer to the following information:

- *Mastering PyCharm,* by Quazi Nafiul Islam, Packt Publishing (https://www.packtpub.com/web-development/mastering-pycharm)
- *Modern Python Development with PyCharm,* by Pedro Kroger (https://pedrokroger.net/pycharm-book/)
- *Django Projects in PyCharm Community Version,* by Andy Knight, Automation Panda (https://automationpanda.com/2017/09/14/django-projects-in-pycharm-community-edition/)
- *Python Virtual Environments: A Primer*, Real Python (https://realpython.com/python-virtual-environments-a-primer/)

4
Editing and Formatting with Ease in PyCharm

So far in this book, we have only covered high-level ideas for using PyCharm and developing Python projects within it. In this chapter, we are going to take a closer look at the editor and its various functionalities for Python development.

Specifically, this chapter serves as a comprehensive compilation of features in PyCharm that facilitate faster and more accurate programming. These features include linting, code completion, refactoring, documentation, and so on. This chapter will offer you a practical understanding of the preceding programming practices. Additionally, you will also learn how to incorporate those practices into your projects and even automate them with the help of PyCharm.

The following topics will be covered in this chapter:

- Real-time code inspection and fixes
- Various code-completion support features in PyCharm and how to leverage them to work faster and make your code more readable as well as accurate
- The concept of refactoring in programming, why it is important to refactor your code, and how to do that in PyCharm
- The details of making documentation in programming and the various options for viewing and creating documentation for your PyCharm projects

Technical requirements

The following is a list of prerequisites for this chapter:

- Ensure that you have both Python 3.6+ and PyCharm installed on your computer
- Download the GitHub repository at `https://github.com/PacktPublishing/Hands-on-Application-Development-with-PyCharm`

- During this chapter, we will be working with the subfolder named `Chapter04` in the downloaded code repository

Code inspection

A large part of the real-time code analyzer that makes PyCharm so powerful is embedded in its code inspection features. Specifically, as you work on your code, potential messages will pop up, displaying various information, including errors and their potential fixes.

Specifics of the code analyzer

In general, PyCharm performs code analysis in real-time as you type in new code into the editor. The executed inspections look for potential syntactical and runtime errors, as well as code styling conventions. Any potential problem that is detected will be highlighted within that specific piece of code and will be indicated in the top-right corner, as well as along the scroll bar of the editor window.

In total, there are three possible levels of severity indicated in the top-right corner of the editor:

- Errors (⬤)
- Warnings (■)
- Nothing detected (✓)

It is generally a good practice to address any problems in your code if the severity is either errors or warnings before using it or committing it to GitHub.

Fortunately, PyCharm not only lists out all problems with our code (using highlighting and severity levels, as we've already mentioned) but also offers a list of potential and relevant fixes for each problem so that you're not left alone in the process of fixing your code. This is done via intention actions, which we will look at in upcoming sections.

Code inspection in a PyCharm project

In this section, we will be considering a number of specific instances where PyCharm's code analyzer points out common errors and warnings in Python programs. We will then address these problems accordingly.

To follow this example, import the `Chapter04/Inspection` project into your workspace and open the `main.py` file, or copy and paste the following code into a PyCharm project:

```
def is_even(x):
    if x % 2 == 0:
        return True
    else:
        return False

    print('Function finished.')


def foo(bar):
    return 0


def main():
    print(math.sqrt(4))

if __name__ == '__main__':
    main()
```

The first thing to note here is that there are several errors and warnings that we need to address in this file, as indicated in the top-right corner and along the scroll bar of the editor window. This is indicated by a green box in the following screenshot:

Code inspection in PyCharm

For each error or warning, you can hover your cursor over the code that is associated with that problem to see more details regarding the issue. For example, if you hover over the `math.sqrt()` function call in the `main()` function, a popup will appear saying **Unresolved reference 'math'** to indicate that we need to import the `math` module to be able to utilize its `sqrt()` function.

> On the topic of hovering, you can also hover over indications of problems in the scroll bar to display the same information. This feature is especially useful in large files and projects.

Now, let's try our hand at resolving each of these problems. The goal, again, is to obtain a green checkmark in the top-right corner of our editor window (which is currently a red exclamation mark).

Dead code

In the `is_even()` function, the `print` statement at the end will never be reached by a Python interpreter since the function will return beforehand. We call this piece of code (which does not affect the execution of our program in any way) dead code. In most cases, a programmer will either try to incorporate that code into the actual function somehow or simply delete it.

We will delete the line of code in this example. Watch the scroll bar on the right as you do so to see the current warning disappear.

Unused declarations

Another nifty feature of code inspection is spotting any unused function parameters or variables. In the `foo()` function of our example, a parameter named `bar` is passed in but never actually used inside the function. By hovering over this parameter, you can see the message **Parameter 'bar' value is not used**. This warning will also be displayed for any unused function, variable, or imported API.

As we are not using this parameter in the function, simply remove it from the function signature. You can also utilize intention actions, which we will consider in more detail after this section.

Unresolved references

Another common problem that PyCharm's code analyzer can detect—and this one is actually an error—is unresolved references. As we mentioned previously, in our example, we are using the `sqrt()` function from the `math` module without importing it. The general error extends to any unimported and undeclared API.

To fix this error, you can manually import the function from the `math` module by typing the `import` statement into the code. On the other hand, you can take advantage of intention actions by performing the following steps:

1. Move your cursor to where the error is, that is, the `math` part of `print(math.sqrt(4))`.
2. A red light-bulb icon will appear shortly at the beginning of the line of code, as shown in the following screenshot. Click on it to open the Intention menu:

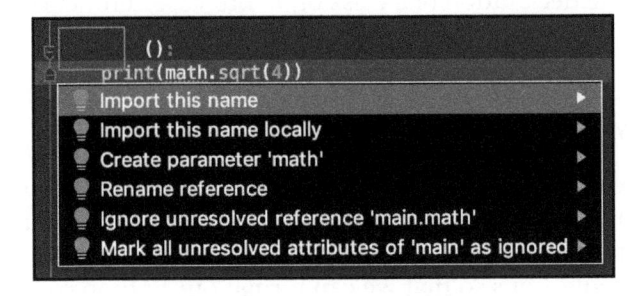

Fixing unresolved references in PyCharm

3. From here, we can choose the appropriate action to take to fix the error. Since we need to import the function from the `math` module, choose the first option, that is, **Import this name**. There will be another menu asking you where to import a module named `math` from (since there are multiple in Python). Choose the first option.
4. After this, an appropriate `import` statement will be automatically inserted at the beginning of the file, and the error will go away.

Again, we can imagine the convenience of this feature in large projects, where it is difficult to keep track of all the libraries and packages that the project uses. PyCharm's intention actions nicely handle these nitty-gritty details for us.

PEP 8 style suggestions

Last but definitely not least, PyCharm will inform you of any improvements that can be made in your code with regard to the official style guide for writing Python code, PEP 8.

> For more information about this style guide, head on over to www.python.org/dev/peps/pep-0008/.

We have already seen an example of using PyCharm to follow PEP 8 conventions with the wrapping limit set to 79 in each line of the editor.

Now, hover over the beginning of the main scope in our current program, `if __name__ == '__main__':`. You will see a message saying **PEP 8: expected 2 blank lines after class of function definition, found 1**. As suggested, following PEP 8, programmers should have two blank lines after the declaration of a class or, in our case, a function before writing new code blocks.

To fix this problem, simply add another blank line after the `main()` function, and the warning will go away.

As you can see, this feature is quite convenient for Python programmers. No one really wants to write bad code that does not follow the official style guide, but not many people really remember all the instances and subtleties of PEP 8 off by heart. Having code inspections offering suggestions so that we can format our Python code in PyCharm effectively takes care of this problem for us.

If, for some reason, you are not seeing the preceding warnings, open PyCharm's settings and navigate to **Editor | Inspections**. From the list included in the main section, expand the Python item and ensure that the two sub-items, that is, **PEP 8 coding style violation** and **PEP 8 naming convention violation**, are enabled, as shown in the following screenshot:

Enabling PEP 8 conventions in PyCharm

After successfully addressing each of these problems, there should be no warnings or error in your current code now, and hopefully the icon on the top-right corner of your editor window is a green checkmark. Again, since we already have a great IDE to detect all potential problems in our code, the least we can do is leverage that and strive for better code quality.

Customizable code completion support

All of us are familiar with code completion support from our editor/IDE in one way or another. This is the functionality that suggests potential ways to complete the line of code that you are currently typing. Text completion is not only limited to programming; we see it in word processing, texting, or typing in general. Even auto-correct functionalities in smartphones are a part of general text completion.

Editing and Formatting with Ease in PyCharm

However, there are still some subtleties in taking advantage of the code completion support in PyCharm, specifically regarding how to adjust various options with the support, as well as how hands-on the suggestions will be. In this section, we will be looking into the advantages of using intelligent code completion functionalities while programming, and how PyCharm assists in this process.

The case for code completion support

Formally, intelligent code completion support is aware of the context of both high-level aspects of programming—the programming language being used and the project/class/method the code that is written belongs to. In general, the purpose of having an intelligent code completion engine is to reduce the number of errors and typos in your code, as well as the development time (specifically, time spent writing code).

The most common form of code completion is showing a pop-up with a list of suggestions regarding how to complete the line of code (or part of the line) that you are writing. You can then choose the item you want to complete your code with. This suggestion list is shown in the following screenshot:

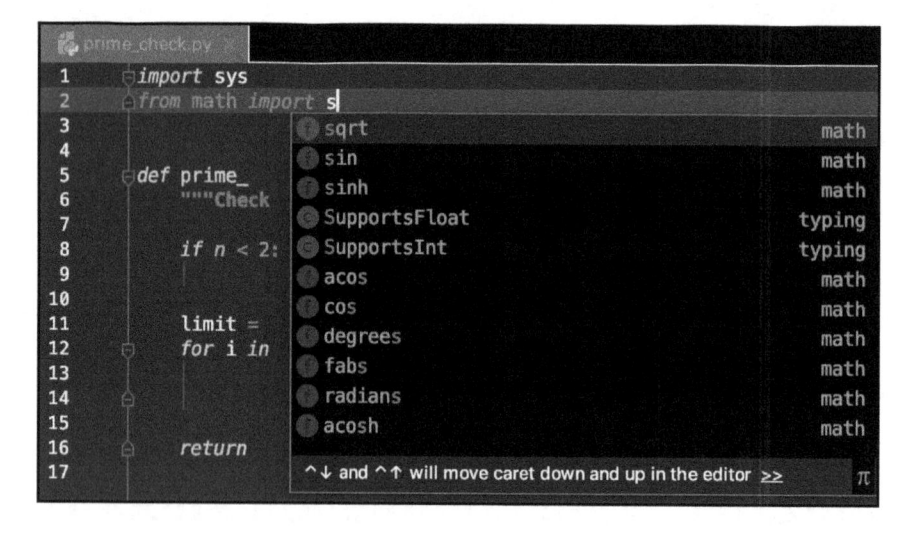

Code completion suggestions

In the preceding example, just from the given information (to the effect that I am trying to import something that has an *s* in its name from the `math` module), PyCharm is able to list all the potential methods and classes, sorted by relevance (we will see how to change the order of these suggestions to alphabetical later in this chapter, in the *Customizing your code completion engine* section). You can then continue typing. Click on an option in this list to complete the sentence, or hit *Enter* or *Tab* to select the first suggested option.

Code completion is widely accepted as a good way to speed up programming and development without bringing about any downsides. Being able to use code completion means that you don't need to memorize all the API and method calls, and you don't have to type as much either. In many IDEs (and certainly in PyCharm), you can dynamically open up documentation saved in the IDE while interacting with the code completion support, so gaining access to the official documentation is still possible.

Code completion specifically doesn't entail the drawbacks that might result from using, as we have already discussed, an IDE. Recall that we have argued that beginner developers, while relying too much on their IDEs, might not have to learn and deeply understand the fundamentals of programming, as well as the general syntax of the language being used. This is not the case for code completion support because, in order to take advantage of its functionality, you have to know what you are looking for and thus be familiar with what you are working with anyway.

Historically, a professor of Computer Science at Columbia University, Gail Kaiser, is considered the creator of many fundamental components of the very first code completion system. While the actual implementation of a good code completion engine can get quite complex, all we need to keep in mind (when using PyCharm specifically) is that the engine relies on the indexing process.

> Recall that this is when PyCharm combs through all relevant code and documentation to gather all the necessary information for various purposes. Code completion is one of them. This is also why code completion, similar to some other functionalities that we have discussed, might not be available when the indexing process is still running.

There is almost no reason for a developer to not utilize a good code completion platform, especially at a time when efficiency and productivity are emphasized and valued. Furthermore, as we've already explained, code completion support can be used as a black box; the developer doesn't need to know how it works in order to take full advantage of it.

Editing and Formatting with Ease in PyCharm

Overall, code completion allows us to efficiently find the correct APIs during the development process. If a developer gets bogged down by miscellaneous and low-level aspects of a project (in this case, looking for API calls), he or she will fail to keep the big picture of the project in mind. However, with the help of a good code completion engine, this problem can be addressed effectively.

In the next subsection, we will be looking at code completion features in PyCharm that make the software stand out.

How is code completion different in PyCharm?

Alongside the generation of boilerplate code, code completion support is indeed one of the most important features of a good IDE, and therefore a big reason why PyCharm is so popular. The main approach to code completion that PyCharm takes is smart code completion, which only looks for the most applicable and most likely APIs to suggest in the pop-up list.

In this subsection, we will go through the code completion features that are commonly used in PyCharm projects. After this, you will be able to leverage and customize various options in PyCharm when it comes to code completion.

Before we move forward, we will set up our workspace by going through the following steps:

1. Navigate to the code repository of this book and go into the `Chapter04/CodeCompletion` folder, which includes examples that we will be examining in this section.
2. Launch PyCharm and import this folder as a project into your workspace.
3. If you are fuzzy on the details, the last section of the previous chapter provides a walkthrough for the process of importing a project in PyCharm.

Once you have successfully imported the necessary example code for this section into PyCharm, it is time to start exploring the various aspects of PyCharm's intelligent code completion engine.

Basics versus smart code completion

Looking back to the preceding screenshot (when I tried to import from the `math` module), the first thing we should appreciate about code completion is the fact that suggestions are not necessarily methods and classes whose names start with an *s*, but ones that have an *s* in their names.

This means that, in general, if a class or a method that contains the word currently being typed is in any part of its name, it will be suggested by code completion. This functionality gives us a better searching capability, but it also generates a large number of suggestions that we might not need.

This is where the distinction between basic and smart code completion in PyCharm comes into play:

- Basic code completion will suggest all the methods, keywords, or classes that are applicable to the line of code the caret is currently on.
- Smart code completion compiles a more filtered list of suggestions by taking into account the types of the variables being used in that line of code.

Let's consider this distinction with an example. Consider the `string_assert.py` file in the `CodeCompletion` folder:

```
def foo(a, b):
    assert isinstance(a, str)

    a

    b
```

The file contains incomplete code—don't panic. This is intentional so that we can see how code completion in PyCharm works. First of all, if the indexing process is still running on PyCharm, be sure to wait for it to complete before moving on to the next paragraph. In fact, if you try to force code completion when indexing is incomplete, you will see the following message:

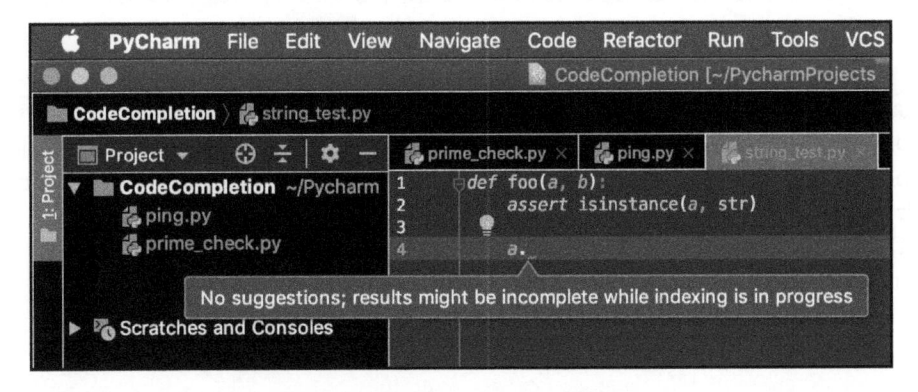

Code completion before indexing completes

Editing and Formatting with Ease in PyCharm

Getting back to our discussion, here, we are considering the difference between basic and smart code completion. In the `foo()` function, which takes in two parameters, `a` and `b`, what we already have is an assertion making sure that `a` is a string. Now, move your cursor to line **4** right after `a`, and enter a dot character (`.`). You should now see a code completion suggestion list pop up, like so:

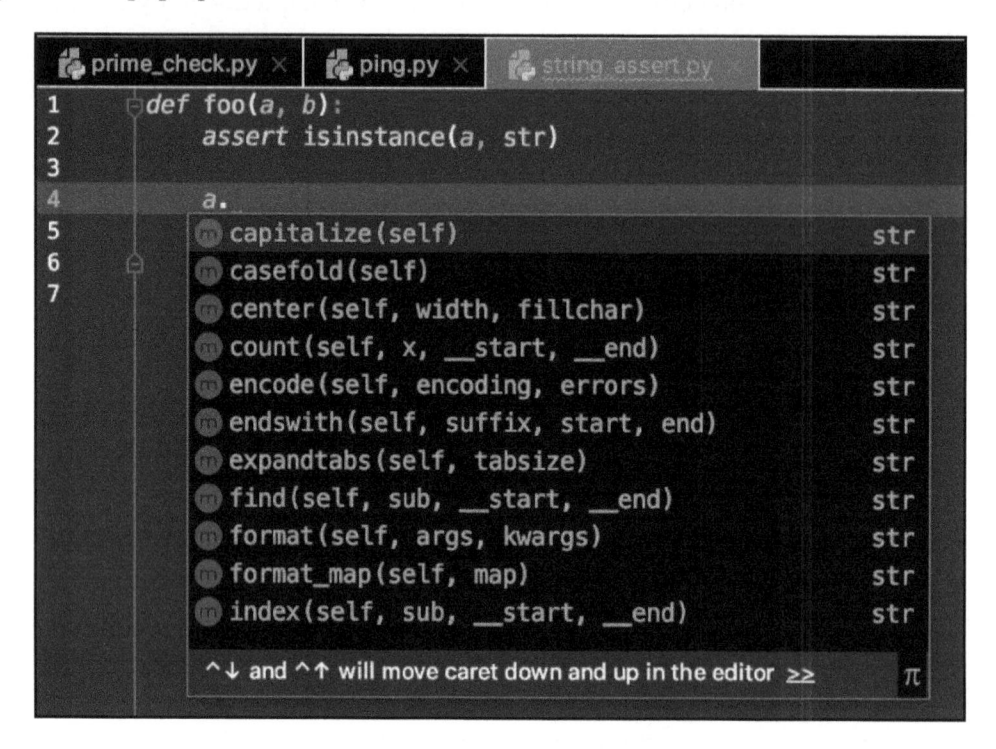

Type-specific code completion

Notice that the items in the preceding suggestion list are all methods for string variables (indicated by the `str` column on the right-hand side of the popup). PyCharm's code completion is able to intelligently narrow down the suggestion list to just string methods because it analyzes the code that we've already entered (specifically the assertion statement) and determines that the `a` variable is a string. Then, it removes all the suggestions that are irrelevant to string variables from the suggestion list.

This distinction becomes more clear when we consider the suggestion list for b—move the cursor to line **6** and enter a dot character (.):

Autocomplete suggestions

You can see that this suggestion list includes many more items and options, simply because PyCharm has no information regarding what datatype variable b is. This goes to show that, if a datatype of a variable in a program is determined, PyCharm can compile a better, more relevant code completion suggestion list.

Postfix code completion

We have seen the general usage of PyCharm's smart code completion engine—looking at a suggestion list and choosing the item that you want. Here, we are considering using the engine for a specific purpose, that is, **postfix code completion**. Still working with the string_assert.py file from the previous example, we look at the suggestion list for variable b, and we enter a dot character after it.

Notice the first suggestion—if (if expr). If you are confused and don't know what the .if expression is in Python, you are completely right in thinking that. In fact, if you go ahead and select the option to complete the line of code, you will see that the code will be transformed into the following:

```
if b:
```

So, `.if` is just another way to express an `if` condition in PyCharm, but why is it necessary and desirable? Well, I know personally—and many might sympathize with me—that I would start an expression, say an `if` condition, by typing in the actual conditional expression (as opposed to the `if` keyword and then the expression), and only afterward move the caret back in front of that expression and add in the `if` keyword to correctly form a Python conditional statement.

This practice helps me organize my thoughts better, especially if the conditional expression is long and complex and consists of multiple components. But it requires me, again, to move the caret to the beginning of the expression and add the `if` keyword afterward. If I were to add together all the time I have spent doing this, I might feel compelled to give up this practice. Luckily, postfix code completion addresses this problem. When I've finished the conditional expression, I simply use the code completion feature, and the line of code will be formatted into a correct `if` statement.

Obviously, postfix code completion is not only limited to `if` statements. If you go to PyCharm's general settings, **Editor | General | Postfix Completion**, and scroll to the section for Python, you will be able to see a complete list of available expressions for postfix code completion. These are illustrated in the following screenshot:

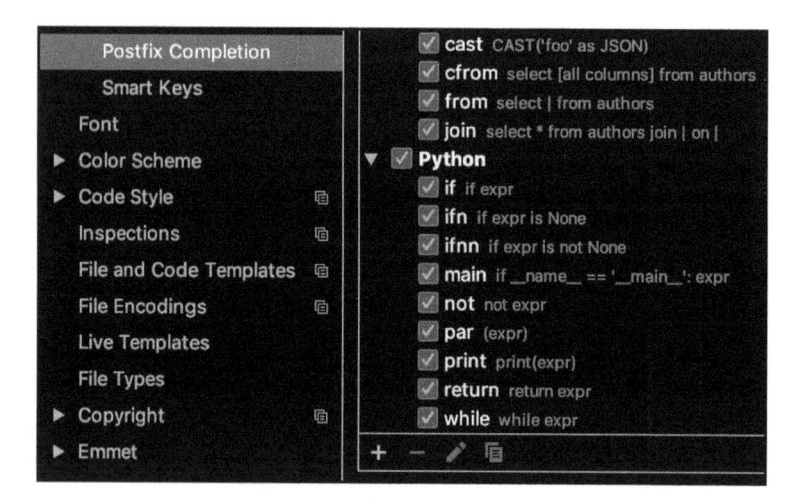

Postfix code completion expressions in Python

You might notice that there are postfix completion options for other languages in that window as well (for example, TypeScript, JavaScript, and SQL). This goes to show that PyCharm realizes the different technologies that Python developers might use in integration with Python, and does its best to support a variety of technologies in the software. We, however, will not consider these options, and only focus on Python development specifically throughout this book.

Hippie completion

Hippie completion denotes code completion where the current *visible* scope and context of your code are taken into account. This is different from general code completion, which produces a suggestion list that includes things outside your current visible context. I emphasize the word *visible* here since what is suggested by hippie completion is dictated by what is currently being opened in PyCharm.

Let's see this feature in action. Close any file you have open in the PyCharm editor and open the `http_status.py` file, which can be found in the `Chapter04/CodeCompletion` folder of our repository. The file currently contains the following code:

```
import requests

SITES = [
    'http://google.com',
    'http://python.org',
    'http://www.python.org/psf/',
    'http://www.packtpub.com/tech/Python'
]

def get_status(url):
    res = requests.get(url)
    return res.status_code

if __name__ == '__main__':
    get_status('http://p')
```

Editing and Formatting with Ease in PyCharm

In the current script, we have a short function, `get_status()`, that takes in the address of a website, attempts to make a `GET` request using the `request` module, and returns the status code of the response the program receives. We also have a list of websites, stored in the `SITES` variable, that we can pass as the parameter for `get_status()`. If you are not familiar with this procedure for using the `requests` library, don't worry, as the point that we are trying to make here does not require you to be.

In the main scope of our program, we are trying to call `get_status()` on one of the websites listed in `SITES`, specifically one that starts with a *p*. Here, we can easily type it ourselves, or move the cursor to the line of code that contains that specific site, and copy and paste it in. However, hippie completion offers the ability to expand the string we are typing efficiently.

While the cursor is right after the letter *p* in the last line of code, evoke the hippie completion shortcut (*option* / for macOS, *Alt* / for Windows). You will see that every time you evoke the action, hippie completion will expand the code with each of the various possible options (`psf`, `python`, `packtpub`) that were included in the current scope. This is because hippie completion looks for anything that starts with a *p* in our scope and context.

Many grow to appreciate the hippie completion feature quickly after they start using it. This is understandable as, generally speaking, looking for what is in the current scope and context will be more likely to give us relevant suggestions than a general code completion option. Doing this is undoubtedly much faster and more efficient than the other two options we listed previously (manual typing and copying/pasting) when we want to look for things in our current context.

I have been using the words `scope` and `context` without explaining their meanings. In general, they are used to denote what you recently typed or have opened. Indeed, similar to how hippie completion suggested applicable options resulting from items in the `SITES` variable in the preceding example, it can do the same thing for external files that have been opened in the PyCharm editor.

This actually opens up a new level of efficiency and flexibility—imagine you are working with a text file in a Python program and you need to hard-code in some strings from that text file. Now, if you have that text file open in another tab in the editor, hippie completion will be able to access that text file and give you relevant suggestions when evoked. Feel free to try out this feature by opening the `sample.txt` file (which contains more random strings that start with the letter *p*) in your PyCharm editor and go back to `http_status.py` to evoke the shortcut again.

Intentions

Code completion support in PyCharm is not limited to typing suggestions. In other words, you can take advantage of various features so that you can format/edit the code after it has already been typed up. Specifically, intention actions are possible ways to analyze and alter a completed line of code; this feature is displayed as a yellow light bulb icon, as illustrated in the screenshot that follows:

1. Open the `sqrt_floor.py` script, which is in the same subfolder that we have been working on, `Chapter04/CodeCompletion`. The script contains the following code, including a function that returns the greatest integer that does not exceed the square root of the input parameter. This is called `sqrt_floor()`:

   ```python
   from math import sqrt


   def sqrt_floor(x):
       return int(sqrt(x))


   if __name__ == '__main__':
       sqrt_floor(10)
   ```

   > Note that `sqrt_floor()` takes advantage of the `sqrt()` function from the `math` module.

2. Now, move your cursor to the first line of the script and leave it there. The intention icon should appear as follows:

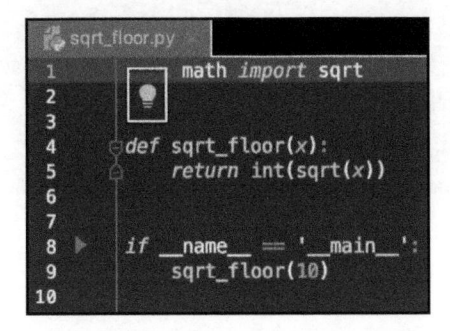

   Intentions in PyCharm

[109]

3. Hover over this icon and open the drop-down menu, which should contain one option saying **Convert to 'import math'**. Here, the intention capability has scanned through the code we currently have and looked for better ways to structure and optimize it. Sometimes, the light bulb is red and has an exclamation point on it, indicating that there are actual errors in the code.

> Not stopping at detecting errors and showing warnings, the intention also suggests a list of actions to take to address the detected problem—this is the drop-down list included in the intention icon.

4. Going back to our example, we can see that intention has suggested that we, instead of importing the `sqrt()` function from the `math` module, import the whole `math` module itself.

> Now, this fix won't make any difference in terms of efficiency for our current small-sized example but imagine a situation where you are importing a large number of classes and methods from the same module. In that case, it might make the code better (and definitely more readable) to simply get the whole module itself.

So, what actually happens when we choose to apply a suggestion from the Intention drop-down menu? For our current example, once we choose the **Convert to 'import math'** option, PyCharm will mutate our current code into the following:

```
import math


def sqrt_floor(x):
    return int(math.sqrt(x))


if __name__ == '__main__':
    sqrt_floor(10)
```

Effect of intention actions

So, instead of `from math import sqrt`, we now have `import math`. However, also notice that, in the `sqrt_floor()` function, `math.sqrt(x)` has replaced `sqrt(x)`. This change is necessary since we are now importing the whole `math` module, so we need to specifically pick out the `sqrt()` function from it. With that being said, PyCharm automatically implements this change for us.

Again, this feature does not seem like much in our current example, but you can imagine and appreciate how much this feature would help in a large project where classes and methods are used from multiple modules and libraries. This intention feature is the perfect example of code completion and its intended functionality—taking all the nitty-gritty away from your development process and keeping you on track with regard to the big picture of your project.

In case you are wondering, intention actions are not limited to just changing the way we import packages and modules into Python programs. In fact, we can customize and adjust which intention actions are available for code completion in PyCharm. This is done in the settings, which we will be discussing in the following subsection.

Customizing your code completion engine

With all the code completion features available in PyCharm, a developer will be able to significantly increase their productivity—specifically their code output. However, not everyone has the same preference for development environments (some people prefer to stick with minimal text editors, however experienced they are at programming); in the same way, not everyone has the same preference for code completion. Some might want a more hands-on code completion engine assisting them with every line of code they write, while others might prefer to work on their own and only evoke code completion when they really need help referencing obscure APIs.

This is why PyCharm provides the option to customize various aspects of its code completion support. In this section, we will be looking into some of these aspects so that you can tailor code completion support in PyCharm to your own preferences.

To open the settings for code completion, go to your PyCharm settings window and navigate to **Editor** | **General** | **Code Completion**.

Editing and Formatting with Ease in PyCharm

The window should now look like the following:

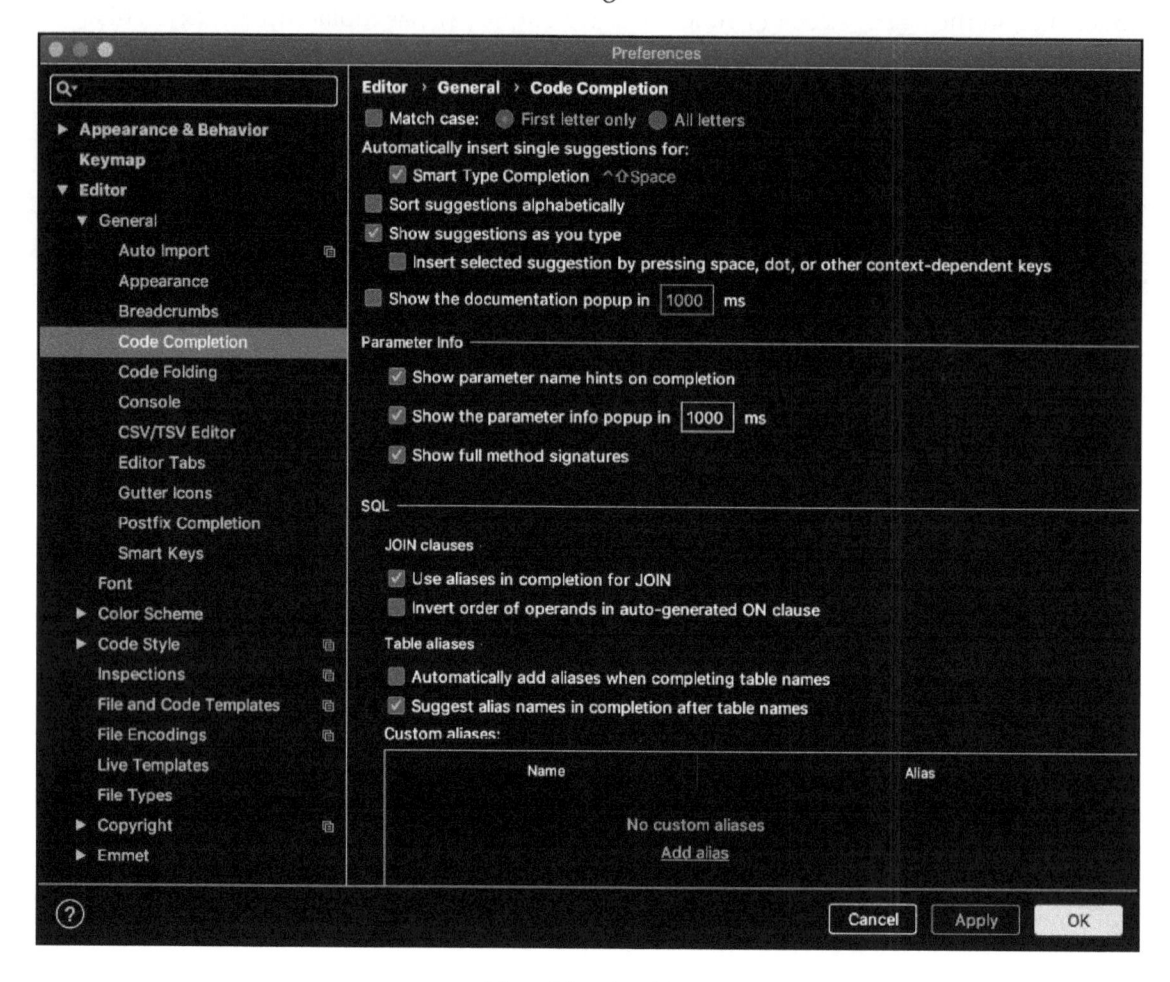

Code completion settings window

As you go through the specific options (which I recommend you do), you will see a comprehensive list of all the customizations and adjustments you can make to your code completion engine. In the following subsections, we are only going through a number of basic and often used options so that you have a better starting point before exploring other, more subtle options.

Match case

Located at the top of the window, this option specifies whether items in the suggestion list should match the case of whatever you are typing. For example, if I wanted to type in an exception expression for the `KeyboardInterrupt` exception in Python and the **Match case** option is enabled, I would have to type a capital letter *K* for the correct class name to be included in the suggestion list. Next to the **Match case** checkbox, you can also choose only the first letter's case should be matched or whether this should apply to all the letters.

I personally always disable this checkbox so that I only have to type in, for example, a lower-case *k* to take advantage of code completion. However, like everything we have seen in code completion (and for that matter, like everything in programming), there is a trade-off to this practice. Specifically, if **Match case** is disabled, sometimes the suggestion list might be populated by many more irrelevant options, which would make finding the correct API more difficult. In this case, you would have to continue typing so that the suggestion list is narrowed down.

Sorting suggestions alphabetically

As its name suggests, this option allows you to sort the items in the suggestion list in alphabetical order. This feature is useful for long suggestion lists that would require the developer to scroll through them carefully to find what he or she is looking for if they were not ordered alphabetically.

On multiple occasions, we have seen the dynamic nature of PyCharm, and it is once again demonstrated in this feature. Specifically, while interacting with a suggestion list in the editor, you can change the order of the items in the list at any time by clicking on the icon located in the bottom-right corner of the suggestion window.

This feature is illustrated in the following screenshot:

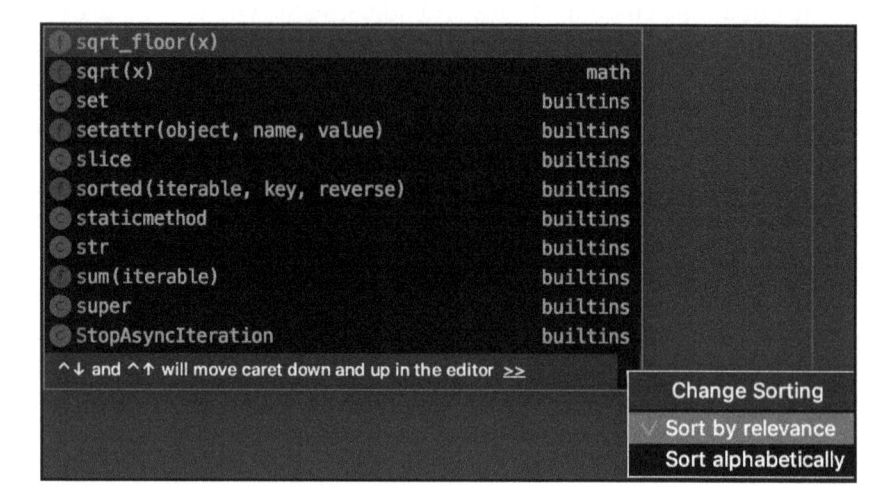

Changing code completion suggestion order dynamically

Showing the documentation popup in [...] ms

If this feature is enabled, every time an item in a code completion suggestion list is highlighted (that is, when you move the cursor to that item), PyCharm will display the documentation for that specific item (after the specified time period). The advantage of this feature is that you can go through the documentation of all the suggested items dynamically as you simply move the cursor down the items.

This is especially beneficial when you are working with classes and methods that have similar APIs. We will discuss this feature, along with other documentation-related functionalities, in the last section of this chapter.

Parameter information

In the middle of the window, we can see various code completion options regarding parameters:

- Show parameter name hints on completion
- Show the parameter info popup in [...] ms
- Show full method signatures

These options are self-explanatory, and the options themselves are generally useful.

> If you are not familiar with the term *method signatures*, it denotes the fully declared method name, along with all the parameters and potentially returned types.

All in all, I suggest that you have all three parameter options on so that you get the necessary information about the parameter of a method or function while interacting with it in your Python programs.

Intentions

We looked at intentions previously. These are predetermined options that can quickly reformat your code with a click of a button. To customize which intention options are available, open the settings window, navigate to **Editor** | **Intentions**, and scroll down to the options for Python:

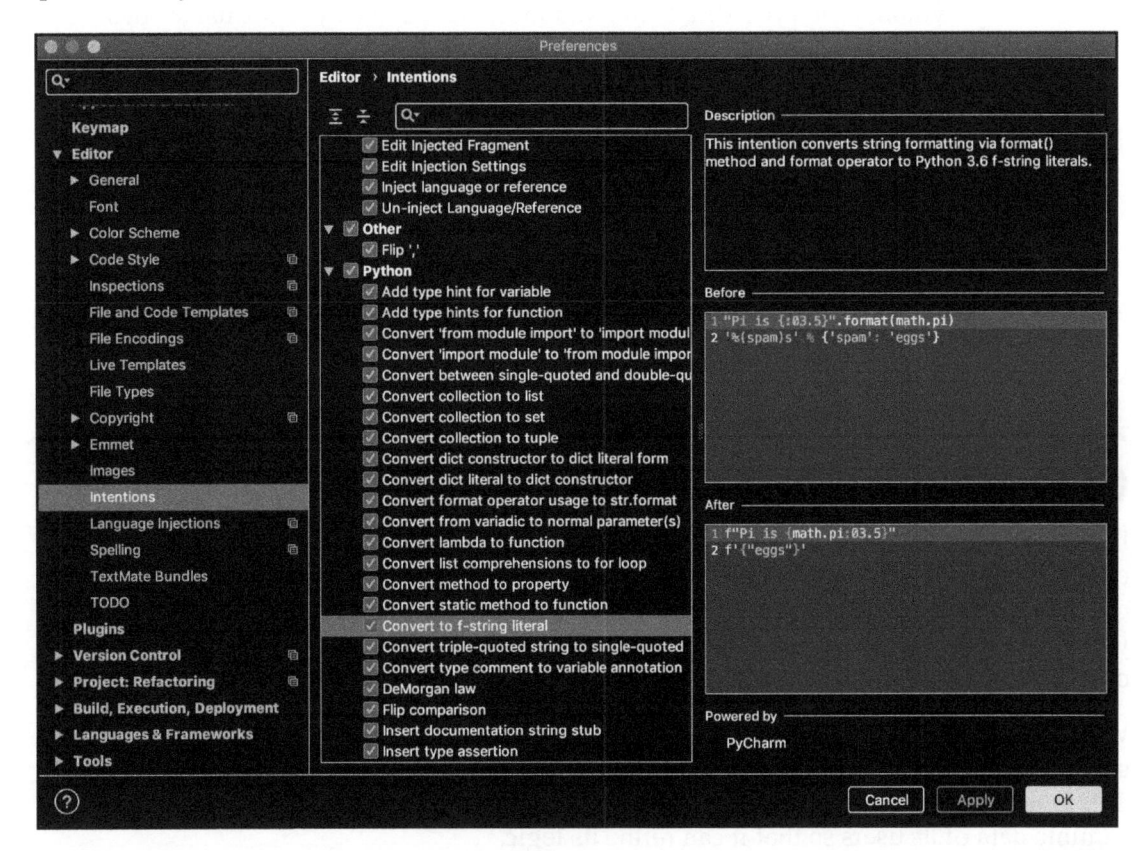

Intentions in PyCharm

As you select/deselect each option, you are choosing whether PyCharm should include that specific option in the drop-down menu whenever an intention popup appears.

The first thing to note is that there are numerous potential options for intentions, even if we are just focusing on Python. Obviously, not all the options will be included in every intention drop-down menu (as we saw earlier); in fact, PyCharm filters out irrelevant options from this list and only leaves behind those that can actually be applied in a specific situation.

Secondly, as you select each option, the panel on the right-hand side of the window will adjust itself to display the appropriate information about the option in question. For example, the preceding screenshot displays information on the option of converting old string formatting APIs into f-string literals.

> For those of you who are not familiar with this f-string is a feature I use throughout the code repository of this book. It was implemented in Python 3.6 to provide a better and more readable way to format strings. However, many online tutorials, articles, and blogs still use %-formatting and `str.format()` in their materials.
>
> This, in turn, discourages other Python users who are reading these materials even more strongly from taking advantage of f-string. However, with PyCharm, you can easily convert those old formatting APIs into f-string literals using PyCharm's intentions.

Again, you have the option to fully specify which options you want PyCharm to utilize in its code completion support. With that being said, similar to my advice with other customizations, it is generally a good idea to leave all the options enabled—you never know when an option will become useful when you are working on a project.

Collecting runtime types

In this section, we will be learning how to improve our experience when using PyCharm code completion—sharing runtime data. In general, the logic that's used for PyCharm's code completion engine is efficient at predicting which suggestions are applicable to what you are currently typing. However, programming conventions and best practices are ever-changing and so the code completion engine needs to adjust itself to meet these changes.

We have seen that one of the most important aspects of code completion is suggesting and encouraging good styling, and failure to adjust quickly will negatively affect this feature. This is why it is important for any good code completion engine to collect and analyze the runtime data of its users so that it can refine its logic.

With that being said, protecting your data is just as, if not more, important than having good, self-adjusting code completion logic. PyCharm, therefore, allows you to choose whether you want your runtime data to be collected (and used for the improvement of its code completion) or not.

> **TIP**
> Note that this option is disabled by default, which means you have to enable this option before PyCharm can collect your data.

Furthermore, the runtime data that's collected simply involves data that's generated when you *debug* a program, as opposed to when you *run* it. All in all, I personally think enabling this feature is an easy and effortless way to help improve code completion in PyCharm. To do this, go to the **General** settings and navigate to **Build, Execution, Deployment | Python Debugger**. Then, check the box that corresponds to the option, as illustrated by the following screenshot:

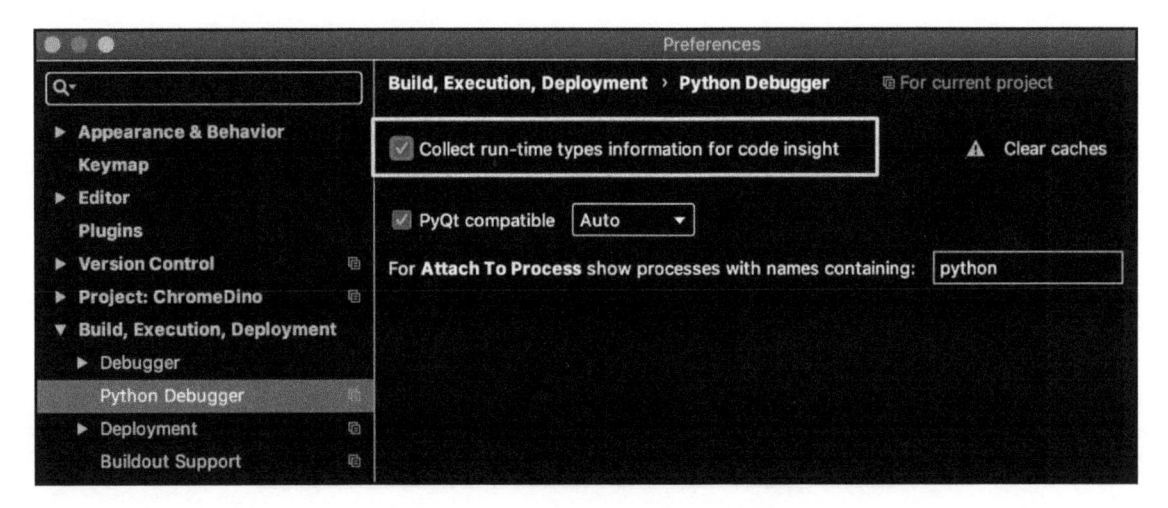

Collecting runtime types

That's all you need to do. From now on, every time you choose to debug your program, data regarding runtime types will be collected and sent to JetBrains. Potential improvements to the code completion engine will be included in future updates of the software.

[117]

Troubleshooting

Just like any feature in any software, sometimes code completion in PyCharm doesn't work as intended, causing frustration and headaches for its users. In this subsection, we'll discuss some common problems PyCharm users often encounter while working with code completion.

Indexing process

We have already emphasized the importance of waiting for PyCharm's indexing process—when PyCharm scans through all the project files and folders to adjust its code completion logic and other support features—to finish before working with various features, but it is worth reiterating again. This is because code completion utilizes the information that was gathered from the indexing process.

Power save mode

Located at **File | Power Save Mode**, this feature, as its name suggests, is used to conserve the power of your computer. When turned on, power save mode will stop running all background tasks, such as error highlighting, inspections, and, of course, code completion, and will display the following message in the bottom-right-hand corner of your project window:

Power save mode and code completion

Simply go to **File | Power Save Mode** again to turn the feature back off, and code completion will be able to function properly again.

Out-of-scope files

If you are confused about why APIs that are included in some external libraries or scripts are not showing up in your code completion suggestion lists, chances are the files containing those APIs are not included as part of your project:

- For an external Python file containing classes and methods you'd like to include in code completion suggestion lists, check to see if it is inside the project folder you are working on and if it is currently marked as a plain text file (it shouldn't be).
- For third-party packages and libraries, make sure to actually install them (globally or in the current virtual environment) and add them to the `requirements.txt` file of your project. We have seen that `requirements.txt` plays an important role in detecting unmet dependency requirements and that that information is used for code completion purposes as well.

Troubleshooting also marks the end of our discussion on code completion in PyCharm. Throughout this section, we have discussed some of the most common and most powerful features offered by PyCharm's code completion support.

There are, of course, many more available features and functionalities included in PyCharm that you might find useful for your development process. Therefore, it is important that you keep exploring and playing around with various options for code completion so that you find the best settings and customizations for your own preferences.

After code completion, the second topic regarding editing and formatting Python code within PyCharm is refactoring. Let's have a look at this in detail.

Refactoring

The ability to effectively refactor your code is a characteristic any good programmer should have, but there can be confusion regarding what actually constitutes refactoring, as well as how to do it well in Python development.

In this section, we will discuss the case for refactoring, see how it helps us structure and format our code (specifically Python), and learn what options PyCharm offers to assist us in this process.

What is refactoring?

As we mentioned previously, there might be confusion as to what the process of refactoring code actually means. Before moving on to discuss any specifics, let's get the definition straight.

Formally, **code refactoring** is the process of changing the structure and organization of your code. The term **factoring** in computer science means splitting/decomposing a given system into smaller components; to refactor, then, is to rework on that decomposition process. The purpose of refactoring is to improve various aspects of a program, such as its readability and the simplicity of its code.

> **TIP**
> Note that these aspects do not directly affect how the program functions, but the process of maintaining and extending the program heavily depends on how readable and simple its code is. This is why refactoring is such an important process in programming and, again, a sign of a good developer.

Let's consider a quick example: the problem of representing and interacting with points on a 2D, Cartesian coordinate system. For example, the origin of the Cartesian plane is (0, 0) (zero for the x-coordinate and zero for the y-coordinate); point (3, 2) is 3 units away from the origin to the right with respect to the x-axis, and 2 units above with respect to the y-axis.

For now, we are looking to write a program to calculate the distance between two given points. Mathematically, the distance between (x_1, y_1) and (x_2, y_2) (with the x's and y's being real numbers) is as follows:

$$d = \sqrt{(x1 - x2)^2 + (y1 - y2)^2}$$

Now, navigate to the `Chapter04/Refactoring` folder and consider the code in the `point_v1.py` file:

```
from math import sqrt


def tuple_distance(tuple1, tuple2):
    return sqrt((tuple1[0]-tuple2[0])**2 +(tuple1[1]-tuple2[1])**2)


if __name__ == '__main__':
    x = (1, 0)
    y = (5, 3)
    print(f'Distance between {x} and {y} is {tuple_distance(x, y)}')
```

In this script, we are using two-element tuples to represent 2D points—the first element is the x-coordinate, while the second is the y-coordinate. Here, we have a function called `tuple_distance()` that takes in two tuples and distributes and applies operations on the elements in those tuples so that a quantity corresponding to the distance between the points the tuples represent is worked out and returned.

Finally, in the main scope of the program, we declare two tuples representing points (1, 0) and (5, 3), calculate the distance between them using `tuple_distance()`, and print it out in an f-string. If you like, run it. You should get the following output:

```
Distance between (1, 0) and (5, 3) is 5.0
```

This program works fine for all intents and purposes right now. But you can imagine the problems that might occur when representing points using tuples in a large system—how to distinguish them from other actual two-element tuples. Accessing the x- and y-coordinates of a point is equivalent to tuple indexing, which is not readable and might cause confusion. We can see that, even in the simple task of calculating the distance between two points, the `tuple_distance()` function has to contain a rather long and awkward line of code consisting of many operations.

Following an object-oriented mindset, we can try to design a class for 2D point objects. In the same subfolder that contains point_v1.py, open point_v2.py, which contains the following code:

```python
from math import sqrt

class Point():
    def __init__(self, x, y):
        self.x = x
        self.y = y

    def __str__(self):
        return f'Point ({self.x}, {self.y})'

    def __add__(self, p):
        return Point(self.x + p.x, self.y + p.y)

    def __sub__(self, p):
        return Point(self.x - p.x, self.y - p.y)

    def distance(self, p):
        diff = self - p
        distance = sqrt(diff.x**2 + diff.y**2)
        return distance
```

```
if __name__ == '__main__':
    p1 = Point(1, 0)
    p2 = Point(5, 3)
    print(f'Distance between {p1} and {p2} is {p1.distance(p2)}')
```

Here, we have a `Point` class whose initializer function takes in two parameters—x and y—which correspond to the coordinates of the specific point, respectively. Inside the class, we have the customized `__add__()` and `__sub__()` methods, which allow us the perform coordinate-wise additions and subtractions. We also have the customized `__str__()` method for better string representation (more on this later).

If you are not familiar with class methods that have double underscores surrounding their names, they are called **dunder (double-under)**, or magic methods in Python. Dunder methods allow you to mutate the default behavior of built-in methods for `class` objects. By using dunder methods in your custom class, you can improve the readability of the corresponding class methods.

For example, the `__add__()` and `__sub__()` methods specify how addition and subtraction between `class` objects is performed; the `__str__()` method specifies the string representation of the `class` object. For more information, you can check out the article titled *Enriching Your Python Classes with Dunder (Magic, Special) Methods* in the *Further reading* section at the end of this chapter.

More importantly, we also have the `distance()` class method, which computes the Cartesian distance between the calling `Point` object and another `Point` object. Note that this method applies the subtraction operation on the two `Point` objects—`diff = self - p`. This is appropriate since we have customized our own class subtraction method in `__sub__()`.

Finally, in the main scope, we declare the two points we used in the previous example that were used as `Point` objects and display the distance between them using the `distance()` class method. Run the program and you will receive the following output:

```
Distance between Point (1, 0) and Point (5, 3) is 5.0
```

The first difference to note between the two versions of the program is the readability that the API of the `Point` class provides. As we have said, the `tuple_distance()` function in the first version of the program contains some awkward operations that might not be descriptive of what we are trying to achieve (which is the distance between two 2D Cartesian points), while the representation of Cartesian points using two-element tuples has problems of its own.

Additionally, using the `Point` class, we can simply call the `distance()` class method to handle all the logic for us. This provides another level of encapsulation for the program so that external users of the `Point` class will not, and cannot, interact with the underlying logic of the class.

Even though we get the exact same information as the old `tuple_distance()` function and we have to write more code, we can see that this way of representing point coordinates in an object-oriented way and making use of the ability to overwrite built-in functions can help future users of the code have a better time working with, maintaining, and extending the program. For example, you can go further and customize the `__str__()` class method to give a different string representation.

This `Point` class is an example of the refactoring process in programming—you take a specific portion of your program (this can be a function, a class, or simply a block of code) and restructure and reorganize it without actually changing the functionality of the code. This gives us better readability and maintainability.

There are, of course, other forms of refactoring aside from creating a new class, as we've already mentioned. While we will not discuss the refactoring process itself and its other forms further (since they are not the focus of this book), we will learn more about various aspects of refactoring from PyCharm's support for this process, starting from the upcoming subsection.

Refactoring in PyCharm

Keeping the fundamentals of refactoring in mind, we will now move on to see how PyCharm supports various tasks and actions in this topic. Still considering and making changes to the current `Point` class that we have, we will go through specific refactoring techniques that are most commonly used and applicable, even outside the context of writing a Python class.

Throughout the following subsections, we will still be working with the `Chapter04/Refactoring` subfolder, specifically the `point_v3.py` file.

Renaming

Before you start wondering—yes, simply renaming things in a program is still an aspect of refactoring. However, there is more subtlety in renaming than you might imagine. For example, say you'd like to rename a variable in a Python program. This process would be trivial if that variable was only used once or twice throughout the whole program, but if the program you are working with was large enough, and the variable is shared among many components of the program, renaming the variable might prove extremely difficult and time-consuming.

One potential solution is to use the find and replace functionality (which is commonly applicable in this case) to find all the locations in the program that contains that specific variable name and then replace it with the new name. However, there is a downside to using the find and replace (or for that matter, find) functionality—false positives.

For example, if you type in the variable name in question in the search box, any places that contain that specific string will be returned. So, if there were string objects in the program that contain that variable name, or if there were other variables whose names correspond to the original variable name (for example, 'x' will be found in 'f_x'), a lot of unintended consequences could result from using find and replace.

Undoubtedly, renaming is not limited to variable names. Often, it's for developers who want to rename specific functions, classes, or even filenames in their program. The same problem is faced in renaming functions and classes if we use find and replace, which will not be able to handle renaming filenames anyway.

So, let's examine the functionality of PyCharm's refactoring support as a way to rename various elements of our Python programs. Navigate to the `point_v3.py` file, which extends from the `point_v2.py` file that we previously considered. This new file contains the same `Point` class API, with the addition of a `draw()` static method, which will be used to draw the corresponding point in the 2D Cartesian plane:

```python
from matplotlib import pyplot as plt

class Point():
    ...

    @staticmethod
    def draw(x, y):
        # set up range of the plot
        limit = max(x, y) + 1

        fig = plt.figure()
        ax = fig.add_subplot(111)
```

```
            ax.set_aspect('equal')

            # lines corresponding to x- and y-coordinates
            plt.plot([x, x], [0, y], '-', c='blue', linewidth=3)
            plt.plot([0, x], [y, y], '-', c='blue', linewidth=3)

            plt.scatter(x, y, s=100, marker='o', c='red')  # actual point

            ax.set_xlim((-limit, limit))
            ax.set_ylim((-limit, limit))

            # axis arrows
            left, right = ax.get_xlim()
            bottom, top = ax.get_ylim()
            plt.arrow(left, 0, right - left, 0, length_includes_head=True,
                    head_width=0.15)
            plt.arrow(0, bottom, 0, top - bottom,
                    length_includes_head=True,
                    head_width=0.15)

            plt.grid()
            plt.show()
    if __name__ == '__main__':
        p1 = Point(1, 0)
        p2 = Point(5, 3)

        draw(p2.x, p2.y)
```

Feel free to look at and study the `draw()` method, but note that it is not necessary to understand its logic for us to carry on our subsequent discussions in this section. For now, we will only focus on what we already discussed in the previous example—the `__add__()`, `__sub__()`, and `distance()` class methods. Each of these methods handles the logic of the interaction between the calling object and another `Point` object, which is represented as the `p` parameter.

In these methods, the character *p* is currently not very readable; you might not be able to guess that the parameter indicates another `Point` object. To make it clear what this parameter represents, we will rename it from `p` to `other`.

Editing and Formatting with Ease in PyCharm

To do this for each method, move your cursor to any occurrence of *p* inside the method and go to **Refactor | Rename...** to start the renaming process:

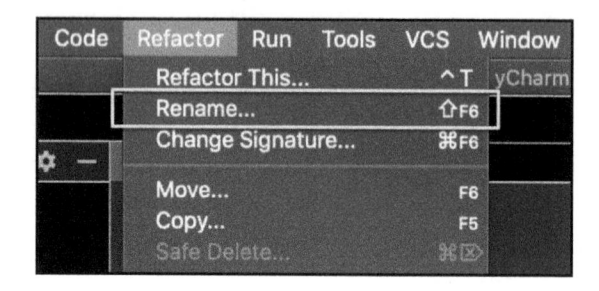

Renaming in PyCharm

> Also notice the keyboard shortcut associated with the action (in my case, as you can see, the macOS shortcut is ⇧ F6). As we mentioned in the previous chapter, remembering shortcuts for tasks and actions that you use often will help you become increasingly productive.

As you choose the **Rename...** action, a pop-up window will appear, asking for the new name of the component in question (in this case, it is our variable, `p`). Type the new name in the box for the variable—`other`—and hit **Refactor**. You will see that all the instances of `p` have been replaced with `other`. For example, the `__add__()` method should look as follows after this process:

```
def __add__(self, other):
    return Point(self.x + other.x, self.y + other.y)
```

Do this for all three methods to improve their readability.

It is important to note that this process can be applied to renaming functions and classes in the same manner. All occurrences of the element to be renamed within the whole project will be changed appropriately so that there is no naming inconsistency.

Let's do the same for filenames:

1. Open the `point_client.py` file, which contains the same usage of the `Point` class as the previous example. However, we are doing this in another file now, so an `import` statement is necessary:

   ```
   from point_v2 import Point
   
   
   if __name__ == '__main__':
   ```

```
            p_x = Point(1, 0)
            p_y = Point(5, 3)
            print(f'Distance between {p_x} and {p_y} is
                {p_x.distance(p_y)}')
```

2. Let's say we'd like to rename the `point_v2.py` file to just `point.py`, but we are wondering how other files that import elements of `point_v2.py` in our project (namely `point_client.py`) will be affected.
3. First, in the **Project** panel (on the left-hand side of the project window), select the `point_v2.py` file and evoke the **Refactor** | **Rename** action again.
4. In the renaming pop-up window, type in `point.py` and you will see that not only the name of the file itself was changed appropriately, but also that the `import` statement in `point_client.py` was converted:

    ```
    from point import Point
    ```

This is quite a powerful feature since it takes care of all the instances that use and interact with the element that we'd like to rename in a consistent way.

Inline variable

Inline variable refactoring is used to remove redundant usage of variables. Consider our current `distance()` method in the `Point` class:

```
def distance(self, p):
    diff = self - p
    distance = sqrt(diff.x**2 + diff.y**2)
    return distance
```

We can see that, after the `distance` variable is declared, it is immediately returned by the method. We would like to combine these two lines of code into one so that we can simply return the `sqrt(diff.x**2 + diff.y**2)` expression.

However, doing this, you might argue, can be seen as the opposite of how we defined the general purpose of refactoring; after all, by getting rid of a variable, we are potentially making our code less readable and extendable. The readability of our code will not be affected since we can easily guess that the expression being returned by a method named `distance()` is a distance quantity. Since the variable is being returned right away, there is no use in making the method extendable and allowing the variable to be used further. All in all, we can safely shorten and make this code simpler without any significant downsides.

Editing and Formatting with Ease in PyCharm

This process is generally known as **inlining variables**. Let's go over this now:

1. Getting back to our specific example in the `distance()` method, go ahead and select the two lines of code that we wish to combine and go to **Refactor | Inline...**, like so:

    Inlining variable

2. A pop-up window will appear, informing us about the total number of instances where the variable will be inlined (there should be only one in this specific case). After this, the `distance()` method will be transformed into the following code, which is what we wanted:

    ```
    def distance(self, p):
        diff = self - p
        return sqrt(diff.x ** 2 + diff.y ** 2)
    ```

We can see that the method is now more concise, but no readability has been lost. In practice, you also have the option of inlining various other components of a Python program (constants, fields, parameters, methods, and superclasses) using the same feature in PyCharm. More information can be found at www.jetbrains.com/help/pycharm/inline.html.

Extracting methods

Extracting methods is arguably one of the most common aspects of refactoring. In general, it is the process of taking a block of code, which specializes in a specific task, outside of the current context it is being used in and converting it into a method/function.

Doing this is generally good practice in programming and has the advantages of readability and extendibility. For example, by moving a specific block of code into its own method/function, that logic can be reused in other places in the program, without the programmer having to copy and paste that block of code. Having some functionality that is used a lot through a program inside a separate function is intuitively a good way to structure your code as well.

Turning our attention to the aforementioned `draw()` method, we can see that the usage of the `arrow()` function from the `matplotlib.pyplot` module to draw the axis arrows (*lines 45 - 48*) is quite repeatable. In other words, we would like to extract these two lines of code into a function that takes in the four measurements of the axis (`left`, `right`, `top`, `bottom`) and evokes the `plt.arrow()` function twice. Let's get started:

1. To do this, select the four lines of code and go to **Refactor** | **Extract** | **Method...** to perform the extraction (note the keyboard shortcut for future use):

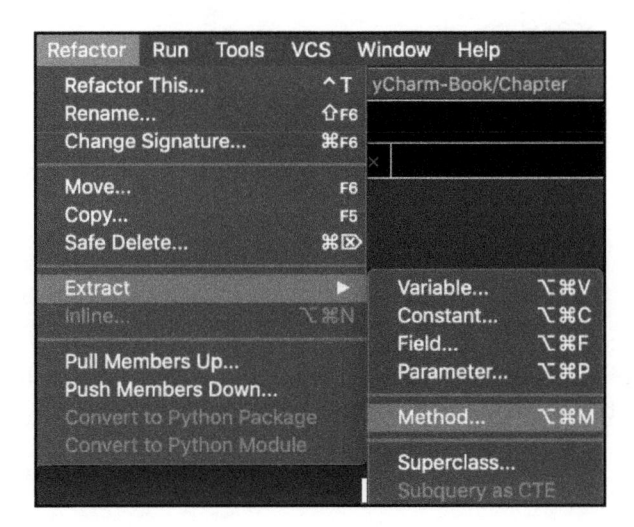

Extracting a method

Editing and Formatting with Ease in PyCharm

2. Another familiar pop-up window will appear and ask for the name of the method to be extracted.
3. We will enter `draw_arrow` for now.
4. Also, note that you can specify which parameters the newly extracted method will take in the **Parameters** section of the pop-up window by checking and unchecking particular options.
5. Finally, **Signature preview** gives you one last chance to check what the signature of the method will look like before we actually extract the code.
6. For now, hit the **OK** button. You will see that not only are the two instances of the `plt.arrow()` function being called moved to a completely new function with the appropriate signature, but also that the code within the old `draw()` function is also edited appropriately (that is, the new `draw_arrow()` function is now being called within `draw()`):

```
...
# axis arrows
left, right = ax.get_xlim()
bottom, top = ax.get_ylim()
Point.draw_arrow(bottom, left, right, top)

plt.grid()
plt.show()


@staticmethod
def draw_arrow(bottom, left, right, top):
    plt.arrow(left, 0, right - left, 0, length_includes_head=True,
              head_width=0.15)
    plt.arrow(0, bottom, 0, top - bottom,
              length_includes_head=True,
              head_width=0.15)
```

Also note that, if the code being extracted returns some value, the new method will also return the same value in a consistent way. This feature allows us to achieve a fairly complex refactoring task with the click of a button.

Conversion between method and function

At this point, `draw()` and `draw_arrow()` are static methods of the `Point` class, and therefore can only be called using `Point.draw()` and `Point.draw_arrow()`, respectively. Let's say we'd like to convert these two methods into functions outside the scope of the `Point` class so that they can be called in a simpler way. To do this, we can take advantage of the *intention* feature that we discussed earlier in this chapter:

1. Specifically, move your cursor to the signature of either method, wait for the Intention drop-down menu to appear, and choose **Convert static method to function**:

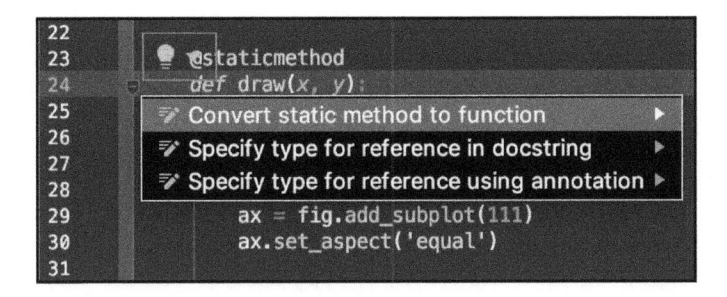

Method/function conversion via intention

2. Do this for both methods. You should end up with them being converted into functions that are beyond the scope of the `Point` class. Specifically, your code should look like the following:

```
class Point():
    ...

    def distance(self, p):
        diff = self - p
        return sqrt(diff.x ** 2 + diff.y ** 2)


def draw_arrow(bottom, left, right, top):
    plt.arrow(left, 0, right - left, 0, length_includes_head=True,
              head_width=0.15)
    plt.arrow(0, bottom, 0, top - bottom,
length_includes_head=True,
              head_width=0.15)

def draw(x, y):
    # set up range of the plot
```

[131]

```
            limit = max(x, y) + 1

        ...


        if __name__ == '__main__':
            p1 = Point(1, 0)
            p2 = Point(5, 3)

            draw(p2.x, p2.y)
```

Notice that the call to `draw()` in the main scope and the one to `draw_arrow()` inside the `draw()` function itself do not involve the `Point` class anymore—the two are now independent functions inside our `point.py` script.

Exporting a function to another file

Sometimes, to create more encapsulation and modularity for your Python program, you might want to move some functions that perform very specific tasks to another file. Then, other programs can simply import those functions and use them inside their logic. We see this the most in Python programming with `util.py` files, which are also in most external packages and modules that contain various miscellaneous utility functions.

To simulate this process, let's try moving the two functions we just converted from class methods—`draw()` and `draw_arrow()`—into another Python script. Let's get started:

1. Move your cursor to the signature of one of the two functions (you can also highlight the whole function) and select **Refactor | Move...** (as always, keep track of the keyboard shortcut for future usage). After this, a familiar pop-up window will appear:

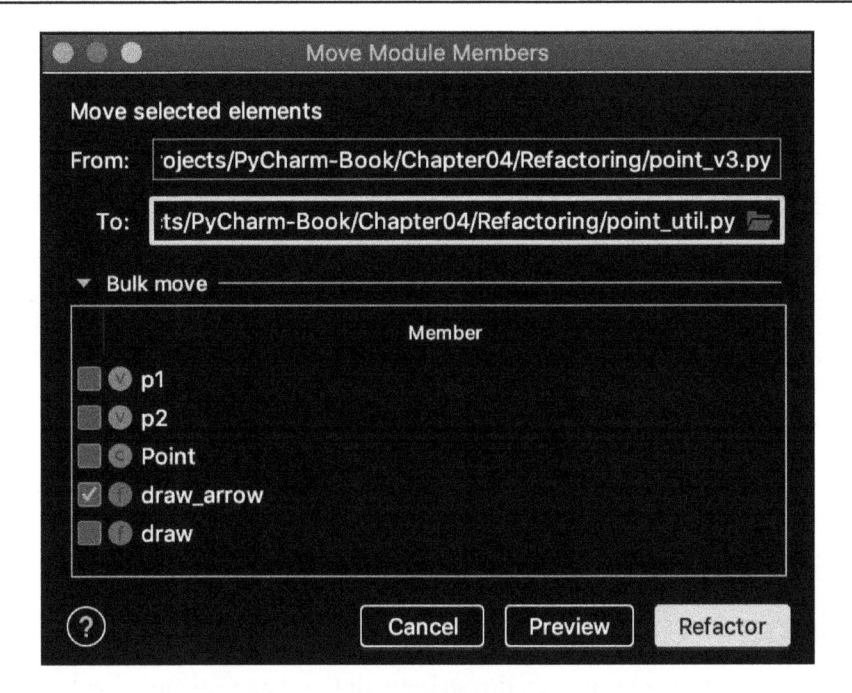

Moving functions to a new file

2. In the **To** prompt (highlighted in the preceding screenshot, where you specify which file to send the selected function to), enter `point_util.py` (or any name for the script that you prefer) within the current path. Note that, even if the file we are specifying does not exist yet, PyCharm will create it automatically for us.
3. Hit **Refactor** and the exporting process starts. Afterward, go ahead and do the same thing for the other function (out of `draw()` and `draw_arrow()`), while making sure that the destination file is the same for the two files. You can also move several components to another file in bulk by checking them in the **Bulk move** section, which is in the middle of the pop-up window (illustrated in the preceding screenshot).

A powerful thing about this feature is that `import` statements are generated according to the interaction between files. In our example, the newly created `point_util.py` file utilizes the `matplotlib` library in its functions, so the library was imported automatically there. The `matplotlib` library was also removed from the `point.py` file as it is not needed in that scope anymore. Instead, `point.py` is now importing the `draw()` function from `point_util.py` appropriately.

Editing and Formatting with Ease in PyCharm

Throughout several topics in this section, we have learned the specifics of some of the most common refactoring techniques in Python programming that PyCharm handles seamlessly.

A dynamic approach to documentation

No programmer can doubt the importance of documentation in software engineering and development. With that said, the process of creating documentation for a program can be quite tedious. Furthermore, the end result might not even be effective if the person doing the documenting was not following standard practices.

Keeping that in mind, PyCharm looks to streamline this process of documentation and make it as straightforward and seamless as possible. Regarding documentation, there are two components we will consider for this process: viewing and creating documentation. We will learn that PyCharm offers great support for both processes.

Docstrings – documentation for Python

Documentation in Python is known as **docstrings**, defined as a string literal that is placed before any of the statements in a module, function, class, or method in Python. You can look at examples of Python docstrings by going into the source code of the various built-in Python functions. It is also recommended that any custom API you write also has the appropriate docstrings for readability and maintainability.

The most noteworthy subtlety in creating docstrings is the practice of using triple-double quotes to surround a docstring (which we will see examples of in the next subsection). For more details about docstring conventions, take a look at this PEP article: www.python.org/dev/peps/pep-0257/.

Creating documentation

In this subsection, we will look into the process of writing a docstring for functions with the help of PyCharm. Let's get started:

1. Copy the following code into a Python script in a PyCharm project. Alternatively, navigate to the `Chapter04/Documentation` folder in our code repository and open the `prime_check.py` file, which contains the same code:

    ```
    import sys
    from math import import sqrt
    ```

```
def prime_check(n: int) -> bool:
    # TODO: docstring goes here

    if n < 2:
        return False

    limit = int(sqrt(n)) + 1
    for i in range(2, limit):
        if n % i == 0:
            return False # return False if a divisor is found

    return True # return True if no divisor is found


if __name__ == '__main__':
    input_ = input('Enter a number: ') # get user input

    # handle invalid inputs
    try:
        num = int(input_)
    except ValueError:
        print('A number was not entered.')
        sys.exit(0) # quit if the input is invalid

    # print out the result
    if prime_check(num):
        print('It is a prime number.')
    else:
        print('It is not a prime number.')
```

In short, the preceding program asks users for an integer, and prints out a message indicating whether that integer is a prime number or not. Again, note that a full understanding of the logic that's included in this program is not necessary.

2. Now, let's turn our attention to the `prime_check()` function, which starts from *line 5* in the script. This function does not have any documentation/docstring inside it yet, and it is our job to enter an appropriate docstring there (as indicated by TODO).

Editing and Formatting with Ease in PyCharm

3. Navigate to the line that contains the TODO, delete it, and type in a triple-double quote (which PyCharm will match-complete by inserting another triple-double quote after the cursor), like so:

```
def prime_check(n: int) -> bool:
    """[Your cursor is here]"""

    if n < 2:
```

4. Again, we are using triple-double quotes because it is a convention of writing Python docstrings. Now, hit the *Return/Enter* key, and PyCharm should expand the current docstring automatically. It should look as follows:

```
def prime_check(n: int) -> bool:
    """
    :param n:
    :return:
    """

    if n < 2:
```

5. We can see that the function parameters are scanned by PyCharm and that that information is used to generate the appropriate template for our docstring here. Our job is to fill in the blanks and complete the docstring with specific information about the function. Finish the docstring by entering the following in your code:

```
def prime_check(n: int) -> bool:
    """
    Check whether an integer is a prime number of not.
    Generally, the function goes through all odd numbers
    less than the square root of the input integer, and
    checks to see if the input is divisible by that number.

    :param n: the integer to prime check
    :return: boolean
    """

    if n < 2:
```

Consider the generated template of the docstring after we hit *Return/Enter* to expand the pair of triple-double quotes. :param and :return: are part of the template, and will be included every time we expand a docstring in the same way. Being highly customizable and accommodating to its users, PyCharm allows us to change this format of docstring templates.

6. Open PyCharm's general settings, go to **Tools | Python Integrated Tools**, and focus on the **Docstrings** section in the window, as shown in the following screenshot:

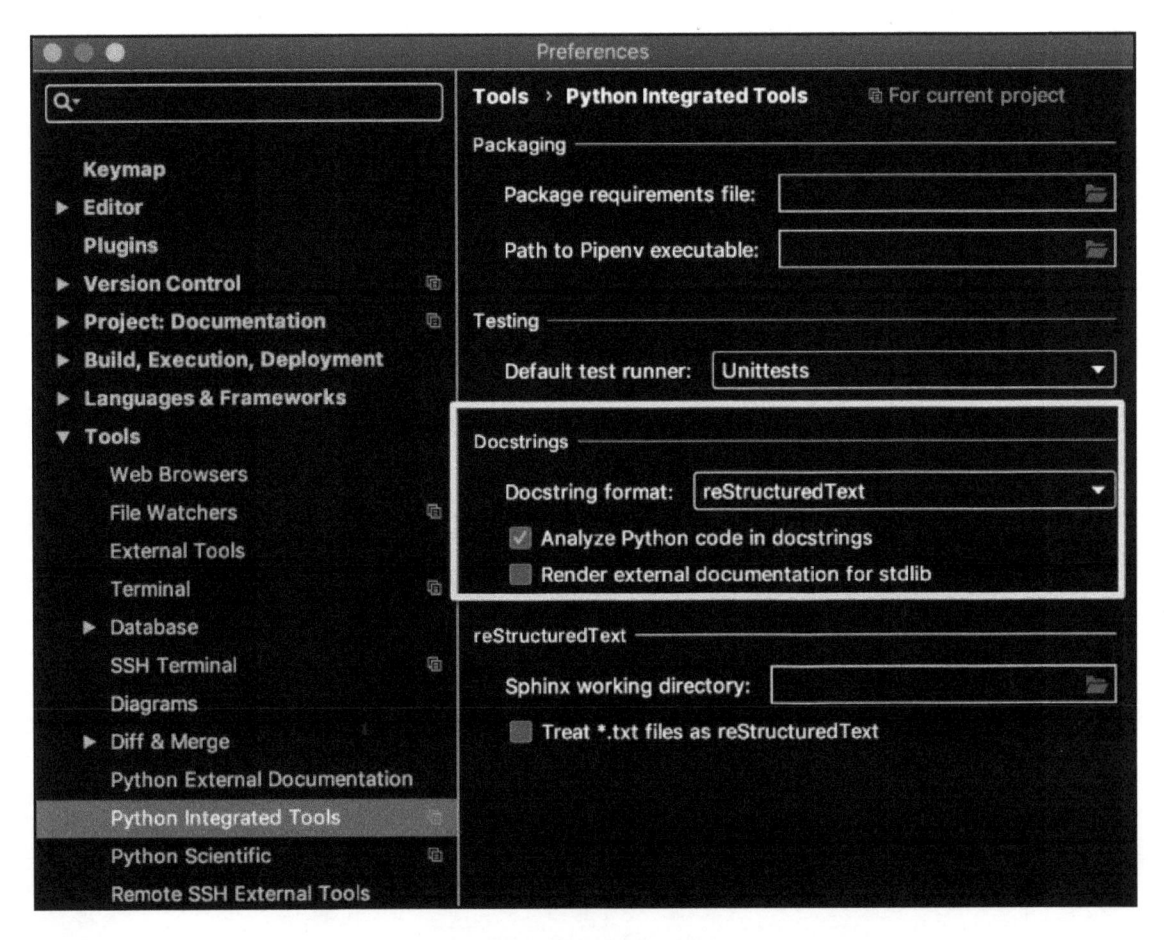

Customizing auto-docstring behaviors in PyCharm

7. Specifically, in the **Docstring format** section, you can change the predetermined template of your docstrings. Aside from **reStructuredText** (the default option), you can choose a **Plain** format (which will not generate anything in your docstrings when you expand them), or various other formats such as **Epytext**, **NumPy**, or **Google**.

In this section, we covered the process of creating documentation in Python. In the next subsection, we will consider viewing Python documentation within PyCharm.

Viewing documentation

Imagine a situation where you are using a specific method from one package, but you are not entirely sure which parameters the method takes in and/or what its return type is. Therefore, you need to go online and look into the documentation of the package for that specific method.

As a PyCharm user, you can achieve the same thing with two simple actions: **Quick Definition** and **Quick Documentation**. Still using the `prime_check.py` script from the previous section, move your cursor to the line where we use the `math.sqrt()` function in the `prime_check()` function; it should be around line **19**.

Quick Documentation

Let's say we'd like to see the documentation of this function. We can choose **View | Quick Documentation** for this (or its corresponding keyboard shortcut). You will see a pop-up window showing that documentation, as follows:

Viewing documentation in PyCharm

What's more, you can also view the documentation for your own functions (or methods, classes, and so on) using the same action since PyCharm scans through all code in its projects. Move your cursor to the call to `prime_check()` in the main scope in the following line (which should be around *line 38*):

```
if prime_check(num):
```

If you evoke the same **Quick Documentation** action, you will be able to see the same docstring that we entered earlier.

Quick Definition

Say the documentation alone doesn't provide enough information and you'd like to see how a specific function is defined. **Quick Definition**, which operates in the same way as **Quick Documentation**, can be utilized for this. While having your cursor at a specific API call, go to **View | Quick Definition** to evoke the action.

For example, the following screenshot was captured when I evoked the feature on the call to `prime_check()` in our example:

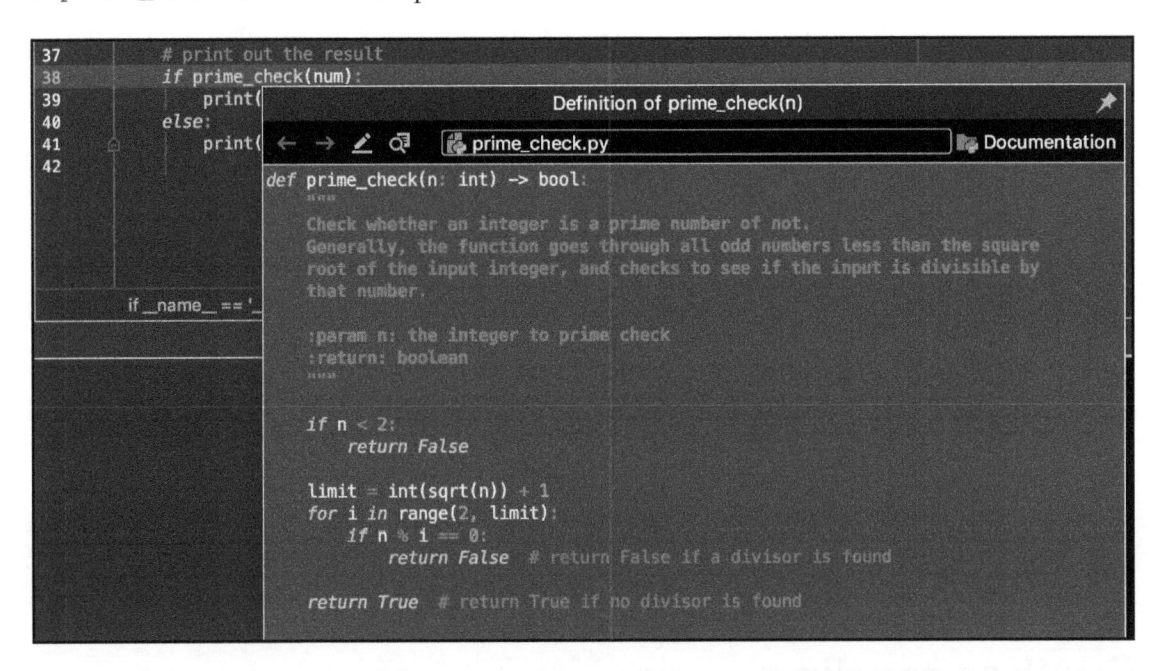

Viewing a definition in PyCharm

Overall, we can appreciate the powerful options PyCharm provides when it comes to dynamically viewing documentation and definitions within the IDE. Significant time and energy can be saved when programmers don't have to switch away from their development environment to look for documentation, say, on the internet.

Summary

Throughout this chapter, we examined PyCharm's features regarding various aspects of programming, including code analysis, code completion, refactoring, and documenting. In all of these processes, PyCharm's intelligent code analyzer provides smart and convenient options for editing and fixing problems in your code in real-time and in a dynamic way.

Aside from a wide number of options the intelligent code analyzer can support, PyCharm also allows users to customize the behavior of the analyzer to their liking. This can be achieved in various sections of the general settings. Overall, these support features look to improve your productivity as a developer in a way that is customized and beneficial to you.

In the next chapter, we will focus on a particular aspect of programming: version control. We will learn about the specifics of the version control process with Git, and how PyCharm supports and streamlines this process.

Questions

1. What levels of severity in terms of problems in a Python program are determined by PyCharm's code analyzer?
2. What are some common problems that PyCharm can detect and help fix via its intelligent code analyzer?
3. How is PyCharm's code completion support different from others?
4. What are some common code completion options that PyCharm offers?
5. What are common causes for PyCharm's code completion support not working?
6. What are some common refactoring options that PyCharm offers?
7. What options does PyCharm provide when it comes to documentation?

Further reading

For more information regarding what you learned in this chapter, you can refer to the following links:

- *Mastering PyCharm*, Quazi Nafiul Islam, by Packt Publishing (https://www.packtpub.com/web-development/mastering-pycharm)
- *Modern Python Development with PyCharm*, by Pedro Kroger (https://pedrokroger.net/pycharm-book/)

- *Code completion*, JetBrains s.r.o. documentation (`jetbrains.org/intellij/sdk/docs/reference_guide/custom_language_support/code_completion.html`)
- *Intelligent code completion*, Wikipedia (`https://en.wikipedia.org/wiki/Intelligent_code_completion`)
- *PyCharm: The Good Parts*, by Nafiul Islam (`http://nafiulis.me/pycharm-the-good-parts-ii.html`)
- *Hippie Completion in Eclipse*, by Cédric Beust (`https://beust.com/weblog/2005/03/11/hippie-completion-in-eclipse/`)
- *Intention actions*, JetBrains s.r.o. documentation (`https://www.jetbrains.com/help/idea/intention-actions.html`)
- *Refactoring Python Applications for Simplicity*, by Anthony Shaw, (`https://realpython.com/python-refactoring/`)
- *Enriching Your Python Classes With Dunder (Magic, Special) Methods*, by Bob Belderbos (`https://dbader.org/blog/python-dunder-methods`)

5
Version Control with Git in PyCharm

Version control is an essential part of software engineering and development, but it is a considerably complex process, and therefore hard to get right. The process, in general, is quite intimidating, especially to beginner programmers. However, as we will learn in this chapter, PyCharm offers an intuitive and graphical interface that helps demystify version control for its users.

This chapter will first cover the idea of version control and why it is important, both in personal projects and group work. You will then learn about the most common version control tool, Git, and how to integrate it into Python projects in PyCharm.

Using PyCharm to take care of our version control process will help us avoid the low-level, nitty-gritty details that are usually involved in the process, leaving us free to focus on the actual development tasks. Knowing how to facilitate version control with PyCharm will also offer us a clearer idea of the extent to which PyCharm assists with almost all aspects of Python software development.

The following topics will be covered in this chapter:

- The idea behind the process of version control and its importance
- How to use Git to facilitate adding, committing, pushing, merging, and branching
- The options and features PyCharm provides to streamline the version control process

Technical requirements

The following is a list of prerequisites for this chapter:

- Ensure that you have both Python 3.6+ and PyCharm installed on your computer
- Download the GitHub repository at `https://github.com/PacktPublishing/Hands-on-Application-Development-with-PyCharm`
- During this chapter, we will be working with the `Chapter05` subfolder in the downloaded code repository

Version control and Git essentials

Hopefully, the fact that you are reading this chapter means that you already acknowledge the importance of the process of version control in software development and in programming in general. If you want to learn the specific options and features, PyCharm offers to assist users during the process of version control, specifically with Git. Feel free to skip to the next section, which is going to be more hands-on.

If, however, you'd like to learn more generally about the process and the details about Git and GitHub, stick around, as this section will provide that information, which will be essential as we move forward with the topic of this chapter.

What does version control mean?

In the general context of programming, version control denotes the process of using a specific system to record and save changes and overall progress in directories and files so that a programmer can come back to it later. If multiple separate changes have been applied to a project that is under version control, you can even switch between these different changes (versions) in the development process.

In software development, we are generally concerned with applying version control to files containing the source code (scripts), but almost any file type in a computer can be version controlled (images, videos, system files, and so on).

The simplest form of version control is something that most of us are already doing—file backups. For example, as you are working on a project, each time you'd like to version control the changes made, you can copy the entire project to a separate location in your local computer. To facilitate multiple versions, each time you back up your project, you can create a new folder with a timestamp containing that version of the project.

This simple method is effective at helping us achieve what we want from version control—progress made to a project is saved in separate version instances and it is possible to go back to each of those versions. However, it is not without its disadvantages—errors can be made and files can be copied to the wrong folders, and if the local drive of your computer is damaged, everything that is version controlled in this way might be lost.

Nowadays, it is standard practice to use methods that take advantage of some sort of database that can be accessed in a network of multiple systems. This is called **distributed version control** and allows multiple agents to collaborate on a common project by applying different changes to that project independently (given that there are no conflicts between the changes).

Situations that require version control

I personally think the easiest and quickest way for a programmer to appreciate version control is to imagine various scenarios, programming-wise, where things will become dire, or even catastrophic if version control is not being implemented.

The scenario that can be imagined easily (which has also probably happened to you) is when a programmer has made too many changes to a project that cannot be easily reverted manually. For example, after two hours of implementing a specific feature for your program, you decide that the feature is no longer desirable and would like to omit any instance in the project where that feature is used. This is not an easy task to do manually, especially if the feature is complicated and has complex APIs that are scattered throughout different files of the project.

The much more efficient way to revert all the changes made is to save the project before any changes of that feature are made and simply revert the project to that stage when you decide not to implement that feature anymore. Instead of going through all the files and folders that have been changed with regard to the feature, you can simply take a step back and use a past version of the project.

Another reason to use version control, especially in today's industry environment, is its efficient facilitation of collaborative work. Backing up your project to, say, a cloud version control service such as GitHub allows others to see and make comments on that project, as well as obtain the source code for themselves. Furthermore, members of a development team can have a centralized code hub for their projects; specific roles can be assigned to different members during the version control process (programming, reviewing, tracking issues).

Using a cloud-based version control method also means that, even if you completely lose everything in a given project on your local computer, you can retrieve it from the web anytime. This practice additionally allows programmers to work on projects in a cross-platform manner.

Git and GitHub

Git (along with its cloud interface GitHub) is undoubtedly the most common version control tool in the field of programming and software engineering today. Even if you are not using Git and GitHub to facilitate version control for your projects, you actually have already interacted with GitHub in a sense when downloading the code repository for this book!

In this section, we will go into details about how to get started as a Git user (if you are not already one), and various options available for the facilitation of version control. Again, if you are already an experienced Git user, feel free to skip to the next section to learn about the integration of Git in PyCharm.

Downloading Git and registering for GitHub

To be able to utilize Git and GitHub for version control, you have to have two components ready—a Git client on your local computer (used to communicate with the cloud service GitHub) and a GitHub account (to be associated with all version control tasks that you will perform).

Let's walk through the following steps to set up our Git and GitHub tools:

1. Go to `git-scm.com/downloads` and choose the download that corresponds to your operating system.
2. By default, Git client is a command-line tool, but it is possible to utilize various GUI tools from Git to make the process more intuitive. We will not be needing these GUI tools, as PyCharm will take care of this process.
3. Next, you need to register for an account on GitHub. Head to `www.github.com` and click on the **Sign Up** button to start the registration process.

With that, you are all set to be able to utilize various version control functionalities with Git and GitHub. In the next few subsections, we will be considering various tasks and commands that programmers commonly use in their version control process.

Setting up a repository

The term **repository** is used to denote an overarching project that is version controlled with Git. Given that there are two main components to working with Git (Git client and GitHub), there are two separate processes you need to go through to set up a repository that is version controlled and these are as follows:

1. Firstly, you need to initialize the project that is to be put under version control as a repository on your local system. This can be done with a simple command (`git init`), which is to be executed at the root directory of the project.
2. Second, you need to create a corresponding repository on GitHub. While logged in with your GitHub account, click on the + button in the top-right corner of the site and choose **New repository**.
3. Next, GitHub will take you through multiple steps to customize various information about your repository. At this stage, you should only enter the name of the repository and leave all the other options as is.
4. Finally, you need to associate the local repository to one stored on GitHub—this process is called **adding remotes**. To do this, you can run the following Git command:

    ```
    git remote add origin
    https://github.com/PacktPublishing/Hands-on-Application-Development
    -with-PyCharm
    ```

The previous steps outline the process for setting up a local Git repository on GitHub. Next, we will learn about the process of transferring data from your local repository to GitHub.

Add, commit, and push

To send any files you have saved and stored in your local repository to GitHub, we need to utilize the add, commit, and push commands, which are to be executed in the same order. Note that these commands can transfer your local repository to GitHub when you first set up the Git repositories and they can also apply any changes you have made locally to the cloud repository on GitHub.

We are now considering these commands one by one:

- The `add` command registers a specific file (or a set of files) to Git, indicating that this file should be a part of the version controlled repository. You can either run `git add [path to some file]`, or run `git add .`, which will register all folders and files inside the root directory into the Git repository.
- The `commit` command applies all the newly created changes in the registered files to Git. This command is run when we'd like to literally commit the changes we have made to version control.
- Finally, the `push` command sends the committed changes to the remote that is associated with the local repository. Normally, this is done via `git push origin master`.

By following these steps in order, you can apply cloud version control to your own projects with Git and GitHub in a simple manner. In the next subsection, we will discuss working with projects that are not your own, which can be group projects or open source projects that you'd like to tinker with.

Fork, clone, and pull requests

The series of commands discussed in the previous section (`add`, `commit`, and `push`) work great if you are only working with and version controlling your own projects and code. However, this is not always the case in the real world, where you need to work with other developers in a common project at work, or you are contributing to an open source project.

In these situations, you are interacting not only with your own GitHub repository but also with others. This process requires you to have multiple remotes for your local repository. Recall from the previous subsection that a remote can be thought of as a link between a local repository and a GitHub one on the cloud. Here, we need to have multiple (at least two) remotes—one associated with our own repository and one with the original GitHub repository.

The process is as follows:

1. Say, there is a GitHub repository called `abc` created by another user named Alice that you'd like to work on. The GitHub repository is located at `github.com/alice/abc`. The first thing you need to do is go to that GitHub repository and **fork** the repository, using the **Fork** button in the top-right corner of the window, as shown in the following screenshot:

Chapter 5

Forking on GitHub

This action, in essence, creates a copy of that given repository as one of your own, in your GitHub account. To learn more about forking, check out the following link: `guides.github.com/activities/forking/`.

2. Now, from your local computer, you will set up a Git repository in a similar way as what we discussed earlier (including adding a remote associated with your GitHub repository, forked from Alice's original one). From here, you will clone the GitHub repository to your local system via that remote; doing this will create a physical copy of the repository on your local machine.

3. In your local repository, you can now make any changes to the project as you'd like, and finally, push them to your GitHub repository. This process is no different from making changes to your own repository. However, note that you can only push the changes made to your repository, forked from the original; you cannot directly push those changes to Alice's repository (unless you have permission to do so on GitHub, which is commonly not the case).

4. From your own updated GitHub repository, you can now create a pull request, which will submit all the changes you have made to your forked repository to the original repository if you'd like to contribute to that original project. This can be done by going to the **Pull requests** tab of your GitHub repository and clicking on the **New pull request** button on the right, as illustrated in the following screenshot:

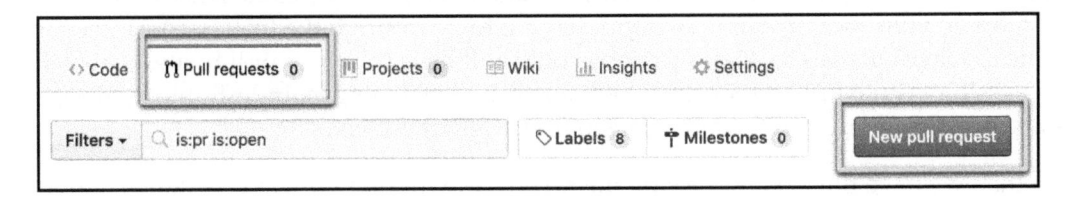

Making a pull request on GitHub

[149]

In short, the whole process can be summed up with the following diagram, with numbered arrows denoting specific steps to be taken in order:

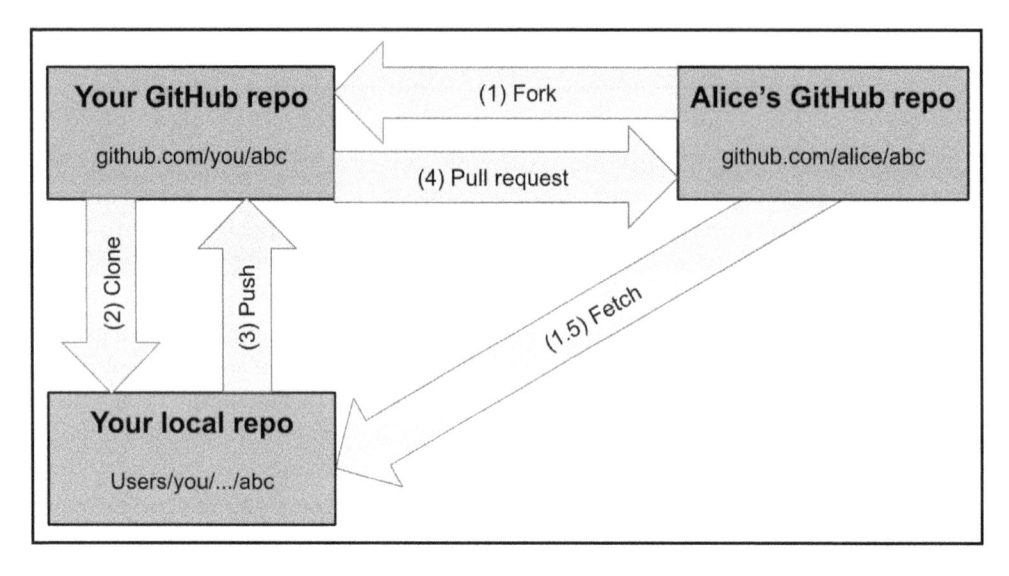

Working with others' GitHub repositories

Specifically, while working with Alice's GitHub repository, we would first fork it to our own account, which will then be cloned to our local environment. Any changes made to our local copy should be applied (or pushed) to our repository, which could finally be applied back to Alice's original project with a pull request. A `fetch` command can also be used to copy Alice's project to our local environment, but the middle-man repository in our GitHub account will not be created in this way.

Note that there is an arrow in the previous diagram that we have not discussed—**(1.5) Fetch**. This arrow represents the fact that you can, in fact, directly clone Alice's GitHub repository to your local machine (without having to go through the fork step). However, to be able to make changes to Alice's project, you'd still have to utilize pull requests, which are only possible with a forked repository of your own. So fetching is undesirable in most instances, unless you simply want a code of the original project.

With that, we have finished discussing the process of working with and making changes to a GitHub repository that is not your own. In the next section, we will move on to discuss the main topic of this chapter—the integration of Git and GitHub as a version control method in PyCharm.

Branching and merging

In addition to forking and pushing, branching and merging are two other processes that directly affect the GitHub repository of a given project. As the name suggests, branching is when we create an entirely separate copy of our repository, and any changes applied to this copy will not affect the main copy (also known as the master branch) or any other copies. The ability to isolate different versions of a project in one repository is significantly useful when experimental changes are made.

When committing them to GitHub, a developer can access different branches in the branch dropdown menu in the top-left corner of the GitHub web page, as shown in the following screenshot:

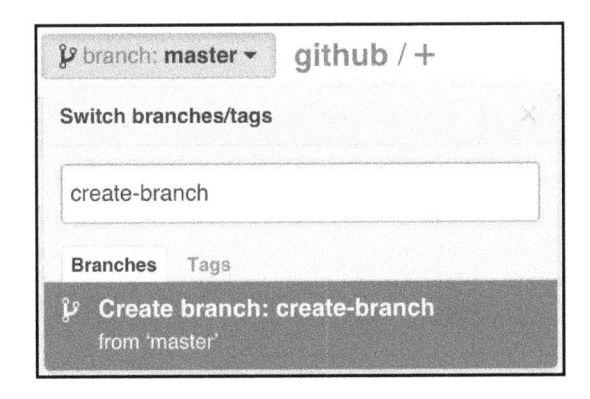

Branches in GitHub

On the other hand, merging is the process of combining two given branches into one, commonly between the master branch and another branch. Merging is done mainly when the developer wants to apply the changes made to a non-master branch to the master branch. This process is typically done via GitHub's online interface and is quite similar to accepting a pull request.

Ignoring files

Most of the time, one would not want to transfer all the folders and files in your local project onto GitHub. For example, if you are working on a data science project and the datasets you are working with are significantly large, it is undesirable to upload these datasets on GitHub. In fact, there is a limit of 100 MB in size for files that you can upload to GitHub. Another reason not to upload everything to GitHub is to avoid leakage of sensitive information such as login credentials and API keys that are stored in your projects.

Version Control with Git in PyCharm

To leave certain files out of the transferring process, you can take advantage of a `.gitignore` file. Treated as a hidden file, only to be interpreted by Git, `.gitignore` can be edited as a text file in which folders and files that should be ignored by Git can be listed out.

> A complete documentation on gitignore can be found at `git-scm.com/docs/gitignore`.

With that, we have learned about the fundamental components of a Git/GitHub workflow. In the next section, we will see how PyCharm can streamline and automate most of this process.

Version control in PyCharm

In this section, we will study various features in PyCharm that facilitate the process of version control with Git and GitHub. As a prerequisite of this exercise, go on to your GitHub account to create a new repository to be the one associated with this current local project. You can name this repository however you like (`GitTest`, `PyCharmVersionControlTest`, or whatever).

Also note that while creating the GitHub repository, you can specify it to be private, which will prevent other people from seeing and accessing the repository—after all, this is a playground repository solely for learning purposes.

Next, either create a new Pure Python project in PyCharm and enter the following sample code into a Python script inside that project or import the `Chapter05` folder from our book repository as a project into your PyCharm:

```
if __name__ == '__main__':
    print('Hello from Version Control!')
```

Our goal in this section is to push this project to GitHub by walking through all the steps that we discussed previously. If at any point you are not sure what a specific command is used for, you can go back to the previous section in this chapter to learn more about Git commands. We will also be looking at the differences between the manual process and doing it via PyCharm so that the advantages of the latter option can be highlighted.

Setting up a local repository

As you might remember from the previous section, the first step to version control with Git is to initialize a local repository.

To do this, go to **VCS** in the menu bar and choose **Enable Version Control Integration**. If you don't see this option in your PyCharm project, this means that you already have your Git integrated, so simply move on to the next step. Otherwise, a pop-up window will appear asking for the version control tool you'd like to use. Choose **Git** for this option, as illustrated in the following screenshot:

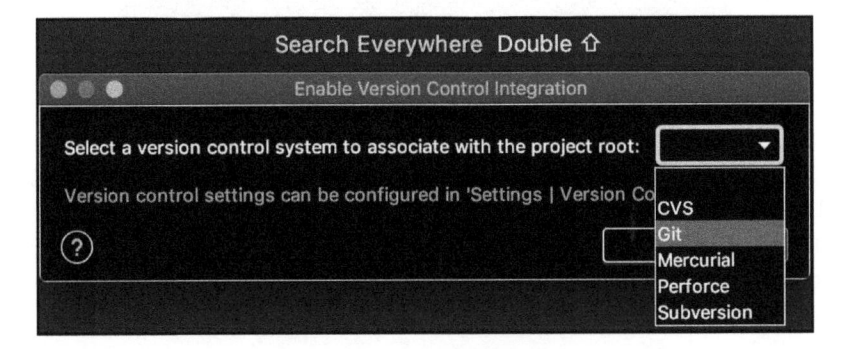

Choosing Git for version control in PyCharm

As you can see, there are other options for version control that PyCharm can support—**CVS**, **Mercurial**, **Perforce**, and so on. Since Git and GitHub, once again, are the most common option for version control nowadays, we will focus on them in this book. However, you always have the chance to take advantage of the other options if you do work with any of them.

To actually create the local Git repository, choose **VCS** | **Import into Version Control** | **Create Git Repository**. In the window that opens immediately after, choose the directory that you'd like to create the Git repository. For this exercise, simply choose the current folder that we are in, `Chapter05`.

The Version Control panel

After creating the Git repository, the tab for the **Version Control** panel will appear in your project window (most likely in the bottom-left corner), though it is minimized by default. (Note that we have talked about PyCharm panels in `Chapter 3`, *Customizing Interpreters and Virtual Environments*, so if you skipped that chapter but would like to learn more, feel free to go back to it before moving forward with this section.)

The **Version Control** panel, when pulled up, will look similar to the following screenshot:

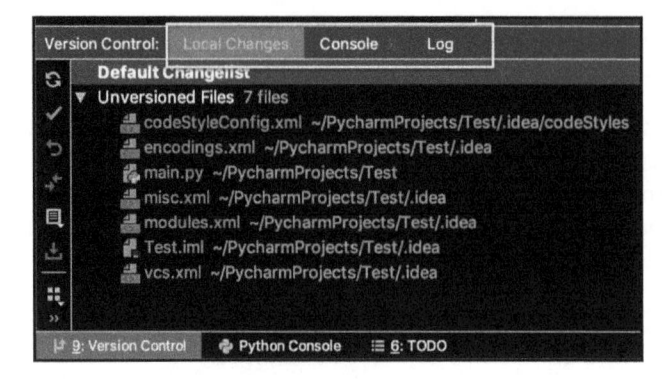

The Version Control panel in PyCharm

First, notice that there are multiple tabs that you can examine in this panel—**Local Changes**, **Console**, and **Log**—as highlighted earlier (note that the **Console** tab might not be available if you haven't run any Git commands yet). Most of the time, we will mostly focus on the **Local Changes** tab, where we will be able to interact with files where we want to apply version control.

In the **Local Changes** tab, you will typically see two separate sections:

- **Default Changelist** lists all files within your project that have been added to Git. A file highlighted in blue indicates that it has been modified since the last commit, while a file in green means that it has not yet been committed.
- **Unversioned Files**, on the other hand, lists all files within your project that have not been added to Git altogether.

For example, in the preceding screenshot, and most likely in the project you currently have open (if you are following with the example), all the files in our project (`main.py` along with other hidden, project-related files) are in the **Unversioned Files** section, since we have not added them to Git yet.

Add, commit, and push

Again, we will try to perform all the tasks in the version control pipeline we have discussed in the previous section using PyCharm. Here, we will see how we can add files to Git, commit them, and finally, push them on the GitHub repository created at the beginning for this section.

[154]

To add a specific file to Git, simply select it within the **Version Control** panel, right-click on the file, and select **Git | Add**, as illustrated, where I was adding the `main.py` file to Git:

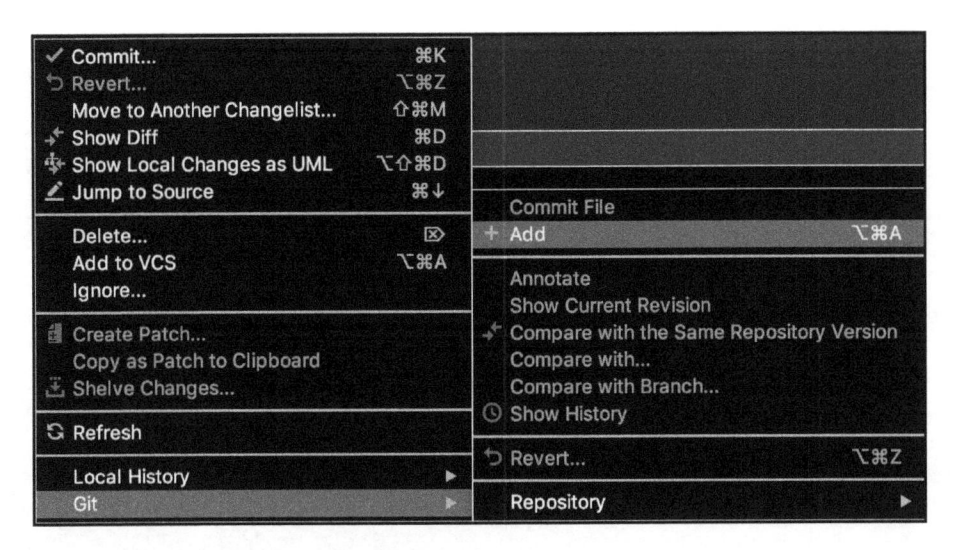

Adding files to Git in PyCharm

Alternatively, you can also go to **VCS | Git | Add** in the menu bar, or use the corresponding keyboard shortcut. After the add is performed, you should be able to see that the file has been moved to the **Default Changelist** section, and is now highlighted in green (again, indicating that it is registered by Git and has not been committed).

Note that you can also select multiple files at the same time in the **Version Control** panel and add them to Git simultaneously. To add all the unversioned files to Git, you can also select the **Unversioned Files** section itself and evoke the add action. For now, just add the `main.py` file to Git.

Furthermore, to remove a file from Git, you can select that file within the **Default Changelist**, right-click, and choose **Revert**. Doing this will have Git unregister the file, and move it back to the **Unversioned Files** section. Again, we only want `main.py` committed in our current example, so go ahead and revert any file that you accidentally committed using this method.

The process of committing files is fairly similar to what we just saw with adding. To commit the files highlighted in green in the **Default Changelist** section (which we only have the `main.py` file for now), right-click on them and select `Commit`, or use the corresponding keyboard shortcut.

Version Control with Git in PyCharm

The following pop-up window will appear, showing information regarding the commit that we are attempting:

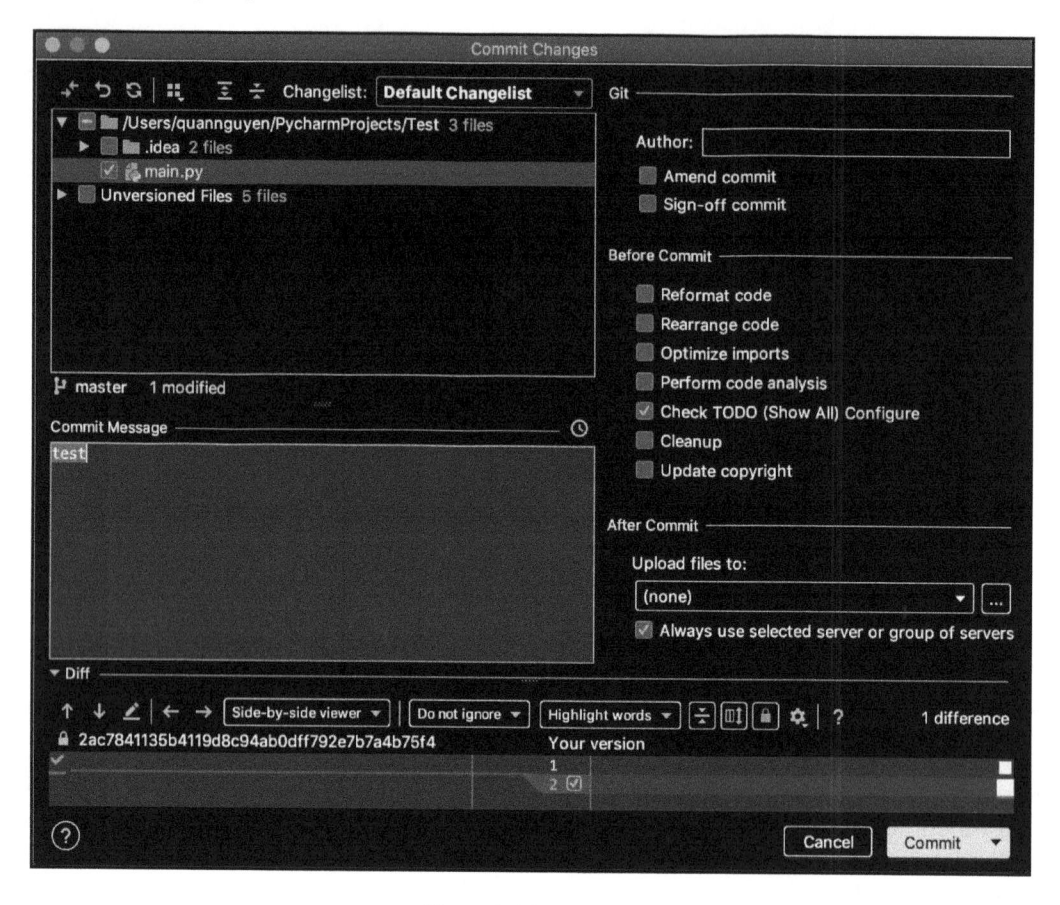

The commit window in PyCharm

In the middle-left section of the window, you can enter a commit message indicating the purpose of the commit, which will be displayed on GitHub. Furthermore, in the bottom section, you can see the differences between the file(s) you are committing and their previous versions; the default comparison is displayed side by side (which you can further customize).

When you have entered a commit message, you can finalize the process by clicking the **Commit** button. After a file has been committed, it will disappear from the **Default Changelist** section.

Additionally, you can also evoke the **Commit** button, conveniently placed in the top-right corner of the project window by default, when files you'd like to commit are selected:

Version Control's Commit button in PyCharm

Finally, the last step is to push the committed portion of the project (which consists of the `main.py` file only for now) to GitHub. Go to **VCS** | **Git** | **Push** to perform this task and another pop-up window will appear.

If you are pushing to GitHub for the first time in this project (which we are if you are following the example), there will be a **Define remote** link in the main section of the window, which we can use to establish the connection between our local project and a GitHub repository:

Adding remotes in PyCharm

Click on the link and input the URL to the GitHub repository that you created at the beginning of this section. After this, you can push the local project you have to this repository on the cloud. You can go to that repository on GitHub to see the pushed `main.py` file after this process is complete.

Branching and merging

Branching and merging processes can be accomplished quite effortlessly in PyCharm. In the bottom-right corner of your project window, click on the **Git** button, which will bring up the following dropdown in which we can manage the branches for our project:

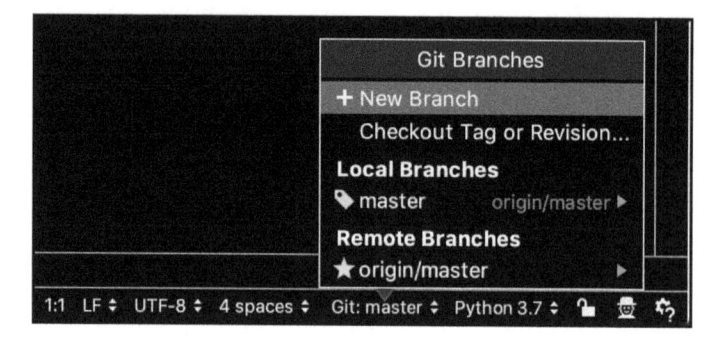

Management of branches in PyCharm

As you can see, in this menu we can create a new branch for our project. Go ahead and create a new branch and make a change to the `main.py` file in our project. For example, I named my new branch **branch1** and changed the code in `main.py` too:

```
if __name__ == '__main__':
    print('Hello from Version Control!')
    print('Change in branch 1.')
```

From here, you can switch back and forth between different branches in the same menu by selecting a specific branch and choose **Checkout**. For example, selecting the following will bring you back to the master branch of our current project:

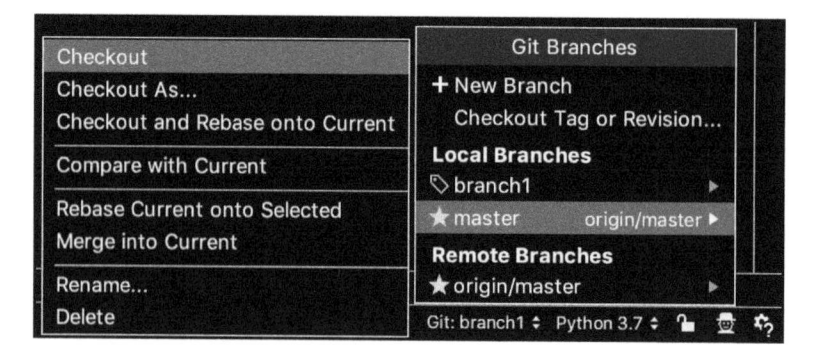

Switching between branches

From the same menu, you can choose to rename or delete a branch, or more importantly, implement a merge between two branches by selecting **Merge into Current**.

Ignoring files

With what we just discussed/will discuss, you will see that there are a lot of useful commands and actions available when one right-clicks on items in the **Version Control** panel, and ignoring certain files is no exception. We have talked about the need of not including specific files in the version control process (because they contain confidential information or they are heavy files).

Again, doing this in PyCharm is quite simple; right-click on the items you'd like to exclude from version control within the **Version Control** panel, and choose **Ignore**. Additionally, you can go to the settings and navigate to **Version Control | Ignored Files** to further customize your preferences for files to be ignored.

So, we have learned about the basic commands in Git and how to implement them in PyCharm. In the last discussion of this chapter, we will consider an advanced functionality of the version control process in PyCharm—creating diagrams.

Version control diagrams

As we have seen, before any changes to Git are committed, a commit message is required to explain how the project being considered has been changed. This practice is quite useful, as we can look through all the different commits in the future and see what progress each of them accomplished.

However, when many changes are made across multiple files and folders within a project, it can be quite difficult to wrap one's head around how the entire project has been altered. This is when the ability to create diagrams to visualize changes across different files can be significantly useful.

Version Control with Git in PyCharm

Similar to class diagrams, which are integral in object-oriented programming, version control diagrams, also drawn in UML style, show any changes that have been made locally in a systematic way across files and folders. This action is called **Show Local Changes as UML**, which can be accessed via right-clicking items in the **Default Changelist** in the **Version Control** panel, as illustrated in the following screenshot:

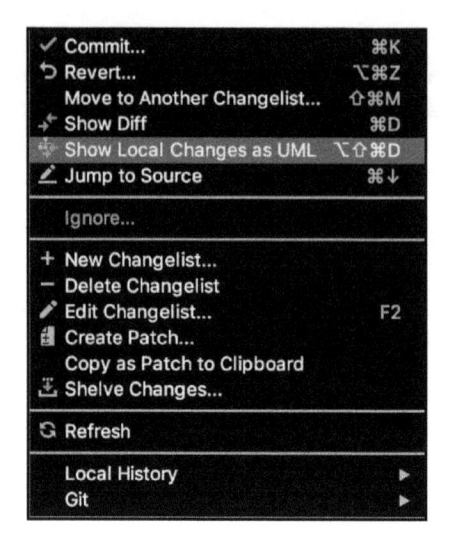

Creating UML diagrams for local changes

When the action is evoked, a window will appear, displaying the UML diagram that visualizes the changes made to the project. Following is a sample class diagram provided by JetBrains in their documentation:

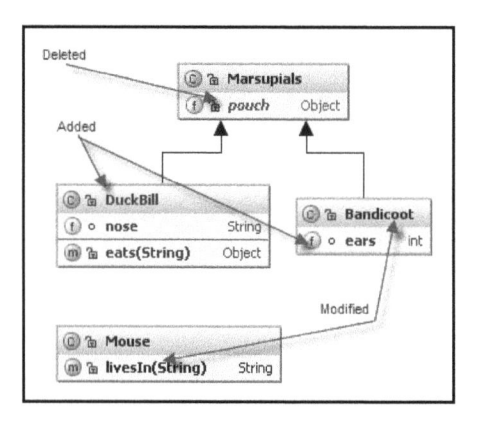

Sample UML diagram for version control

As indicated, any changes in a class diagram will be color-coded so that modified items are highlighted in blue, newly added items in green, and deleted ones in gray. From any UML diagram, you can further interact with elements in it (for example, dragging and dropping), or even save the diagram for future reference. All in all, it is a great feature for documenting and reporting changes that you have made to, say, a work group project or an open source project.

Also, note that since our current project only contains the `main.py` file, the usefulness of the feature cannot be illustrated. With that said, you can try using it on other projects you might have or after creating some additional sample files in your project.

And that is it! You have learned the process of working with Git and GitHub for version control within PyCharm projects. As you have probably noticed, the options offered by PyCharm allow a more intuitive way of thinking as well as a dynamic workflow in the version control process for your applications.

Summary

In this chapter, we have covered two main topics—the idea of version control in application development and programming and its importance, as well as how to practice it using Git and GitHub within PyCharm. Specifically, we have learned how to carry out version control using Git and GitHub in two different ways: manually and with PyCharm.

With this knowledge, PyCharm users can apply version control to their own projects in a flexible way, skipping over the manual and tedious process in the Terminal/command line. We see that, by offering these features, PyCharm allows us to focus on the actual development process in any given software engineering project.

Aside from version control, there are other practices in application development— which PyCharm provides intuitive, straightforward commands to facilitate. Without these commands, application development be quite complex and intimidating. These processes are testing, debugging, and profiling, all of which will be discussed in the next chapter.

Questions

1. What does the term version control entail, specifically in the context of programming?
2. What are the benefits of doing version control?
3. What are the basic steps to version control for your own projects with Git and GitHub? What additional steps are needed for collaborative work?
4. What are the options that PyCharm's **Version Control** panel provides?
5. What is the significance of being able to create version control UML diagrams for changes in files and folders in a project?

Further reading

More information can be found in the following articles and literature:

- *Getting Started - About Version Control*, Git (git-scm.com/book/en/v2/Getting-Started-About-Version-Control)
- *PyCharm documentation: GitHub*, JetBrains s.r.o. (www.jetbrains.com/help/pycharm/github.html)
- *PyCharm documentation: Version Control with PyCharm*, JetBrains s.r.o. (www.jetbrains.com/help/pycharm/version-control-integration.html)
- *PyCharm documentation: Viewing Changes as Diagram*, JetBrains s.r.o. (www.jetbrains.com/help/pycharm/viewing-changes-as-diagram.html)

6
Seamless Testing, Debugging, and Profiling

esting, debugging, and profiling are three of the more advanced practices in programming. They are generally difficult to implement, and there can be significant confusion regarding how to facilitate them.

This chapter goes through a myriad of PyCharm tools that can streamline these three processes, and make them as seamless as possible. PyCharm users who take advantage of these features can greatly improve their productivity.

The following topics will be covered in this chapter:

- Testing in general and specifically unit testing
- How to facilitate debugging in PyCharm
- Code optimization in PyCharm with performance survey and profiling

Technical requirements

The following is a list of prerequisites for this chapter:

- Ensure that you have both Python 3.6+ and PyCharm installed on your computer
- Download this book's GitHub repository at https://github.com/PacktPublishing/Hands-on-Application-Development-with-PyCharm
- In this chapter, we will be working with the subfolder named Chapter06 in the downloaded code repository

Testing

We will open this chapter with the topic of testing, specifically **unit testing**. As usual, we will examine the theoretical background of the practice in Python and then move on to learn about how PyCharm helps facilitate the process. You are welcome to skim through the theoretical discussion if you are already familiar with the concept and practice of unit testing, but a full read-through is still encouraged.

Unit testing fundamentals

Intuitively, testing in software development is used to look for inconsistencies and errors in our programs and code. The difference between testing and debugging, which is discussed in the next section of this chapter, is that testing is about looking for the indication of bugs in our code, while debugging is when we hope to identify the bugs themselves.

As we will see later in this section, testing mostly involves the comparison between the results that are produced by our programs and what they should actually be. In short, testing is all about determining whether our programs are functioning as we intended.

Again, the main goal of testing is to raise any potential bugs and errors in our programs. However, if a test does not look for specific bugs in its logic, chances are it will not be able to offer the programmer any indication of those bugs. This is to say that test results are only as good as the tests themselves, and effective testing is equivalent to effective test design.

The question is, then, how to design effective tests that can give us a good indication of the performance of our programs. One of the most common ways to do this is unit testing, where, as the term suggests, individual units of a specific program will be considered and tested (a unit here indicates the smallest testable component of the said program—this can be a class, method, or function.).

Unit testing offers us a systematic way to write and implement tests for our programs: since we are going to look at individual program units, if an error is to arise, we will be able to easily narrow down which specific individual unit is responsible for the error. From there, we only have to focus on debugging that specific unit. This ability to isolate errors and bugs to individual units can save developers significant time during the testing process.

Of course, aside from unit testing, there are other methods with which you can design tests for your programs: integration testing (where groups of program units are tested while working together) or system testing (where the whole piece of software is considered). However, all these testing methods are higher leveled than unit testing, and should only be used after the program has passed all of its unit testing cases. For the same reason, these methods do not offer the same insights as unit testing (that is, the mentioned isolation of bugs and errors to individual units).

Overall, unit testing is the first—and sometimes the most important—step to a complete, systematic testing procedure for your software. Therefore, we will only concern ourselves with unit testing in this chapter, which, in fact, is highly supported by PyCharm. Next, we will move on to see how unit tests are implemented in Python.

Unit testing in Python

In this section, we will be using examples from the Chapter06/Testing subfolder in this book's code repository. Go ahead and import the folder into PyCharm as a project, or create a new project and enter the code as we move along with our discussions.

First and foremost, unit testing in Python is supported by the unittest module, which offers similar functionalities to those in common unit testing frameworks in other programming languages. Generally, tests for a specific unit component of a program are organized into a subclass of the TestCase class from the module.

As an example, consider the test_example.py file in this book's repository, which contains the following code:

```python
from unittest import TestCase


class MathTest(TestCase):
    def test_add(self):
        self.assertEqual(1 + 1, 2)

    def test_mul(self):
        self.assertEqual(2 * 5, 10)


class StringTest(TestCase):
    def test_stringcase(self):
        self.assertTrue('FOO'.isupper())
        self.assertFalse('Bar'.isupper())
```

As we mentioned earlier, the `MathTest` and `StringTest` classes, where our unit tests are stored, both inherit from the `TestCase` class of the `unittest` module. To implement different unit tests, we simply put testing methods in the corresponding classes. For example, the `test_add()` method in the `MathTest` class tests for the equation 1 + 1 = 2 (which, obviously, is just a toy example), while the `test_stringcase()` method in the `StringTest` class tests for the uppercase-ness of the `FOO` and `Bar` strings.

Note that in each of these methods, we use various asserting methods from the `TestCase` class. For example, `assertEqual()` looks to see if the two arguments that are passed to it are indeed equal, while `assertTrue()` and `assertFalse()` make sure that the arguments that are passed to them are `true` and `false` booleans, respectively.

The most common way to run these Python unit tests is via the command line; in fact, the `unittest` module is designed to have a good command-line interface. Specifically, the module can be included in a `python` command to run tests from modules/files, classes, and even individual test methods via the following interfaces:

```
python -m unittest test_file1 test_file2
python -m unittest test_file.TestClass
python -m unittest test_file.TestClass.test_method
```

With this interface in mind, let's try running our tests via the command line. Either use the **Terminal** panel of your PyCharm or open the actual command line of your system and navigate to the folder we are working with. First, we can run the whole file by using the following command:

```
>> python -m unittest test_example
...
----------------------------------------------------------------------
Ran 3 tests in 0.000s

OK
```

We can see that three tests were run in total (which is consistent with the fact that we have three tests in our current Python script) and that all of them were successful. Again, we can also run individual test classes and methods, as opposed to the whole test file. For example, run the following command in the command line to only run tests in the `MathTest` class:

```
>> python -m unittest test_example.MathTest
..
----------------------------------------------------------------------
Ran 2 tests in 0.000s

OK
```

To run the `test_stringcase()` method in the `StringTest` class, use the following command:

```
>> python -m unittest test_example.StringTest.test_stringcase
.
----------------------------------------------------------------------
Ran 1 test in 0.000s

OK
```

We have seen how to run unit tests in Python via the command-line interface for the `unittest` module. In the next subsection, we will learn how to implement the same process using PyCharm's powerful testing features.

Unit testing in PyCharm

Still considering the `test_example.py` file in the `Chapter06/Testing` folder, let's see how PyCharm helps facilitate the process of unit testing in Python.

PyCharm's run arrows

Since you have the file opened in the editor within PyCharm, you will see multiple green arrows to the left of your code, as illustrated here:

```
from unittest import TestCase


class MathTest(TestCase):
    def test_add(self):
        self.assertEqual(1 + 1, 2)


    def test_mul(self):
        self.assertEqual(2 * 5, 10)



class StringTest(TestCase):
    def test_stringcase(self):
        self.assertTrue('FOO'.isupper())
        self.assertFalse('Bar'.isupper())
```

Run arrows in PyCharm

Seamless Testing, Debugging, and Profiling

You might remember from Chapter 2, *Installing and Configuring PyCharm*, that by using a similar green arrow located at the beginning of the main scope of a Python program (the `if __name__ == '__main__'` condition), we can run the whole program. In general, these green arrows are indeed used to run, not just whole Python programs, but also code snippets and, in this case, unit tests. I personally like to call them *run arrows*.

As you click on any of these run arrows, a list of options will appear, displaying various actions you can have PyCharm perform with the code snippet that corresponds to that arrow:

Running tests in PyCharm

For now, we can select the first option, **Run 'Unittests for test_e...'**, to execute a specific test class or method. For example, when I chose the option to run the `test_mul()` method in the `MathTest` class, PyCharm executed that specific test method and opened the **Run** panel to display the output that's produced by the test. The following is my output after the execution:

```
Testing started at 14:17 ...
/usr/local/bin/python3.7
/Applications/PyCharm.app/Contents/helpers/pycharm/_jb_unittest_runner.py --target test_example.MathTest.test_mul
Launching unittests with arguments python -m unittest test_example.MathTest.test_mul in /Users/quannguyen/PycharmProjects/PyCharm-Book/Chapter06/Testing


Ran 1 test in 0.001s

OK

Process finished with exit code 0
```

Looking closely at the output, specifically the line that starts with **Launching unittests...**, we can see that PyCharm is acting as the middleman between the programmer and the command line. In particular, PyCharm specified that the argument that was used was `python -m unittest test_example.MathTest.test_mul`, which is the exact command we would use via the command line to execute the same test.

This is quite a useful feature: instead of having to type out the whole command in the command line, we can now simply visually locate the specific tests that we'd like to run and take advantage of the corresponding run arrows to execute them in PyCharm. This visual, graphical approach is also friendlier toward new Python programmers/testers.

The Run panel in the context of unit testing

We have said that, when we choose to run a specific set of unit tests, PyCharm will open up the **Run** panel to display the results. You may have already noticed that this **Run** panel is different from ones that display the output of regular Python programs. Specifically, the **Run** panel for the execution of unit tests should look similar to the following:

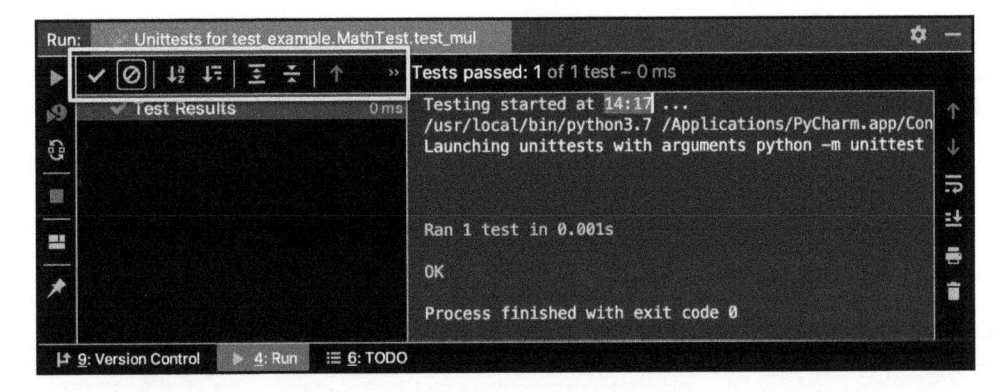

PyCharm's Run panel when unit testing

Aside from the output section on the right (which is what the **Run** panel typically displays), we can also see other additional navigation options on the left in the panel. Firstly, we can see a toolbar at the top of this section (highlighted in the preceding screenshot). Among the buttons in this toolbar, there are a number of noteworthy features:

- Displaying passed tests (disabled by default, since we typically only care about failed tests)
- Displaying ignored tests
- Sorting test results alphabetically

Seamless Testing, Debugging, and Profiling

- Sorting test results by the time the tests took (that is, test duration)
- Expanding/collapsing test suites
- Exporting test results to an output file

Directly following the toolbar on the left-hand side section of the **Run** panel, is a tree view of the results of the tests we just ran. Again, only results from failed tests will show up in this view by default (this behavior can be changed using the toolbar), so you shouldn't see anything in this section for now.

Let's look at an example of a failed test. Go ahead and enter the following test method *inside* the `MathTest` class of your code:

```
def test_exp(self):
    self.assertEqual(2 ** 3, 9)
```

Alternatively, you can enter your own custom tests however you like; keep in mind that we are trying to look at an example of a test that would fail upon being executed. Using the `test_exp()` test method, I obtained the following output after hitting the run button that corresponds to the whole `MathTest` class:

```
Testing started at 13:48 ...
/usr/local/bin/python3.7
/Applications/PyCharm.app/Contents/helpers/pycharm/_jb_unittest_runner.py -
-target test_example.MathTest
Launching unittests with arguments python -m unittest test_example.MathTest
in /Users/quannguyen/PycharmProjects/PyCharm-Book/Chapter06/Testing


Ran 3 tests in 0.013s

FAILED (failures=1)


9 != 8

Expected :8
Actual   :9
 <Click to see difference>

[...]


Process finished with exit code 1
```

We can see that this output is rather long, but not entirely unreadable. Specifically, we can see that, out of the three tests that were run, one failed at an `AssertionError`, where a value of 9 was returned when 8 was expected.

Additionally, in the tree view on the left-hand side of the panel, you can expand the tree deep enough to get to the specific tests that failed. For example, my PyCharm showed the `test_exp` test, as follows:

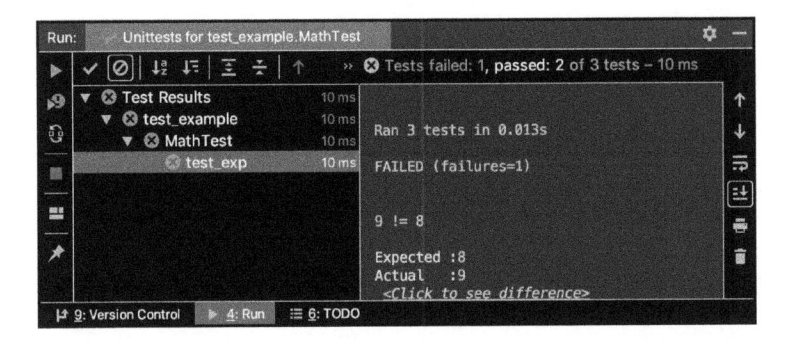

Failed tests in PyCharm's Run panel

We can see that by combining the printed output on the right and the comprehensive view on the left of the **Run** panel, PyCharm offers its users an easy way to navigate through Python test results, especially when there are failed tests.

Another great feature in PyCharm when working with tests is the option to examine differences between entities when a test using an `assertEqual()` method fails. Specifically, right-click on the failed test—in this case, this is `test_exp`—and choose the **View assertEquals Difference** option (note that you can also click on the corresponding link, **<Click to see difference>**, in the printed output on the right, to evoke the feature).

A popup window will open, detailing the differences between the two quantities that should have been equal. Using the toolbar of this popup window, you can customize how these differences are displayed (for example, in a side-by-side view or a unified view, or to highlight lines or words that are different, and so on).

Creating unit tests with PyCharm

We have talked about various features when it comes to examining the results from previously created unit tests in PyCharm. However, the support for testing from PyCharm does not stop there, and in this section, we will learn how to create unit tests within PyCharm.

In the same folder that we have been working with, `Chapter06/Testing`, open the `counter.py` file, which contains the following code:

```
import threading
import sys; sys.setswitchinterval(.000001)


class Counter:
    def __init__(self, target, num_threads):
        self.value = 0
        self.target = target
        self.num_threads = num_threads

    def update(self):
        current_value = self.value
        self.value = current_value + 1

    def run(self):
        threads = [threading.Thread(target=self.update)
                   for _ in range(self.target)]

        for t in threads:
            t.start()

        for t in threads:
            t.join()
```

This file contains a class called `Counter`, which is a multi-threaded class utilizing the `threading` module. Note that you don't need to understand this code in depth; we will only be using this class as the starting point to create our tests in PyCharm. With that said, the following are a few more details regarding the `Counter` class:

- Upon initialization, the class takes in two integers: `target` and `num_thread`.
- When the `run()` class method is invoked, it will increment its `value` field (which starts at 0) until the field reaches the `target` parameter using the `update()` class method.
- The `value` field will be incremented across multiple threads (the number of which is specified by the `num_threads` parameter).

- At the beginning, we are setting the switch interval of the system to 0.000001 seconds. Don't worry about this for now.

Now, we would like to test this class to see whether it is actually able to do the incrementation process we described previously correctly, using unit tests. To do that, perform the following steps:

1. Move your cursor/caret to the class declaration (line 5 in the original file).
2. From the menu bar, choose **Navigate** > **Test** or evoke the corresponding keyboard shortcut. From here, a small popup window will appear, listing all available tests that involve the `Counter` class:

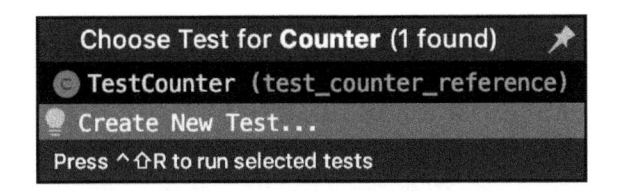

Creating tests in PyCharm

3. As we illustrated previously, there should already be one available test called `TestCounter` (stored in the `test_counter_reference.py` file). This is a reference script for the tests that we are attempting to create, so ignore that option for now and go ahead and choose the **Create New Test** option.
4. Another popup window will appear, this time listing out the specifications of the test file. In this window, you can customize the test file name, its location, and the name of the test class. Generally, the default options that are automatically filled in by PyCharm are already appropriate.

   The most important option in this window is the **Test method** section, in which we can choose which methods are to be tested. As you select a specific method in this section, a corresponding boilerplate test method will be generated inside the target test class. For now, we will simply hit the **OK** button without choosing either of the two methods included.

5. PyCharm will then generate the test file accordingly and open it in the editor. The code that's included in this file should be similar to the following:

   ```
   from unittest import TestCase


   class TestCounter(TestCase):
       pass
   ```

6. The preceding is the skeleton for our test class, which is named `TestCounter` and inherits from the `TestCase` superclass from the `unittest` module. To complete this test file, our job is to design individual test methods in the `TestCounter` class. In each test method, we need to check whether a `Counter` object (in the `counter.py` file) can correctly increment its value to the desired target.

    With that in mind, modify your current `TestCounter` class in the newly created test file to contain the following test methods (you can also reference the `test_counter_reference.py` file):

    ```python
    from unittest import TestCase
    from counter import Counter


    class TestCounter(TestCase):
        def test_small(self):
            small_counter = Counter(5, 5)
            small_counter.run()

            self.assertEqual(small_counter.value, 5)

        def test_med(self):
            med_counter = Counter(10, 8)
            med_counter.run()

            self.assertEqual(med_counter.value, 10)

        def test_large(self):
            large_counter = Counter(500, 20)
            large_counter.run()

            self.assertEqual(large_counter.value, 500)
    ```

And that is how unit tests are created in PyCharm. We can see that, with the generation of boilerplate code and a code skeleton, PyCharm offers ways for developers to effectively save time from manually creating scripts and entering repetitive code patterns, thus increasing their productivity.

Additionally, there is a theoretical discussion on the test methods we just created for the `Counter` class, which I include in the next subsection. This discussion does not pertain to PyCharm and its usage, but covers some abstract points about generally designing test cases, as well as specifically in concurrent Python programs.

I recommend going through this if you are interested in learning more about the theory of testing in programming. If, on the other hand, you would like to simply move on to the next main sections, you can do so—we will be discussing the process of debugging in PyCharm.

Tests for the Counter class

Unlike unit tests that you might have seen from other sources, where you typically only have a single test for a given class, method, or function, in the example of the preceding `Counter` class, we entered three different unit tests in our test class to test the same functionality.

Recall the point that we made earlier—the test results are only as good as the test themselves, and it is entirely possible for the tests we design to be unable to detect some specific bug that the program to be tested has. Therefore, it is good practice to have multiple test cases for the same functionality that you'd like to test so that we can see whether that functionality is able to handle various different situations and edge cases. This is especially true for concurrent programs, where the working between multiple components might give rise to bugs in some situations but not others.

Indeed, if you run the whole `TestCounter` class, you might see a peculiar case where the first two tests (`test_small` and `test_med`) pass successfully, but the third test (`test_large`) fails. (Sometimes, the third test may successfully pass as well; you can re-run the whole test class multiple times until you see the test fail.)

This is an example of an infamous bug in concurrent systems called **race condition**, which tends to manifest itself when a concurrent system has to handle a large number of components (this is why the large test encounters this bug while the smaller two tests do not).

The lesson here is that, in order to catch as many potential errors in a program as possible, we need to try to anticipate various scenarios in which our program might fail, and test those scenarios in our unit tests. Additionally, if you are interested in the design and implementation of concurrent programs in Python, I highly recommend the *Mastering Concurrency in Python* book, which is included in the list of *Further reading* section of this chapter.

This discussion also concludes the topic of testing in PyCharm. In the next section, we will begin talking about the process of debugging.

Debugging

After completing the process of testing your programs, if no bug or error has been found, you can feel confident enough to move forward with code review, deployment, or production. However, if there are issues that need addressing, the next step in the application development pipeline is debugging. In this section, we will learn more about the theoretical background of the practice and then the various ways of debugging using PyCharm.

Debugging fundamentals

As we mentioned previously, debugging typically comes after testing, when errors and bugs are detected. The general goal of debugging is to identify the specific causes of those bugs and errors that are detected in testing processes, and, from there, adjust the program accordingly.

More specifically, in a debugging process, a developer watches the interactions between, and the changes taking place in, the variables of their program. By seeing how each different function, method, or even line of code alters the value and functionality of the variables, the developer can narrow down the potential causes for the bugs and errors in the program. To that end, there are a number of common debugging methods that programmers utilize in Python:

- **Print debugging**: This is the simplest yet most intuitive debugging method. In print debugging, we simply add in print statements between commands in our programs to display the values of the variables that we think are causing the bugs. By looping through the printed values of the variables and how they change over time, we can visually see the effects of each different line of code on the variables under consideration.
- **Logging**: In the most general sense, logging is equivalent to the process of keeping track of various events that take place during the execution of the program we are trying to debug. In terms of the output logs that are produced in this process, it is quite similar to print debugging, but programmers typically store the output in log files that can be viewed later on. Logging is quite common among server administrators, who often have to handle server crashes and other site-reliability issues.

- **Tracing**: In the process of tracing, low-level machine language details regarding the execution of the program to be debugged are tracked. The results that are produced in this process are fairly useful in terms of actually getting to the bottom of the cause for a specific bug that is embedded deep in a programming language.
- **Using a debugger**: The last common method of debugging is to utilize a separate program to debug your own program; these programs are called **debuggers**. This is typically the most powerful method as debuggers are designed to be multipurpose and to provide various approaches when it comes to keeping track of the changes taking place in your programs.

Most of the time, print debugging might be sufficient for your debugging purposes in small to medium programs. However, in a large system with many moving parts interacting with each other, using a debugger might prove useful to save time and improve your productivity. In the following subsection, we will be learning how to use the debugger provided by PyCharm and the various interactive functionalities it offers in the process of debugging.

Debugging in PyCharm

Let's see how we can implement various debugging practices while working with PyCharm. In this subsection, we will be working with the example that's included in the Chapter06/Debugging folder of this book's code repository. Specifically, we will consider the main.py file inside this folder, which contains the following code:

```
def change_middle(my_list):
    print('Start function')
    x = int(input('Enter a number: '))
    my_list[1] = x
    print('End function')


if __name__ == '__main__':
    a = [0, 1, 2]
    b = a

    change_middle(a)

    print(a)
    print(b)
```

Seamless Testing, Debugging, and Profiling

The preceding code is a simple Python program where we can explore the referencing mechanism in Python while learning about PyCharm's debugging functionalities. Either copy the code directly into a PyCharm project or import the file into your PyCharm.

In this file, we have a function called `change_middle()`, which takes in a Python list as the only parameter, asks for a number in the console using the `input()` function, and finally assigns that numerical value to the second element in the input list.

In the main scope of our program, we initialize a list of three numbers (0, 1, and 2) and assign it to the `a` variable. The `a` variable is assigned to the `b` variable so that the two have the same value (the list of three mentioned numbers). Next, we call `change_middle()` on `a` so that we can modify the second element in the list from the console. Finally, we print out the values of both `a` and `b`.

Without running the programming, let's hypothesize about the output that will be produced by our program. For example, you might—especially if you are familiar with C and C++—expect that, in the end, since we called `change_middle()` on `a`, the list will be `[0, x, 2]` (x is whatever we input in the console), and `b` will simply remain `[0, 1, 2]`.

However, as we run the program, the output that we will obtain (if we were to input, say, 3 in the console when asked) is as follows:

```
Start function
Enter a number: 3
End function
[0, 3, 2]
[0, 3, 2]
```

We can see that both `a` and `b` have been modified, which contradicts our initial hypothesis. In the rest of this subsection, we will explore various debugging tools in PyCharm and attempt to debug this problem. (If you already know the cause of the aforementioned behavior, simply follow the discussions to learn about PyCharm's debugging features.)

Starting a debugging session and the Debug panel

One of the many great things about PyCharm is that relevant features and functionalities can be found under the same interface so that even if you don't remember how to navigate to a specific feature, you will have no problem finding it again. One example is the run arrows, which we discussed earlier in the *Testing* section.

In the same way that we start a test in PyCharm (or even run a program, for that matter), run arrows can be used to start a debugging session. When you click on the run arrow at the beginning of the main scope, choose the **Debug 'main'** option, as shown here:

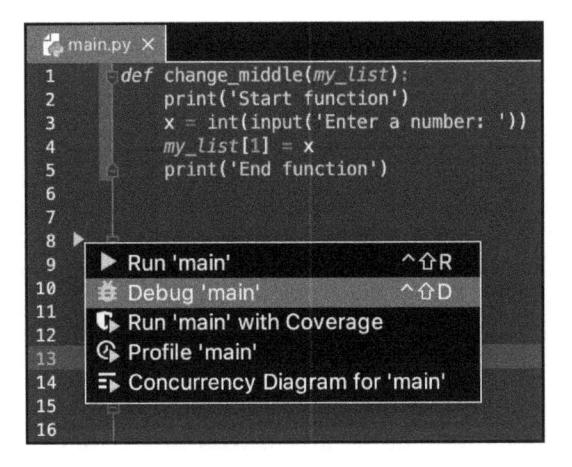

Starting a debugging session in PyCharm

The **Debug** panel will then automatically open (most likely in the bottom section of your project window), which should look similar to the following:

The Debug panel in PyCharm

With that, your debugging session has started. The first thing to notice in the **Debug** panel is that you can switch between two tabs, the debugger and the console, that are located at the top of the panel by clicking on them. Their roles are as follows:

- The **Debugger** tab lists various information and statistics regarding the execution of our program and any variables it might have.
- The **Console** tab, in essence, has the same functionalities as the normal console in the **Run** tab. In other words, it is used to display the printed output of the program as well as where we can enter any input.

[179]

Seamless Testing, Debugging, and Profiling

Since we are already familiar with the console, let's turn our attention to the **Debugger** tab. By default, the tab should have two separate sections (similar to the preceding screenshot) called **Frames** and **Variables**:

- The **Frames** section allows us to view, examine, and navigate between different items in the stack frame of a specific thread of your program. In most programming languages, when a program is run, the execution takes place in the execution stack, and the components of your program (method/function calls, different scopes) are arranged in order in this stack. The stack frame, as such, gives you the ability to see this aspect when the program you'd like to debug is executed.
- In the dropdown menu at the top of the **Frames** section, you also have the option to switch between different threads of your program. In this example, since our program runs on a single thread, we only have the **Main Thread** option in this menu.
- The **Variables** section on the right displays the value of any and all variables that are in the selected frame on the left. You can use this **Variables** section to inspect the changes in your variables while debugging a program.

Aside from these sections, we should also take note of the toolbars along the left and the top edges of the **Debug** panel, as highlighted in the following screenshot:

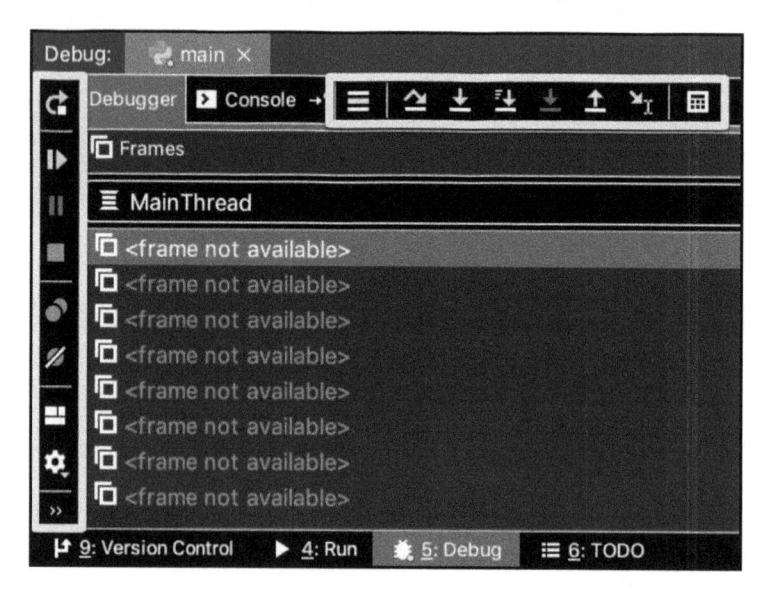

Debugging toolbars in PyCharm

[180]

These two toolbars contain different sets of functionalities:

- The vertical toolbar along the left edge of the panel provides general control options for your debugging session. Specifically, the important options are rerunning sessions, pausing, resuming, and stopping sessions.
- The horizontal toolbar at the top offers stepping features while a specific Python program is being debugged. We will look into these features later in this section.

One thing to note about debugging sessions, both generally and in PyCharm specifically, is that the execution of a given program is to be paused at various places. For example, in the session for our example, the execution of our sample program is currently paused (you can see this because, in the console, the program is not asking for our input in the `change_middle()` function yet).

So, to resume the execution of the program, we need to continually click on the resume button in the vertical toolbar we discussed previously. Alternatively, you can choose the corresponding action, that is, **Run > Resume Program**, in the menu bar. As you evoke this action over and over, you will notice, in the **Frames** section, that the execution of our program is moving across the different frames in the stack.

At one point, the frame stack will display a message stating **Frames are not available**. Switch to the **Console** tab; we will see that we have reached the point that we discussed earlier (when the `change_middle()` function asks for our input integer). Here, simply enter any number other than 1 (again, 3 is what I use throughout this example), and the entire program will be executed as normal.

Remember that our goal is to find out how our variables (`a` and `b`) are changed during the execution of our program. However, as of now, we are not able to gain any insight regarding how those changes take place. Therefore, we need to add breakpoints into our debugging process, which we will discuss in the next subsection.

Placing breakpoints

Breakpoints, as the term suggests, are markers to be placed in our programs to indicate places where the execution in a debugging session should pause. While a program being debugged is paused, developers then can examine that frozen state of the program as well as its variables, with the goal of gaining insight into how those variables are mutated at a specific step of the program. We will see that this is the exact tool we need to debug our example program.

Breakpoints are to be placed at specific lines of code in our program. To insert a breakpoint in PyCharm's editor, click on the region between the line numbers and the actual code, called **the gutter**, at a line where you'd like to place a breakpoint. Once placed, PyCharm's breakpoints are represented as red circles. In our current example, let's place breakpoints at lines **3**, **5**, and **12**, as shown here:

```
 1  def change_middle(my_list):
 2      print('Start function')
 3      x = int(input('Enter a number: '))
 4      my_list[1] = x
 5      print('End function')
 6
 7
 8  if __name__ == '__main__':
 9      a = [0, 1, 2]
10      b = a
11
12      change_middle(a)
13
14      print(a)
15      print(b)
16
```

Placing breakpoints in PyCharm

The general strategy of using breakpoints is to freeze the program after each time the variables we are interested in are mutated. Again, we are trying to see what happens when the a variable is changed inside the `change_middle()` function, and why the b variable is also changed. For this reason, we have the following breakpoints:

- The breakpoint at line **12** pauses the program before the function is called
- The ones at lines **3** and **5** help us inspect the program right before and after the mutation of the a variable at line **4**

Now, let's start our debugging session with these breakpoints added. Slowly, click on the resume button to step through the program again, but stop when you have reached the frame that displays **<module>, main.py:12**. This is the first breakpoint that our program reaches (at line **12**):

Chapter 6

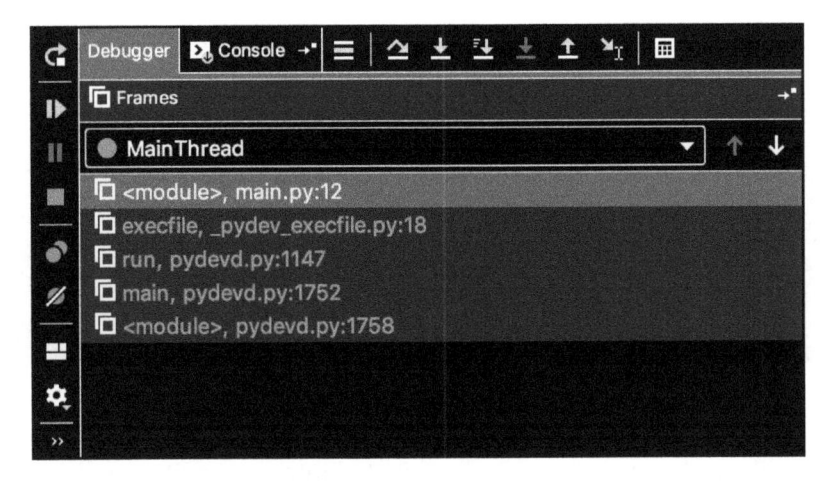

Walking through a program in debugging mode

There are a number of elements that we should notice:

- The line highlighted in blue is where the execution is currently at. Again in our example, it should be at line **12**.
- The **Variables** section in the **Debug** panel: At the current frame, we can see that this section displays the corresponding variables, which are a and b. We can see that they both hold the same value—a Python list, [0, 1, 2], as shown here:

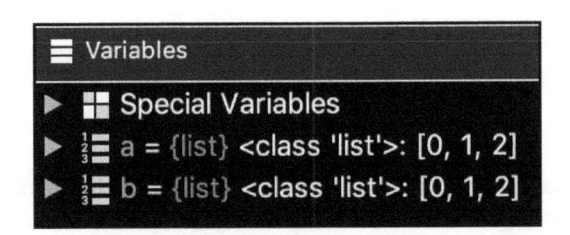

Variables at breakpoints

Notice that you can also expand each variable in this section to further inspect the individual elements in the list.

[183]

- Inline debugging: Information regarding the variables of our program is also displayed inside the editor. For example, at this point, you will notice the following at lines **9** and **10** of your editor:

```
 8  ▶  if __name__ == '__main__':
 9         a = [0, 1, 2]   a: <class 'list'>: [0, 1, 2]
10         b = a           b: <class 'list'>: [0, 1, 2]
11
12  ●       change_middle(a)
13
```

Inline debugging in PyCharm

These comment-like codes are automatically inserted into your editor to display the current variable values at each specific breakpoint. After you have fully examined your program at a breakpoint and want to move on with the execution, you can use the resume button again.

After clicking the resume button once, the current execution should move into the `change_middle()` function and jump to line 3 (which is our second breakpoint). Let's keep our debugging session paused at this point to discuss other debugging features in PyCharm—specifically the various stepping functionalities in the next subsection.

Stepping functionalities

Stepping functionalities are a way to control how the execution of your program should proceed. Going from left to right in the toolbar, we have the following functionalities:

- Show execution point/Show the current program execution point: This will move the caret in the editor to the line where the execution is currently at, as well as jump to the corresponding frame in the **Debug** panel.

- Step over/Step to the next line in this file: This will move the execution to the next line of code in the current scope (function or the main scope). If it is the last line of a function, the execution will return to the parent scope that called the current function.

- Step into/Step to the next line executed: This will move the execution into any method that's called at the current line of code. This feature is useful when we'd like to inspect external APIs, and we will come back to it after this list.

- **Step into my code/Step to the next line executed ignoring libraries** : This is somewhat the opposite of the previous functionality. This will move the execution to the next line of your own code.
- **Force step into/Step into, ignore stepping filters for libraries, constructors, and so on** : This will allow the execution to step into any external method that's being used in the current line of code, even if the method was previously ignored. This button is appropriately disabled if you haven't ignored an API yet (which is the case in our example).
- **Step out/Step to the first line that's executed after returning from this method** : This will have the execution step out of the current function or method and return to the parent scope.

Let's look at some of these functionalities in action:

1. With the execution of our example program currently at line **3** (where the built-in `input()` function is used), click on the step into button, and you will see that the `parse.py` file, which implements the `input()` function, is opened in the editor, and the execution moves to the first line of the `quote()` method in that file.

   Again, this functionality is quite useful when you'd like to inspect built-in or external APIs that you are not familiar with.

2. Now, click on the step out button, and the execution will return to our own code. Here, the console is waiting for our input, so simply enter a number and move forward with our debugging session. Note that after entering your input, other built-in files might be opened in the editor by PyCharm. This is because the step into button is still active. Simply use the step out button until you get back to our example file, which should now look similar to the following:

```
main.py
1   def change_middle(my_list):   my_list: <class 'list'>: [0, 1, 2]
2       print('Start function')
3       x = int(input('Enter a number: '))   x: 3
4       my_list[1] = x
5       print('End function')
6
```

Inline debugging inside a function

3. Let's focus on the current inline debugging output inside our `change_middle()` function: at line **1**, we can see the value of the `my_list` parameter that's been passed to the function, which is the list `[0, 1, 2]`; at line **3**, we can see the value of the `x` variable that's been entered by the user from the console. Again, this inline debugging feature is significantly helpful, especially in large functions and programs where there are many values for the debugging programmer to keep track of.
4. We have discussed the most common stepping functionalities in support for debugging purposes in PyCharm. For now, simply step through the rest of the example program using either the resume button or the step over button.

In the rest of this section, we will look into more advanced features when it comes to keeping track of variables.

Watches

Regarding the stepping functionalities we discussed earlier, they are significantly useful for controlling the execution of the program we'd like to debug, but we were unable to truly examine the value of the variables we care about (`a` and `b`), even if we could control our program execution, in our current example. To do this, we can use watches.

Watches in debugging are a mechanism that programmers can use to follow the changes that are taking place in specific variables. Once a watch has been created for a variable, the value of that variable will be updated at each stage as you step through the program you are debugging. In comparison to inline debugging, watches are a more active and in-depth way to monitor your variables.

Much like the **Variables** section, watches will display the specified variables and their respective values. But these variables are kept throughout the program, as opposed to in the **Variables** section, where the list of displayed variables is changed with respect to the frame the program execution is currently at.

In the **Debug** panel, you may only have the **Frames** section and the **Variables** section. There is also an additional section called **Watches**, which is activated when the watches button 👓 (located in the top right corner of the panel) is clicked. Let's get started:

1. Once the **Watches** section is open, click on the **+** button, and you will see a prompt appear where you can enter the names of the variables you'd like to track.

2. If you click on the dropdown button in this prompt, all the available variables in our program will be listed, as shown here:

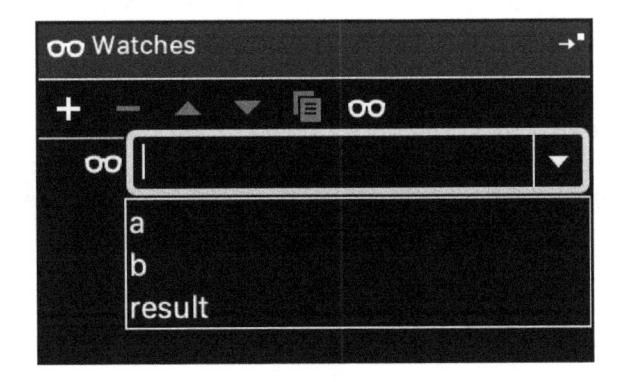

Watches in PyCharm

3. Here, enter **a** and **b** individually to specify that you'd like to track these variables through the debugging process.
4. Now, start a debugging session as normal. First, you will see messages stating that the variables associated with the watches we have specified are not (yet) defined. Simply step through these first few frames.
5. Having reached the first breakpoint (at line 12), you will see that our watches will be updated accordingly. Specifically, both watches will display the correct values of the variables and the Python list, [0, 1, 2].
6. Focusing on the **Watches** section, slowly step through the second and third breakpoints. Note that you will have to enter some input into the console between these two breakpoints. Now, when the execution of my program is at the third breakpoint (line 5), my **Watches** are as follows:

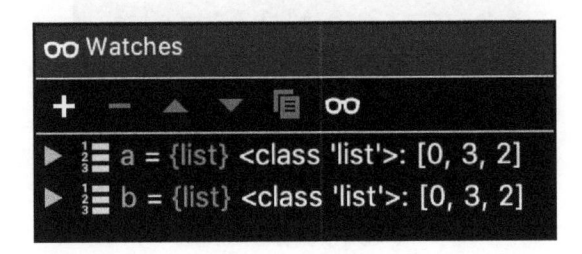

Updated watches in PyCharm

7. This indicates that, as soon as the a variable is changed inside `change_middle()`, the b variable is also changed in the same way.

This is because of how referencing in Python is implemented—when a is assigned to b (line 10), these variable names, in essence, reference, or point to, the same Python object. So, when a is mutated inside `change_middle()`, it is the object referenced by a (`[0, 1, 2]`) that is changed. Since b references the same object, the value of b is also changed in the same way.

This is a common source of confusion for beginner Python programmers, so we have seen how PyCharm's debugging features help us examine this behavior more closely. Before ending your debugging session, we will consider another powerful debugging feature in PyCharm.

Evaluating expressions at all times

During a debugging session, you can take advantage of the evaluate expression feature.

This is evoked with the ⊞ button, which is located on the far right of the stepping toolbar, at the top of the **Debug** panel. A popup window will appear to facilitate this process. In the prompt at the top of the window, you can enter any Python expression (variables, operations on and between variables, built-in methods, and functions) to evaluate and examine your program on the fly.

For example, the following is my output after entering `sum(b)` to get the sum of the elements in b (when the program execution is at line 5, after the two variables have already been changed):

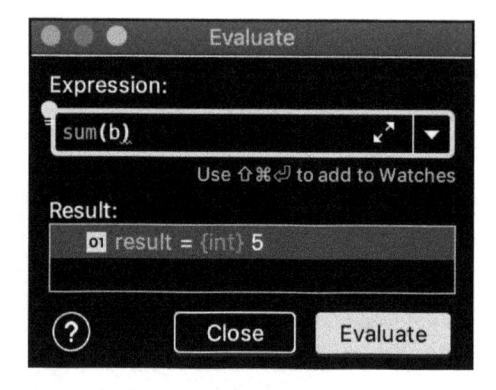

The window for evaluating expressions

This feature is helpful when you'd like to apply more complex logic on the current variables of your program, as opposed to simply printing their values.

As indicated in the popup window, you can additionally add the expressions you have entered to the **Watches** section as well (in macOS, you can use the ⇧ ⌘ ↵ keyboard combination), and these expressions will be updated as the execution of the program proceeds throughout a debugging session.

Evaluating expressions in the middle of a debugging process marks the end of our discussion on the debugging support that PyCharm offers. In general, PyCharm purposefully provides a wide range of debugging tools that facilitate different functionalities, and programmers can combine them in a dynamic way during their debugging sessions.

In the final section of this chapter, we will be learning about the process of profiling in Python, and how PyCharm streamlines and supports the process.

Profiling

Aside from testing and debugging, profiling is another high-level process where programmers analyze their applications to find ways to improve them. However, as opposed to errors and bugs, the goal of profiling is to analyze the performance of our program, identify potential bottlenecks, and, in general, find where the actual execution of the program can be improved efficiency-wise.

Profiling fundamentals

As you probably already know, making sure that your programs work as intended and compute the correct outputs (testing and debugging) is only part of the development process; there is also an additional aspect that's equally as important—optimizing the actual performance of your programs.

This process is typically called profiling, where various statistics regarding the execution of a specific program are computed and analyzed so that programmers can identify potential bottlenecks and other performance-related inefficiencies and address them to improve the overall quality of the software. In turn, a profile is a set of statistics representing the overall performance-related quality of that program.

Performance—especially execution time is an important factor to keep in mind when you work on your software projects. In the tech industry, sometimes speed is even valued more than accuracy, given that the computed outputs are in an acceptable range of accuracy.

Seamless Testing, Debugging, and Profiling

For example, in a large system that interacts with a corresponding database, it is fairly inefficient to have the system update its data *each time* there is an update for the database. Specifically, most of the computing resources will be allocated to facilitate this updating process, and other tasks that the system is also responsible for might be negatively affected. It is more desirable if the system is updated not as often as its database (for example, every hour, every day, for every 10 updates made to the database, and so on). This is actually the case for many systems in real life.

Performance is even more important in Python, which is typically viewed as one of the slower programming languages. In `Chapter 1`, *Introduction to PyCharm – the Most Popular IDE for Python*, we discussed the fact that this is one of the very few disadvantages of using Python for your development, and that is why Python developers need to pay special attention to profiling and performance analysis.

In Python, there are a number of profiling tools that are favored and commonly used by the community—**yappi**, **cProfile**, and **VMProf**, to name a few. cProfile is the most simple and fundamental profiling tool in Python, and it is also a built-in feature of the language. yappi contains similar functionalities but further supports multithread and CPU time profiling, while VMProf offers statistical sampling features to achieve a more comprehensive profile for your programs.

Luckily, all of these profiling tools are supported by PyCharm. However, it is important to note that PyCharm will look through all the Python profilers that you have installed within your project and will see if yappi or VMProf is included or not (remember that cProfile is already built-in). The default option, when a profiling session is started, is VMProf if it is available, yappi if it is available, or cProfile.

The discussion in the next subsection will examine the usage of cProfile within PyCharm so that you can profile your code as it is the most fundamental option of the three, on top of already being built into Python.

Profiling in PyCharm

For this discussion, we will be considering the example that's included in the `Chapter06/Profiling` subfolder of this book's repository. This subfolder contains a `main.py` script, which provides the following code:

```
def custom_sum(n=1000000):
    result = 0
    for i in range(n):
        result += i
```

```
    return result


def built_sum(n=1000000):
    result = sum(range(n))
    return result


if __name__ == '__main__':
    print(custom_sum())
    #print(built_sum())
```

As you can probably guess from the code, we will be comparing and contrasting the two ways of computing the sum of the integers going from one to a specific n (whose default value is 1,000,000). The first way (the `custom_sum()` function) is to loop through all the elements to be summed and add them to a running sum. The second way (the `built_sum()` function) utilizes the built-in `sum()` method of Python.

In the main scope, we will be commenting/uncommenting one of the two function calls to test both methods. We will be looking at our custom summing function first, so the call to `built_sum()` is commented out for now.

The typical claim is that built-in functions are generally faster than custom ones; in this example, we will be able to fact-check that claim and further qualify it with runtime statistics through our profiling process. Let's get started:

1. Just like in testing and debugging, we can start a profiling session by using the run arrow:

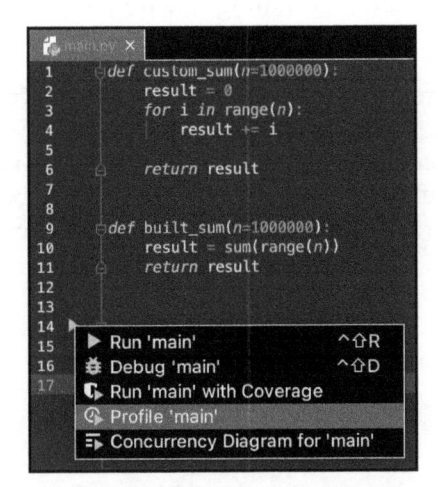

Starting a profile in PyCharm

2. When the profile has completed, another tab will be opened inside the PyCharm editor, listing various statistics about the runtime of our program. Your output should look similar to the following screenshot:

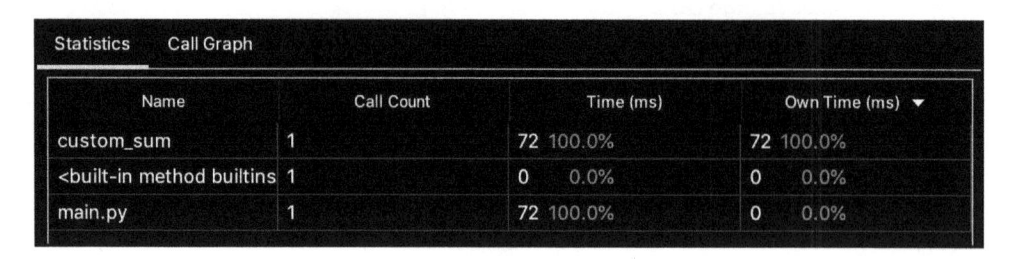

Name	Call Count	Time (ms)	Own Time (ms) ▼
custom_sum	1	72 100.0%	72 100.0%
\<built-in method builtins	1	0 0.0%	0 0.0%
main.py	1	72 100.0%	0 0.0%

A generated profile in PyCharm

This list contains all the functions that are used during the execution of our program and their respective running time. The list is sorted by **Own Time** (the last column in the report) in descending order by default. As you can see from my report, the program on my system took **72** ms to run (almost), all of which was done by the `custom_sum()` function.

3. Now, let's go back to our original script and switch to the call to the built-in function (comment out line 15 and uncomment line 16). Start a profiling session in the same way that we did earlier. A similar report will be generated, this time for our second summing function.

On my computer, this version of the program took only 24 ms to complete; this is strong evidence suggesting that the built-in summing function is somewhat three times faster than our custom one.

Within any given generated report, you can also navigate between the two tabs, that is, **Statistics** and **Call Graph**. While the **Statistics** tab, as we saw, includes the running time of the functions that were executed by the program, the **Call Graph** visualizes the flow of execution of that program, helping developers follow its logic better. For example, the following is the call graph for the call to the first summing function, `custom_sum()`:

Chapter 6

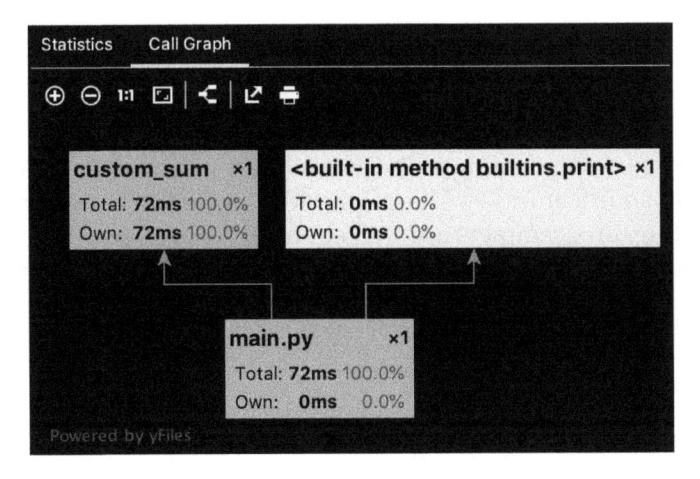

Call graph in PyCharm

Within this **Call Graph** tab, you can move around, zoom in and out, and even print out the graph as you like, using the toolbar at the top of the tab.

Additionally, emphasizing the ease of navigation, PyCharm also offers developers the option to further examine a specific method or function in the context of a profile. Specifically, in the **Statistics** tab of a profile, you can right-click on a specific entry that you'd like to examine in detail, as shown here:

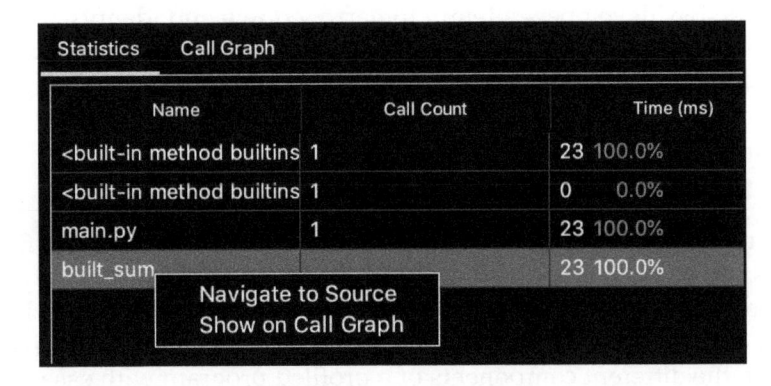

Examining a specific function in a profile

As you can see, you are given two options:

- You can navigate straight to the source code of the function that's currently selected. This is particularly useful when you'd like to find out, for example, which specific part of your code is causing a bottleneck in execution.

[193]

- You can also jump to that specific function in the call graph. This offers a bird's-eye view of the execution flow of your program, as well as the role of the function you are considering within that flow.

With that, our discussion on profiling in PyCharm has been concluded. We can see that with the various dynamic features PyCharm provides, not only in profiling tasks but also in debugging and testing, programmers are well equipped to examine the behavior of their programs and look into potential bottlenecks, bugs, and errors productively.

Summary

Testing, debugging, and profiling are high-level tasks we can use to analyze applications to look for improvements in correctness and performance, but they can be quite confusing to beginner developers. PyCharm offers straightforward and intuitive interfaces for these processes, thus making them more accessible and streamlined.

Unit testing is the process of making sure individual components of a large system work as intended. PyCharm has convenient commands to generate test skeletons/boilerplate code that usually takes time for developers to manually write. While testing a program, it is important to anticipate and test for edge cases to ensure the overall correctness of that program.

In a debugging session, developers attempt to narrow down and identify the causes of bugs and errors that are detected during testing. With a graphical interface combined with various options to track the values of variables throughout a program, PyCharm allows us to debug our programs in a dynamic way with considerable freedom. The various stepping functions also provide a flexible way for us to step through the program we are trying to debug.

Lastly, the goal of profiling is to analyze the performance of a program and find ways to improve it. This can be looking for faster ways to compute a value or identifying a bottleneck in the program. With the ability to generate comprehensive statistics on the running time of each function executed as well as call graphs, PyCharm helps developers navigate through the different components of a profiled program with ease.

This chapter also marks the end of the second part of our book, where we focused on improving our development productivity. From here, we will be considering the usage of PyCharm in more specialized fields, namely web development and data science projects. In the next chapter, we will cover the basics of three universal web dev tools—JavaScript, HTML, and CSS within the context of PyCharm.

Questions

1. What is testing in the context of software development? What are the different testing methods?
2. How does PyCharm support testing processes?
3. What is debugging in the context of software development?
4. How does PyCharm support debugging processes?
5. What is profiling in the context of software development?
6. How does PyCharm support profiling processes?
7. What is the significance of run arrows in PyCharm's editor?

Further reading

More information can be found in the following articles and readings:

- *PyCharm documentation: Testing*, JetBrains s.r.o. (https://www.jetbrains.com/help/pycharm/testing.html)
- *Unit testing, Software Testing Fundamentals* (http://softwaretestingfundamentals.com/unit-testing/)
- *Python documentation: Unit testing framework* (https://docs.python.org/3/library/unittest.html)
- *PyCharm documentation: Debugging Python Code*, JetBrains s.r.o. (https://www.jetbrains.com/help/pycharm/part-1-debugging-python-code.html)
- *PyCharm documentation: Thread Concurrency Visualization*, JetBrains s.r.o. (https://www.jetbrains.com/help/pycharm/thread-concurrency-visualization.html)
- *Python documentation: The Python Profilers* (https://docs.python.org/3/library/profile.html)
- *PyCharm documentation: Optimize your code using profilers*, JetBrains s.r.o. (https://www.jetbrains.com/help/pycharm/profiler.html)
- *Mastering Concurrency in Python*, by Quan Nguyen, Packt Publishing (https://www.packtpub.com/application-development/mastering-concurrency-python)

Section 3: Web Development in PyCharm

This section starts with Chapter 7, *Web Development with JavaScript, HTML, and CSS*. This section mainly deals with various aspects of web development projects in Python and how PyCharm facilitates support in those regards. First, we will discuss editing web development languages such as JavaScript, HTML, and CSS, as well as how to work with the Django framework (which is one of the two most popular web frameworks in Python, along with Flask) within PyCharm. We will look at all of the important features in PyCharm that help to streamline and support Python web development tasks.

We will learn how to use PyCharm to work with databases and integrate them into our web development projects. We will also look at options in PyCharm that allow the visualization of relational databases, making thinking/rationalizing about the data included in databases easier and more intuitive. We will finally end the section by going through a specific use case of developing a complete Python web application using PyCharm.

This section includes the following chapters:

- Chapter 7, *Web Development with JavaScript, HTML, and CSS*
- Chapter 8, *Integrating Django in PyCharm*
- Chapter 9, *Understanding Database Management with PyCharm*
- Chapter 10, *Building a Web Application in PyCharm*

7
Web Development with JavaScript, HTML, and CSS

This chapter marks the beginning of a series of four chapters on web programming with PyCharm, covering the development of general web applications. The topics discussed in this chapter include the integration of common web programming languages (JavaScript, HTML, and CSS) in PyCharm and how to debug them in straightforward and intuitive ways. By the end of the chapter, you will have gained a comprehensive knowledge of how to use the three languages to get started with a web development project using PyCharm.

The following topics will be covered in this chapter:

- Introducing JavaScript, HTML, and CSS in the process of web development
- The options for working with JavaScript, HTML, and CSS code in PyCharm
- How to implement live editing and debugging for web projects

Technical requirements

The following is a list of prerequisites for this chapter:

- Ensure that you have both Python 3.6+ and PyCharm installed on your computer.
- Download the GitHub repository at `github.com/PacktPublishing/Hands-on-Application-Development-with-PyCharm`.
- We will be working with the `Chapter07` subfolder in the downloaded code repository.

Introduction to JavaScript, HTML, and CSS

To understand and appreciate the benefits PyCharm brings to the process of web development, we will examine the general use of the three most common web development languages—JavaScript, HTML, and CSS—in this section. If you are already familiar with these languages, feel free to skip ahead to the next section to see how PyCharm supports them.

The examples discussed in this section are included in the `Chapter07/Intro` subfolder of the code repository for this book.

Understanding the importance of HTML and CSS

In general, HTML and CSS serve to provide customizations for the *appearance* of a web application or page. **Hypertext Markup Language** (**HTML**) concerns itself with the overall structure of the web elements, while **Cascading Style Sheets** (**CSS**) is used to specify the visual presentation of those elements. It is important to note that HTML and CSS are *not* programming languages; they are simply types of markup tools that are used to style the data that one wants to display.

Writing our code with HTML

In an HTML file, individual elements are included inside tags, which are a way to specify the type of content each element contains. For example, HTML tags can be `<p></p>` for paragraphs, `<table></table>` for tables, or `<li></li>` for lists. As you can see, HTML tags are typically created in pairs to indicate the beginning and the end of each element.

HTML files are directly interpretable by web browsers; in fact, one can use web browsing software to read custom HTML code. For example, in the current subfolder of our repository, there is an HTML file named `index.html` that contains the following code:

```html
<!DOCTYPE html>
<html lang="en">
<head>
    <meta charset="UTF-8">
    <title>HTML Test</title>
</head>
<body>
<p style="color: red">Hello, World!</p>
</body>
</html>
```

Regarding the HTML code itself, aside from some particularities (for example, the UTF-8 character encoding scheme in the `meta` tag, which we don't need to worry about), we can speculate, to some extent, the contents of the web page created with this file:

- The `<title></title>` tag: A title saying `HTML Test`, which will be displayed as the name of the tab in your browser
- The `<p></p>` tag: A sentence saying `Hello, World!` that is also red in color

> **TIP**: Note that just like any text-based files that contain code, HTML files can be opened and edited with most text editors and IDEs. For now, feel free to open the file with your favorite text editor (Atom, Sublime, Notepad, and so on), as we will save PyCharm for the discussion in the next section.

As we have said before, HTML files can be interpreted and displayed by most browsers. With your favorite browser, evoke the **Open** action (**File** | **Open**), and navigate to the `index.html` file that we are considering, and you will see data specified by HTML code interpreted by a web browser. For example, the following screenshot is from my Chrome browser:

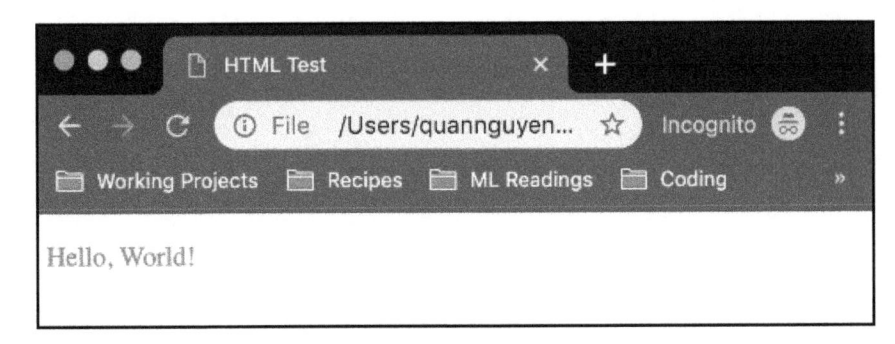

Opening HTML files in web browsers

Similar to how one refreshes a web page so that any potential updates to the website can be displayed, you can also refresh this offline HTML page to reflect any changes. For example, you can change the `<p>` tag in *line 8* of the previous HTML code to the following and then refresh the page:

```
<p style="color: red; text-align: center">Hello, World!</p>
```

After doing this, the displayed content will be updated so that the text is appropriately center-aligned.

We have considered the most basic aspects of the HTML language. In the next subsection, we will learn more about CSS and how it works together with HTML in a web application.

Writing our code with CSS

While HTML can be responsible for specifying the actual content of a web page, CSS is again about customizing the visual aspects of that content. Looking at the `<p></p>` tag in the previous HTML example, you might say that we already have the ability to customize the styling of HTML content (for example, the color and the alignment of the text).

However, the way we applied the style to the text in the previous example—while it can work for small, simple web pages—is not efficient and extensible in large web projects. Instead, we can have a separate file to specify the styling of individual HTML elements in a systematic way, and that is the problem CSS addresses.

Inspect the `external.html` file in our current folder, which contains the following HTML code:

```
<!DOCTYPE html>
<html>
<head>
    <meta charset="UTF-8">
    <title>External CSS</title>
    <link rel="stylesheet" href="styles.css">
</head>
<body>

<h1>This is a heading</h1>
<p>This is a paragraph.</p>

</body>
</html>
```

The thing to notice in this file is the `<link></link>` tag inside the `<head></head>` tag:

```
<link rel="stylesheet" href="styles.css">
```

This code is used to specify that we would like to use the `styles.css` file as a style sheet for this HTML file. In the same folder, you should see that particular CSS file:

```
body {
  background-color: powderblue;
}
h1 {
  color: blue;
}
p {
  color: red;
}
```

A typical CSS file, similar to the preceding one, contains separate sections, each specifying how an HTML element should be styled. In our current example, we have the whole background of the body of our web page as a powder blue color, while the text in the `<h1></h1>` (heading) tags should be in blue, and the regular `<p></p>` text should be in red.

In the same way, as we did before, use your browser to open this `external.html` file to see how the resultant web page is styled accordingly.

With that, we have learned the basics of the HTML and CSS languages. Next, we will discuss the final one of the three common web development tools: JavaScript.

Understanding the importance of JavaScript

Despite the similarity in their names, JavaScript and Java barely share any commonalities in their purpose and usage. **JavaScript** (or **JS** for short), unlike HTML and CSS, is indeed a programming language, typically used to process and manipulate data, which is then to be displayed by HTML and CSS. What makes it so universal among web projects is its ability to integrate and work with HTML/CSS as well as other web development tools so well.

In our current folder, let's examine the `script.js` file, which contains the following code:

```
class Person {
    constructor(name) {
        this.name = name;
    }

    sayHi() {
        alert("Hello, I'm " + this.name)
    }
}

let p = new Person("Quan");
p.sayHi();
//document.body.innerHTML = "<p>Hello, I'm " + p.name + "</p>"
```

Being a programming language, JS allows web developers to implement object-oriented development ideas, which, in this case, is the design of classes.

[203]

Web Development with JavaScript, HTML, and CSS

In this example, we have a class named `Person`, whose constructor takes in a string as the name of the person. The `Person` class also has a method called `sayHi()`, which will create an alert on the web page that implements it with a `hello` message. Outside of the class declaration, we initialize an instance of the `Person` class with the `Quan` name, and then call the aforementioned `sayHi()` method.

This file on its own cannot create and display a web page; instead, it would have to be called from an HTML file. Let's turn our attention to an example of such a file, `person.html`:

```
<!DOCTYPE html>
<html>
<head>
    <meta charset="UTF-8">
    <title>Person</title>
</head>
<body>
</body>
<script src="script.js"></script>

</html>
```

Different from the other HTML examples we have seen so far, this file has a `<script></script>` tag that, via the `src` attribute, points to a JavaScript script, which in this case is our `script.js` file. Now, open the HTML file in a browser, and you will see the effect of the JS code we entered in the action. Specifically, the `alert()` function in JS creates a pop-up window in a web page with a specified message:

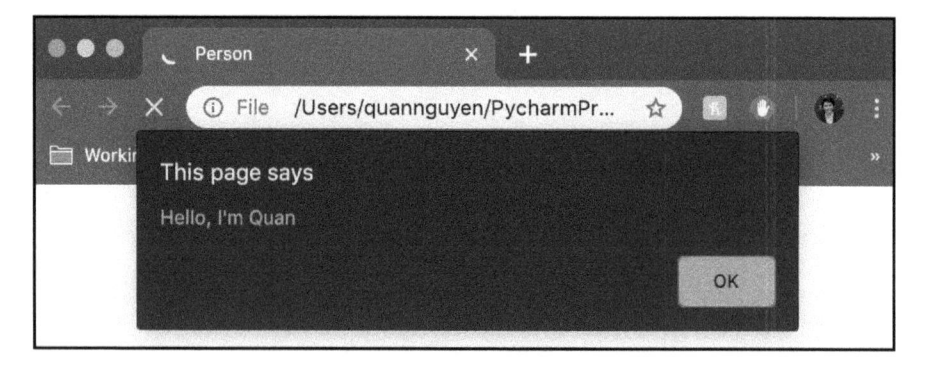

The alert function in JavaScript

[204]

Additionally, JS can modify the HTML content of a web page in its code. For example, in the `script.js` file, uncomment the last line of code by removing the `//` double forward slashes from the last line of code, and put the slashes in front of the second-to-last line (where we used the `alert()` function) so that the code becomes as follows:

```
let p = new Person("Quan");
//p.sayHi();
document.body.innerHTML = "<p>Hello, I'm " + p.name + "</p>"
```

As you can see, instead of creating an alert pop-up, this time, we are using JS to create an actual HTML element inside a `<p></p>` tag. Since JS is a programming language, we are free to perform string concatenation and access attributes of class objects (`p.name`). We see that we are able to include the `<p></p>` tag inside the string itself, which is a convenient method of manipulating the content of our HTML code within JavaScript.

This discussion concludes our brief introduction to the web development trio: JavaScript, HTML, and CSS. We see that with JS, web developers can dynamically perform complex calculations and data processing and then finally display the results using customizations in HTML and CSS.

In the next section, we will find out how PyCharm supports web development with these languages through various features and functionalities.

Implementing web pages in PyCharm

Similar to the approach we have taken many times in this book, we will now try to contrast the topics/tools we are discussing with and without the support of PyCharm. In this section, we will examine various features in PyCharm that facilitate faster and more efficient web development with JavaScript, HTML, and CSS.

As for the code examples used in this section, we will be looking at the `Chapter07/PyCharmSupport` subfolder. First, we will discuss the features that apply to HTML and CSS.

Using HTML and CSS in PyCharm

In this subsection, we will go over a number of ways that PyCharm streamlines the process of writing HTML and CSS code. You will see that, with the help of PyCharm, working with HTML and CSS code is significantly easier than doing so in a minimal text editor.

Creating new HTML files

Generating boilerplate code has been a recurring theme about the advantage of using an IDE during software development processes in this book, and web development is not an exception. Here, let's see how PyCharm can help us generate HTML boilerplate code:

1. Now, within a newly created PyCharm project (or it can be any project that you currently have opened), right-click on the project name within the **Project** panel (the project directory) and choose **New** > **HTML File**, as illustrated here:

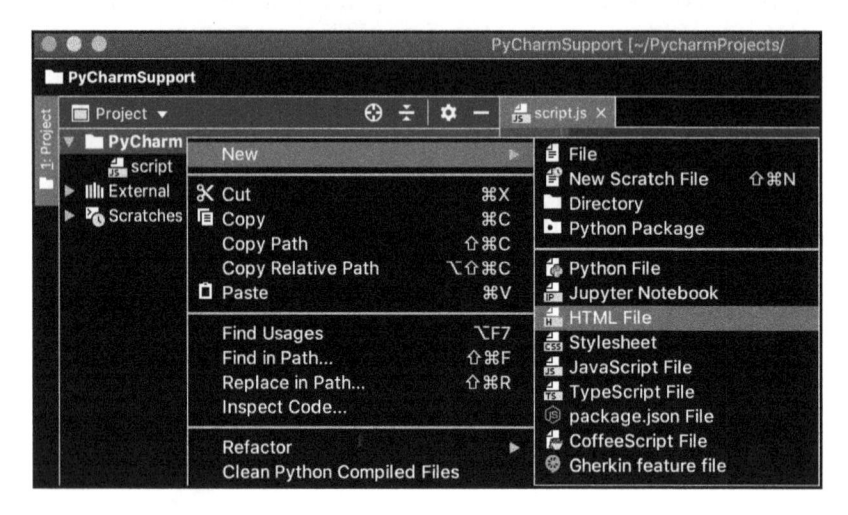

Creating HTML files in PyCharm

2. After entering any name for our new HTML file, it will be opened within the PyCharm editor. You will see the HTML-specific boilerplate code that was automatically generated:

```
<!DOCTYPE html>
<html lang="en">
<head>
    <meta charset="UTF-8">
    <title>Title</title>
</head>
<body>

</body>
</html>
```

With this skeleton, we can continue to add in further HTML code with ease.

Including external files in HTML code

We have seen in the previous section that in order to use the code implemented in JS and CSS files in our resultant web page, we would need to specify them in the corresponding HTML file. PyCharm provides easy navigation to facilitate this process. Let's say we'd like to include a JS script in an HTML file within the same PyCharm project (in the `Chapter07/PyCharmSupport` folder, it is the `script.js` file):

1. You may recall that we need to wrap the JS file inside a `<script></script>` tag. You will find that as you type in the tag, PyCharm's code completion engine will be able to generate a suggestion list that only consists of relevant scripts:

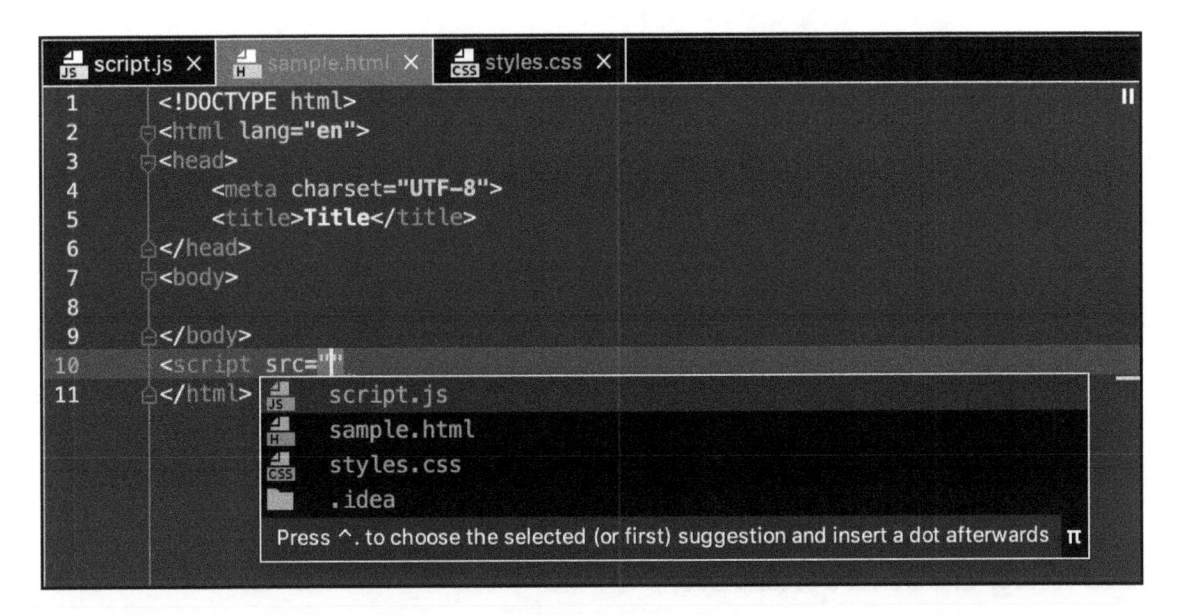

Code completion in HTML

2. Alternatively, from the **Project** panel (mostly on the left-hand side of your project window), you can drag a file that you'd like to reference and drop it in the HTML file in the editor, and PyCharm will automatically generate the appropriate tag for the element to be included.

For example, the following is the result produced after I dragged and dropped the `styles.css` file inside the `sample.html` file (note the new line at line **6**):

```
1   <!DOCTYPE html>
2   <html lang="en">
3   <head>
4       <meta charset="UTF-8">
5       <title>Title</title>
6       <link rel="stylesheet" href="styles.css">
7   </head>
8   <body>
9
10  </body>
11  </html>
```

Dragging and dropping files into HTML

The second method is extremely convenient, especially in large projects where specifying the path to a specific file can be time-consuming if the path is long and complex.

Furthermore, in addition to JS scripts and CSS style sheets, we can apply these two methods to image files as well (in the second method, the `width` and `height` attributes will be automatically generated along with the `<img></img>` tag).

Viewing documentation

If you are somewhat familiar with HTML tags and attributes, you will most likely agree when I say that there are too many of them, and sometimes it can be quite confusing to know which is the correct one to use in a specific situation.

To address this problem, PyCharm offers a way to dynamically view documentation for these tags and attributes as we write them. For example, in the previous section, we skipped over the purpose of the `<meta>` tag in our examples; we now would like to find out what it is:

1. Move the cursor/caret to the tag and go to **View** | **Quick Documentation** (or its corresponding keyboard shortcut), and you will see something similar to the following screenshot:

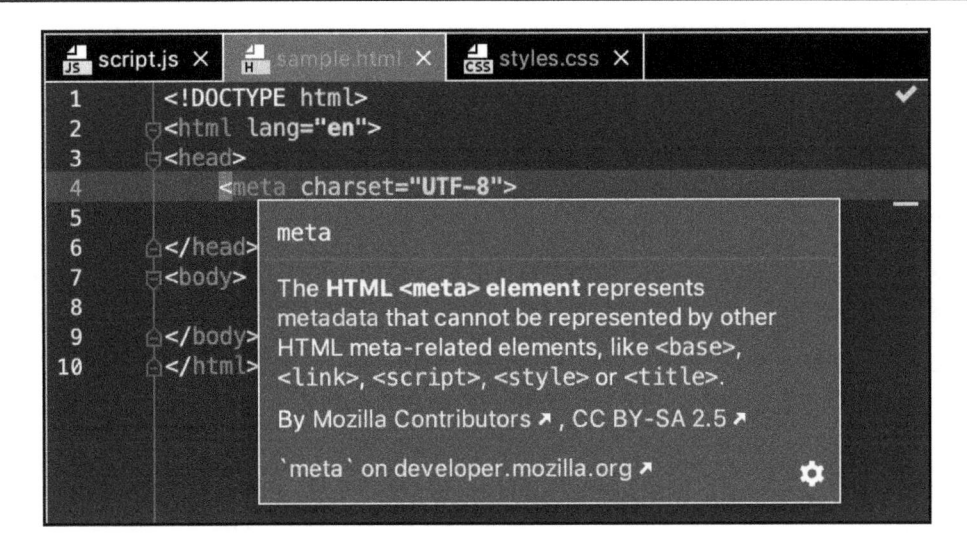

Viewing documentation for HTML code

2. Additionally, there are particular HTML tags that are only supported by some browsers and not others. The preceding documentation pop-up window will display which browsers support the tag for the documentation we are reading.
3. If a tag is supported by all standard browsers, like the `<meta>` tag in our example, then this information will be excluded. One can also click on the link included at the end of the pop-up window to go to the **Mozilla Developer Network** (**MDN**) documentation web page.

Emmet

If you are an experienced web programmer, you know that **Emmet** is a valuable tool in web development. In essence, Emmet provides powerful options to shorthand while writing HTML and CSS code; the support Emmet offers allows for faster writing and editing. Quite similar to general code completion, you type the shorthand for a piece of code in PyCharm and hit the *Tab* key, and the complete code will be inserted.

For example, you'd like to create an HTML table of two rows and three columns, which typically corresponds to the following code:

```
<table>
    <tr>
        <td></td>
        <td></td>
        <td></td>
```

```
            </tr>
            <tr>
                <td></td>
                <td></td>
                <td></td>
            </tr>
        </table>
```

In this case, with Emmet, you can simply type `table>tr*2>td*3` in an HTML file and hit the *Tab* key, and you will see that the appropriate code is generated.

Emmet is not a part of the Python web development process or of the PyCharm IDE. It is simply a general toolkit that can be installed and utilized in web projects. However, since Emmet is such a powerful and widely used tool, PyCharm offers its full support for Emmet in its web development projects. Additionally, you can configure the behavior of Emmet within PyCharm by going to the settings and navigating to **Editor** | **Emmet**.

To learn more about Emmet itself outside the context of Python and PyCharm, you can also go to `https://emmet.io/`.

Viewing HTML output in browsers

As discussed in the previous section, to be able to see how a browser will display code in a given HTML file, we normally have to open the HTML file from the browser. This process can be very time-consuming (and frustrating) if the file you want to display is buried deep inside a project directory. Let's see how PyCharm streamlines that process in the following steps:

1. In PyCharm, as you hover your cursor over the top-right corner of the editor, a pop-up toolbar will appear with icons for various browsers:

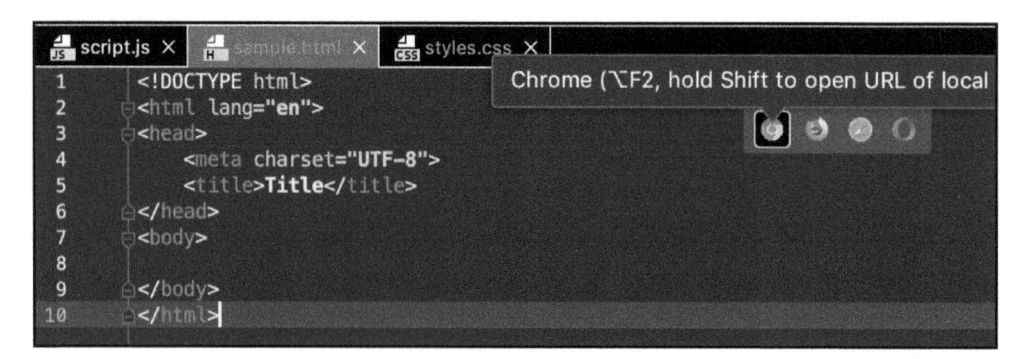

Opening HTML in browsers

2. Simply click on the desired browser to have the HTML file displayed. Unlike manually using a browser to open an HTML file offline, PyCharm automatically creates a local server on your machine to host the HTML code (note the URL when the HTML file is opened).
3. Additionally, it is possible to configure this list of browsers available to use. Go to the PyCharm settings and navigate to **Tools** | **Web Browsers**, and you will be taken to this window:

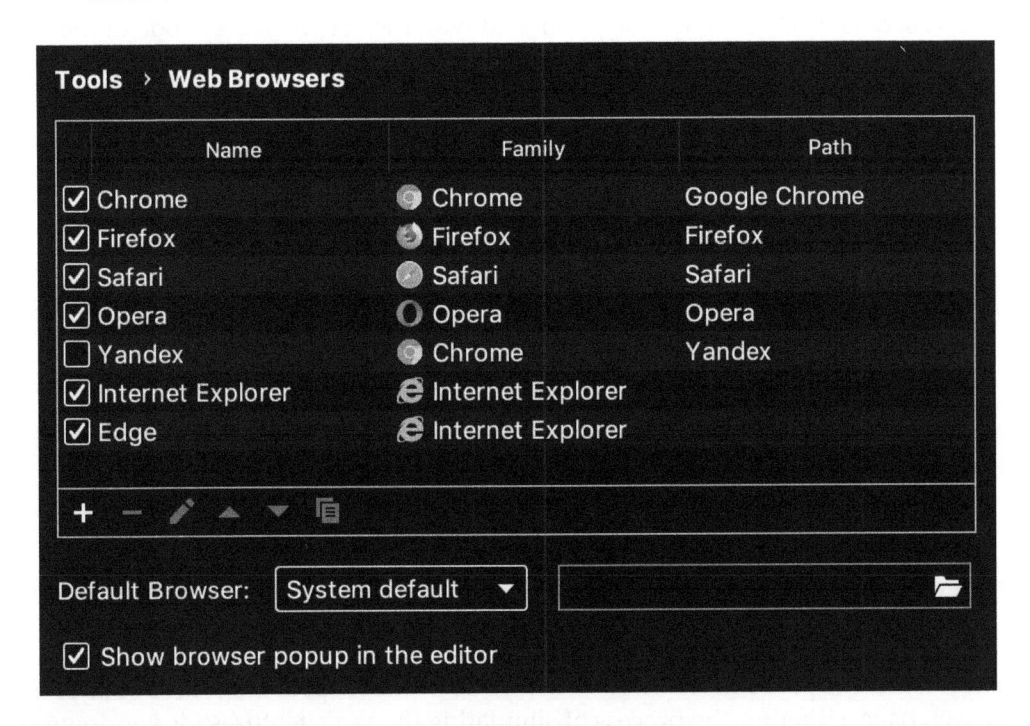

Customizing browsers in PyCharm

From here, you can check/uncheck items in the list displayed to customize the items in the pop-up toolbar, and add in browsers that are not yet included.

Extracting HTML source code in PyCharm

As you are working on your web project, you might notice a display or feature from another website that you'd also like for your own site. Typically, you would go to that web page, inspect its source code, and try to apply the appropriate portion of code to your own project.

When using PyCharm, you can have the IDE facilitate this process and fetch the HTML source code for you:

1. Go to **File** | **Open URL**.
2. Type in the address of the website from which you'd like to extract the HTML source code.
3. Hit **OK**.
4. A scratch HTML file will be populated with the HTML source code of the site, and opened in the editor. For example, the following screenshot is my output after fetching the source code of https://www.packtpub.com/:

Fetching HTML code in PyCharm

Again, this feature is particularly useful when you have to inspect the source code of a specific web page, either for the process of simulating the same features for your own site, or for web scraping.

We have considered a number of important features in PyCharm when it comes to writing and editing HTML and CSS code. In the next subsection, we will learn about the options available for JavaScript and how they can help us become more productive in our web projects.

Using JavaScript in PyCharm

In this section, we will see features that facilitate developing JavaScript code within PyCharm. With JavaScript being a programming language, we will focus on familiar topics such as editing, code completion, and debugging.

Choosing the version for JavaScript

There are multiple versions for the JavaScript language, just as for Python (2.7, 3.5, 3.6, and so on). It is obvious that in order to produce a correct and reliable web program in JavaScript, you need to configure the correct version for the language:

1. Go to the PyCharm settings.
2. Navigate to **Languages and Frameworks | JavaScript**.
3. From the drop-down menu at the top of the main window, you can now select the version of JavaScript that you are using, as illustrated here:

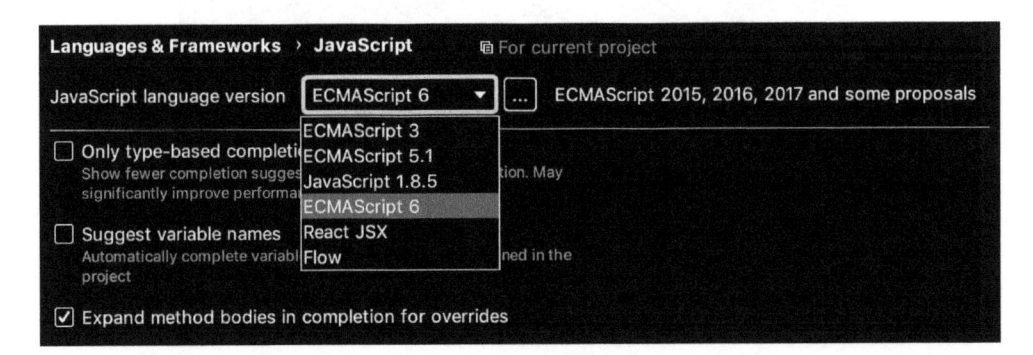

Choosing JavaScript version

From the main window, you can further customize various aspects of the code completion logic for JavaScript.

Hints about parameters

PyCharm offers the feature that displays parameter names when methods, functions, or classes are called, which can improve the readability of our code considerably. Let's consider the `script.js` file in our current code folder:

```
class Person {
    constructor(name) {
        this.name = name;
    }

    sayHi() {
        alert("Hello, I'm " + this.name)
    }
}
```

This file contains the same `Person` class that we saw in the example in the previous section. Now, in a new line in this file, we will initialize a new `Person` instance by entering the following code:

```
let p = new Person("Quan");
```

You will see that as you type in the initialization of the new `Person` instance, PyCharm automatically reformats the appearance of our current line of code:

```
script.js
1   class Person {
2       constructor(name) {
3           this.name = name;
4       }
5
6       sayHi() {
7           alert("Hello, I'm " + this.name)
8       }
9   }
10
11  let p = new Person( name: "Quan");
```

Parameter hints in JavaScript

As always, you can further configure this behavior in the PyCharm settings:

1. Navigate to **Editor** | **General** | **Appearance**.
2. Click on the **Configure** button next to the **Show parameter name hints** option.
3. Another window will open. Check the appropriate boxes in the bottom **Options** section of the window.

Debugging the code

Debugging is perhaps one of the most important features of any IDE. As it turns out, debugging JavaScript code is quite similar to debugging Python code, especially for graphical interface and navigation.

As discussed in the *Debugging* section in Chapter 6, *Seamless Testing, Debugging, and Profiling*, there are specific steps to a debugging session in PyCharm. If you want a refresher on the specifics during such a debugging session, give the *Debugging* section in Chapter 6, *Seamless Testing, Debugging, and Profiling*, a quick read-through before continuing.

With that said, to debug JavaScript code, you can do the following:

1. Place breakpoints at specific stages of the code you'd like to debug. The execution of the program will stop at each breakpoint so that you can examine its current state. Breakpoints are represented as big red dots in the left-hand gutter of the PyCharm editor.
2. Find the HTML file that contains the JS script you'd like to debug in the **Project** panel (the project directory tree, typically on the left-hand side of the window).
3. Right-click on the file, and choose **Debug 'sample.html'**, as illustrated here:

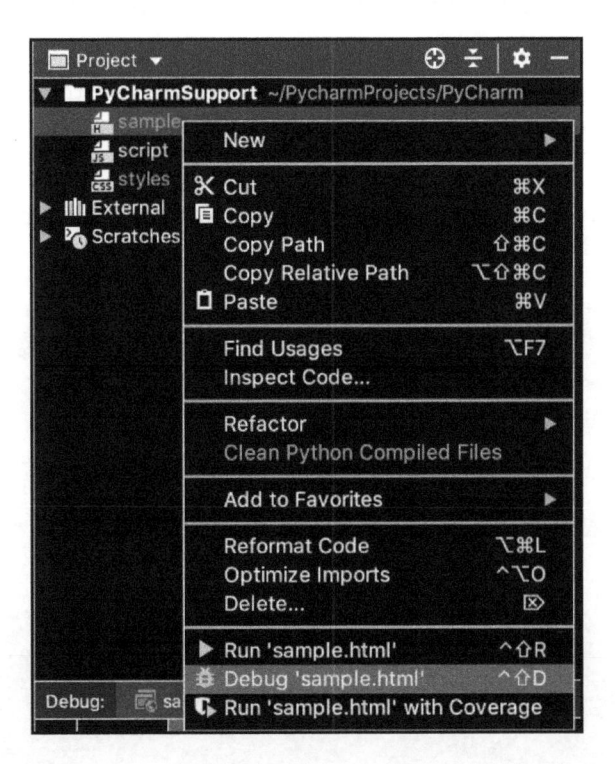

Debugging JavaScript from an HTML file

4. PyCharm will open that HTML file in a web browser, and the **Debug** panel will appear in your PyCharm window, much like a debugging session with traditional Python code.

With the web browser and various control features in the **Debug** panel, you can choose to step through your JavaScript code in multiple ways and examine the behavior of the code at each placed breakpoint.

Live editing

Recall what we saw earlier in the first section: when an HTML file you are working with is being displayed by your browser and a change has just been made to the file, you will have to manually refresh the page in your browser for the displayed content to be updated.

LiveEdit is a PyCharm feature that updates the web page for you automatically every time there is a change to the source code. This is quite a useful feature, as it will save web developers significant time, not having to manually reload a web page. It is also important to note that *LiveEdit* can only be utilized during a debugging session.

With that said, *LiveEdit* does not come with PyCharm by default, but it is a free plugin developed by JetBrains that can be installed free of charge. Note that we will go into the details regarding PyCharm plugins in `Chapter 14`, *More Possibilities with PyCharm Plugins*, and for now we will only consider the process of installing *LiveEdit* specifically:

1. Go to the PyCharm settings and navigate to the **Plugins** tab. You should see the following window:

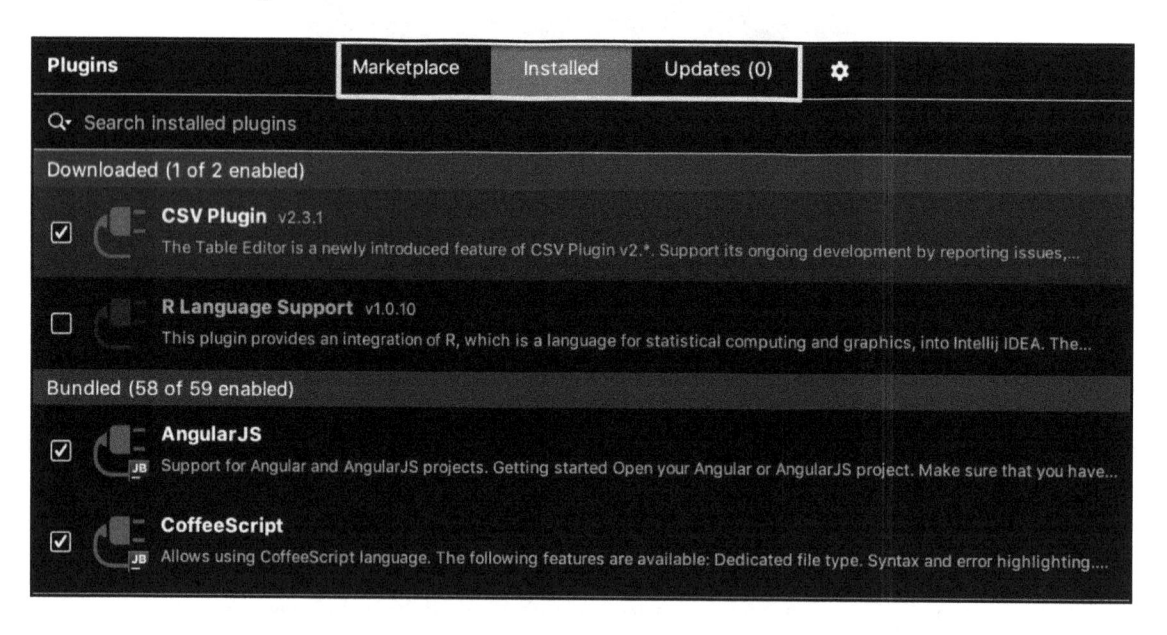

PyCharm plugin manager

2. Note the three tabs available in this window, highlighted in the preceding screenshot: we are currently in the **Installed** tab. Since *LiveEdit* is not installed by default, we will have to navigate to the **Marketplace** tab.

Chapter 7

3. In the **Marketplace** tab, you will see various plugins that you can install for your PyCharm. Type in `LiveEdit` (no spaces) in the search bar, and choose the option **LiveEdit by JetBrains**, as illustrated here:

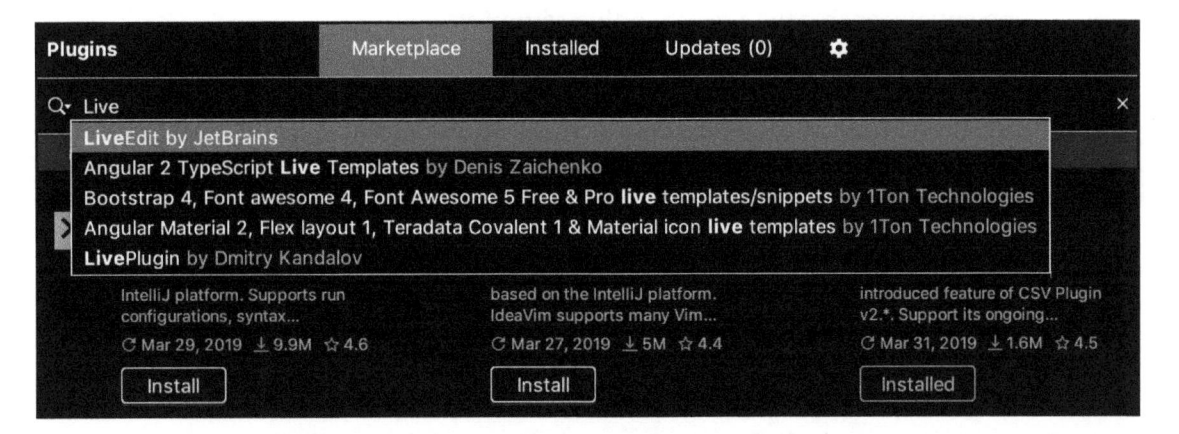

Searching for and installing LiveEdit

4. Click on the **Install** button in the next window to install *LiveEdit*. You might also have to restart your PyCharm for the plugin to activate.
5. After the restart, you can further customize the behavior of *LiveEdit*. From the settings, go to **Build, Execution, Deployment** | **Debugger** | **Live Edit**, and you will see this window:

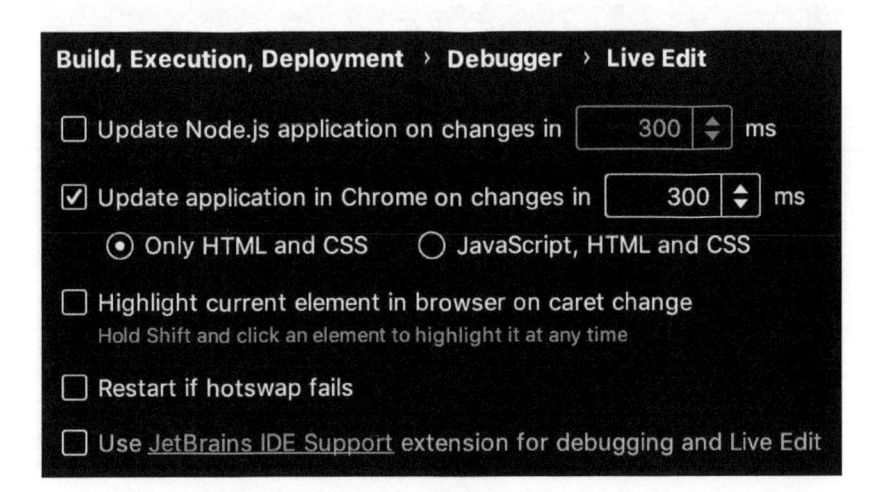

LiveEdit settings

[217]

The options are relatively self-explanatory, and the default selections are generally optimal for most web development projects:

- If you are working with a Node.js application within PyCharm, you could potentially enable the corresponding setting as well.
- By default, *LiveEdit* will only update the displayed web page when changes in HTML and CSS are made, but not JS—this is because changes in JS might require a complete restart of a given web application. However, you still have the option to apply *LiveEdit* to JS in this setting window.

With that, you are ready to utilize *LiveEdit* in your web applications. Within the current repository folder, start a debugging session with the `sample.html` file, or any HTML file you are interested in, to see *LiveEdit* in action.

Specifying a framework for new applications

In this last subsection on the PyCharm support for JavaScript, we will discuss the various frameworks available to be implemented in PyCharm for web projects. As mentioned before, if you are using the professional edition of PyCharm, you will be asked to specify the project type when you create a new PyCharm project:

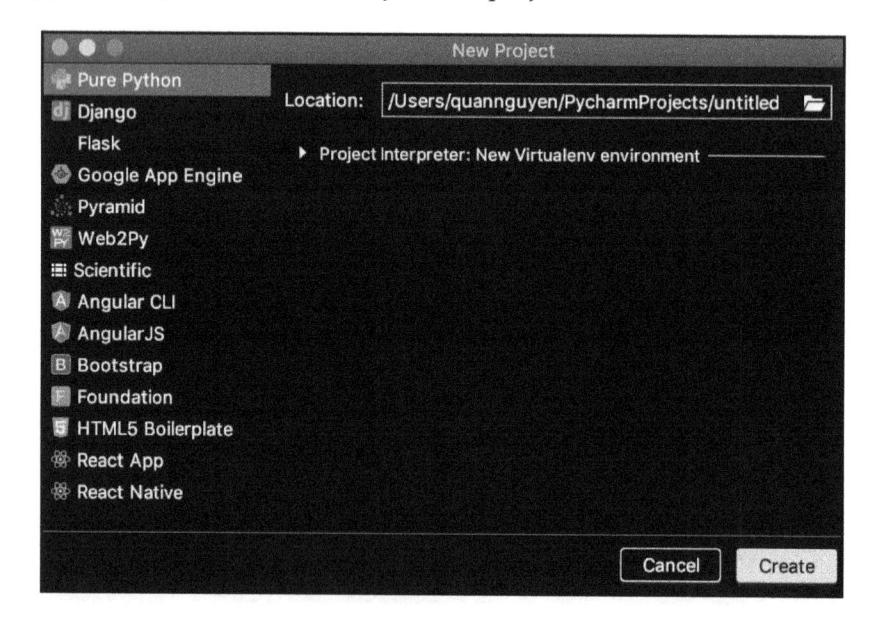

Project types in PyCharm

In this window, you can choose any project type that facilitates JavaScript application development, such as Angular CLI, AngularJS, React App, or React Native. As a specific option is chosen, you can further customize the initiation of your project in the **More Settings** section of the window.

We have covered a number of important features in PyCharm that facilitate the development of web applications. Overall, PyCharm offers extensive and convenient functionalities that streamline various processes in web development.

Summary

Throughout this chapter, we have learned the basics of the three most common web development languages: JavaScript, HTML, and CSS. While HTML and CSS deal with the display and styling of a web page, JavaScript is mainly used to process and manipulate data that will produce the final content of the page.

PyCharm offers numerous options in terms of streamlining web development processes. HTML and CSS can be written and edited with higher accuracy and speed using PyCharm's boilerplate code generation, documentation viewing features, integration of Emmet, and live editing options. JavaScript, on the other hand, is supported by multiple versions, a hands-on, graphic debugging toolset, as well as a wide range of available JS frameworks.

With this knowledge, we are now able to start developing simple, bare-bones web applications with PyCharm. However, this process does not involve our main language of choice, Python, just yet. In the next chapter, we will move on to the topic of web development with Python and Django specifically. We will discuss the ecosystem of Python web applications, the specifics of the Django web framework, and finally how PyCharm supports Django web projects.

Questions

1. What is the purpose of HTML code? How is an HTML file structured?
2. What is the purpose of CSS code? How is a CSS file structured?
3. What is the purpose of JavaScript code? In general, what makes it one of the most popular web programming languages?
4. How can one include a CSS style sheet or a JS script in an HTML file in PyCharm?

5. What is Emmet? How is it supported by PyCharm?
6. What options are available when it comes to debugging JavaScript in PyCharm?
7. What is the purpose of the *LiveEdit* feature in PyCharm?

Further reading

More information can be found in the following articles and documents:

- *PyCharm documentation: Web Frameworks*, JetBrains s.r.o. (https://www.jetbrains.com/help/pycharm/web-frameworks.html)
- *Web Design 101: How HTML, CSS, and JavaScript Work*, HubSpot (https://blog.hubspot.com/marketing/web-design-html-css-javascript)
- *Emmet documentation: Emmet — the essential toolkit for web-developers,* (https://docs.emmet.io)

8
Integrating Django in PyCharm

The Django framework is one of the most common, if not the most common, web development tools in Python. However, due to the wide range of functionalities it offers, Django can be very confusing and frustrating to work with, especially for beginners.

This chapter discusses various ways PyCharm addresses this problem, showing us why the PyCharm IDE is known as one of the best support systems for Django. By the end of the chapter, you will be able to fully integrate and work with the Django framework in PyCharm web projects.

The following topics will be covered in this chapter:

- A brief introduction to the Django framework and some preliminary comparisons with its counterpart, Flask
- Various features and functionalities offered by PyCharm that make Django easy to work with, including Jinja and the run/debug configuration for a PyCharm project

Technical requirements

The following is a list of prerequisites for this chapter:

- Ensure that you have both Python 3.6+ and PyCharm installed on your computer.
- Download the GitHub repository at https://github.com/PacktPublishing/Hands-on-Application-Development-with-PyCharm.
- During this chapter, we will be working with the Chapter08 subfolder in the downloaded code repository.

An overview of Django

To fully appreciate how PyCharm simplifies various processes in a specific Python programming task, we will first briefly discuss the given task outside of PyCharm. In this section, you will learn about the basics of the Django web framework, which Python web development problems it addresses, and its pros and cons with respect to the other most popular Python web framework, Flask.

As always, if you are already familiar with the workings of Django, simply skip forward to the next section about the PyCharm support.

Django and the idea of web frameworks

First of all, let's discuss the idea of a framework, specifically in the context of web development. As you already know, a web application consists of multiple interconnected aspects—frontend code specifying the appearance of web pages, backend logic to process and handle data, and a server to keep the application online so that others can access and interact with it.

A web framework handles the heavy-lifting and repetitive aspects of this process. This allows web developers to focus on the specific logic of their applications. Web frameworks usually implement common design patterns and good practices into their structure, so that a web application developed with a framework will be up to common standards by default, without its developer having to manually integrate those standards into the application.

Django, titled *the web framework for perfectionists with deadlines*, is a Python web framework dedicated to building robust, complex web applications in simple and minimal APIs. The following are a few notable high-level priorities accommodated by Django, as outlined in its documentation:

- **Speed**: Similar to Python itself, Django emphasizes the ease of developing and translating ideas into actual code. With straightforward yet extensive APIs, Django aims to accommodate a wide range of web applications and features.
- **Security**: Web development is one of the topics in programming in which security is the highest priority. The Django framework offers features that navigate web developers, beginners, and experts alike, away from security flaws in their applications.
- **Scalability**: When a website gains more clients, scalability becomes more and more important. Scalability in Django can be achieved in flexible and intuitive ways; in fact, some of the largest sites on the internet (Bitbucket, Instagram, Pinterest, and so on) are built with Django for that reason.

Needless to say, there are other web frameworks aside from Django, both in general web development and in Python web development, specifically. For example, AngularJS is one of the most popular frameworks for JavaScript projects, while Flask, as mentioned, is another commonly used Python web framework.

Each web framework is typically set out to solve a specific problem, and, in the next subsection, we will learn about the specific features of the Django framework.

What makes Django special?

Going from other web frameworks to Django, you will notice the following differences, which distinguish Django in special ways.

Django models

Django uses models to structure and organize the data of a web application. Typically written as a class in Python inheriting from the `django.db.models.Model` class, a model supports object-oriented thinking in a web development project, containing attributes and class methods that are used to store and process data for the given website.

For example, the following code is for a Django model, implementing the same `Person` class that we considered in the previous chapter:

```
from django.db import models

class Person(models.Model):
    name = models.CharField(max_length=30)

    def say_hi(self):
        return f"Hello, I'm {self.name}."
```

Additionally, each model corresponds to a database table in the backend of a Django project, and Django handles the creation of any database table automatically. Still looking at the preceding class model, the equivalent of the following SQL code will be executed by Django:

```
create table myapp_person (
    "id" serial not null primary key,
    "name" varchar(30) not null
);
```

Integrating Django in PyCharm

Additionally, Django can specify relationships between different tables, commonly used in database management. Specifically, the following are used:

- `django.db.models.ForeignKey` can be used instead of a regular `Field` type to indicate a many-to-one relationship in the class model declaration.
- `django.db.models.ManyToManyField` can be used instead of a regular `Field` type to indicate a many-to-many relationship in the class model declaration.
- The same goes for `django.db.models.OneToOneField` and a one-to-one relationship.

All in all, the Django Pythonic model design makes it as easy as possible for Python developers to get into the field of web development, while still ensuring the correctness and robustness of the project structure.

Admin access in Django

One aspect of creating a website that some might not think about often is designing and implementing administrative access. An example of an admin access can be to add, change, or delete content in an online blog. Since setting up admin privileges (and the corresponding interface) is somewhat tedious and repetitive, Django believes it should be automated.

After you have created a Django application in your website, you can access the admin page by going to the `/admin/` site (this is applicable even to the Django server run locally). After logging in successfully, you will be taken to a dashboard where you can customize the content available on your website. The following screenshot in the official Django documentation shows an example of this dashboard:

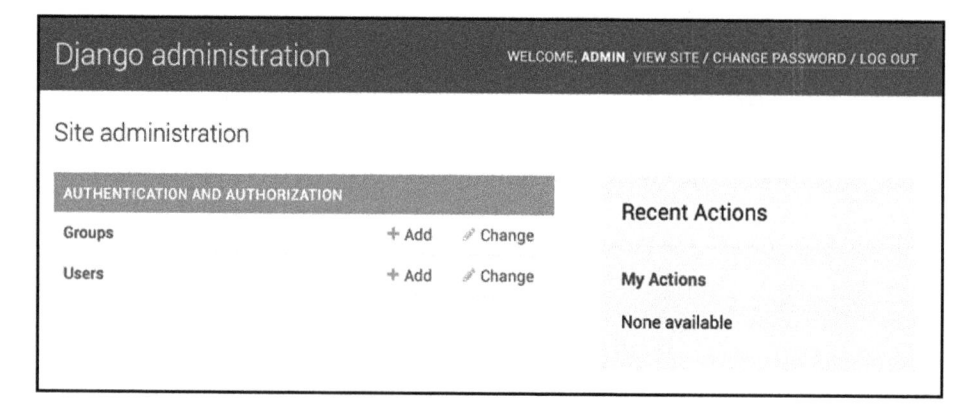

Django's admin access

Again, this graphical interface allows for faster and more accurate customization of data for your web application.

Django templates

The third notable feature that Django provides is the ability to generate HTML code in a dynamic way—with Python. Specifically, you would have a basic structure for your web page in an HTML file, parts of which are static and can be specified directly within the HTML file, and parts are the dynamic content that will be populated later on by Django, working with Python in the backend.

For example, within a Python file, you can have the framework load the base HTML file and directly feed to it some data specified in a Python dictionary (if you are familiar with sending web requests via Python, this process is quite similar to making a POST request to a website). For example, in the following code snippet, we are using the `render_to_string()` method to load the `base_template.html` file and pass in a variable named `foo` that is holding the `'bar'` string:

```
from django.template.loader import render_to_string

rendered = render_to_string('base_template.html', {'foo': 'bar'})
```

Notice that this is the opposite way of having backend and HTML code interact with each other—compared with the JavaScript example in the previous chapter—instead of including an HTML tag that points a given web page to a specific backend code, we are now loading an HTML template and rendering it with our backend data.

The resulting HTML code will be the same for client browsers; in other words, they will receive the same information either way. However, using HTML files as base templates makes them more readable.

Jinja

This is the last feature to be discussed that makes Django a special web development framework in Python. It is also quite relevant to the idea of HTML templates discussed previously.

In general, Jinja is a template engine in Python, independent of the Django framework. However, it is inspired by the Django template system to provide web developers with a powerful Python syntax for working with web templates. Jinja2 (the second version of Jinja) is considered to be one of the most popular template engines for Python, and Jinja is used by tech giants such as Mozilla, Instagram, and SourceForge.

Integrating Django in PyCharm

The most attractive feature of Jinja, again, is its Pythonic syntax, which results in the ability to interact with and process data in ways that Python programmers are already used to. The following example is provided in the official documentation of Jinja code:

```
{% extends "layout.html" %}
{% block body %}
  <ul>
  {% for user in users %}
    <li><a href="{{ user.url }}">{{ user.username }}</a></li>
  {% endfor %}
  </ul>
{% endblock %}
```

As you can see from the preceding snippet, Jinja supports the following powerful features:

- Extending a base template: In our example, we are extending the `layout.html` file. By extending a base HTML file, we produce a web page that includes both the base template and the output of code specified in the current file.
- Looping: Notice the `{% for user in users %}` line of code. Here, `users` might be a variable specified by the Django backend via a template (similar to the example we saw in the preceding subsection). As you can see, the syntax for this `for` loop is identical to one in Python, thus providing a powerful way to read through iterable data.
- Combining HTML tags: Inside the same `for` loop, we see the code attributes of each element in `users` (such as `url` and `username`) are being placed into various HTML elements. This is quite a convenient feature, facilitating a dynamic and flexible generation of HTML code.

Jinja is the perfect way to tie Pythonic syntax in the context of web development. It gives traditional Python programmers an approachable method to tackle web projects, as well as web developers a dynamic way to process, manipulate, and display their data.

Overall, models, admin functionalities, templates, and Jinja create a powerful combination that sets Django apart as the premiere web framework in Python. With that said, there are still considerations regarding the pros and cons of Django, specifically in comparison with another Python web framework—Flask. In the next subsection, we will look into the differences further.

Django versus Flask

Normally when comparing it with Flask, Django users point to a feature of the framework that emphasizes the biggest difference between the two: Django is to be used with the batteries-included approach. The term *batteries included* denotes the fact that Django comes with considerable support for common repetitive tasks such as user authentication, URL routing, or even the migration of database schema.

Flask, on the other hand, is significantly more lightweight, offering minimal design structures. As a result, web applications developed with Flask are relatively simple and can be easily plugged into other types of applications. However, a lot of heavy-lifting features that we mentioned earlier have to be implemented by the web developers themselves.

The distinction between Django and Flask is also mirrored in the one between PyCharm and other editors/IDEs. As we discussed extensively at the beginning of the book, the wide range of features offered by PyCharm, while incredibly useful, can be intimidating for beginner programmers, who should only focus on the core structure and syntax of the language. In Django, one could easily get lost in the complex project structure and various powerful functionalities that will streamline large web applications, especially if one is new to web programming.

For that reason, the same answer can be applied to the question of which one is better, Django or Flask—it depends on your current level of expertise and the end result you want from your chosen framework. Flask will keep your applications to the minimum and emphasize the core functionality of the application logic, while Django will build upon that core and add in multiple layers that will produce a full-fledged web application with features conforming to current standards in the industry.

If you are new to Python web programming, it is advisable to look at Flask first. After you have familiarized yourself with the process with Flask, Django will prove to be even more useful, especially if a full-stack application is what you want to achieve.

If you are starting out with Django straightaway, don't be discouraged—even though the learning curve might be relatively steep at the beginning, having to learn the core concepts of web development as well as how to implement them with Django, things will become much clearer after you have mastered the core concepts.

This discussion also marks the end of our brief overview on Django and its place in the ecosystem of Python web development. In the next section, we will look at PyCharm and how it integrates the framework into its projects.

Django in PyCharm

PyCharm provides powerful and convenient support for Django projects through various functionalities. Following an example of an online library containing information on books and authors, we will be examining these functionalities one by one. After this section, we will have a better understanding of the way PyCharm facilitates the process of developing web applications in Django.

You can additionally find the complete code for this section in the `Chapter08/mysite` subfolder in the repository of the book. Note that, if you do decide to import the whole project instead of doing the steps yourself while following the discussion, you will need to create an appropriate virtual environment for the project to be imported. With that in mind, you can utilize the `requirements.txt` file of the project to correctly install all dependencies.

(You can head back to the *Importing an external project into PyCharm* section in `Chapter 3`, *Customizing Interpreters and Virtual Environments* if you need a refresher on this process.)

Typically, it is important to make sure the version of Django you will be using is compatible with that of the Python interpreter you have. This is because similar to other Python external libraries such as OpenCV or TensorFlow, not all versions of Django are compatible with all versions of Python. You can head to the official Django documentation at `https://docs.djangoproject.com/en/2.2/faq/install/#what-python-version-can-i-use-with-django` for the complete list of compatibility between Django and Python.

With that in mind, let us start this section with our first step—creating a Django project.

Starting a Django project

As discussed many times previously, to create a new Django project in PyCharm, you can start with either step 1 or step 2 in the following list:

1. Choose **Create New Project** from the welcome window.
2. Go to **File | New Project** within an existing workspace.
3. In the **New Project** window, choose **Django** in the left-hand side menu as your project type.
4. In the main window, expand the available two sections, **Project Interpreter** and **More Settings**, as illustrated here:

Chapter 8

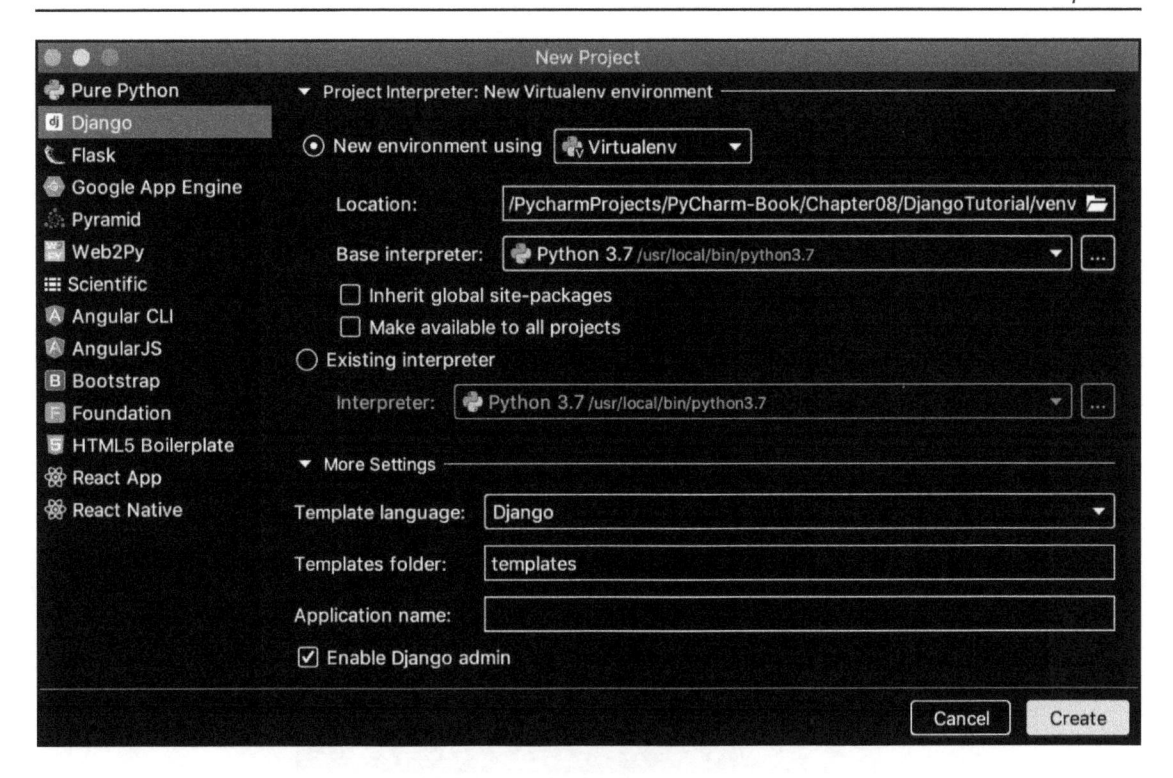

Creating a Django project

We will then make the following selections:

- At the top of the window, you can specify the name of your project and its path. Note that `mysite` is the convention for Django project names, so that is what I named the project in the code repository as well.
- Typically, we would like to create a new virtual environment for any web project, so choose the **New environment** option in the **Project Interpret** section.
- Check the two boxes in the same section if you want to include all the packages installed with your global Python interpreter in this project, and have this interpreter available for other PyCharm projects.
- In the **Template language** prompt in the **More Settings** section, you can have your templates managed by either **Django** or **Jinja2**. For our purposes, we will use the default option, Django.
- You can also rename the folder containing the templates of your project. Again, we will simply use the default name.

Integrating Django in PyCharm

- In the **Application name** prompt, you can specify if you'd like to start an application for your project at this point. Since we already know we'd like to implement our library application, we will input library in this prompt.
- The **Enable Django admin** box, if enabled, allows us to have an admin interface after the project is created (this is the admin feature discussed in the previous section). We will thus leave this box checked.

With everything ready, we will now click the **Create** button, and PyCharm will start the process of creating the project with the specified settings for us. You might notice that during this process, PyCharm makes sure to install the appropriate version of Django.

In the next subsection, we will take a closer look at the generated project and its structure.

Structure of a Django project

When PyCharm finishes creating our Django project, we will be taken to the corresponding project window. Let's now examine the various elements in this window. First, if you expand the directory tree in the **Project** panel on the left-hand side, you will see the general structure of the generated Django project:

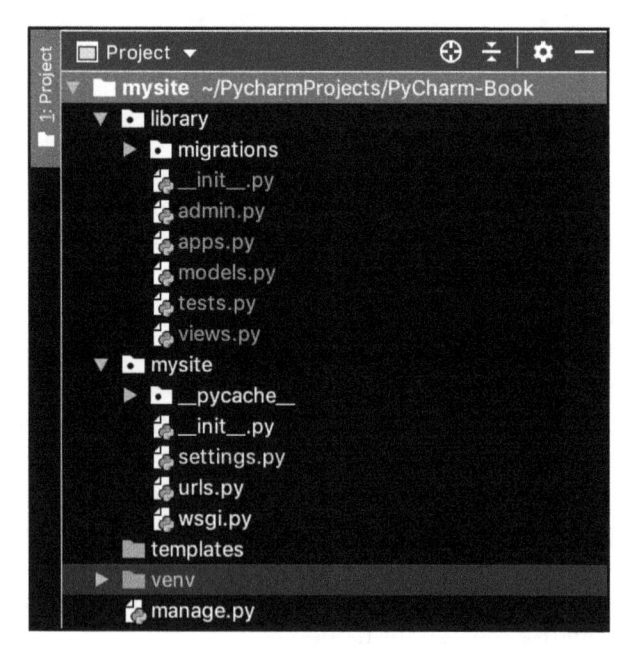

Django project structure

Let's have a look at some of the folders we see in this directory:

- `mysite` contains information and customizations for the general project.
- `library` contains settings for the library application itself. Note that a Django site can contain multiple applications, and `library` is the only one we currently have for `mysite`.
- `migrations` (a subfolder inside `library`) contains scripts that apply customizations and changes in your models to the corresponding databases.
- `templates` contains templates for the whole web project. A brief discussion on the Django template engine was included in the previous section.

Notice that most of the files in the folders are empty for now. As we move forward with the development of our application, we will be editing a number of the files to implement various features of the application.

In addition to the directory tree, you can also see that PyCharm automatically opens `settings.py` and `urls.py` in the editor. These files, included in the `mysite` folder, specify the configurations and URL routings for our project, respectively. Since we will be working with these files quite frequently, it is generally a good idea to keep them opened in the editor.

Initial configurations

For now, we can briefly consider the `settings.py` file and look through all the various settings that we currently have, for example, as follows:

- Production-related configurations (lines 22 - 26):

    ```
    # SECURITY WARNING: keep the secret key used in production secret!
    SECRET_KEY = ...

    # SECURITY WARNING: don't run with debug turned on in production!
    DEBUG = True
    ```

    The information included in these lines should be changed when we are at the production stage of our site. However, we can leave it as is for now.

- Database configurations (lines 75 - 83):

    ```
    # Database
    # https://docs.djangoproject.com/en/2.2/ref/settings/#databases

    DATABASES = {
    ```

Integrating Django in PyCharm

```
        'default': {
            'ENGINE': 'django.db.backends.sqlite3',
            'NAME': os.path.join(BASE_DIR, 'db.sqlite3'),
        }
    }
```

Note that we are using `sqlite3` as our database engine. Aside from that, you can of course utilize other engines such as MySQL or Oracle by specifying the value of `'ENGINE'` (line 80); for now, we will stick with `sqlite3`. On the other hand, you can freely customize the name of the database, as specified by the value of `'NAME'` (line 81). In particular, simply change the second parameter string (which is currently `'db.sqlite3'`) to the desired name. (I personally changed it to `'LibraryDatabase'`.)

Running manage.py and launching the server

Next, we will see how we can interact with the `manage.py` file in Django. If you are experienced with Django, you might remember that we typically work with the `manage.py` file when we'd like to run project-wide tasks, such as launching the server or applying database migrations.

Typically, you would have to run a terminal command to evoke functionalities in the `manage.py` file. For example, to launch the server for your Django project, you would run the following:

```
python manage.py runserver
```

In PyCharm, you can open a separate panel within your Django project window that is solely dedicated to interacting with the `manage.py` file. This is quite similar to having a panel for the terminal within our project window; since `manage.py` is something we would have to work with frequently, this feature will prove convenient in any Django project.

To open the panel, go to **Tools** | **Run manage.py Task** from the menu bar, and you will see the **manage.py** panel for the current Django project pop up, similar to the following:

Chapter 8

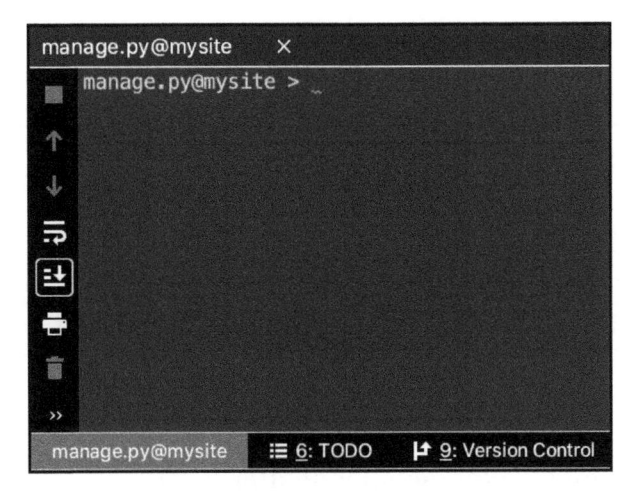

The manage.py panel for Django

Much like any other panel (tool window) in your project, you have the ability to relocate this **manage.py** panel around your project window however you want.

Finally, let's see how we can launch the server of our current Django project using this panel. In the prompt, type in the command:

```
runserver
```

After hitting *Enter*, you will obtain an output that is completely identical to the one produced by the native Django/terminal `manage.py` command:

The manage.py panel for Django

[233]

Integrating Django in PyCharm

Now, if you go to the URL of our local server (which, in my case, was `http://127.0.0.1:8080/`), you will see the Django welcome webpage for our project:

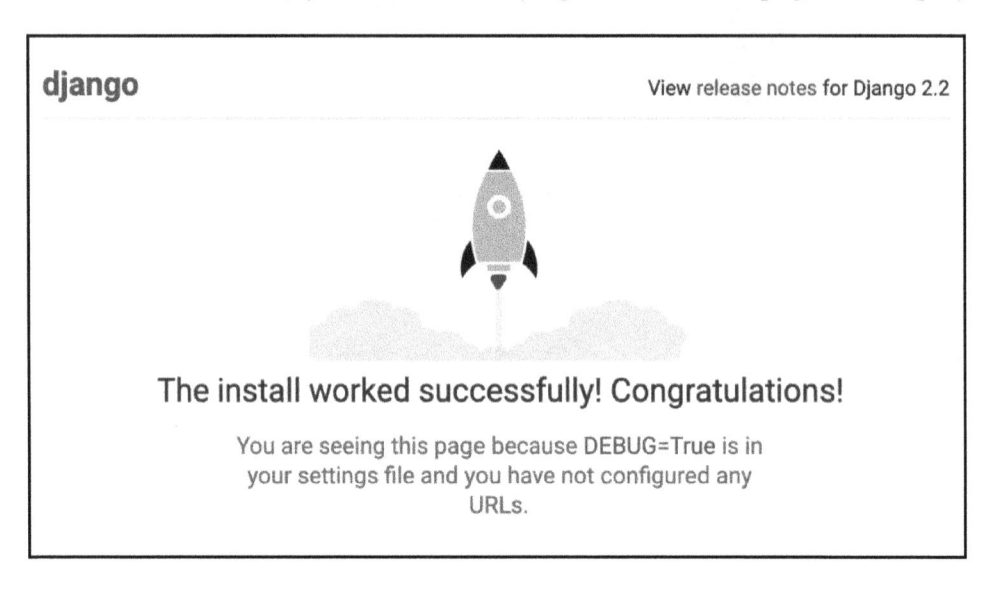

The Django welcome webpage

This webpage tells us that everything is working perfectly, and we can implement additional features into our web project. Again, everything we did could be achieved with the terminal, but the PyCharm **manage.py** panel makes it more convenient for us to have, and organize, all the tools we need in one window while working on the project.

Creating Django models

We have discussed in the previous section that Django's logic is implemented in a model-oriented way, which means that each entity in our web application should be designed as a Django model. In this section, we will examine the specific process of writing a model in Django.

Navigate to the `library` folder within our project, and open up its `models.py` file, which was generated automatically when the library application was created. As the name suggests, we will keep all the models that pertain to the library application and their respective logic in this file. The file should already contain the following code:

```
from django.db import models

# Create your models here.
```

Now, we will implement two separate models—`Author` and `Book`. Imagine the kind of information we would like for our library to hold; a library should consist of multiple books, and each book in turn should be written by a specific author. We will thus have a model for the books and one for the authors.

While you can copy the following code and paste it in your current project, or you can even simply import the project from the code repository of the book, I highly recommend manually typing the code in your `models.py` file; doing this will help you mentally walk through the code as you type each line in, and you will also be able to experience first-hand PyCharm's powerful code-completion features.

First, the `Author` model will contain various information about the author. Its implementation is as follows:

```
class Author(models.Model):
    first_name = models.CharField(max_length=100)
    last_name = models.CharField(max_length=100)

    def __str__(self):
        return f'{self.last_name}, {self.first_name}'
```

Considering the implementation of the preceding simple `Author` model, we see that it has two fields—first and last name of the author. We are also overwriting the `__str__()` method to return the string representation of an `Author` instance in the format we have specified.

Note that all the data structures commonly used in web applications are incorporated in Django. Specifically, we see that `models.CharField` (and `models.DateTimeField` in the next code block) handle nicely all the logic behind the respective data structures (text string and timestamp data); Django developers simply need to import and use them in an appropriate way.

Next, we implement the model for the choices to the questions:

```
import datetime
from django.utils import timezone


class Book(models.Model):
    title = models.CharField(max_length=200)
    author = models.ForeignKey(Author, on_delete=models.DO_NOTHING,)
    pub_date = models.DateTimeField('date published')

    def __str__(self):
        return f'{self.title} by {self.author}'
```

Integrating Django in PyCharm

```
def was_published_recently(self):
    now = timezone.now()
    return now - datetime.timedelta(days=1) <= self.pub_date <= now
```

In the `Book` model, we have a text field for the title of a given book, as well as a `DateTimeField` attribute holding the time the given book is/was published. In addition, each book has a many-to-one relationship with an author in our library (since each author might have one or more book that they have written), so we are using `models.ForeignKey` to implement this relationship just online. The behind-the-scenes implementation of the corresponding database logic is all handled by Django.

Again, these two models are both implemented inside the `models.py` file of the library application, keeping a simple and straightforward yet powerful structure for our web project.

Making migrations

As mentioned before, each model will be associated with a database table, which needs to be implemented via *migrations*:

1. This task is also done using the **manage.py** panel; therefore, if it is not in your project window already, go ahead and open it up via **Tools** | **Run manage.py Task** or its corresponding keyboard shortcut.
2. Next, type in the following command in the **manage.py** panel:

   ```
   makemigrations library
   ```

   (As you type in the command, notice the intelligent code-completion suggestions.) You should get the following output in the **manage.py** panel:

   ```
   Tracking file by folder pattern: migrations
   Migrations for 'library':
     library/migrations/0001_initial.py
       - Create model Author
       - Create model Book

   Following files were affected
   [...]/mysite/library/migrations/0001_initial.py
   ```

After this, data for the two models we implemented has been registered inside the `library/migrations/0001_initial.py` file. You can navigate to that file and examine its content; in general, that file is used by the Django backend to handle the implementing of the database tables, which we don't need to worry about.

3. In the **manage.py** panel again, type in the following command:

   ```
   sqlmigrate library 0001
   ```

   This command will, in turn, run SQL-related functions to create the database tables with the specified fields. You will see the following output, which contains SQL commands:

   ```
   Tracking file by folder pattern: migrations
   BEGIN;
   --
   -- Create model Author
   --
   CREATE TABLE "library_author" ("id" integer NOT NULL PRIMARY KEY
   AUTOINCREMENT, "first_name" varchar(100) NOT NULL, "last_name"
   varchar(100) NOT NULL);
   --
   -- Create model Book
   --
   CREATE TABLE "library_book" ("id" integer NOT NULL PRIMARY KEY
   AUTOINCREMENT, "title" varchar(200) NOT NULL, "pub_date" datetime
   NOT NULL, "author_id" integer NOT NULL REFERENCES "library_author"
   ("id") DEFERRABLE INITIALLY DEFERRED);
   CREATE INDEX "library_book_author_id_d9a3b67e" ON "library_book"
   ("author_id");
   COMMIT;
   ```

   With that, the specifications for the database tables in the backend have been registered.

Integrating Django in PyCharm

4. Finally, we apply all the changes and create the preceding tables by running `migrate` in the **manage.py** panel. At this point, you should see something similar to the following screenshot in your **manage.py** panel:

```
manage.py@mysite    ×
Tracking file by folder pattern:    migrations
Operations to perform:
  Apply all migrations: admin, auth, contenttypes, library, sessions
Running migrations:
  Applying contenttypes.0001_initial... OK
  Applying auth.0001_initial... OK
  Applying admin.0001_initial... OK
  Applying admin.0002_logentry_remove_auto_add... OK
  Applying admin.0003_logentry_add_action_flag_choices... OK
  Applying contenttypes.0002_remove_content_type_name... OK
  Applying auth.0002_alter_permission_name_max_length... OK
  Applying auth.0003_alter_user_email_max_length... OK
  Applying auth.0004_alter_user_username_opts... OK
  Applying auth.0005_alter_user_last_login_null... OK
  Applying auth.0006_require_contenttypes_0002... OK
  Applying auth.0007_alter_validators_add_error_messages... OK
  Applying auth.0008_alter_user_username_max_length... OK
  Applying auth.0009_alter_user_last_name_max_length... OK
  Applying auth.0010_alter_group_name_max_length... OK
  Applying auth.0011_update_proxy_permissions... OK
  Applying library.0001_initial... OK
  Applying sessions.0001_initial... OK

Process finished with exit code 0

manage.py@mysite >
```

Applying migrations in PyCharm

We have thus learned how to apply migrations within PyCharm. Again, we see the considerable convenience achieved via using the **manage.py** panel, which is also supported by the PyCharm intelligent code-completion engine.

The admin interface

We briefly discussed the admin feature of Django in the previous section. Again, Django automatically sets up a powerful interface for admins of a given web project, making the process of customizing various specifications of our website effortless. There are several steps to the process of managing our website via the admin interface, which will be discussed in the following sections.

Creating a superuser and logging in

The first step is to declare an admin user for our website in the backend using the **manage.py** panel:

1. In the **manage.py** panel, type in the following command to create a superuser:

   ```
   createsuperuser
   ```

   Django will then also ask for your email address and password for the superuser. You will obtain an output saying **Superuser created successfully.** when the process is completed.

2. Now, we will take a look at the admin interface that Django has prepared for us. From the **manage.py** panel, execute the `runserver` command.

3. From your localhost (where the current web project is being hosted), add `/admin` to the URL to go to our admin interface. For example, since my site was running on the `8000` port, my URL was `http://127.0.0.1:8000/admin`.

4. From here you will see an admin login page:

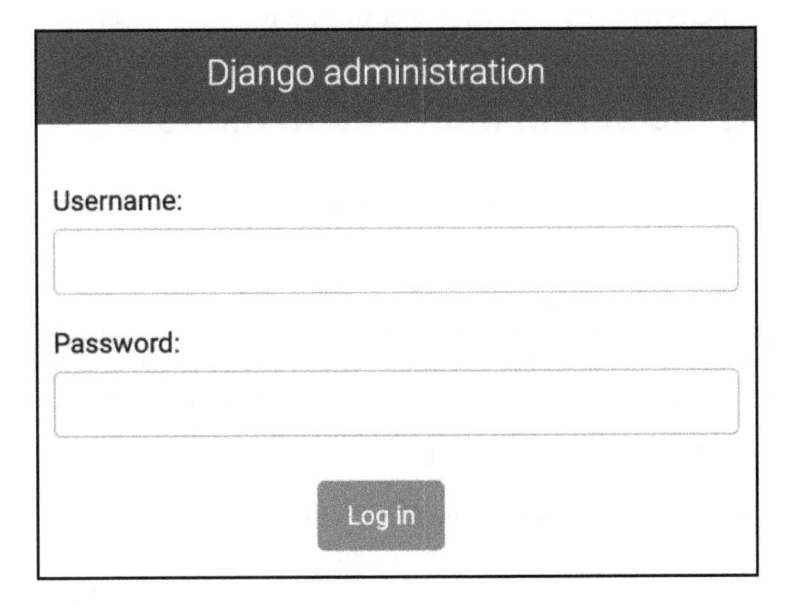

Django's admin login page

Integrating Django in PyCharm

5. Enter the information for the superuser you just created, and you will be taken to the admin dashboard for your website:

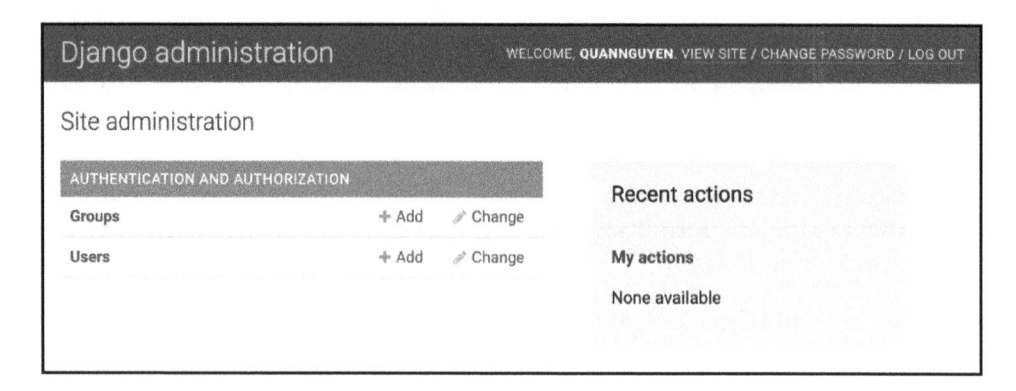

Django's admin dashboard

We see that, even with the simple web application we just created, Django automatically generates a fully functioning admin interface for the app. This goes to show the extent to which Django supports its users with its powerful features.

Connecting the admin interface to models

You might have noticed from the preceding admin dashboard that there is a section called **AUTHENTICATION AND AUTHORIZATION**, in which we, as an admin, could add and customize privileges of various groups of users. However, the models that we created (`Book` and `Author`) are not there.

This is because, as a result of the automatic nature of its generation, the admin interface was created independently of our models. Therefore, we will need to connect our models to this admin interface, which, in fact, is also a Django application in itself, called `admin`.

First, we will implement the `Author` model:

1. Make sure that our current server is still running.
2. In the `admin.py` file of the `library` folder, enter the following code (note that the first line should already be added in automatically by Django):

```
from django.contrib import admin

# Register your models here.
from .models import Author
admin.site.register(Author)
```

Here we are registering the `Author` model with the admin application using `admin.site.register()`.

3. Go to your browser and refresh the page of your admin interface, and you should see that the `Author` model has been successfully added to the dashboard:

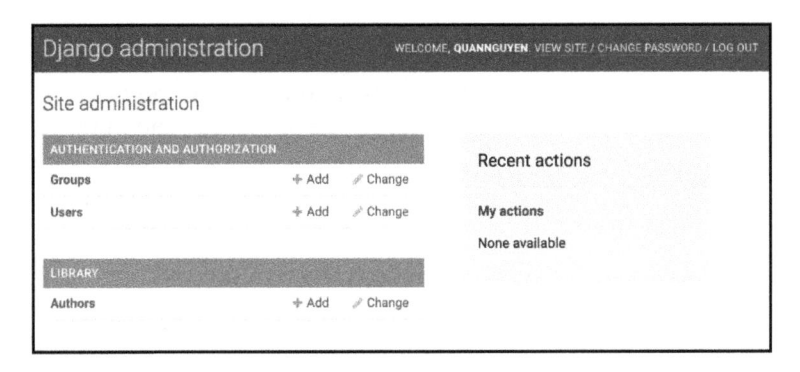

New models in the admin dashboard

From here, click on the **Add** button in the **Authors** section to create some entries for our author database table. You will see the **Add author** prompt, which will ask you to enter the attributes for each author that we specified in our Django `Author` model, namely, the first and last names.

Go ahead and enter the sample authors for your database. As an example, I entered the following four names:

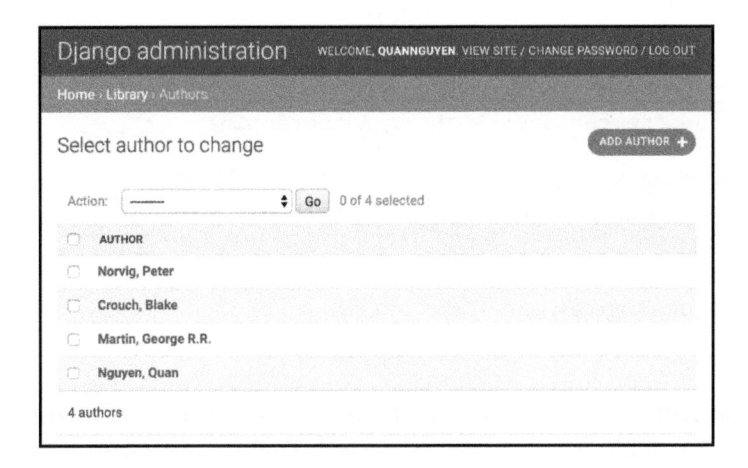

A view on created database entries

[241]

Integrating Django in PyCharm

And that's how we populate a simple database table for our Django application. It is important to note that we did not implement the same logic for the `Book` model, since each `Book` instance has to reference one instance from the `Author` model (due to the many-to-one relationship between these models). This is also why we needed to create entries for the `Author` table first in a way that was independent from the `Book` table.

Next, we will populate the `Book` table:

1. Stop the server on your localhost by using the *Ctrl + C* keyboard combination or clicking on the stop button in the toolbar on the left in the **manage.py** panel.
2. Modify the `library/admin.py` file so that it now contains the following code:

   ```
   from django.contrib import admin

   # Register your models here.
   from .models import Author, Book


   class BookInLine(admin.TabularInline):
       model = Book
       extra = 1

       fieldsets = [
           (None, {'fields': ['title']}),
           ('Date information', {'fields': ['pub_date']})
       ]


   class AuthorAdmin(admin.ModelAdmin):
       inlines = [BookInLine]


   admin.site.register(Author, AuthorAdmin)
   ```

   The preceding code implements the `Book` model in the admin interface, while ensuring the many-to-one relationship between itself and the `Author` model is preserved.

3. From the **manage.py** panel, execute `runserver`.
4. Go to the `/admin` site of our web application.

> **TIP**
>
> You will still initially see that there is only the section to add and edit our `Author` table. This is because we technically cannot create an instance of the `Book` model without involving the `Author` model (due to the `Book` model referencing the `Author` model).

[242]

5. Click on the **Authors** section (or go to `/admin/library/author`) to go to our current `Author` table.
6. Click on any author that you have previously created, and you will see a different interface that was implemented by our changes to the `admin.py` file. Specifically, you will notice a new section in which you can customize the books that are associated with the given author:

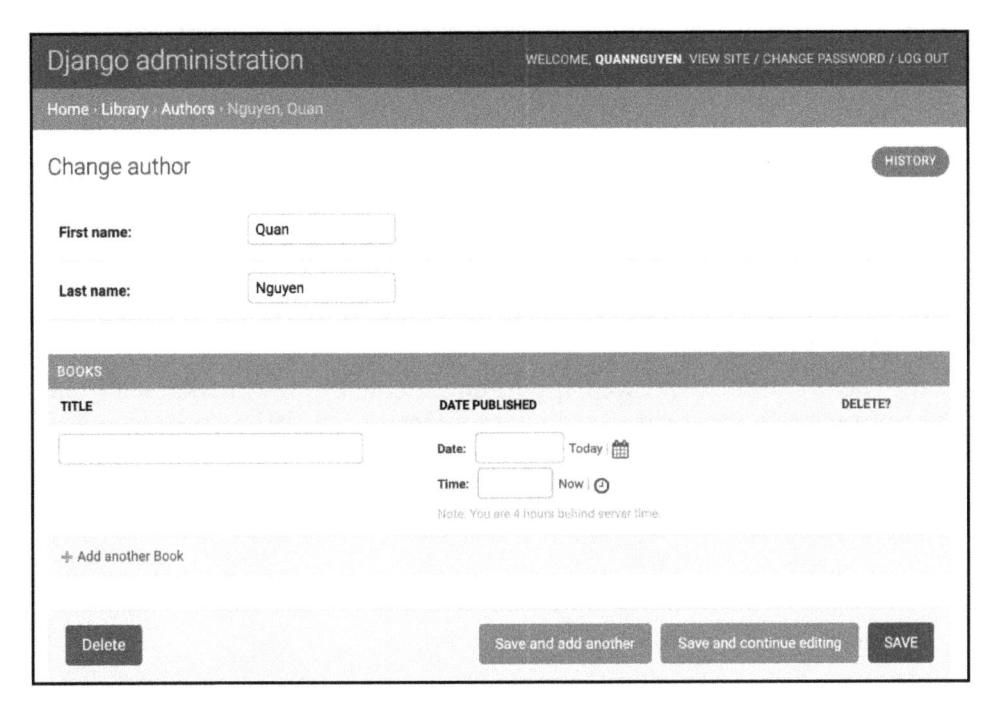

Customizing books and authors from the admin interface

7. Additionally, when we choose to create a completely new author, the corresponding book section is still included.

In short, in order to enter a new instance of the `Book` model, we can do either of the following:

- Add a new book to the list of books of a given author by modifying the specific author entry, if the new book we are creating is written by an author who is already in the `Author` table.
- Add a new author and specify the corresponding book during the process, if the `Author` table does not contain the author for the book.

The limitation set out by this process, again, makes sure that the many-to-one relationship between `Book` and `Author` is preserved. Specifically, we have seen that a new instance of the `Book` model cannot be created without referencing an `Author` instance. For now, go ahead and add any number of `Book` instances that you like; we will be seeing an example where we work with the `Book` entries in the next section.

This concludes our overview of the admin interface provided by Django. Overall, the admin interface offers powerful options in terms of creating and customizing entries in our database tables, while still protecting any constraints implemented by the design of our models.

For the rest of the subsections in this chapter, we will turn our attention to frontend-related aspects of the Django web development process. Next, we will examine the PyCharm support for creating views for our web applications.

Creating Django views

Views are the way for users of our web applications to see the information we would like to display from our models and databases. In the simplest sense, the purpose of views is to connect the data accessed and computed from the backend to the templates in the frontend. In this section, we will learn the process of creating initial views for our current web project example:

1. Open the `views.py` file in the `library` folder, and enter the following code:

    ```
    from django.http import HttpResponse


    # Create your views here.
    def index(request):
        return HttpResponse('Currently at the library index')
    ```

    The preceding `index()` function specifies the output one will see when visiting the `/library` site.

2. Next, we need to register this view with our library application. To do this, create a new file within the `library` folder named `urls.py`, which will contain the following code:

    ```
    from django.conf.urls import url
    from . import views
    ```

```
urlpatterns = [
    url(r'^$', views.index, name='index'),
]
```

You can see that we are including the `index()` function of the `views.py` file inside the `urlpatterns` variable, which will let Django know to use the specific function we just wrote.

3. Now, open the `mysite/urls.py` file and add a line pointing to our newly created `library/urls.py` file. In the end, we should have the following code:

```
from django.contrib import admin
from django.urls import path
from django.conf.urls import url, include   # add this line


urlpatterns = [
    path('admin/', admin.site.urls),
    url(r'^library/', include('library.urls'))   # add this line
]
```

Doing this, we are connecting the URL pattern of our library application with the main project.

4. Finally, run the server and go to the `/library` site and you will be able to see the message **Currently at the library index** that we specified in our views earlier within the browser.

You might have noticed that, if you simply go to the main site of our web project (for example, `http://127.0.0.1:8000/` as opposed to `http://127.0.0.1:8000/library`), Django will display an error message indicating that a view is not available for this page yet. This is to be expected since, in the URL pattern of our main site (the `mysite/urls.py` file), we are only handling the `/admin` and `/library` sites.

Since we are only considering the library application at the moment, we would like to customize the default page of the web project to the `/library` site, so that we will not have to enter the URL ourselves every time we run the server. Fortunately, PyCharm offers the ability to do this via its run/debug configuration, which we will discuss next.

Integrating Django in PyCharm

Customizing the run/debug configuration

Among various other advantages, customizing the run/debug configuration of a PyCharm project is helpful when it is a web development one and we would like to specify the default page for our web application, as explained in the previous subsection.

1. To open the configuration window, select the following section within the main toolbar of your project window, and choose **Edit configurations** as illustrated here:

Opening the run/debug configuration

2. In the new window that just appeared, enable the **Run browser** option, and edit the corresponding URL so that it points to our desired default page, which, in this case, is `http://127.0.0.1:8000/library` and hit **Apply**:

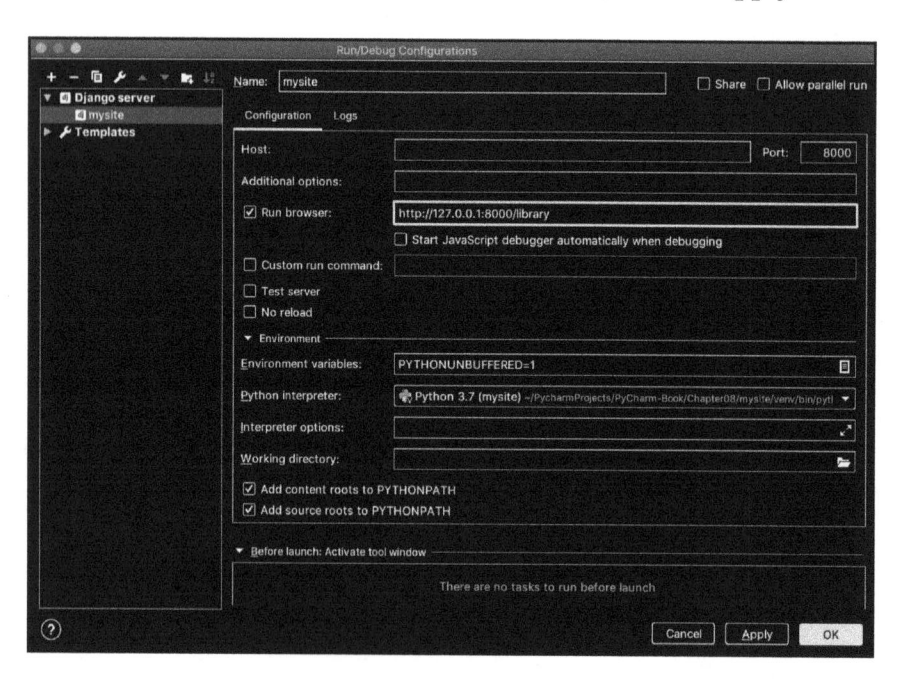

Specifying the default page for a Django project

[246]

3. Now, whenever we would like to run the server, we can utilize this run configuration by clicking on the **Run** button (instead of using the **manage.py** panel, whose default page is still http://127.0.0.1:8000/) and PyCharm will take us to the page that we specified earlier:

Running a Django server using a run configuration

In this case, we will be taken to the index of our library application and we'll see the **Currently at the library index** message again.

Note that clicking on this **Run** button is a significantly faster process than opening the **manage.py** panel and executing the runserver command. So, even within PyCharm, we still have a wide range of options to achieve the same goal. Most of the time, customizing a run/debug configuration for your web project will prove to be more efficient in the long run.

Making templates

In the final section of this chapter, we will see how PyCharm supports the process of making Django templates within a web project. To see the power of these features in action, we will be extending the index view of our current library application.

1. Open the library/views.py file and modify its content to the following:

   ```
   from django.shortcuts import render
   from .models import Book


   # Create your views here.
   def index(request):
       latest_books = Book.objects.order_by('-pub_date')[:5]
       context = {'latest_books': latest_books}
       return render(request, 'library/index.html', context)
   ```

   Here we are creating a dynamic view for our library application. Specifically, we access the Book database table and retrieve the latest five entries, according to their publication date (the pub_date attribute in reverse, hence the minus sign). Finally, we send that information to a template named library/index.html via the render() function.

[247]

Integrating Django in PyCharm

2. Notice that there is now a warning within the current `library/views.py` file, saying that the template `library/index.html` we specified does not exist:

```
# Create your views here.
def index(request):
    latest_books = Book.objects.order_by('-pub_date')[:5]
    context = {'latest_books': latest_books}
    return render(request, 'library/index.html', context)
                                  Template file 'index.html' not found more... (⌘F1)
```

Django template not found warning

If you have worked with Django before, you know that we now need to manually create this file within the `templates` folder of our web project. However, since we are using PyCharm, things are much simpler!

3. With your cursor at the error, click on the corresponding intention action icon (the yellow lightbulb to the left), and select the first option from the drop-down list to create the template in question:

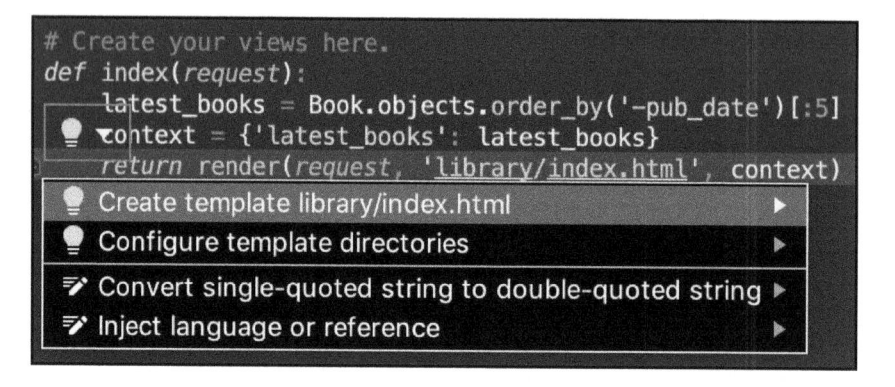

```
# Create your views here.
def index(request):
    latest_books = Book.objects.order_by('-pub_date')[:5]
    context = {'latest_books': latest_books}
    return render(request, 'library/index.html', context)
    Create template library/index.html                    ▶
    Configure template directories                        ▶
    Convert single-quoted string to double-quoted string  ▶
    Inject language or reference                          ▶
```

Django-specific intention actions

4. Choose to create a new folder in the `templates` folder in the pop-up window if prompted, and, after the process, the `library/index.html` template should be created accordingly. It will also be opened in the editor automatically.

[248]

Chapter 8

5. Now, enter the following code for our template, which lists all the entries we currently have in our `Book` database table:

```
{% if latest_books %}
    <ul>
        {% for book in latest_books %}
            <li>{{ book }}</li>
        {% endfor %}
    </ul>
{% else %}
    <p>No books available.</p>
{% endif %}
```

Again, I highly recommend manually writing the code yourself, so that you can experience PyCharm's excellent code-completion features. In this case, we see that code completion is able to support HTML and Jinja syntax, making writing Django templates an effortless process.

6. Now, either use the run configuration customized earlier, or run the server directly from the **manage.py** panel and go to the `/library` page. Here, you should see the corresponding output that we specified in our views and templates—a list of entries from our `Book` database table, printed out via the `__str__()` method of the `Book` model.

The last element of note while working on a Django project with PyCharm is the convenient navigation between views and templates. Specifically, notice the icons at the top of the gutter of our current views and templates: in the `templates/library/index.html` file, and in the `library/views.py` file.

As we know, one is a Django view that utilizes another, which is a template. These two kinds of files are therefore interconnected in their logic and are likely to be worked on concurrently by Django developers generally. Via the aforementioned icons, you can jump back and forth between a view and its corresponding template with a mouse click, which will undoubtedly prove considerably useful.

And that concludes our current discussion on the PyCharm support for Django applications. Note that there are a number of other great features that we can explore, and we will come back and further expand on this topic later in `Chapter 10`, *Building a Web Application in PyCharm*.

Integrating Django in PyCharm

Summary

In this chapter, we examined various PyCharm features regarding supporting and automating tasks in the process of web development with Django. While this list of features is in no way exhaustive, I hope it can offer you a solid starting point to continue discovering other powerful features for your web development process.

First, we see that, by specifying the PyCharm project type as Django, an extensive project skeleton will be generated with convenient boilerplate code already filled out. With the implementation of the **manage.py** panel inside the project window as well as its run/debug configuration, PyCharm additionally allows for a higher level of development, with various tasks traditionally achieved via the command line, such as running the server or making migrations. Finally, by acknowledging integrated views and templates in Django, PyCharm makes it as easy as possible for developers to work with them in the editor—be it generating a missing template, code completion even in HTML and Jinja, or even dynamically switching between views and templates.

In the next chapter, we will tackle the last major component of any web application: database. We will see which tools and features from PyCharm can help with the management of databases in web applications.

Questions

1. What are the major characteristics of Django, and how do they set Django apart from another popular Python web framework, Flask?
2. What is the purpose of the PyCharm **manage.py** panel in a Django project, and how does one open and utilize it?
3. What is the purpose of the Django admin interface? How does one create an instance of a model (that is, a new entry in a database table) in this interface? How does the process change if the model references another model?
4. What is the purpose of the run/debug configuration in PyCharm in the context of running a Django server?
5. Does PyCharm's code completion logic only apply to Python code in Django projects?
6. What is the significance of being able to switch between Django views and corresponding templates in PyCharm?

Further reading

More information can be found in the following articles and readings:

- *Modern Python Development with PyCharm*, by Pedro Kroger (https://pedrokroger.net/pycharm-book/)
- *Two Scoops of Django: Best Practices for Django*, by Audrey Roy and Daniel Roy Greenfeld (www.twoscoopspress.com/)
- *PyCharm documentation: Creating and Running Your First Django Project*, JetBrains s.r.o.
  (www.jetbrains.com/help/pycharm/creating-and-running-your-first-django-project.html)
- *PyCharm documentation: Django*, JetBrains s.r.o.
  (www.jetbrains.com/help/pycharm/django-support7.html)
- *Django: Keeping logic out of templates (and views)* (https://openfolder.sh/django-keeping-logic-out-of-templates-and-views)

9
Understanding Database Management with PyCharm

Databases are ubiquitous, not only in web applications but also in data and business analytics projects. Throughout this chapter, we will learn about the various tools and features available in PyCharm that facilitate the process of working with the database systems used by your Python projects. These tools include powerful features such as the SQL editor, graphical interfaces with data sources, and making query diagrams.

All web developers should have a solid understanding of how to work with databases, and learning how to do that with PyCharm will be a good conclusion to our discussions on the process of web development in Python with PyCharm.

The following topics will be covered in this chapter:

- Connecting PyCharm to a given database
- Relational databases
- Utilizing the **Database** panel in PyCharm
- Data manipulation via the SQL console
- Creating database-related diagrams

By the end of the chapter, you will have a comprehensive understanding of how to utilize PyCharm's powerful support for database management processes.

Technical requirements

The following is a list of prerequisites for this chapter:

- Ensure that you have both Python 3.6+ and PyCharm installed on your computer.
- Download the *Database Tools and SQL* plugin for PyCharm.
- Download the GitHub repository at `https://github.com/PacktPublishing/Hands-on-Application-Development-with-PyCharm`.
- During this chapter, we will be working with the `Chapter09` subfolder in the downloaded code repository.

The first step in working with any database is to import the corresponding data source into our environment.

Connecting to a data source

First, the term **data source** indicates a given method of accessing a database from a server. Recall from the previous chapter that the database used by our web project is named `LibraryDatabase`. There is a file with the same name within the project folder, which is the data source for that database.

Throughout this chapter, we will be working with the corresponding folder in the code repository `Chapter09/DatabaseTutorial`. Go ahead and import the folder into your PyCharm workspace. As the first step of the database management process, we will learn how to import a data source into a PyCharm project:

1. In general, if the data source file you'd like to work with is not in your current project, then open up the **Database** panel by going to **View** | **Tool Windows** | **Database** and click on the + icon within the window, as illustrated in the following screenshot:

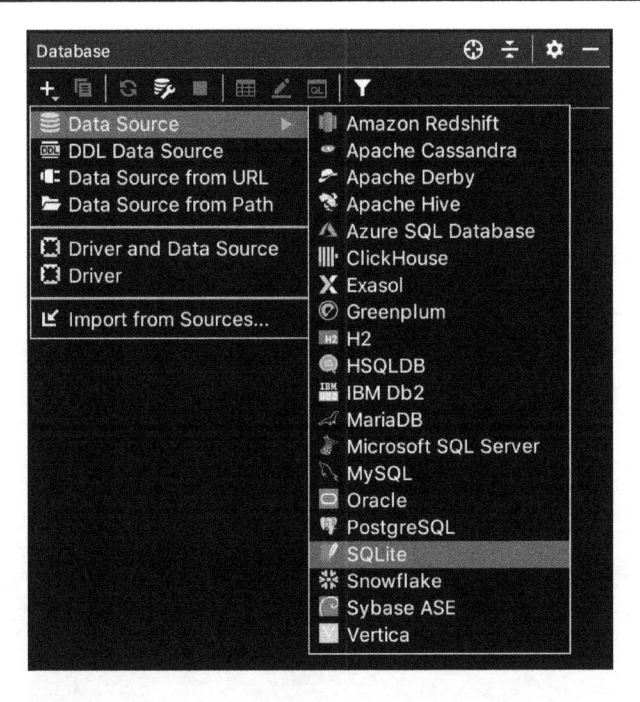

Adding new data sources into PyCharm

2. In our current example, we already have a file named
   `Chinook_Sqlite.sqlite`, which is the data source that we will be working
   with, so the preceding step is not applicable to our specific case.

   > **TIP**
   > Chinook is a sample database, commonly used for demo and testing tasks
   > for database projects and tools. It is available for SQL Server, Oracle,
   > MySQL, and many more. You can find more information regarding
   > Chinook at https://archive.codeplex.com/?p=chinookdatabase.

3. From the **Project** panel of your PyCharm window, double-click on the file to
   open the PyCharm **Database** panel. You can do this because PyCharm can
   automatically detect that the file you are opening is a data source. Your **Database**
   panel should look similar to the following:

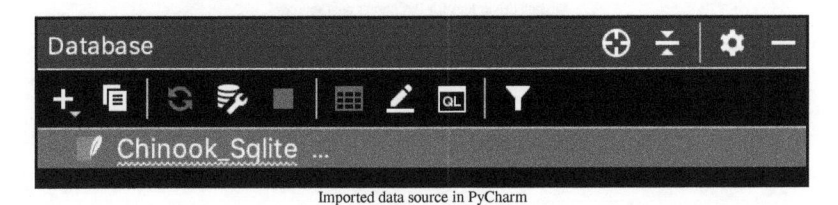

   Imported data source in PyCharm

   [255]

Understanding Database Management with PyCharm

4. We cannot interact with this data source just yet, as some initial configurations are necessary. Within the toolbar at the top of the **Database** panel, click on the Data Source Properties icon, which will open the configuration window for our data source.
5. The first thing you might notice is the bottom section of the window indicating that the driver appropriate for our data source is currently missing, as highlighted in the following screenshot:

Missing driver files for PyCharm's data sources

[256]

6. The beauty of PyCharm is that, as we have seen multiple times, not only does it look for potential errors and warnings for our programs (as in the previous screenshot), but it also provides simple commands to address the problems. In this case, a simple click on the hyperlink in **Download**, and PyCharm will take care of all of the nitty-gritty details on its own. If, on the other hand, you don't see this message, it means your PyCharm already has all the necessary driver files for your data source, and you can simply move on to the next steps.

> Note that in our current example, the data source corresponds to an SQLite database, but the same process applies for other database systems such as Oracle, MySQL, or PostgreSQL.

7. With the driver files downloaded, we have successfully imported our data source into PyCharm. We can test out the connection to this data source by clicking on the **Test Connection** button in the configuration window we opened earlier. If everything goes well, you will see the following output:

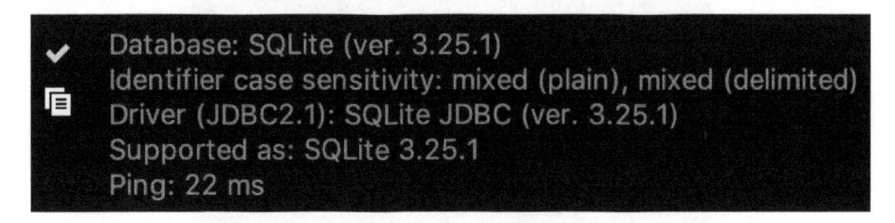

```
Database: SQLite (ver. 3.25.1)
Identifier case sensitivity: mixed (plain), mixed (delimited)
Driver (JDBC2.1): SQLite JDBC (ver. 3.25.1)
Supported as: SQLite 3.25.1
Ping: 22 ms
```

Testing connection to a data source

8. Now, simply click **Apply** and **OK** in the configuration window to apply the specifications we have made to our data source.
9. Now, we need to customize the schema for our data source. In the **Database** panel, click on the icon next to our current data source highlighted (note that instead of saying **0 of 1**, the icon can display ... as well):

Choosing the schema for the data source

10. This will open up a pop-up window with a number of checkboxes. Select the **Current schema (main)** option within the window, and you will see that with the correct schema our data source can now be expanded and examined within the **Database** panel:

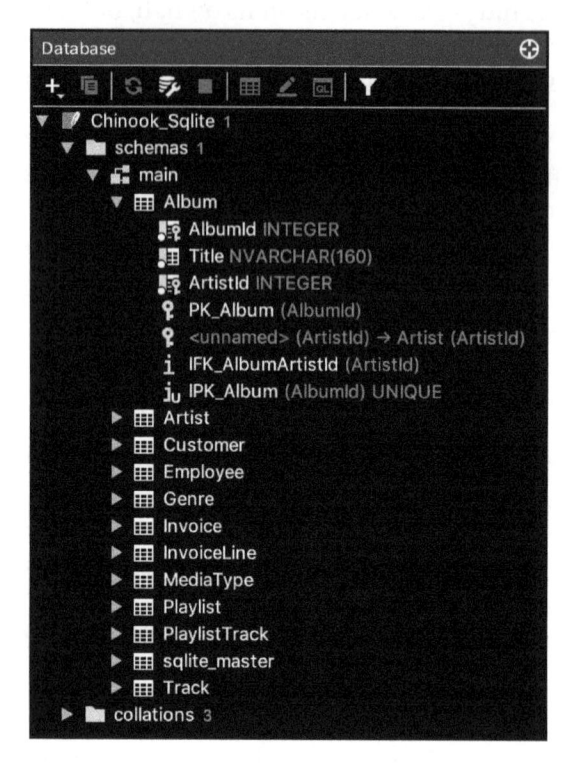

Examining database schemas

With that, we have successfully connected a sample data source to our PyCharm project. The different sections in the main schema are the database tables included in the data source. So in our current Chinook example, we have various different database tables such as `Album`, `Artist`, `Customer`, and so on.

We see that the **Database** panel offers quite a powerful feature, giving us the ability to inspect not only the different tables we have but also their respective fields (as well as any relationship between the tables). For example, the preceding `Album` table has a foreign key referencing the `Artist` table, indicating the creator of the given album. If you are not familiar with these concepts involving relational databases, don't worry because we will have that discussion later in this chapter.

Additionally, if you have gone through the last chapter where we worked on a Django web project, you might remember that we also implemented our own data source called `LibraryDatabase`. If you were to go back to the project and walk through the same steps for that data source (still using SQLite), you would be able to examine the schema for the database tables created, as shown here:

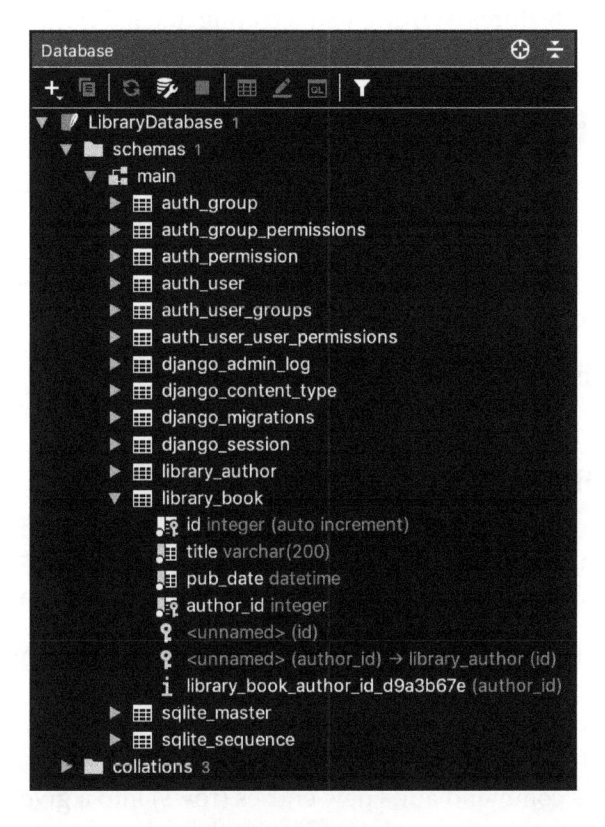

<figure>

Inspecting a Django data source

</figure>

Again, we are able to inspect all the fields in any given database table from the data source, including the many-to-one relationship via a foreign key from the `Book` table to the `Author` table. You might also notice that there are multiple other tables in a Django data source, such as `auth_group`, `django_admin_log`, or `sqlite_sequence`. These are database tables used by Django to handle complex backend logic such as user authentication or logging for admin users.

We have seen how to import a given data source into our PyCharm projects. Still using the current Chinook example, we will discuss the various options to work with our database tables via the PyCharm **Database** panel in the next section.

Working with a database in PyCharm

When a data source has been added to PyCharm via the **Database** panel, PyCharm users will have multiple options to view, interact, and even change the content of the tables included in the data source via PyCharm's intuitive interface. In this section, we will go over the details of these features, starting with creating and submitting SQL queries.

Working with SQL

If you are not familiar with the technology, **SQL** (short for **Structured Query Language**) is the most common tool for developers and data engineers who interact with databases, as well as the standard language for relational database management systems, according to the **American National Standards Institute** (**ANSI**). With SQL queries, you can retrieve data from and submit changes to a database table.

First, let's briefly discuss the basic usage of this language.

SQL fundamentals

A comprehensive discussion on SQL will not be covered here, as it is beyond the scope of this book. However, there are a few common SQL commands to create and manipulate entries in a database table that you can try on our current data. They are as follows:

- `SELECT`: This command is used to query data from one or multiple tables. By specifying attribute (row) names in this command, you can specify which attributes from the tables to be queried should be returned. You can also use * to indicate that all attributes should be returned.
- `INSERT`: This command adds new entries (rows) into a given database table. Within an `INSERT` command, you specify the value of each attribute the new entry should hold; otherwise, the default values (which are determined by the database table) will be used.
- `UPDATE`: This command is used to modify entries that already exist in a given database table. Using this command, we are able to assign specific attributes of any entry to new values. This command is typically used with a `SET` command for that assignment process (as we will see later).
- `DELETE`: Finally, this command deletes specific entries from a given table. Once a `DELETE` command is executed, there is no way to recover the deleted data.

When using these commands, we typically combine them with a `WHERE` clause, with which we can specify a condition to filter out the entries in a database table we want to manipulate. For example, with the following command we can go into the database table named `student`, look for the entries that have the `location` attribute holding `"Indiana"`, and finally change the value of the `age` attribute to `18`:

```
UPDATE student
SET age = 18
WHERE location = "Indiana";
```

Additionally, to execute SQL commands, we need a platform in which we can enter and run the commands. Normally, these platforms come preinstalled with any database management tool that you use for your databases. However, as we will see later on, PyCharm actually offers an editor for SQL as well as the option to execute them within a given PyCharm project.

Needless to say, this is simply a brief overview of what SQL is and what a number of SQL commands can help us achieve. To learn more about this tool on your own, I recommend tutorials from `https://www.codecademy.com/learn/learn-sql` or `https://www.khanacademy.org/computing/computer-programming/sql`.

Next, let's see how PyCharm supports the use of SQL.

Using SQL in PyCharm

PyCharm allows us to write, edit, and run SQL commands within a console. In addition to being able to work with the console as a simple text file, PyCharm users also have the added bonus of code completion and syntax checking when using the console.

Let's see an example of this by following the steps mentioned here:

1. First, to open the console in our PyCharm workspace, click on the Jump to Console icon from the toolbar of the **Database** panel as illustrated here:

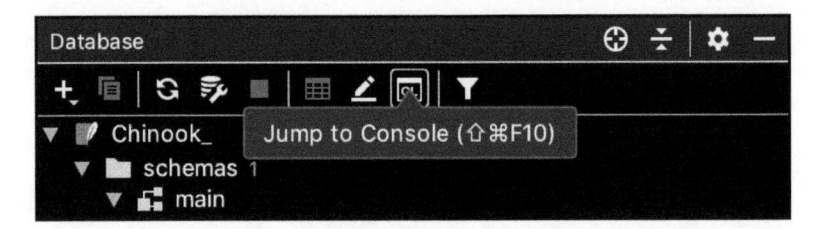

Opening a database console

Understanding Database Management with PyCharm

2. If there is more than one available console within your project, select the one that corresponds to the database that you would like to work with. In the current Chinook example, we simply have a SQLite database, so the corresponding console will be opened in the editor.

   To send a query to your database and have it executed, enter the actual query into the console. For example, enter the following SQL command:

   ```
   SELECT a.Title FROM Album a
   ```

   This command queries and returns all the entries in the `Title` column of the `Album` table. Note that the `a` variable in the command here is being used as a placeholder for `Album`. In other words, `a.Title` is a shorthand for `Album.Title`, which, again, corresponds to the data in the `Title` column of `Album`. Similar to what we have discussed for Python, JavaScript, and HTML, it is recommended that you manually type in the command to experience PyCharm's code completion support, in this case, for SQL. Now, let's execute the query and see what is returned afterward:

3. Click on the Execute button in the toolbar of the console:

Executing a query

4. As the query executes and returns, PyCharm's **Database Console** panel will pop up (most likely at the bottom of your project window), displaying the output of our query:

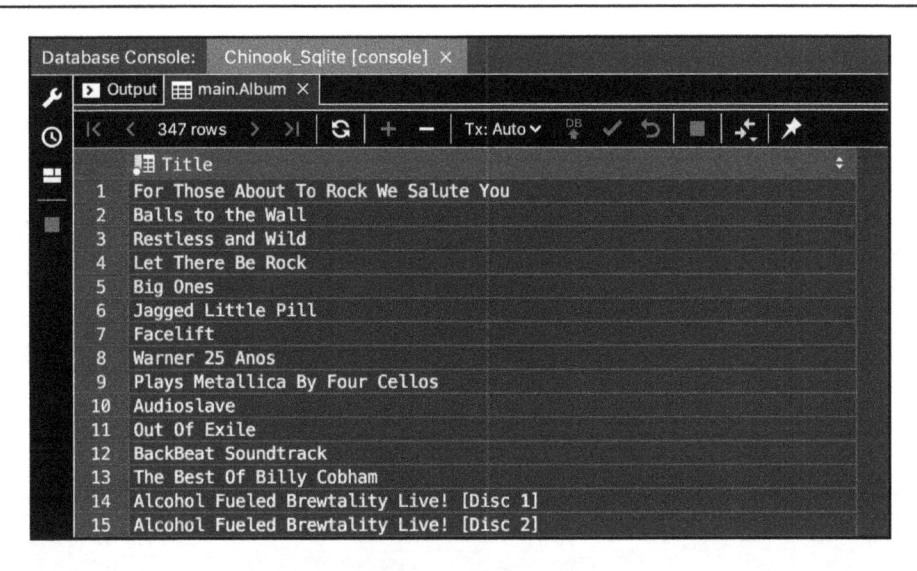

The output from database queries

This panel will contain any output produced by your database queries. You might also notice that there are multiple tabs within this panel—the tab in the preceding screenshot displays the actual result of the executed query, while the **Output** tab (to the left) contains performance-related information about the queries.

Additionally, you can save SQL commands in a console to a SQL script file; simply go to **File** | **Save as** and select the location to which you would like to save the file:

Saving SQL queries

Conversely, we can open a given SQL file, edit, and execute it in our PyCharm console in the same way. We have seen this ability to work with scripts of different languages simultaneously in the PyCharm editor multiple times before with JavaScript, HTML, and Jinja in previous chapters; this ability is quite powerful while working with databases as well.

Understanding Database Management with PyCharm

The PyCharm table view

In the previous subsection, we saw that when using a query console we can execute queries to a database included in a given data source in PyCharm. This means that we can retrieve data as well as submit changes to our connected database tables using the console. Alternatively, as we will see in this subsection, PyCharm offers another way to work with database tables—the table view—that is more graphical and thus more intuitive:

1. To evoke the table view and apply it to a given table in our database, we can simply double-click on the table in the PyCharm **Database** panel, and the table view will be opened in the editor. For example, I obtained the following screenshot after double-clicking on the Album table in the **Database** panel:

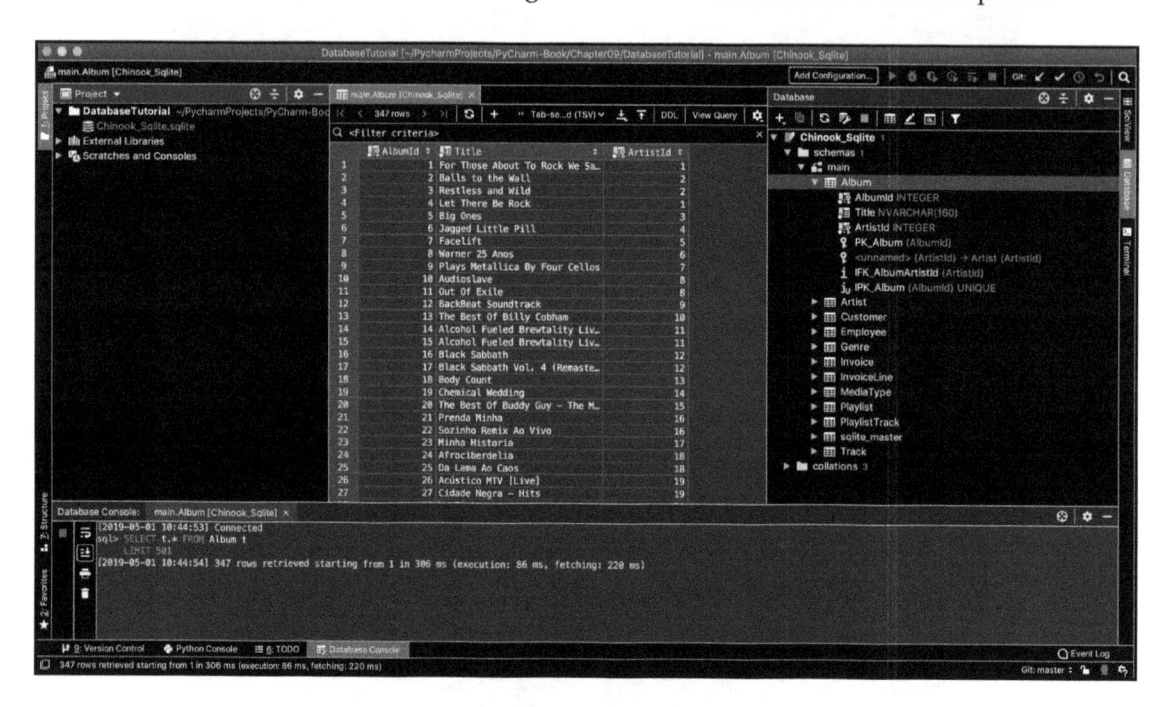

The table view in PyCharm

Notice that the corresponding executed query is displayed in the **Database Console** panel (at the bottom of the project window). Since I opened the whole Album table in my table view, the query executed was SELECT t.* FROM Album t.

[264]

You might have noticed that this table view is identical to the output we obtain by running queries from the console in the **Database Console** panel, discussed in the previous subsection. In fact, all the features included in the following discussion also apply to that table view as well.

2. Now, using the toolbar at the top of the table view, we have multiple ways to display the result table we have in our view. For example, we can transpose the result table, sort the rows using ORDER BY, or apply a custom filter, using the following options:

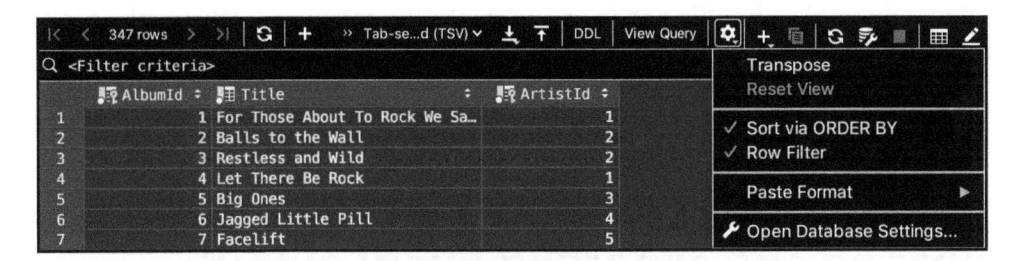

Different options to manipulate a table in the table view

3. Specifically, we can insert a new row or remove a row from the table, using the buttons in the following console toolbar, highlighted:

Adding/removing a row in the table view

> **TIP**
> Similar to how we can make changes to a database table via queries, we can also achieve the same results via this graphical interface of the table view.

4. We can also double-click on a specific cell to alter the content of that cell. Simply try this feature with any cell in the current table in our table view.
5. Note that by changing the content of a cell, we have not made any actual changes to the corresponding database table. To manually submit the changes we have made to the actual database, click on the Submit icon, also included in the console toolbar.

> You will also see the corresponding query to mutate the database in the **Database Console** panel.

6. With that said, you can also tell PyCharm that you want all changes made to the table in the table view to also be applied to the actual database. To do this, go to the settings and navigate to **Tools** | **Database** | **Data Views**, and enable the **Submit changes immediately** box.

Now, you might think submitting changes automatically made to database tables is a convenient feature. However, doing so would prevent us from being able to revert any unintentional changes made in the table view. Specifically, we can use the keyboard shortcut ⌥ ⌘ Z in macOS (or *Ctrl* + *Alt* + *Z* in Windows) to revert a change that has not been applied to the actual database yet.

Comparing and exporting query output

While considering the result from multiple queries as well as table views, we might want to compare two tables to further understand the effects of two given queries. To do this, from the toolbar at the top of one table view, click on the Compare with icon.

If you are following the examples used in our current discussion, then follow these steps:

1. Evoke this feature from either the table view (the graphically created one or the one resulting from running the SQL query).
2. Select the other table view from the drop-down menu that appears subsequently:

```
Output    main.Album  ×
   347 rows                  Tx: Auto
   Title                                     Album [Chinook_Sqlite]
1  For Those About To Rock We Salute You
2  Balls to the Wall
3  Restless and Wild
4  Let There Be Rock
5  Big Ones
6  Jagged Little Pill
7  Facelift
8  Warner 25 Anos
9  Plays Metallica By Four Cellos
10 Audioslave
```

Comparing table views

3. This will, in turn, open a pop-up window displaying the two selected result tables with any differences highlighted. Again, this feature is quite useful for the process of comparing two different queries and their effects on a given database table.
4. While the PyCharm table view offers a wide range of options in terms of viewing and manipulating tables resulting from queries, sometimes we would like to simply copy or export those tables to files. From the table view toolbar, click on the Dump Data icon. Here, you can choose to either export the data to a file or copy it to a clipboard:

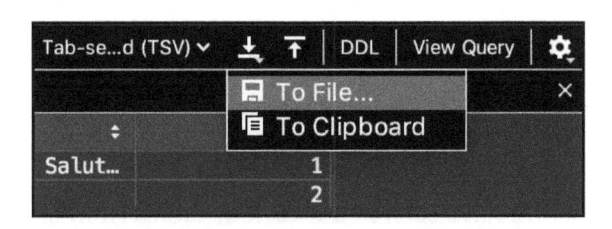

Dumping data from the table view

If you choose to export a given table to a file, note that the default format for the output file is `.tsv`. You can change the format of your table in the corresponding drop-down list in the table view toolbar:

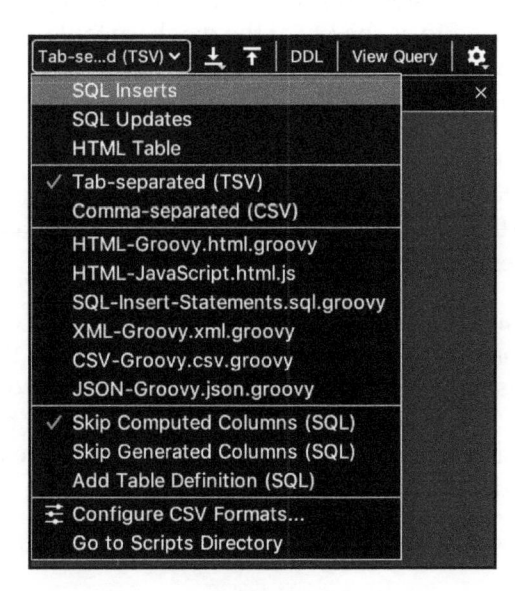

Changing table format

We can see that there are multiple options available, including HTML, **tab-separated values** (**TSV**), CSV, and so on, further proving PyCharm's dynamic features, especially in the context of web development.

Diagrams for databases

In the last discussion of the chapter, we will examine the creation and use of diagrams while working with databases in PyCharm. But first, since diagrams are mostly used to explain and represent relationships among database tables, let's briefly discuss that topic.

Relational database

In general, the term **relational database** denotes a specific form of storing and managing data. In a relational model, databases (which might be related to each other) are stored as tables, in the same way as we have seen in the various tables from our current example (`Album`, `Artist`, `Customer`, and so on). Each attribute of an entry in the database is formalized as a column in the database table, and all entries in the table must therefore share the same set of attributes.

In a database table, each entry must have a unique identifier, which will be used by the underlying data management system to keep track of all the existing entries. Such a unique identifier can often be referred to as the *key* of the database table, and no two unique keys can hold the same value in a common database table. In the `Album` database we considered earlier, the `AlbumId` attribute is used as the key for the table.

The most important aspect of a relational database is the ability to represent any relationships between different databases. A relationship is represented as a reference by an entry in a given database table to one in another table. Generally, a relationship denotes a connection between entries in different database tables.

For example, in the database system of a university, there are two different database tables: one containing information on its students, and one on professors that teach there. Each student has a faculty advisor assigned to him or her, which is one of the professors in the university, and we would like to store that information in the first database for the students. Each entry in that database should then have an attribute that references a professor or, in other words, an entry in the second database.

This kind of reference is typically done via a **foreign key**. Basically, in the attribute for the advisor information, each student entry will hold the identifier for the corresponding professor entry in the professor database. This way the underlying system can always go from a student entry in the first database and look up the information on their advisor in the second database. The term *foreign key* is used since the keys in another table are being used as data for an attribute in a given table.

This design is illustrated in the following diagram:

StudentId	StudentName	...	Advisor
1	Alice	...	101
2	Bob	...	409
3	Caroll	...	101

ProfessorId	ProfessorName	...
101	Ken	...
205	Brian	...
409	Richard	...

Student-advisor relation diagram

We can interpret the preceding information as the following:

- **Alice** has Professor **Ken** as her advisor.
- **Bob** has Professor **Richard** as his advisor.
- **Caroll** also has Professor **Ken** as her advisor.

Coming back to our current example with the `Album` database table, we see that each entry denoting each album object has an attribute called `ArtistId`, which references the `Artist` table. This relationship denotes an album and the artist that produced that album.

Now, we see that by visualizing the student-advisor relationship with arrows pointing from the referencing table (the student database) to the referenced table (the professor database), we can quickly understand the nature of the relationship. In the next subsection, let's see how PyCharm can streamline that process for us.

Diagrams for database objects

When you are working with a database system, there might be multiple tables that are connected to one another via different relationships (one-to-one, many-to-one, or many-to-many). Most of the time, keeping track of these relationships analytically might prove to be very difficult, but graphically visualizing them in a diagram can offer easy ways to understand and gain valuable insights into our database tables.

Understanding Database Management with PyCharm

Let's see an example of creating a visualization for our current database tables:

1. To create a diagram for database objects, be it individual tables or the whole schema, right-click on an object in the PyCharm **Database** panel, and choose **Diagrams** | **Show Visualization**. For example, I right-clicked on the **main** schema in the following screenshot to create a diagram for all the available database tables:

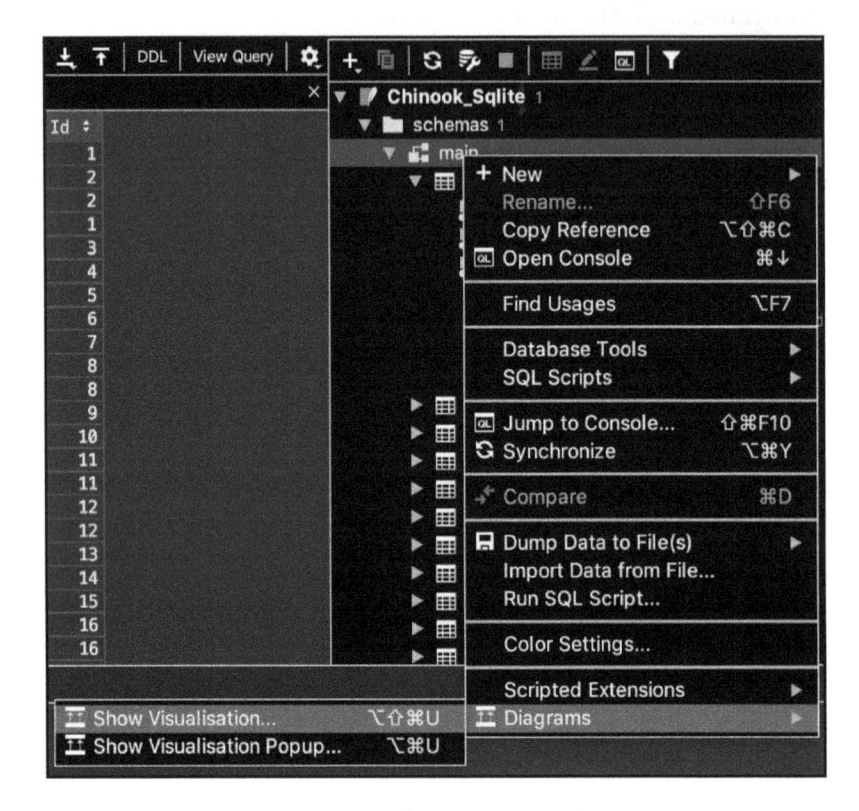

Creating diagrams for database objects

2. This will open the corresponding diagram in the editor. If you choose to visualize the whole schema as I did, you should obtain a diagram similar to the following:

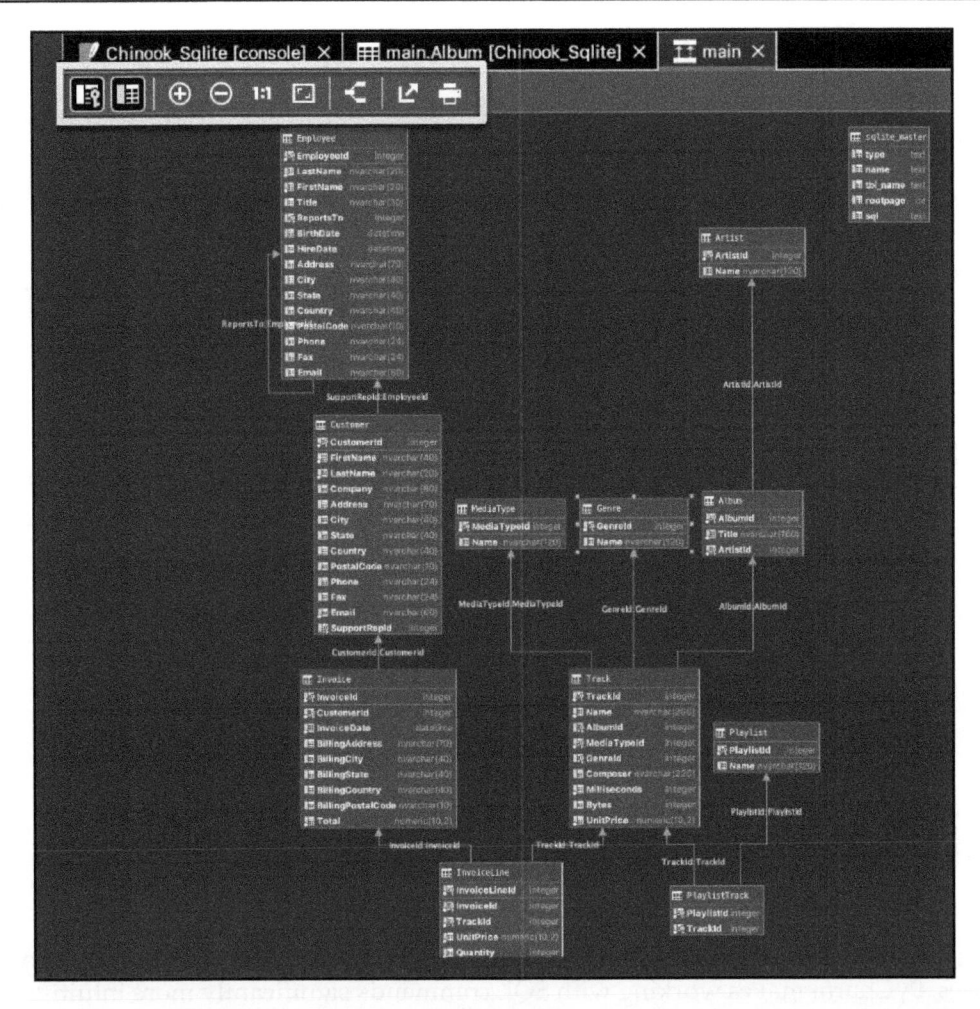

Database diagrams

The blue arrows in the diagram denote relationships between different database tables. Similar to the preceding diagram, most of the time we will have one-directional arrows indicating many-to-one relationships. For example, we see a blue arrow going from the `Album` table to the `Artist` table, which corresponds to the foreign key in `Album` that references `Artist`.

Finally, from the toolbar on top of a diagram (as highlighted in the previous screenshot), we can choose to exclude key columns or other columns from our diagram to obtain a simpler visualization. Various options to export or print the diagram are also included in the toolbar.

Diagrams for queries

While visualizing relationships between database tables is quite a convenient feature, PyCharm further offers the ability to create diagrams for your queries:

1. For example, in your SQLite console, enter the following query that asks for the title of each album in our database as well as its corresponding artist:

    ```
    SELECT a.Title, ar.Name FROM Album a, Artist ar WHERE a.ArtistId = ar.ArtistId;
    ```

2. Within the console, right-click on the command you just entered, and select **Explain Plan**. Doing this will open a new tab in the **Database Console** panel named **Plan**.
3. From this tab, click on the **Show Visualization** button within the toolbar on the left of the tab, and you should obtain the following diagram the corresponds to our query:

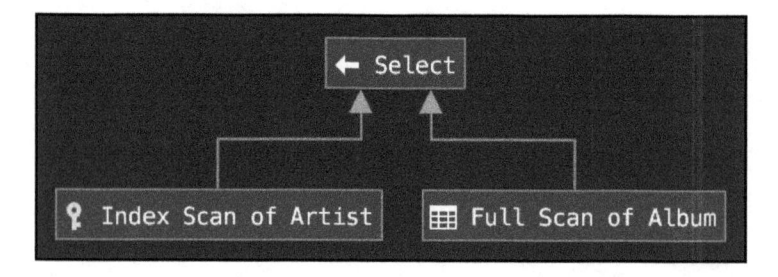

Visualization of a query plan

With this ability to visualize the logic of a query, which is especially valuable for reporting purposes, PyCharm makes working with SQL commands significantly more intuitive. Similar to what we saw with other diagrams, we can also print or export this visualization to a file using the corresponding toolbar.

Summary

We have thoroughly discussed some of the most powerful features in PyCharm that allow us to work with databases seamlessly. These include the ability to create, retrieve data from, and make changes to database tables via console queries and a graphical interface with the table view. Furthermore, PyCharm offers the ability to create diagrams that visually explain database relations, as well as query logic. All of these features combined help streamline the process of working with and analyzing databases and their relations.

By using the tools we have discussed, Python web developers can effortlessly interact and work with databases from within PyCharm. Given the important role that database management plays in medium- to large-sized web projects, this ability will significantly improve the level of productivity for any web developers using Python.

In the next chapter, we will conclude this part of the book on web development by walking through a hands-on example of building an actual web application in PyCharm. Specifically, we will combine what we have learned throughout the last few chapters to build a complete web project, as well as consider the process of deploying your Python web applications. This process will serve as the conclusion for the topic of web development in PyCharm, and it will solidify what we have learned so far about the different features and tools PyCharm offers to help us build Python web applications.

Questions

1. In the context of database management, what is a data source, and how do we connect to one in PyCharm?
2. What purpose does the PyCharm **Database** panel serve?
3. What is SQL?
4. What purpose does the **Database Console** serve in PyCharm?
5. How is the table view different from the **Database Console** in PyCharm?
6. In the context of database management, what kinds of diagrams can one make in PyCharm?

Further reading

More information can be found in the following articles and documents:

- *PyCharm official documentation: Databases and SQL,* by JetBrains s.r.o. https://www.jetbrains.com/help/pycharm/relational-databases.html
- *PyCharm official documentation: Database Tool Window,* by JetBrains s.r.o. https://www.jetbrains.com/help/pycharm/database-tool-window.html
- *What is SQL? Structured Query Language explained,* by Martin Heller. https://www.infoworld.com/article/3219795/what-is-sql-the-first-language-of-data-analysis.html
- *PyCharm official documentation: Creating diagrams,* by JetBrains s.r.o. https://www.jetbrains.com/help/pycharm/creating-diagrams.html

10
Building a Web Application in PyCharm

This chapter will walk you through the entire process of building a Django blog application from scratch in PyCharm. It combines all the topics that we discussed in the previous chapters regarding Python web development while introducing a number of new technologies from the Django web framework and explaining how they are integrated by PyCharm.

The following topics will be covered in this chapter:

- Understanding the model-view diagram in Django
- Working and interacting with a database
- The deployment of a Python web project

This discussion will help us tie in several important topics we have learned about so far in the context of web development, and serve as a conclusion for this section of this book. By the end of this chapter, you will also have a working version of a new web application in PyCharm that can also be extended further so that you can use it for similar projects that you might work on in the future.

Technical requirements

The following is a list of prerequisites for this chapter:

- Ensure that you have both Python 3.6+ and PyCharm installed on your computer
- Download the GitHub repository at https://github.com/PacktPublishing/Hands-on-Application-Development-with-PyCharm
- During this chapter, we will be working with the Chapter10 subfolder in this book's downloadable code repository

Starting a web project in PyCharm

To build a blog application with the Django web development framework in PyCharm, it is recommended that you follow the discussions in this chapter and create the project on your own system. That way, you will be able to experience first-hand the support options that PyCharm offers during the process of building the application.

With that said, all the code for this project is included in the `Chapter10/mysite` folder of this book's repository, which you can use as a reference point while following our discussions. If you are already familiar with the various topics we've discussed in this chapter, you can also simply make use of that folder as a base for your web project and plug in additional features.

Furthermore, note that I will be making many references to the topics we discussed in previous chapters regarding Django and general web development in Python. I highly suggest that you read through the previous three chapters on Python web development, especially `Chapter 8`, *Integrating Django in PyCharm*, which includes in-depth discussions about working with Django in PyCharm, before moving forward with this chapter.

With that out of the way, we will begin building our blog application.

Creating a Django project

As a refresher, Django is a heavy-duty, battery-included web framework in Python. It is one of the most (if not the most) common web development tools in the language. While there are multiple aspects in the ecosystem of a Django project such as the model-view-template paradigm, writing templates, and database integration, PyCharm can actually take care of a significant amount of the heavy lifting, leaving us free to focus on high-level ideas.

As we have seen in previous chapters, to create a new PyCharm project, we need to follow these instructions:

1. We can click on the **Create New Project** button from the welcome window, or go to **File** | **New Project** within an existing project window.
2. Within the next window, choose Django as our project type, `mysite` for the name of the project (as per Django convention), as well as the option to create a new virtual environment for our project:

Chapter 10

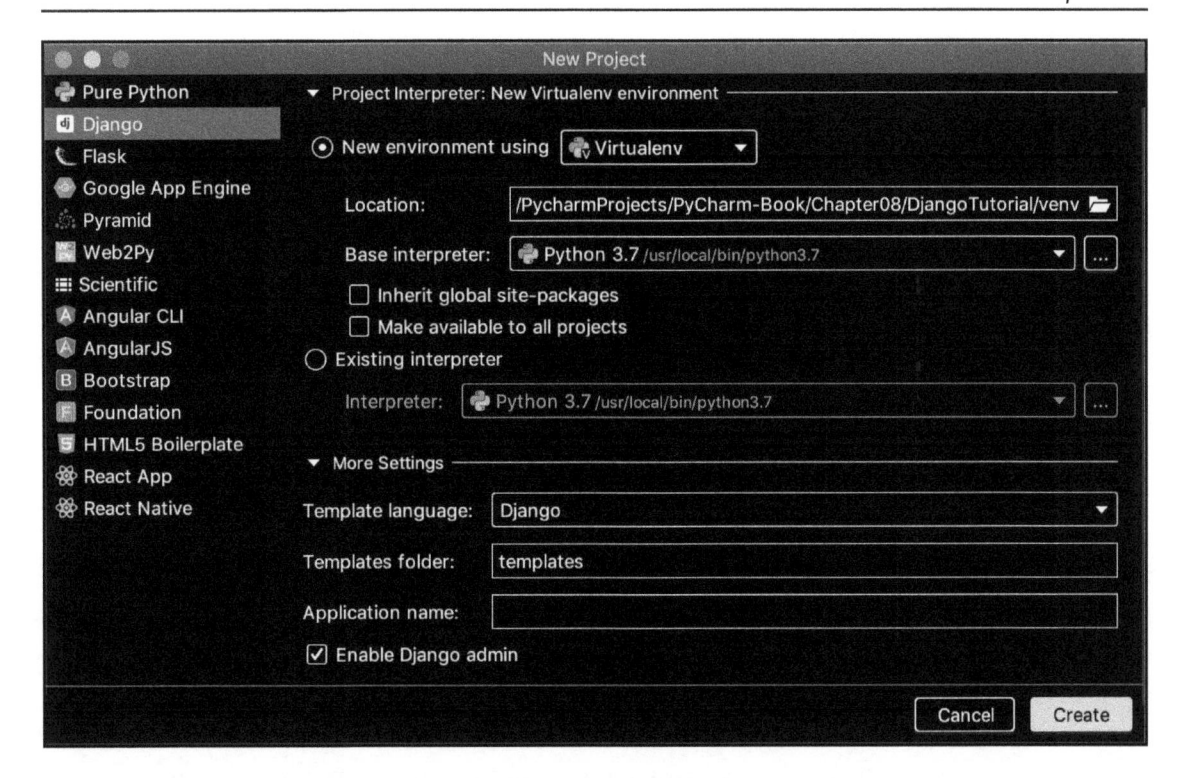

Creating an isolated Django project

3. As the creation of our new project finishes, our project window will open with two files, `mysite/settings.py` and `mysite/urls.py`, in the editor. For now, we don't need to worry about these two files, but feel free to keep them in your editor.

4. To finalize the process of setting up our Django application, open the `manage.py` panel in PyCharm (by going to **Tools** | **Run manage.py** task or by using its corresponding keyboard shortcut), and enter the following command to apply various initial migrations for our project:

    ```
    manage.py@mysite > migrate
    ```

5. Finally, we will run the server for our project to make sure everything is working perfectly. In the same `manage.py` panel, enter the following command:

    ```
    manage.py@mysite > runserver
    ```

6. Now, either go to `http://127.0.0.1:8000/` directly from your browser or simply click on the URL in the output of the `manage.py` panel. From here, you should see the following web page, which is Django's version of a `Hello, World!` program:

Django's welcome web page

That is how we start a Django project and get it up and running in PyCharm. In the next subsection, we will begin working on our blog application and its models.

Creating a Django application and models

In this section, we will implement our blog application as well as a Django model called `Post`, which contains the object-oriented logic for the posts in our blog:

1. First, in the `manage.py` panel, enter the following command:

    ```
    manage.py@mysite > startapp blog
    ```

2. This, as we have seen, will create a subfolder within our current project directory named `blog` with all the various Django-specific Python scripts for our blog application. Now, within the `blog/models.py` file, enter the following code (again, manually typing in the code is highly recommended):

    ```
    from django.db import models
    from django.utils import timezone
    from django.contrib.auth.models import User
    ```

```python
class Post(models.Model):
    STATUS_CHOICES = {
        ('draft', 'Draft'),
        ('published', 'Published'),
    }

    title = models.CharField(max_length=250)
    slug = models.SlugField(max_length=250,
                            unique_for_date='publish_date')
    author = models.ForeignKey(User, related_name='blog_posts',
                               on_delete=models.DO_NOTHING)
    body = models.TextField()

    publish_date = models.DateTimeField(default=timezone.now)
    created = models.DateTimeField(auto_now_add=True)
    updated = models.DateTimeField(auto_now=True)
    status = models.CharField(max_length=10,
                              choices=STATUS_CHOICES,
                              default='draft')

    class Meta:
        ordering = ('-publish_date',)

    def __str__(self):
        return self.title
```

This `Post` class (which inherits from the `models.Model` class in Django) implements the model for our post objects.

While most of the preceding code is self-explanatory, there are a few things we should note within the model:

- All of the attributes of the `Post` class (for example, `title`, `slug`, `author`, and so on) are implemented by Django's built-in classes. Once again, we can see the powerful features that Django offers when it comes to implementing complex data structures for our web applications.
- We haven't seen the `models.SlugField` class before in this book. This class offers a way to generate a valid and readable URL from other attributes of a specific class instance. We will look at an example of this feature later on in this chapter when we launch this blog application.
- The `author` attribute is a foreign key referencing the built-in `User` model of Django.
- Finally, in the `Meta` class, we specify that we want the order of these `Post` instances to be descending (using the minus sign) with respect to the `publish_date` attribute so that newly added instances will appear first.

3. Next, we need to register this new blog application with our main project. To do that, locate the `INSTALLED_APPS` list variable in the `mysite/settings.py` file and add the `'blog'` string to that list. The variable should now look as follows:

```
INSTALLED_APPS = [
    'django.contrib.admin',
    'django.contrib.auth',
    'django.contrib.contenttypes',
    'django.contrib.sessions',
    'django.contrib.messages',
    'django.contrib.staticfiles',
    'blog'
]
```

4. Finally, we will apply the relevant migrations and create a corresponding database table for our new model. From the `manage.py` panel, run the following commands sequentially:

```
manage.py@mysite > makemigrations blog
manage.py@mysite > sqlmigrate blog 0001
manage.py@mysite > migrate
```

While executing these commands, you will see corresponding SQL statements being used to generate our table in the printed output of the `manage.py` panel. With everything executing successfully, our blog application has been officially created and set up.

Using the admin interface

To be able to create and edit different blog posts in our application, the easiest way is to make ourselves a superuser and create those posts via Django's admin interface. Let's walk through that process with the following steps:

1. In the `manage.py` panel, enter the following command:

```
manage.py@mysite > createsuperuser
```

2. Django will then ask for the login credentials for this superuser. Simply input your information to finalize this process. Next, we have to register our `Post` model with the admin interface. To do this, go to `blog/admin.py` and enter the following code:

```
from django.contrib import admin
from .models import Post
```

```
# Register your models here.
admin.site.register(Post)
```

This script basically lets Django know that the `Post` model that we implemented should be included in the admin interface.

3. Now, we will launch the server by using the `manage.py` panel:

   manage.py@mysite > runserver

4. When the server has been launched, navigate to the `/admin/` site (typically `http://127.0.0.1:8000/admin/`) to access Django's admin interface. Here, you will see a login prompt:

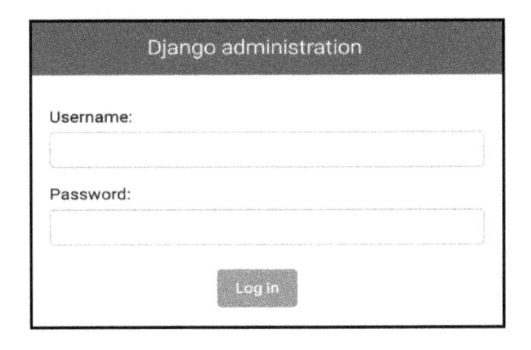

Django's admin login page

5. Now, enter the credentials that you used to create the superuser in *step 2*. You will be taken to your admin dashboard, which should look similar to the following screenshot:

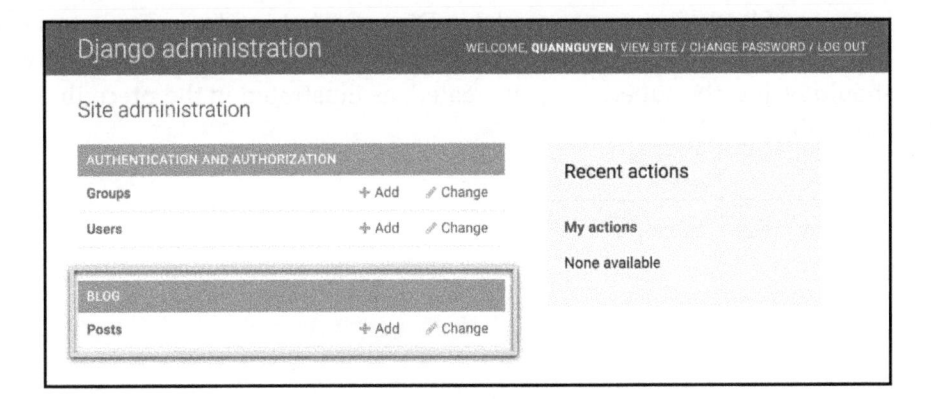

Django's admin dashboard with registered models

> Note that we are seeing a section named **BLOG** that contains `Post` objects, as highlighted in the preceding screenshot. This section would not be available if we did not register the `Post` model in the `blog/admin.py` file.

6. From the dashboard, we can now create an entirely new blog post by clicking on the **Add** button that corresponds to the `Post` model. To create a new `Post` object, we will be filling in the information in the following creation form (note that the user interface is handled by Django):

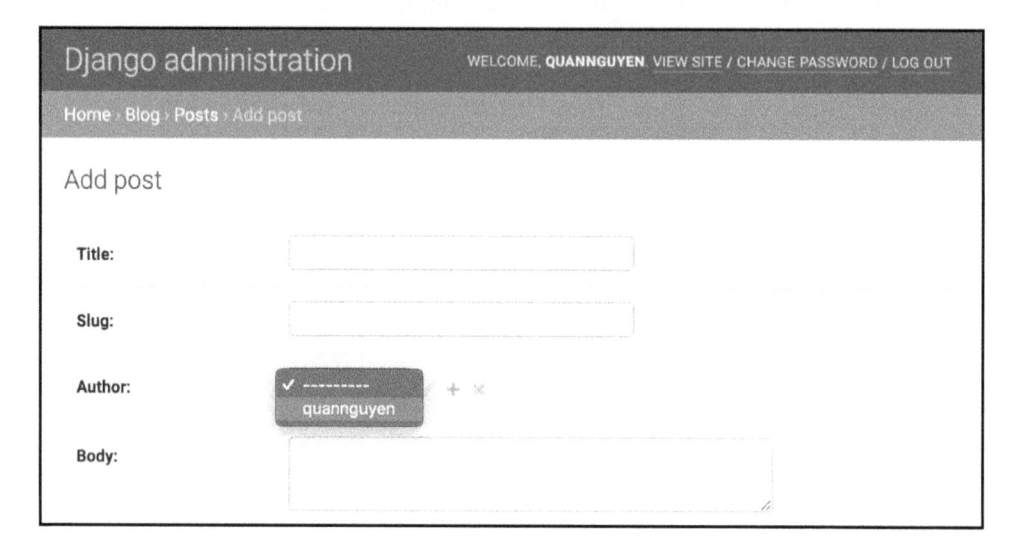

Creating a new blog post

7. Recall that each instance of the `Post` model has a foreign key referencing an instance of the built-in `User` model in Django. That is why we have to select the data for our `Author` field from a dropdown containing the valid users (which should be just the superuser you created, as illustrated in the preceding screenshot).

8. The same also goes for the **Status** field of the `Post` model, this time because we have specified the choices in our implementation in the `blog/models.py` file. Go ahead and create a sample blog post with any appropriate data that you'd like. For example, the following is what I filled in for my sample post:

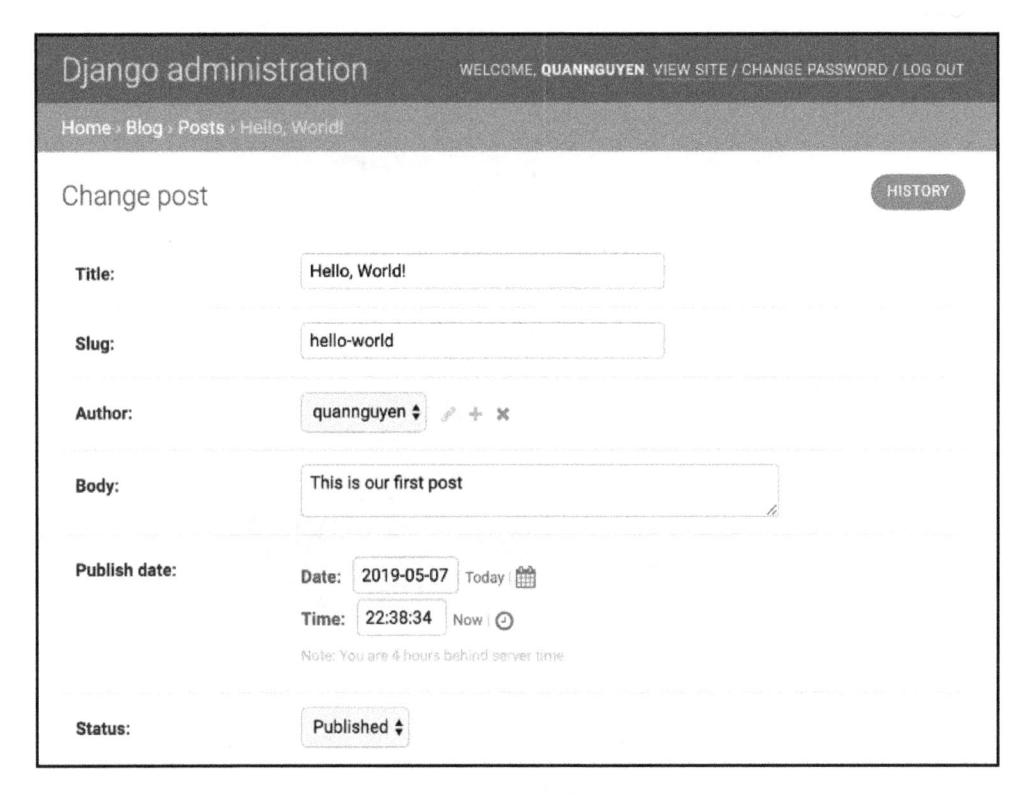

Creating a sample blog post

Note that we are able to customize the `slug` attribute of our `Post` object to correspond to its title, and I specified mine as `hello-world`. Again, this `slug` attribute will help generate the URL to this specific post later on. As you finalize the creation of this post, the data of the `Post` object will be saved to the corresponding database table. As such, we will consider the process of database management in the next subsection.

Building a Web Application in PyCharm

Working with the Database panel

In the previous chapter, we saw that the **Database** panel in PyCharm offers a convenient graphical interface so that we can interact with our databases. Let's see how we can do the same for our current project:

1. Within the **Project** panel of your project window, locate the db.sqlite3 file, which is the data source for our databases:

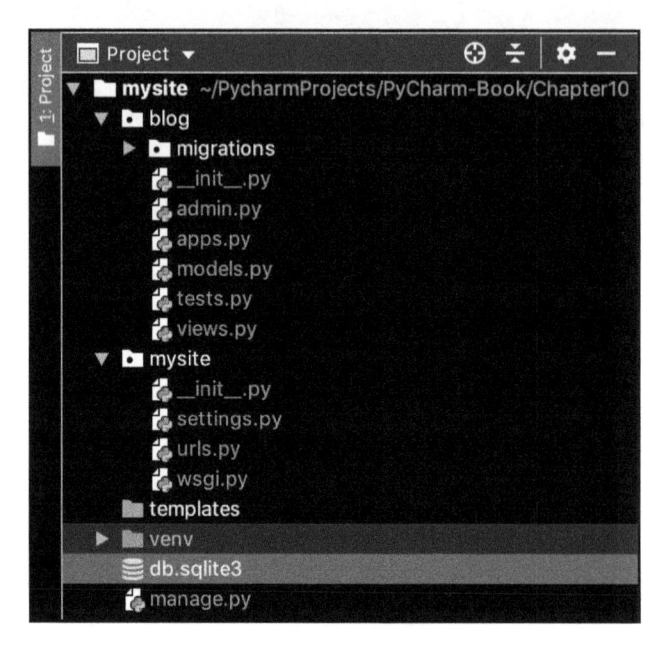

A data source file in a Django project

2. Double-click on the file and it will be opened in the **Database** panel. If you have walked through our discussions in Chapter 9, *Understanding Database Management with PyCharm*, it's likely that your version of PyCharm has been configured to be able to interpret the schema for this specific SQLite data source already. If not, head back to that chapter for the specific steps on how to do so.
3. After everything has been successfully configured, you should be able to expand the main schema of our current database, which will look similar to the following screenshot:

Chapter 10

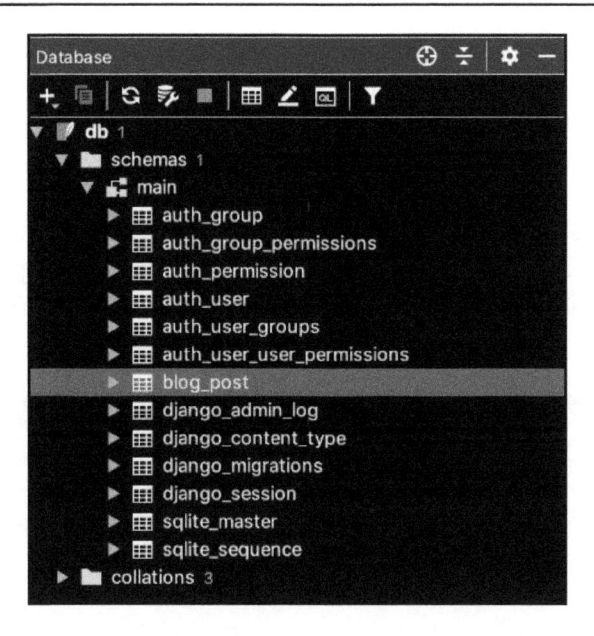

Inspecting a data source in the Database panel

4. As highlighted in the preceding screenshot, this database contains the table for our `Post` objects. Double-clicking on this item in the **Database** panel will open up the table view in our editor, which should only contain the post that we created earlier.

5. Additionally, we can insert a new entry into this table using the graphical interface of the table view by clicking on the **Add New Row** button from the toolbar:

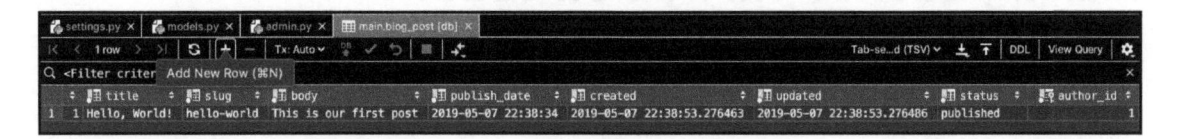

Adding a new database entry using the table view

6. After a new row has been created, you can directly edit the data in individual cells (except for the `id` cell, whose data will be determined by the database itself). Just like in any other table-editing software such as Microsoft Excel or Google Spreadsheets, you can copy and paste the data among different cells (which is what I did for the cells holding date-time information, from the first we entry created earlier to the one currently being created).

[285]

Building a Web Application in PyCharm

> 💡 **TIP**
> Also note that for the `author_id` cell, we have to input `1` to reference the only `User` object that we have created. Alternatively, you can also create another user.

7. Finally, click on the ![DB] **Submit** button (in the table view toolbar) to add that new row to your database. For example, I specified the second post in my project to hold the following information (note that `2` in the `id` cell was automatically generated):

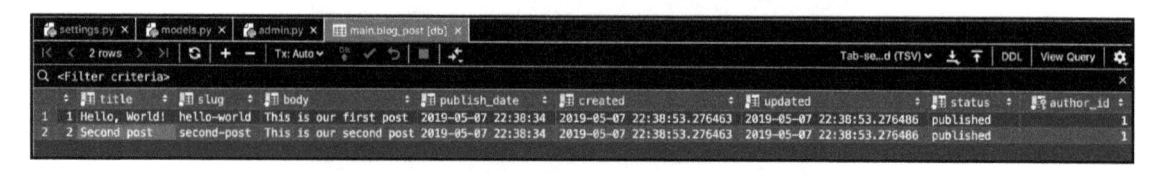

Editing a database table via the table view

8. Now, if you run the server again, go back to your admin dashboard, and look at the entries of our `Post` objects, you will see that this second post has been successfully added to our database.

That is how we modify our database entries using the powerful graphical interface that PyCharm offers. In the next section, we will look at how we can interact with and manipulate database objects using actual Python code.

Making queries via Python code

Database objects in a Django project can also be accessed and modified in a Python script using various Django APIs. In this section, we will automate the process of populating our `Post` database table using this feature.

We will be making Python queries to our database table via the **Python Console** panel. To access it, go to **View** | **Tool Windows** | **Python Console**. Now, we will create a few `Post` objects in our database manually by entering in the following code, line by line:

```
>>> from django.contrib.auth.models import User
>>> from blog.models import Post


>>> user = User.objects.get(username='quannguyen') # replace with your
    username
```

[286]

```
>>> for i in range(10):
...     post = Post.objects.create(
...         title=f'Automated post number {i}',
...         slug=f'auto-post-{i}',
...         body=f'This is the body of post number {i}',
...         author=user
...     )
>>>     post.save()
```

In essence, we are creating 10 new `Post` objects using the `Post.objects.create()` method (within the `for` loop). Each of these new posts also references our superuser, which is queried via the `User.objects.get()` method. Just like how changes to a database table in the table view are not committed to the actual database automatically by default, in order to apply these new posts to the `Post` database table, we call the `save()` method on each object.

Again, you can confirm the creation of the new posts, view the database table in the table view, and access the objects via the admin dashboard. So far, we have examined a number of ways to create and edit database objects for our web applications. In the next section, we will implement a view for these blog posts that we created.

Creating Django's list views

We briefly considered the creation of a Django view in `Chapter 8`, *Integrating Django in PyCharm*. However, there are a number of different options when it comes to designing a view for your applications. In this subsection, we will implement an aggregated view for multiple blog posts (a list view) so that users of the application can see and iterate through all the available blog posts in our Django project.

As we have learned, a Django view is defined as a function that takes in a web request and returns some form of response. The logic within the function specifies the data included in the response, as well as how it might be structured. First, let's create that list view:

1. Open the `blog/views.py` file and edit it to include the following code:

    ```
    from django.shortcuts import render
    from .models import Post


    # Create your views here.
    def post_list(request):
        posts = Post.objects.filter(status='published')
        return render(request, 'blog/post_list.html', {'posts': posts})
    ```

Here, we are querying all the blog posts we created whose status is also published. Then, we're using the `render()` method to send the queried list of posts to the `blog/post_list.html` template file. There should actually be a warning from PyCharm saying that this template file is currently unavailable (since we haven't created it yet).

As we saw in Chapter 8, *Integrating Django in PyCharm*, here, we can utilize PyCharm's Intention feature to automatically create this template:

Creating templates with Intention

2. Inside this newly created HTML template (in the `templates` folder at the root of our entire project), enter the following code:

```
{% extends "blog/base.html" %}
{% block title %}My Blog{% endblock %}
{% block content %}
    <h1>My Blog</h1>
    {% for post in posts %}
        <h2>
            <a href="{{ post.get_absolute_url }}">
                {{ post.title }}
            </a>
        </h2>

        <p class="date">
            Published {{ post.publish }} by {{ post.author }}
        </p>

        {{ post.body|truncatewords:30|linebreaks }}
    {% endfor %}
{% endblock %}
```

In the `content` block, we use Jinja logic to loop through the list of posts (stored in the `posts` variable) and display various pieces of information regarding each item. Each blog post also has a `get_absolute_url()` method that we will implement later on in our detail views.

> We can see several instances of the `block` keyword in this template; this keyword (together with the `extends` keyword) offers a way to define a section in a parent template that can be filled in (or extended) by one of its child templates. Here, `blog/post_list.html` is a child template of `blog/base.html` (as specified in the first line of code), which we will come back to immediately after this.

Now, let's work on the parent template (the `blog/base.html` file that we are extending from in the preceding file):

1. Utilize the Intention feature again or manually create the `templates/blog/base.html` file and input the following code:

    ```
    {% load staticfiles %}
    <!DOCTYPE html>
    <html lang="en">
    <head>
        <title>{% block title %}{% endblock %}</title>
        <link href="{% static "blog.css" %}" rel="stylesheet">
    </head>

    <body>
    <div id="content">
        {% block content %}
        {% endblock %}
    </div>

    <div id="sidebar">
        <h2>My blog</h2>
        <p>This is my blog.</p>
    </div>

    </body>
    </html>
    ```

    Here, the relationship of parent-child templates becomes clear to us: in `base.html`, various blocks are defined as placeholders so that the general structure of the template is specified, but the child templates can still fill in their own data in a dynamic way when they are used by the application.

> You might see a warning given by PyCharm at this point, indicating that we currently don't have the `blog.css` static file (which we are using as the style sheet for this template) defined yet.

Static files in a Django project can be CSS style sheets, images, or any other form of non-dynamic data that is used by individual Django applications.

2. To implement this static file, create a folder named `static` at the root of your Django project and create the `blog.css` file inside this folder. Since this style sheet contains various styling options that are not quite relevant to our discussions, you can simply copy the code from our repository to your own project.
3. Furthermore, in the main settings of our project (the `mysite/settings.py` file), add in the following code:

```
STATICFILES_DIRS = (
    os.path.join(BASE_DIR, 'static'),
)
```

This points the main Django engine to the folder we just created for static files. If, in the future, you would like to have multiple folders to store your static files (for example, if you want to have a separate folder in each Django app), then you can add the path to those folders to the `STATICFILES_DIRS` tuple variable in the same manner.

That's how we can create a list view and the appropriate templates in a Django project. Now, we will configure the URL of our blog application, as well as this list view:

1. First, add the following code to the `mysite/urls.py` file, which specifies that any URL that starts with `blog` will be redirected to the logic in the `blog/urls.py` file:

```
from django.contrib import admin
from django.conf.urls import include, url
from django.urls import path

urlpatterns = [
    path('admin/', admin.site.urls),
    url(r'^blog/', include(('blog.urls', 'blog'),
namespace='blog'))
]
```

2. As such, we will edit the `blog/urls.py` file further, as follows:

   ```
   from django.conf.urls import url
   from . import views
   
   urlpatterns = [
       url(r'^$', views.post_list, name='post_list'), # list view
   ]
   ```

The `urlpatterns` variable in any Django `urls.py` file specifies which view is associated with which URL. Here, we are saying that any time the base URL of the blog application is accessed, we will serve the `post_list` view. That is the entire process of creating a (list) view in Django.

To see what we have implemented, launch the server and go to the `/blog/` site. You will see the following screen:

My Blog

Hello, World!

Published by quannguyen

This is our first post

Second post

Published by quannguyen

This is our second post

My blog

This is my blog.

A list view in Django

> If you are wondering why we are only seeing those two posts that we manually created (and not the others that we created via the Python queries), it is because the latter posts were created as drafts. Recall that the default status for a `Post` object is a *draft*, and in our list view, we only query the *published* posts.

[291]

Here, we can choose to publish all of those blog posts by making the appropriate Python queries in the **Python Console** panel. Open the **Python Console** panel and enter the following code (line by line):

```
>>> from blog.models import Post


>>> for post in Post.objects.all():
...     post.status = 'published'
...     post.save()
```

With this code, we are essentially accessing each object in the `Post` database and changing its status to `'published'`, thereby effectively making it available in our views.

3. Reload the current web page and you will see that all the blog posts are now included in our list view. At this point, we are faced with another potential problem—as the number of published blog posts increases, our list view becomes longer and longer, making navigation more difficult.

4. Here, we would like to implement pagination for this list view so that all the available posts can be viewed and accessed across multiple pages. To do this, go to the `blog/views.py` file and extend our current list view, as follows:

```
from django.shortcuts import render
from .models import Post
from django.core.paginator import Paginator, EmptyPage, PageNotAnInteger


# Create your views here.
def post_list(request):
    all_posts = Post.objects.filter(status='published')
    my_paginator = Paginator(all_posts, 5) # each page will contain 5 posts

    temp_page = request.GET.get('page')
    try:
        posts = my_paginator.page(temp_page)
    except PageNotAnInteger:
        posts = my_paginator.page(1)
    except EmptyPage:
        posts = my_paginator.page(my_paginator.num_pages)

    return render(request, 'blog/post_list.html', {'posts': posts})
```

Similar to the powerful features offered by Django we have seen so far, we are using various Django built-in interfaces to implement pagination for our list view. Specifically, the `Paginator` class provides easy APIs to handle the backend page logic, and we simply need to pass in the number of items we want on a single page (in this case, it is five items). We are also using two different exception classes to handle situations where things can go wrong with pagination.

> Note that the `posts` variable that we are passing to our list view is no longer simply an iterator of `Post` objects; instead, it is an object that's returned by a `Paginator` instance.

Now, let's extend the HTML template for this view and see how we can utilize this `posts` variable. Add the following code at the end of the content block in the `post_list.html` template (right before `{% endblock %}`):

```
<div class="pagination">
    <span class="step-links">
        {% if posts.has_previous %}
            <a href="?page={{ posts.previous_page_number }}">Previous</a>
        {% endif %}
        <span class="current">
            Page {{ posts.number }} of {{ posts.paginator.num_pages }}.
        </span>
        {% if posts.has_next %}
            <a href="?page={{ posts.next_page_number }}">Next</a>
        {% endif %}
    </span>
</div>
```

This is to specify that if we are currently at a page that is not the first (determined via the `posts.has_previous` method), we will create a button to go to the previous page, and the same goes for the potential next page. We can also access the current page number that we are on, as well as the total page number (via `posts.number` and `posts.paginator.num_pages`, respectively).

We can do this because, again, `posts` is now a pagination-specific object, offering those mentioned convenient APIs. Furthermore, we can still iterate through this `posts` variable to access the individual queried `Post` objects. That's why we don't have to modify the Jinja `for` loop that we have in our current same template. This all goes to show the powerful features and capabilities of the `Paginator` class, as well as Django.

From this web page, if we were to click on any blog post, we would be taken to the home page of this blog application. This is because the URLs were defined with the `get_absolute_url()` method from the `Post` objects, which we will implement immediately in the next subsection.

Creating Django's detail views

A detail view is a way to specify what should be included and displayed on a web page. This corresponds to one specific model object. Here, we will add in the logic for listing and viewing the content of the individual blog posts that have been saved in our database. First, we need to extend the logic of the `Post` class:

1. In the `blog/models.py` file, add the following method to our current `Post` class:

    ```
    from django.urls import reverse


    class Post(models.Model):
        ...
        def get_absolute_url(self):
            return reverse('blog:post_detail', args=[
                self.publish_date.year,
                self.publish_date.strftime('%m'),
                self.publish_date.strftime('%d'),
                self.slug
            ])
    ```

    Here, we are specifying that when a `Post` object calls its `get_absolute_url()` method, we will redirect that request to the `post_detail` view of the blog application, with a set of arguments for the date-time data for that post, as well as its slug.

Chapter 10

2. As such, we will continue by creating the `post_detail` view (which is a detail view for individual blog posts in our application) by adding the following code to the `blog/views.py` file:

   ```
   from django.shortcuts import render, get_object_or_404


   def post_detail(request, year, month, day, post):
       post = get_object_or_404(Post, slug=post, status='published',
                                publish_date__year=year,
                                publish_date__month=month,
                                publish_date__day=day)

       return render(request, 'blog/post_detail.html', {'post': post})
   ```

   With the arguments passed from the `get_absolute_url()` method, we use the `get_object_or_404()` function to query for that specific post from our `Post` database table. This function offers a shortcut for implementing the task of querying an object with specific information or raising a `404` error if there is no such object.

   > Note that, in the three last arguments for the `get_object_or_404()` function, we add `__year` (with double underscores), `__month`, and `__day` to the `publish_date` attribute of the `Post` class. This is to specify to Django that we are only considering the year, month, and day of the `DateTimeField` object that is stored in the `publish_date` attribute of a given `Post` object.

3. Finally, we send this queried post to the `blog/post_detail.html` template, which has not been created yet. Again, utilize PyCharm's Intention feature to quickly create and open this file in your editor, and input the following code:

   ```
   {% extends "blog/base.html" %}
   {% block title %}{{ post.title }}{% endblock %}
   {% block content %}
       <h1>{{ post.title }}</h1>
       <p class="date">
           Published {{ post.publish }} by {{ post.author }}
       </p>
       {{ post.body|linebreaks }}
   {% endblock %}
   ```

[295]

Building a Web Application in PyCharm

This file is also a child template of `blog/base.html` (as we can see in the first line). Additionally, we specify the title of the current web page to be the title of the blog post in the `title` block while populating the `content` block with the appropriate information.

4. We need to specify the URL pattern for these individual detail views within our `blog/urls.py` file:

```
from django.conf.urls import url
from . import views


urlpatterns = [
    url(r'^$', views.post_list, name='post_list'), # list view
    url(
        r'^(?P<year>\d{4})/(?P<month>\d{2})/
        (?P<day>\d{2})/(?P<post>[-\w]+)/$',
        views.post_detail, name='post_detail'
    )   # detail view
]
```

In the detail view, we are using a regular expression to specify that if a URL is in the form of "`{year}/{month}/{day}/slug`", then we will return the `post_detail` view that we just implemented. This is also the last step of the process for creating a detail view for our Django application.

Next, let's see what we have implemented in action when the application is launched:

1. Run the server and access the list view by going to the `/blog/` page. Here, as you hover over the title of any blog post, you will notice that the hyperlink now contains the URL to the list view of that specific post. For example, the URL for the **Hello, World!** post is `/blog/2019/05/07/hello-world/`, which is also in the correct format that we specified in our URL patterns.

2. Finally, as you click on a specific blog post, you will be taken to its individual web page, which was not available until just now. For example, the following screenshot is the web page that I obtained for the **Hello, World!** blog post:

A detail view in Django

[296]

We can also see that by using the parent template (the `base.html` file) as a base, we have a unified appearance across multiple views in our blog application. Implementing these parent-child templates is a general good practice in web development, and Django facilitates this task very well.

Throughout this section, we have successfully implemented the foundation for a blog application using Django and PyCharm. However, there are still a number of aspects in building a functional web project that we need to discuss.

In the next section, we will see how we can implement a sharing-via-email feature in our current blog application.

Forms and emails

In this section, we will create a feature that lets a blog reader share a post with another person. Specifically, this reader will fill out a form, entering the email address of the person with whom they'd like to share the given blog post, and our website will send an automatically generated email to that address. This is a common feature in modern blogs and it will be a good addition to our web project.

Now, let's see how the share feature works.

Creating the interface for the share feature

We will implement the form feature, which, in essence, is another view in our blog application. To do this, perform the following steps:

1. First, create a new Python script inside the `blog` folder in the `forms.py` directory, as follows:

    ```
    from django import forms


    class EmailPostForm(forms.Form):
        name = forms.CharField(max_length=25)
        email = forms.EmailField()
        to = forms.EmailField()
        comments = forms.CharField(required=False,
    widget=forms.Textarea)
    ```

You can see that this file resembles a model declaration in Django; while the basic implementation is similar, Django forms are organized in the `forms.py` directory, separate from models. Here, we can see that, once again, Django offers an easy and straightforward API that implements the backend logic for complex tasks. In this case, this is for the input field for emails, as well as for specifying widgets for character fields (for the comments).

2. Next, we will implement a view for this form by adding the following code to the `blog/views.py` file:

```python
from .forms import EmailPostForm
from django.core.mail import send_mail


def post_share(request, post_id):
    post = get_object_or_404(Post, id=post_id, status='published')
    sent = False

    if request.method == 'POST':
        form = EmailPostForm(request.POST)

        if form.is_valid():
            cd = form.cleaned_data
            post_url = request.build_absolute_uri(post.get_absolute_url())
            subject = f'{cd["name"]} ({cd["email"]}) sent you a blog post: "{post.title}"'
            message = f'Read "{post.title}" at {post_url}\n\n'
            message += f'Comments from {cd["name"]}: {cd["comments"]}'
            send_mail(subject, message, 'quannguyen@mysite.com',
                [cd['to']])
            sent = True
    else:
        form = EmailPostForm()

    return render(
        request,
        'blog/post_share.html',
        {'post': post, 'form': form, 'sent': sent}
    )
```

Here, our new view, `post_share()`, takes in an ID number for a specific blog post (in addition to a request). Then, we query our database to obtain this post and check to see if it is indeed a published one.

Next, there are two possible scenarios/cases that we need to handle in this view:

- If the request that's passed to the view is a `POST` request (checked by the first `if` statement), then that indicates to us that a reader has submitted their data via the implemented form. In this case, we will retrieve the submitted data by wrapping the `EmailPostForm` class around the `POST` request and accessing its `cleaned_data` attribute. After this, we need to write the code that actually sends out an email to the intended receiver. From the submitted data, we obtain the appropriate information, such as sender name (`cd['name']`) and email (`cd['email']`), what specific post to share (`post.title` and `post_url`), as well as any potential comments (`cd['comments']`). Finally, we pass all of this information to the `send_mail()` method from Django, which will facilitate the actual process of sending the email. Note that I'm specifying the sender of the email to be quannguyen@mysite.com, which will not be the case for you. Don't worry about this for now, as we will come back to this point in the next section.
- If this view did not receive a `POST` request, we simply initialize a new `EmailPostForm` object to be displayed on the appropriate page.

3. As always, we will pass the processed data, along with the template that corresponds to this view, to a file. In this case, we are talking about the `blog/post_share.html` file, which hasn't been created yet. Simply use PyCharm's Intention feature to create and open the template in the editor. Enter the following code into the template:

```
{% extends "blog/base.html" %}
{% block title %}Share a post{% endblock %}
{% block content %}
    {% if sent %}
        <h1>E-mail successfully sent</h1>
        <p>
            "{{ post.title }}" was successfully sent to {{ cd.to
            }}.
        </p>
    {% else %}
        <h1>Share "{{ post.title }}" by e-mail</h1>
        <form action="." method="post">
            {{ form.as_p }}
            {% csrf_token %}
            <input type="submit" value="Send e-mail">
        </form>
```

```
        {% endif %}
    {% endblock %}
```

In this template, we are also handling the two cases that correspond to the logic we discussed in the view. The distinction between these two cases is stored in the variable that's sent (initialized in the `post_share` view), which indicates whether an email has been successfully sent from a submitted form or whether a reader is simply requesting a new form.

In the former case, we simply display an appropriate message indicating that an email has been sent. In the latter case, we render the form variable as a paragraph HTML element using the `as_p` method inside a `<form></form>` tag that contains a `POST` method.

Additionally, the `{% csrf_token %}` tag is a way to generate a token that counters **CSRF** (short for **cross-site request forgery**) attacks. Keeping things at a high level, we don't need to understand this point in depth, but it is important to remember that this tag is required in a Django application in any given form element.

4. Next, we need to add the link we just implemented in each detail view. In the `post_detail.html` template, add the following code, just before the `{% endblock %}` tag at the end of the file:

    ```
    <p>
        <a href="{% url "blog:post_share" post.id %}">
            Share this post
        </a>
    </p>
    ```

5. Finally, we specify another item in our list of URL patterns, redirecting any applicable request to the `post_share` view in the `blog/urls.py` file:

    ```
    urlpatterns = [
        ...
        url(r'^(?P<post_id>\d+)/share/$', views.post_share,
            name='post_share'), # share view
    ]
    ```

    With that, the interface for our share feature is complete.

6. Go ahead and launch the server and go to any individual blog post. Here, you will see the share button at the end of the post, as highlighted in the following screenshot:

The share button in the blog application

7. Next, click on the URL. You will be taken to the page associated with the share feature. Since we are filling out a new form for the first time (as opposed to submitting a form), we will see the following page:

A form element rendered in Django

This is when we can fully appreciate the powerful `as_p` method that we used earlier—our form element is automatically rendered with the individual questions (attributes of the `EmailPostForm` class) with the appropriate response sections.

Furthermore, since `name`, `email`, and `to` are required questions, you won't be able to submit a form if any of those questions are not answered. Similarly, `email` and `to` are email fields, so if their responses are not in the correct email format (for example, not containing an @ character), then those responses will not be accepted either.

Now, say you have filled out this form with responses of the correct format and click the **Send Email** button to submit the form. At this point, we will receive a `ConnectionRefusedError` exception, which has been raised by Django. This is because we haven't configured the backend of our emailing protocols yet. We will discuss this in the next section.

Configuring Django emails

In this subsection, we will finish the share feature for our blog application by configuring the underlying protocols for Django's emailing APIs. First of all, we will need to add a number of variables to the main `settings.py` file of our Django project, namely the following:

- `EMAIL_HOST`: This variable specifies your SMTP host server
- `EMAIL_PORT`: This variable specifies your SMTP port
- `EMAIL_HOST_USER` and `EMAIL_HOST_PASSWORD`: This pair of variables specifies the credentials for the SMTP server
- `EMAIL_USE_TLS`: This variable specifies whether a **Transport Layer Security** (**TLS**) protocol should be used

The values of these variables depend on your **Simple Mail Transfer Protocol** (**SMTP**) usage. If you already have, or will have, your own custom SMTP server set up and associated with this web application, you can simply input that custom information in the aforementioned variables.

If you are like me and would like to use the SMTP server of your email provider (in my case, Gmail), then you don't have to set anything up. Instead, you will specify those variables, as follows:

```
# SMTP credentials for emailing
EMAIL_HOST = 'smtp.gmail.com'
EMAIL_HOST_USER = ...  # your own Gmail address
EMAIL_HOST_PASSWORD = ...  # password to the Gmail address
EMAIL_PORT = 587
EMAIL_USE_TLS = True
```

Coming back to the code where emails are actually sent out, we now need to change the `post_share()` view in the `blog/views.py` file. Specifically, when the `send_mail()` method is called, change the sender address to the same address that the `EMAIL_HOST_USER` variable holds:

```
send_mail(subject, message, 'EMAIL ADDRESS GOES HERE', [cd['to']])
```

Note that if you are indeed using Gmail as your SMTP server, you will need to go into the settings of that specific Gmail account and allow external applications to access the account. This is required because Gmail automatically blocks unrecognized applications from signing in to its accounts; more information can be found at `https://support.google.com/mail/answer/7126229`.

Now, with everything set up, go back to the form and try submitting it again, this time sending it to an email account that you also have access to so that you can verify the receipt of the email. After the form has been submitted successfully, you will see the following message:

Email successfully sent

Note that the current page is still at the same address as the initial form (for me, it was `blog/1/share/`) and that this is the output that's produced by our template when a form is successfully submitted. Again, by using the if statement inside the view function, as well as in the template, we can handle the two cases we mentioned in one web page.

Furthermore, if you check the recipient email that you used in the form (in response to the **To:** question), you will also see the corresponding email that was generated by the submitted form. For example, I received the following email from a Gmail SMTP server:

Email sent via the Gmail SMTP server

And that is how a sharing feature is implemented in a Django project. Now, when a reader of your blog would like to share your content with others via email, he or she can do that using this feature via Django's SMTP protocols.

Note that, so far, we have only worked on and examined our web project in our local server (`localhost` or `127.0.0.1`). In the next and final section of this chapter, we will discuss the process of deploying a complete Django web application online.

Deploying your web project

To be able to make our website available for other people globally, we need to deploy our project into the cloud. In this section, we will discuss various aspects of this process, namely the different hosting services you can choose from, as well as Django-specific considerations when going to the production stage.

Hosting services

As you can imagine, there are a large number of hosting services that you can deploy your Django web project on. In this section, we will consider some of the most common methods to do so and weigh the pros and cons of each option.

Amazon Web Services

Amazon Web Services (**AWS**) is undoubtedly one of the biggest, most common options when it comes to anything cloud-related. In terms of hosting a Django project, AWS offers a powerful capacity for processing large amounts of requests and processing power. Additionally, as it is an extensive web service, AWS provides analytics and mobile tools that can be applied to your website, which will prove useful as the website grows in size and demand. Other advantages of using AWS include considerable security measures and a fast, responsive support team.

With that said, AWS can sometimes be quite difficult for beginner web developers to use as the options it offers come in large numbers. Furthermore, the amount of money that's charged to your account for using the service has been reported to be hard to predict, and sometimes users have to pay for more than they anticipated. All in all, AWS is suitable for medium-to-large projects that can take advantage of the extensive features AWS provides and require significant processing power.

Google Cloud

Another one of the biggest online computing platforms on the internet, Google Cloud also offers a way to host your Django website in the cloud. The advantages of using this specific service are powerful analytics and storage capabilities. A unique feature of using Google Cloud is the fact that you can integrate other Google products (such as Google Docs or Spreadsheets) into your website with ease; this is because Google's cloud platform is an overarching system extending to multiple tools.

Similarly to using AWS, you may find it difficult to predict how much you will be charged when hosting an application on Google Cloud. The service also doesn't have the extensive features and capabilities that AWS offers. However, if the Django website is a small- or medium-sized one, Google Cloud will be able to host it in the cloud perfectly (and most likely with a very small price as well).

DigitalOcean

Albeit not from a big tech company like the two services we've discussed, DigitalOcean is just as powerful and straightforward as those two. It is commonly utilized by web developers for its simplicity, responsiveness, and security. One notable aspect of DigitalOcean is that it's likely that it won't have any hidden charges that might surprise its users.

Overall, this tool is perfect for beginners as well as professionals with simple websites and processing needs.

Heroku

The last hosting service we will discuss is Heroku, a straightforward, to-the-point tool that you will find extremely simple to use. Even though some might call it too simple of a service for complex websites, Heroku still offers powerful features such as application rollback and analytics. Furthermore, Heroku works closely with GitHub, so you can integrate version control and the deployment of your web project with Heroku effortlessly.

On the other hand, since Heroku is intended for small-to-medium websites, it charges significantly more when a website grows larger; therefore, it is only really suitable for basic web applications and experiments. I personally deployed my first Django project to Heroku and I still use it today to run miscellaneous applications in the cloud.

The hosting services we've mentioned here are among the most commonly used platforms that you can use to deploy your web applications. Needless to say, there are other good services out there that I am not mentioning, such as Microsoft Azure or PythonAnywhere, that will host your Django website just as well as the other tools. In the end, your decision will depend on your needs, that is, the specific size and requirements of the website. Finally, you shouldn't be afraid to switch to a new hosting service if the one you're using isn't suitable.

Overall, choosing your hosting service is only the first step of the deployment process. In the next section, we will consider aspects that are specific to Django when our project is moved to production.

Production-specific settings

There are particular settings in our current Django project that we will need to change. In general, our current settings allow a significant amount of data to be leaked across various components of our project. This is because, while being developed locally, we can afford to have these settings the way they are so that the debugging and testing processes will be easier and more intuitive.

In production, potential attackers and malicious users might be able to take advantage of those data leaks. Furthermore, since no debugging or testing will be done in production, those settings need to be modified accordingly.

These settings are generally called the Django deployment checklist, which needs to be completed regardless of which hosting service you're using. They include the following:

- **Hiding keys and passwords**: It is no surprise that we shouldn't hardcode various keys and passwords for our project within the actual project code. This includes the secret key of our whole project (in `mysite/settings.py`), as well as any passwords and secret credentials that are used by any of our applications (such as the email address and password for our SMTP emailing server).
  One of the easiest ways to address this problem is to hide these keys and passwords in environment variables that are specific to the hosting platform or text file.
- **Disabling debugging**: Simply change the value of the `DEBUG` variable in `mysite/settings.py` to `False`.
- **Listing valid hosts**: Use the `ALLOWED_HOSTS` list variable to include the domain of the sites that will serve your web applications. Any site not listed in this variable will be rejected by Django if it attempts to access the project code.
- **Implementing logging**: As you push your fully functioning website to production, there is still a chance that it will encounter some error in the future. Make sure to configure your logging settings so that you can obtain the appropriate information after potential crashes.
- **Making views for errors**: We saw an example of a site displaying various pieces of information when an error was encountered in our earlier discussions. This is undesirable in production as that output might include important information that will make our website vulnerable to attacks. Instead, we would like to simply create an appropriate view for each of the potential errors that might occur.

To do this, simply create the following files in our `templates` folders: `404.html`, `500.html`, `403.html`, and `400.html`. Then, put in any error message that you'd like. Django will automatically know to use these templates accordingly should an error occur.

The aforementioned points apply for most Django web applications, but your project might have other particularities that need to be addressed. Refer to the official documentation from Django to learn more: `https://docs.djangoproject.com/en/2.2/howto/deployment/checklist/`.

Most of the time, the process of deploying your Django project into the cloud, including these Django-related settings, will be very specific to the hosting service you are using. However, most services have extensive documentation and guides that will walk you through the whole process.

This concludes our discussion on building an example web application using Django and PyCharm. Moving forward, you can choose to either create new Django projects while referencing what we have learned here or simply use the blog application that we built, extend it further, and add more applications to the project itself.

Summary

Creating a website in Django is an involved and complex process, but we have seen that PyCharm offers great support features that streamline various tasks in this process. In this chapter, we have considered a high-level view of using Django in PyCharm by walking through the complex process of building a blog application.

Most notably, we have learned how to generate the basic skeleton for the project directory when a new Django project is to be created, which includes various code-completion features that ensure the consistency between models, views, and templates in a Django project. Furthermore, there are multiple tools in PyCharm, such as the `manage.py` panel or the **Database** panel, that allow for a hands-on and intuitive method of working with swap components of a web project.

Overall, we can see that the combination of Django and PyCharm makes implementing a website and achieving those specific web-oriented goals easy. Now, you are ready to leverage PyCharm to create the perfect Django application for your website.

Building a Web Application in PyCharm

This hands-on guide also concludes the web development section of our book. Moving forward, we will consider the second of the most common use cases in Python programming: data science projects. In particular, the next chapter will examine various interface options and navigation aspects when we turn on *Scientific Mode* in PyCharm.

Questions

1. Aside from SQL queries and using the graphical table view, what is another option we can use to make changes to database records in a PyCharm project?
2. What is the significance of double underscores in the context of working with database records?
3. What is the significance of the `{% csrf_token %}` tag in a form element in Django?
4. What configurations are necessary for the main `settings.py` file if we wish to set up an emailing feature in a Django project?
5. What is the Django deployment checklist and what does it include?

Further reading

More information regarding what was covered in this chapter can be found in the following articles and readings:

- *Django by Example [Video]*, by Antonio Melé, Packt Publishing (https://www.packtpub.com/in/application-development/django-example-video)
- *Django official documentation: Managing static files* (for example, images, JavaScript, and CSS) (https://docs.djangoproject.com/en/2.2/howto/static-files/)
- *Modern Python Development with PyCharm*, by Pedro Kroger (https://pedrokroger.net/pycharm-book/)
- *Two Scoops of Django: Best Practices for Django*, by Audrey Roy and Daniel Roy Greenfeld (https://www.twoscoopspress.com/)
- *PyCharm official documentation: Django*, JetBrains s.r.o. (https://www.jetbrains.com/help/pycharm/django-support7.html

- *Django official documentation: Deployment checklist* (`https://docs.djangoproject.com/en/2.2/howto/deployment/checklist/`)
- *MDN web documentation: Deploying Django to production* (`https://developer.mozilla.org/en-US/docs/Learn/Server-side/Django/Deployment`)
- *Django Starts: Top 6 Django Compatible Hosting Services* (`https://djangostars.com/blog/top-django-compatible-hosting-services/`)

Section 4: Data Science with PyCharm

This section starts with Chapter 11, *Turning on Scientific Mode*. Data science is arguably the field that has made Python increasingly popular in the programming community in the past few years (and the trend is projected to continue further). This is why a focus on data science and scientific computing tools is necessary for any good editor/IDE for Python programming. This section is therefore dedicated to the analysis of PyCharm's support for various scientific computing tasks.

The chapters in this section will discuss the specifics of SciView, the unique view in PyCharm that facilitates scientific computing practices. The integration of widely used scientific tools such as NumPy, pandas, IPython, and Jupyter Notebook will also be discussed in detail. At the end of the final chapter, we will analyze the process of building a complete data pipeline for a Python project using various functionalities of PyCharm.

This section includes the following chapters:

- Chapter 11, *Turning on Scientific Mode*
- Chapter 12, *Dynamic Data Viewing with SciView and Jupyter*
- Chapter 13, *Building a Data Pipeline in PyCharm*

11
Turning on Scientific Mode

We are now starting the third main section of this book, *Data Science with PyCharm*. In this chapter, we will discuss the various features of PyCharm that support scientific computing and data analysis projects. These include a specialized Scientific Mode that streamlines the process of working with data structures, variables, and documentation.

The following topics will be covered in this chapter:

- Starting a scientific project in PyCharm
- Understanding the advanced features of PyCharm's scientific projects

By the end of this chapter, you will understand how these features can improve productivity in scientific computing projects. This chapter will serve as a general, high-level discussion on the various tools PyCharm offers and will help you understand scientific computing and how these tools are integrated and work with each other.

Technical requirements

The following is a list of prerequisites for this chapter:

- Ensure that you have both Python 3.6+ and PyCharm installed on your computer
- Download the GitHub repository at https://github.com/PacktPublishing/Hands-on-Application-Development-with-PyCharm
- In this chapter, we will be working with the Chapter11 subfolder, which can be found in this book's downloadable code repository

Turning on Scientific Mode

Starting a scientific project in PyCharm

Not all PyCharm projects are created equally; this is especially true for any scientific/data science projects. While examining the various features in PyCharm's Scientific Mode in this section, we will consider the process of starting a scientific project in PyCharm.

Additionally, all the projects and code that are used as materials during the discussions in this chapter are included in the `Chapter11` folder of this book's GitHub repository. Again, following the actual discussions and working with your own environment is recommended, but the files in the code repository can always be used for further reference.

Creating a scientific project in PyCharm

Similar to what we have seen at various points in this book, PyCharm has a whole project type dedicated to scientific computing. Let's see how we can create such a project:

1. From PyCharm's welcome window, click on the **Create New Project** button. Alternatively, if you are already within an existing project, go to **File** | **New Project**.
2. From the **New Project** window, select the **Scientific** item from the left-hand panel to create a new scientific project. Here, I am creating a project with the name `SciTest` that's in the `Chapter11` folder of our code repository with a **Virtualenv** virtual environment:

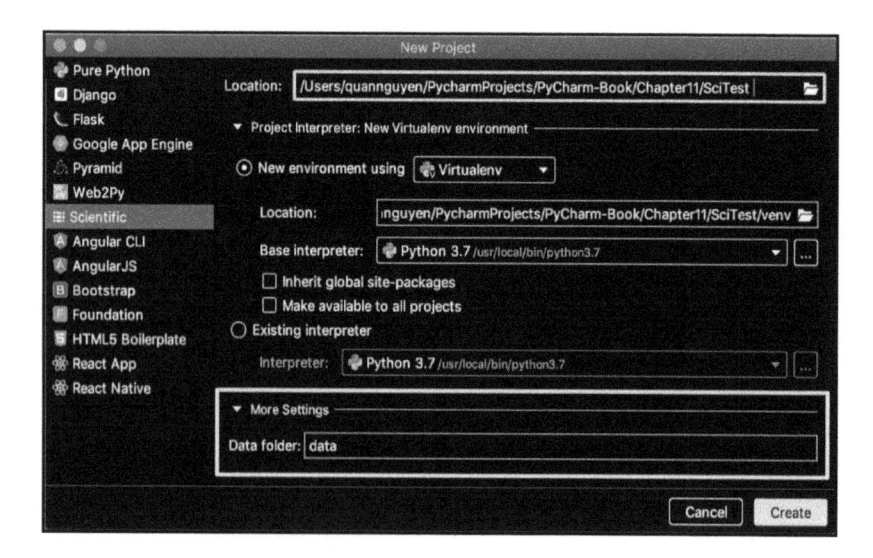

Creating a scientific project in PyCharm

[314]

> **TIP**
> Note that in the **More Settings** section of this window (as highlighted in the preceding screenshot), you can specify the name of the default folder containing all the data for the project to be created.

3. With everything specified to your preferences, simply click on the **Create** button to have PyCharm generate this new project. Once completed, the resultant project window will open. Let's explore the **Project** panel, which contains our current directory tree:

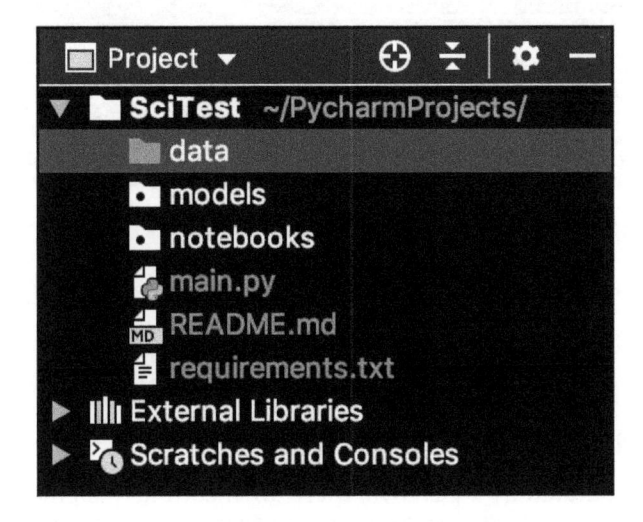

Generated directory tree of scientific projects

We can see that, apart from the boilerplate files (main.py, README.md, and requirements.txt), the three folders (data, models, and notebooks) that are commonly used in scientific and data science projects have been automatically generated by PyCharm. (A brief discussion on the README.md file is included in the next section of this chapter, just in case you're not familiar with it.)

Furthermore, the data folder is excluded from version control tasks by default; this is because this folder will likely contain significantly large files that are unsuitable for a typical version control workflow with Git and GitHub. In the last chapter of this data science section, Chapter 13, *Building a Data Pipeline in PyCharm*, we will discuss the process of applying version control to large data files in detail.

Turning on Scientific Mode

4. On the other hand, if you would still like to include the `data` folder in your version control and/or GitHub repository, right-click on the folder within the **Project** panel and choose **Mark Directory as | Cancel Exclusion**, as shown here:

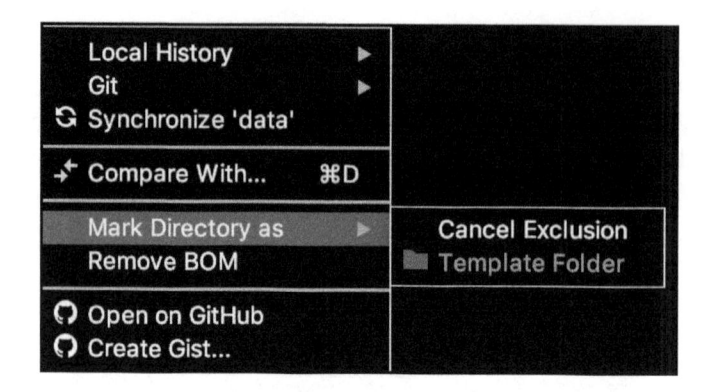

Adding the data folder to VSC

So far, we have learned how to create a scientific project in PyCharm. In the next subsection, we will explore the various aspects of our current project.

Setting up a scientific project

In the project that's generated by PyCharm, there are a couple of elements that we should pay attention to before actually diving into any specific development. First, we will consider the `README.md` file, which you might have already noticed among the generated files and folders within our new project (at the root of the project directory).

The README.md file

This is a markdown file that will be displayed on the main page of the repository by GitHub, as well as other cloud version control services. In other words, `README.md` is the summary of a given repository, and is used to introduce other developers to that repository using the markdown markup language.

To be able to take full advantage of PyCharm's support for markdown files, you will need to download its **Markdown** plugin (if you haven't already). Let's see how we can do that:

1. Open PyCharm's settings, go to **Plugins**, and click on the **Marketplace** tab. From here, you can look for and install the plugin by typing `markdown` in the search bar at the top of the window, as follows:

Chapter 11

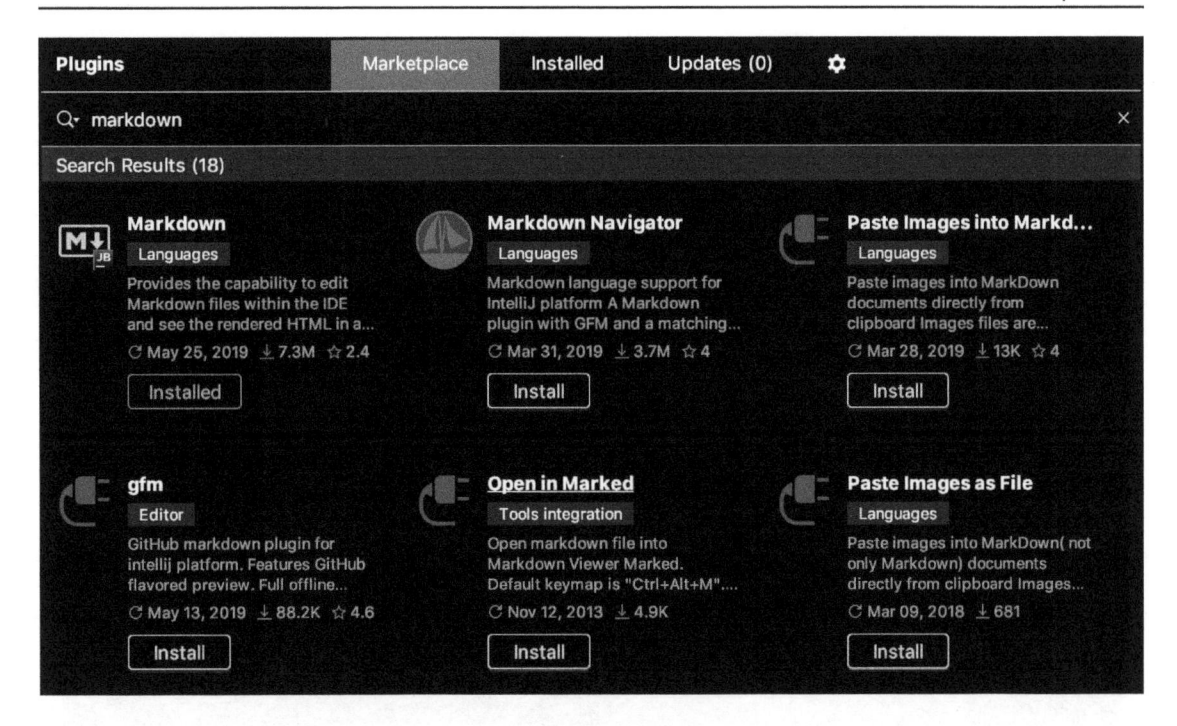

Installing PyCharm's Markdown plugin

2. Now, go ahead and open the README.md file in the editor. You can see that when a markdown file is edited within PyCharm's editor, the changes that are being made to the file are displayed in real time. For example, as markdown code is entered in the left-hand section of the editor (which contains the actual source code of a given markdown file), the right-hand section will display the corresponding output, as illustrated here:

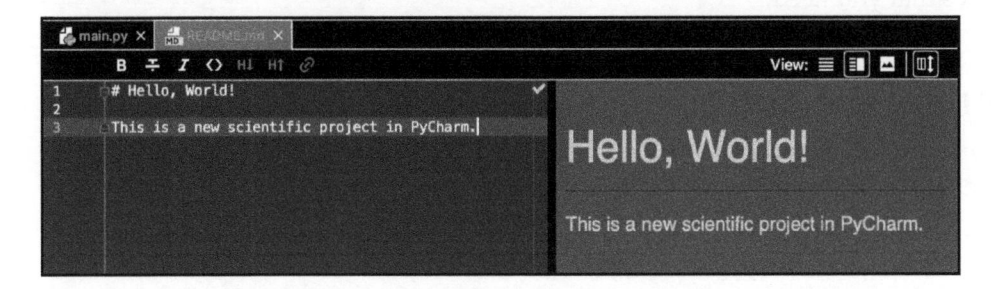

Working with markdown in PyCharm

Turning on Scientific Mode

This is quite a powerful feature that PyCharm offers, allowing for real-time markdown editing and adjusting. To find out more about the syntax of the markdown language, you can reference the cheat sheet at `https://github.com/adam-p/markdown-here/wiki/Markdown-Cheatsheet`.

Installing packages

Next, we will install two Python packages that are required for our scientific project: NumPy and Matplotlib. As a refresher, PyCharm offers various methods so that you can install libraries and packages for your project environment. You need to do the following:

1. Go to **Project** | **Project Interpreter** in **Settings** and use the graphical package manager.
2. Alternatively, you can open the **Terminal** panel and execute the appropriate `pip` commands.
3. As another alternative, you can enter the package names in the `requirements.txt` file and use the **Install requirements** button, as shown here:

Installing packages via the requirements.txt file

The same process can be applied if you wish to install any other external libraries and packages that you need.

Running the code

Following our discussion on working with a scientific project in PyCharm, in the `main.py` file, we will input the following sample code:

```
import numpy as np
import matplotlib.pyplot as plt


N = 100
x = np.random.normal(0, 1, N)
```

```
y = np.random.normal(2, 3, N)

plt.hist(x, alpha=0.5, label='x')
plt.hist(y, alpha=0.5, label='y')
plt.legend(loc='upper right')
plt.show()
```

Using NumPy, we are simply creating two sample 100-element datasets from normal distributions (x from a distribution with a mean of 0 and a standard deviation of 1, y from a distribution with a mean of 2 and a standard deviation of 3). Then, we draw their corresponding histograms using Matplotlib.

Now, execute the program. You will see the corresponding output appear in your project window, similar to the following screenshot (the histograms might be somewhat different from my own due to randomness):

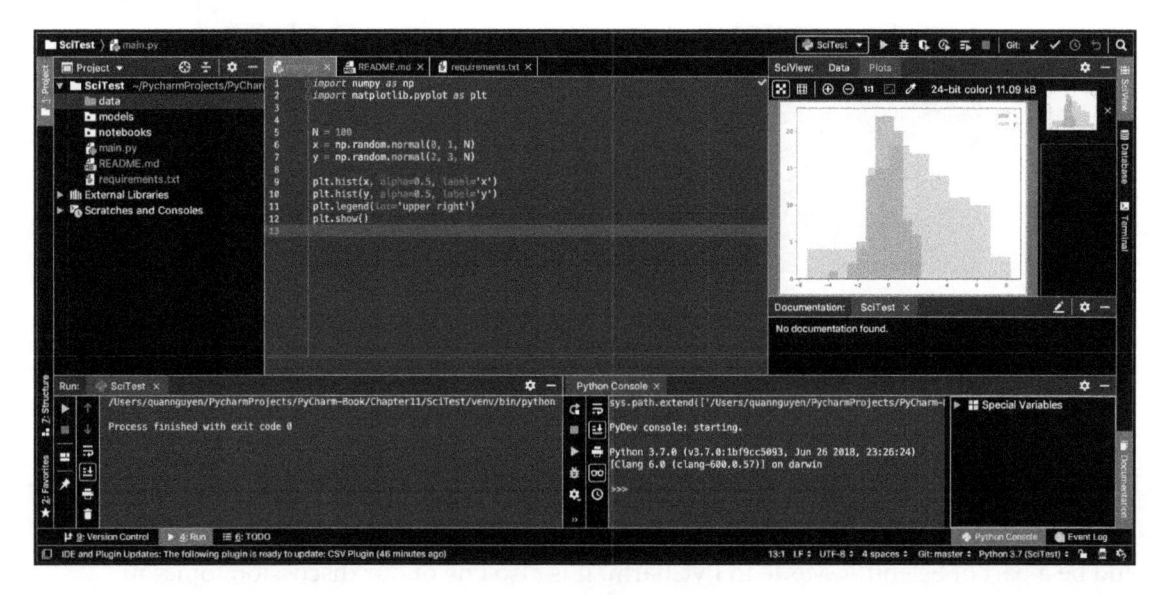

An example scientific project in PyCharm

Turning on Scientific Mode

Note that, by default, a scientific project might be run in the **Python Console** (as opposed to being run via the **Run** panel that we've seen in the previous examples in this book). Additionally, you can right-click on the background of the editor and choose **Run 'SciTest'** to run the program normally via the **Run** panel. You can also set the default run configuration of your project by accessing the **Edit Configurations** feature, which is located in the top window toolbar, as illustrated here:

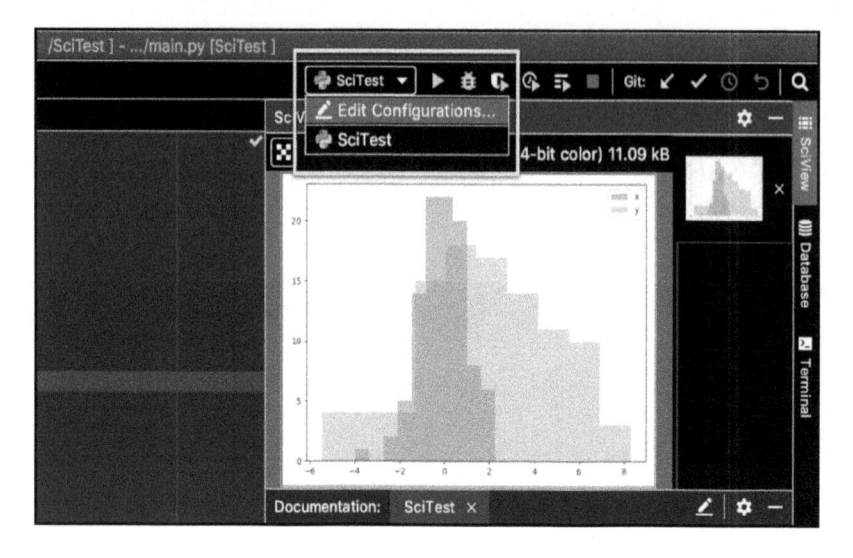

Editing run configurations in PyCharm

You might have noticed that the generated plot is being opened in a panel called **SciView**. This panel is a powerful feature that's specific to PyCharm's scientific projects. For this reason, we are saving it as a topic for the next chapter.

Additionally, we also have the **Documentation** panel in our project window. This panel is likely to be located directly below the **SciView** panel (similar to the preceding screenshot) and be a part of Scientific Mode in PyCharm. It is also one of our discussion topics in the *Understanding the advanced features of PyCharm's scientific projects* section of this chapter, but for now, we will consider Scientific Mode in more depth.

Toggling Scientific Mode

I have mentioned the term Scientific Mode a couple of times before; now, we will see the significance of this mode in PyCharm projects.

In PyCharm, Scientific Mode consists of multiple components that we will be exploring in this and the upcoming chapters, the most notable being the **SciView** and **Documentation** panels. It is important to note that this special mode in PyCharm is not equivalent to having a scientific project. Moreover, it is more of a configuration setting where various PyCharm features that support scientific computing are easier to access and use.

You might be familiar with the idea of a focus or distraction-free mode in Google Chrome (or even programming IDEs) where various components in a window are hidden away to maintain a focused, minimal interface. Scientific Mode uses the same idea, but the interface in this mode is optimized for scientific computing practices such as viewing variables and documentation. Specifically, it reorganizes the panels in your PyCharm workspace and displays the commonly used tools in scientific projects.

By default, this mode is enabled in any PyCharm scientific project, but you can turn it on and off by navigating to **View | Scientific Mode** from PyCharm's menu bar.

After turning Scientific Mode off in our current project, you will see that the **SciView** panel becomes a floating element instead of a pinned section within our project window. The **Documentation** panel is also hidden away when Scientific Mode is turned off. Turning it on again will restore these panels.

Scientific Mode can also be turned on in non-scientific projects in PyCharm using the same navigation. What's more, if you are using NumPy, one of the most common scientific-computing libraries in Python, and don't have this mode turned on in a project, PyCharm will even display a message suggesting that you use this mode, as shown in the following screenshot:

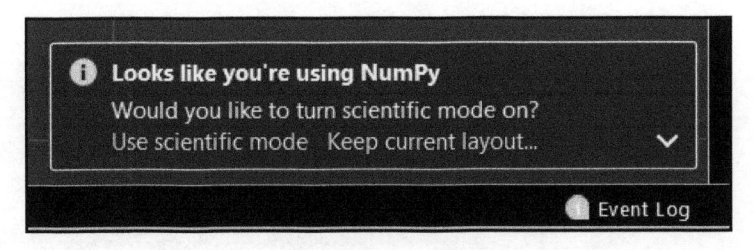

PyCharm's automatic detection of NumPy

Overall, Scientific Mode offers an intuitive interface that can improve your productivity in scientific computing projects. In the next section, we will examine other advanced features within a scientific project in more detail, namely the **Documentation** panel and PyCharm's code cells.

Understanding the advanced features of PyCharm's scientific projects

Equipped with the features we discussed in the previous section, you can navigate and work with PyCharm's scientific projects efficiently and productively. However, there are still other subtle features that PyCharm offers that can prove to be useful in this context. First, we will consider the **Documentation** panel and its usage.

The documentation viewer

As we discussed in `Chapter 4`, *Editing and Formatting with Ease in PyCharm*, documentation is an essential part of programming and software development, and PyCharm offers the most powerful and straightforward features to support the task of working with documentation in Python.

In a scientific project, the **Documentation** panel, as we have seen, is pinned as one of the main panels of the project window. This documentation viewer displays real-time documentation data in a dynamic way. Specifically, as you move your caret to a particular method or function call in the editor, the **Documentation** panel will show the official documentation corresponding to that method/function.

For example, the following screenshot was taken when my cursor was at the `legend()` method from the Matplotlib library (line **11** of our current code):

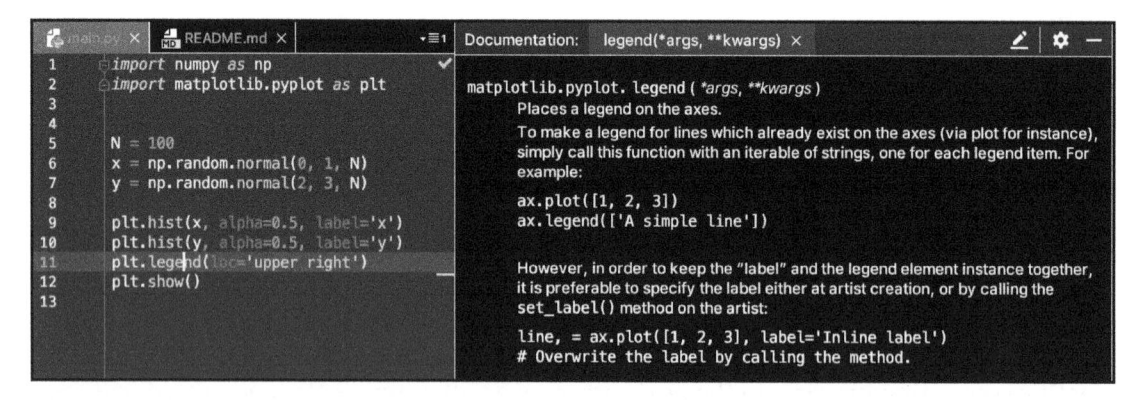

Dynamic documentation in PyCharm

This functionality is also applicable mid-editing: this means that as you type in part or all of a method or function, the **Documentation** panel will also display its corresponding documentation. Combined with an intelligent real-time code-completion feature, this **Documentation** panel allows PyCharm users to have comprehensive knowledge of what they are typing at a given moment.

Additionally, you can use the toolbar of the **Documentation** panel—specifically the Show Options Menu icon—to adjust how the output should be displayed in terms of font size or location and size of the panel. There is also an option in the Edit Source icon that allows users to jump directly to the source code of the method/function that's currently being displayed in the panel.

Next, we will examine a unique feature in PyCharm when it comes to executing Python code, that is, implementing code cells.

Using code cells in PyCharm

PyCharm's code cells are a way to separate and execute different portions of a large Python program sequentially. If you are familiar with Jupyter notebooks, code cells are, in essence, the bare-bones version of executing Python code (if you're not familiar with Jupyter notebooks, then don't worry—we will be discussing them in the next chapter). This ability is specifically valuable in scientific computing projects when different sections of a program are run in order, allowing programmers to follow the logic of the program in an incremental way.

Implementing PyCharm code cells

Code cells in PyCharm are defined by lines of code that start with the following characters: `#%%`. These lines are treated as standard comments in the low-level execution of Python, but PyCharm will recognize them as code cell separators in its editor. Let's see this feature in action:

1. In our current program, add those lines so that your program is similar to the following:

    ```
    import numpy as np
    import matplotlib.pyplot as plt
    
    #%% generate random data
    N = 100
    ```

Turning on Scientific Mode

```
x = np.random.normal(0, 1, N)
y = np.random.normal(2, 3, N)


#%% plot data in histograms
plt.hist(x, alpha=0.5, label='x')
plt.hist(y, alpha=0.5, label='y')
plt.legend(loc='upper right')
plt.show()
```

As you can see, we can actually put comments in these code cell separators, which will help with readability in the future.

2. More importantly, looking at the left-hand gutter of our editor, we will see several Run buttons at the beginning of each code cell that we defined via the separators:

Code cells in PyCharm

Now, we can execute individual code cells by clicking on the Run buttons in sequence.

Chapter 11

> **TIP:** Note that these buttons will execute the code they correspond to in the **Python Console** (as opposed to in the **Run** panel). Using these Run buttons will achieve the same effect as typing and running individual lines of code in the console.

3. On the topic of code cells, there is also a PyCharm plugin available for download that is dedicated to working with Python code cells. From the **Plugins** settings, you can search for and download the plugin named **PyCharm cell mode** in the same way as the **Markdown** plugin:

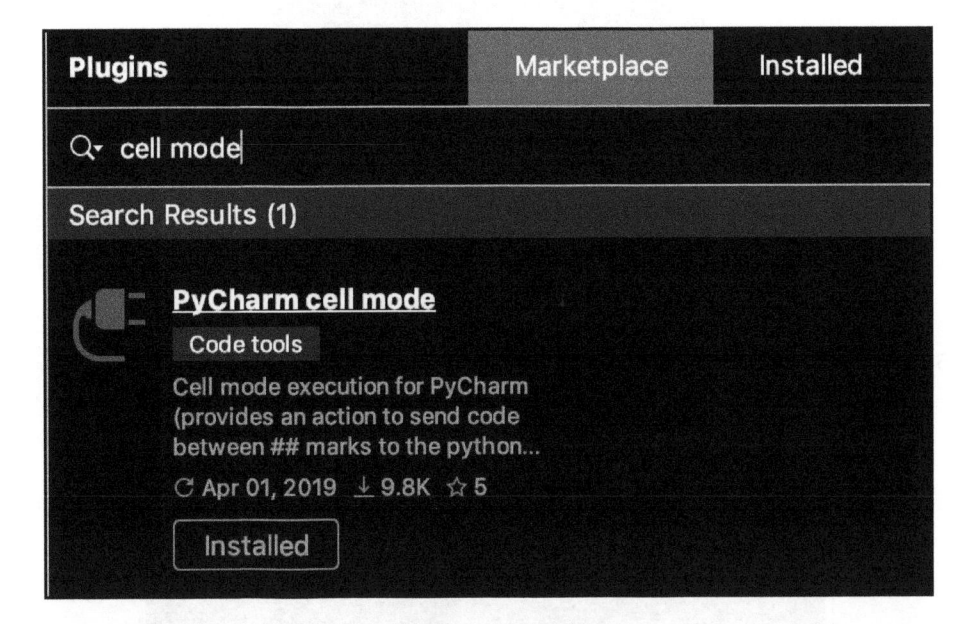

PyCharm cell mode plugin

This plugin provides an easier interface and more options when it comes to executing individual code cells. For example, you can simply use a double pound sign ## (no spaces) to indicate the beginning of a code cell.

Turning on Scientific Mode

4. What's more, when you click on a Run button corresponding to a specific cell, you can choose to either simply run that cell or to move to the next one afterward. The preceding screenshot was taken from the `cell_mode_test.py` file in our current code folder, which contains the same code that we have been looking at but with double pound signs to separate code cells:

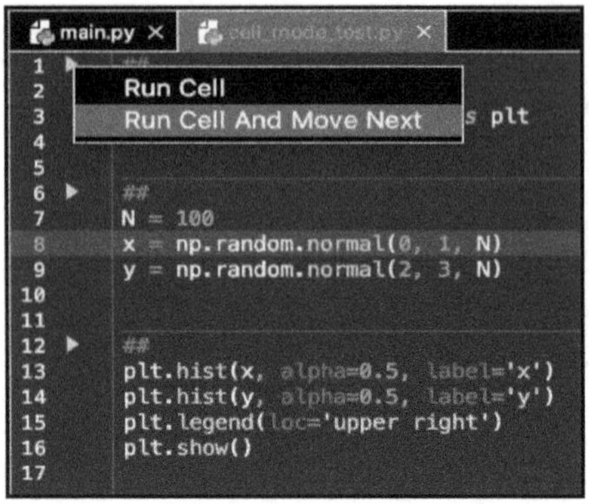

More options with the Cell Mode plugin

5. The **Cell Mode** plugin also offers even more options when it comes to executing your code cells. It's located in **Code | Cell Mode** from PyCharm's menu bar:

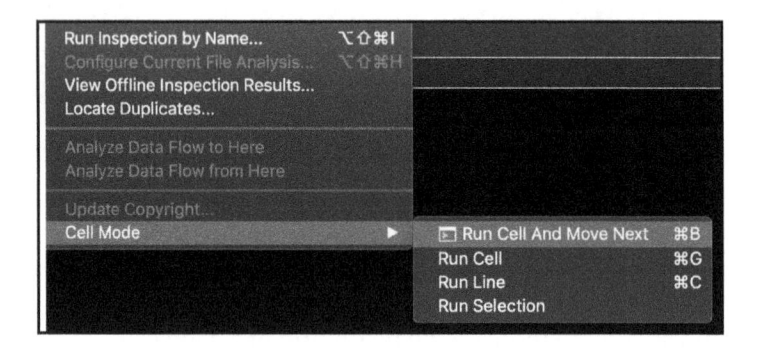

More options with the Cell Mode plugin

6. Another great feature that is accessible when we use these code cells is that we also have the option to debug the cells in the same way that we would debug a whole program. Specifically, we can still place the breakpoints in the gutter to the left of a code cell, as follows:

[326]

Chapter 11

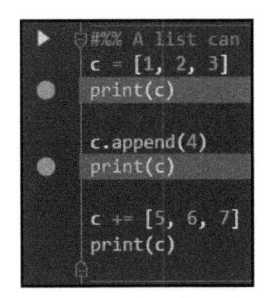

```
#%% A list can
c = [1, 2, 3]
print(c)

c.append(4)
print(c)

c += [5, 6, 7]
print(c)
```

Combining code cells with debugging

When this specific code cell is run, the program's execution will still pause at those particular breakpoints, at which time we can inspect the current values of our variables. Considering that, while debugging, we might need to narrow down a specific portion of our code and inspect the changes it makes to our variables, we can see that the use of a code cell in a debugging process perfectly helps us in that regard.

Overall, we can see that this plugin offers all the advantages of using Jupyter notebooks without having to actually switch to Jupyter applications (again, if you are not familiar with Jupyter notebooks, we will be discussing them in detail in the next chapter).

Working with CSV data

While working on a scientific computing/data science project, it's likely that you'll need to interact with datasets that have been saved in CSV files. In the context of examining the data within a CSV file, a simple text editor can only display that data in text format, which isn't very readable. On the other hand, software that can show the content of CSV files in a nicely formatted table (such as Microsoft Excel) can be quite troublesome to work with in addition to the current IDE or text editor that's being used for code development.

As the premier IDE for Python, one of the most popular programming languages for scientific computing and data science, PyCharm looks to address that problem by offering its own table viewer via the **CSV** plugin. This plugin allows us to inspect CSV files in formatted tables within PyCharm's editor.

First, we need to install the plugin since it doesn't come with PyCharm by default. Similar to the process of installing the **Markdown** plugin in the previous section of this chapter, you can go to the **Plugins** section in **Settings** to have the **CSV** plugin installed in your version of PyCharm.

Using the CSV plugin

To see the **CSV** plugin in action, let's consider a sample CSV file:

1. In the `data` folder of our current project code folder, open the `sample.csv` file in PyCharm's editor (alternatively, you can also use any other CSV file that you'd like). The `sample.csv` file contains the following sample data:

   ```
   a,b,c
   1,2,3
   4,5,6
   ```

2. With the file open in the editor, you will see that the preceding raw data is displayed by default in **Text** mode. However, if we were to switch to **Table Editor** mode (using the navigation bar at the bottom of the editor, as highlighted in the following screenshot), we would be taken to the graphical display of the table data:

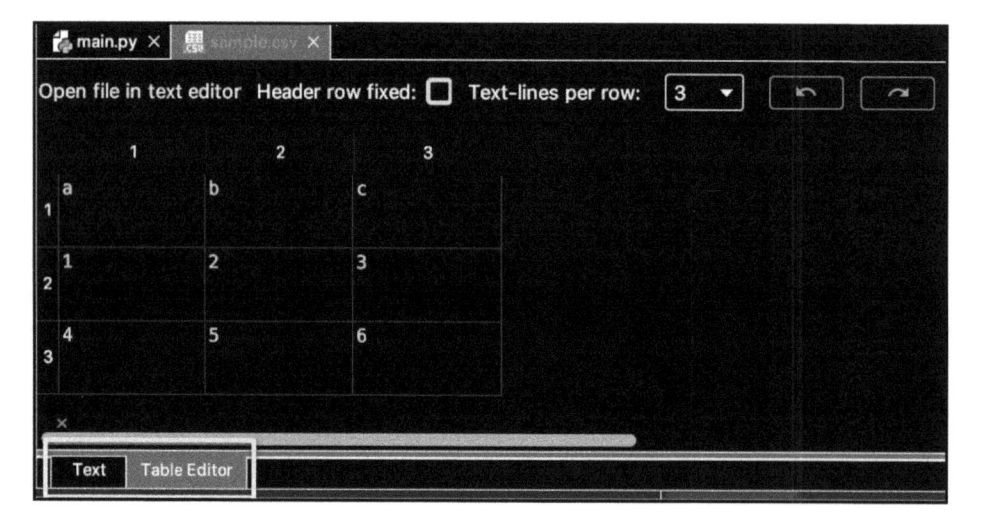

The table editor in PyCharm

3. As you can see, the CSV data being displayed in the formatted table will allow data scientists to inspect their data better.

4. Furthermore, you can edit the content of the considered CSV file by clicking on the individual cells of the displayed table and directly changing their values. This method of altering the data in a CSV file is considerably better than doing so via a text editor, where it could be quite difficult to identify which column a specific data point belongs to.

5. The toolbar at the top of this **Table Editor** also allows for various navigation and display options. For example, the **Header row fixed** checkbox specifies whether the first row should be used as the header of the table, while adjusting the number in the **Text-lines per row** prompt will change how compact or loose the rows appear.
6. Finally, it is also possible to work with files in other delimiter-separated formats such as **tab-separated values** (**TSV**) in the same manner. However, most data files are formatted to CSV in data science projects, so chances are, you will only need to worry about CSV files.

> **TIP**
> Note that one potential downside to using the **CSV** plugin is that it is unable to parse extremely large files (for obvious reasons). Most of the time, the plugin can handle tens of thousands of CSV rows, so most scientific computing/data science projects will have no problem taking advantage of the **CSV** plugin.

The **Table Editor** is also the last feature we will consider in this chapter regarding PyCharm's Scientific Mode. In general, by combining and using the features we have discussed simultaneously in a scientific computing/data science project, we gain the dynamic ability to view and work with both the code and the data within the project.

Summary

A scientific project in PyCharm is created with a general structure that is common among projects in real life, including good practices such as a `data` folder that is excluded from version control, the `README.md` file, and the `requirements.txt` file. As you can imagine, having to manually create this setup for every project can prove to be difficult and time-consuming. This feature helps PyCharm users get right down to the development process after the project has been created so that they don't have to worry about taking care of miscellaneous details. This will allow us to be faster and more productive in our development workflow.

Additionally, PyCharm's Scientific Mode includes various features that support the development process of scientific computing or data science projects, namely the **Documentation** and **SciView** panels. In combination with this mode, you can also take advantage of other powerful features, such as code cells and the **CSV** plugin, to streamline various tasks and effectively improve your productivity in data science projects.

However, these features only mark the beginning of what PyCharm has to offer when assisting us in data-related projects. Building on these topics, in the next chapter, we will look into the usage of the **SciView** panel and Jupyter notebooks, which are a big part of the Python data science ecosystem within PyCharm.

Questions

1. What is the markdown language? What purpose does a `README.md` file in a GitHub repository serve?
2. Why is the `data` folder in a scientific project in PyCharm excluded from version control?
3. How can you turn Scientific Mode on and off in PyCharm? What effect will this have on a given project window?
4. What features are available within PyCharm's **Documentation** panel?
5. What are code cells in PyCharm and how can you implement them?
6. What features are available within the **CSV** plugin in PyCharm?

Further reading

More information regarding the subjects we covered in this chapter can be found in the following articles:

- *JetBrains official documentation: Scientific Mode*, JetBrains s.r.o. (`www.jetbrains.com/help/pycharm/matplotlib-support.html`)
- *Mastering PyCharm* online course, by Michael Kennedy, `https://training.talkpython.fm/courses/explore_pycharm/mastering-pycharm-ide`
- *JetBrains official documentation: Scientific Tools*, JetBrains s.r.o. (`www.jetbrains.com/help/pycharm/scientific-tools.html`)
- *JetBrains official documentation: Editing CSV and TSV files as tables*, JetBrains s.r.o. (`www.jetbrains.com/help/pycharm/editing-csv-and-tsv-files.html`)
- *NumPy official documentation home page*, SciPy.org (`https://docs.scipy.org/doc/`)

12
Dynamic Data Viewing with SciView and Jupyter

This chapter walks you through two of the most important functionalities of PyCharm in the context of data science projects—the **SciView** panel and Jupyter notebooks. Both of these functionalities offer a great interface so that we can view and work with the data and variables we have in a given data science project.

First, we will discuss the process of using the **SciView** panel, another PyCharm-specific panel or window tool, to inspect common data science-related data structures such as NumPy arrays and Pandas DataFrames. We will then learn about the integration of interactive Python computing tools such as Jupyter notebooks in PyCharm and how to use them in our own projects.

The following topics will be covered in this chapter:

- Viewing and interacting with data via the **SciView** panel
- Understanding the integration of **Interactive Python** (**IPython**) within PyCharm
- Using Jupyter notebooks for interactive programming, especially in a PyCharm project

By the end of this chapter, you will be armed with the knowledge of how to integrate PyCharm into your scientific computing workflow using two of its most powerful features—the **SciView** panel and support for Jupyter.

Dynamic Data Viewing with SciView and Jupyter

Technical requirements

The following is a list of prerequisites for this chapter:

- Ensure that you have both Python 3.6+ and PyCharm installed on your computer
- Download this book's GitHub repository at https://github.com/PacktPublishing/Hands-on-Application-Development-with-PyCharm
- You need to know how to install NumPy, Pandas, and Matplotlib in a Python project
- In this chapter, we will be working with the subfolder named Chapter12 from this book's downloaded code repository

Data viewing made easy with PyCharm's SciView

We already encountered the **SciView** panel in PyCharm briefly in the previous chapter. In this section, we will fully explore the support for data-related tasks offered by this feature. By the end of this section, I hope you will be able to appreciate the **SciView** panel, which I personally consider to be PyCharm's best feature when it comes to scientific computing and data science projects.

The code example we will be working with in this section is included in the Chapter12/SciViewPanel folder of our code repository and looks as follows. In essence, this program is the same as the one we were working with in the previous chapter.

However, instead of simply plotting the histogram to indicate the distribution of the x and y variables once, here, we will randomly generate x and y five times using the range function and draw the corresponding histogram at each iteration of the for loop, as we will see immediately after this section:

```
import numpy as np
import matplotlib.pyplot as plt


N = 100
for _ in range(5):
    x = np.random.normal(0, 1, N)
    y = np.random.normal(2, 3, N)

    plt.hist(x, alpha=0.5, label='x')
    plt.hist(y, alpha=0.5, label='y')
```

```
plt.legend(loc='upper right')
plt.show()
```

> **TIP**: Note that, as per Python's best practices, we are assigning the iterator to _ in our `for` loop since we don't need that value anywhere.

We will be using this program to examine various features in the next section, starting with a more in-depth look at the **Plots** tab of the **SciView** panel.

Viewing and working with plots

The **Plots** tab offers a convenient way to browse through and manage any and all plots that are generated by our Python programs. Now, let's see it in action by executing our current program to generate the plots.

Note that, in order to take full advantage of the various features we are discussing, we will run this program in the console. To do this, right-click on the background of your editor and choose the **Run File in Console** option. As the program executes, you will see that the histograms that Matplotlib generates are included in the **SciView** panel, specifically in its **Plots** tab (as highlighted here):

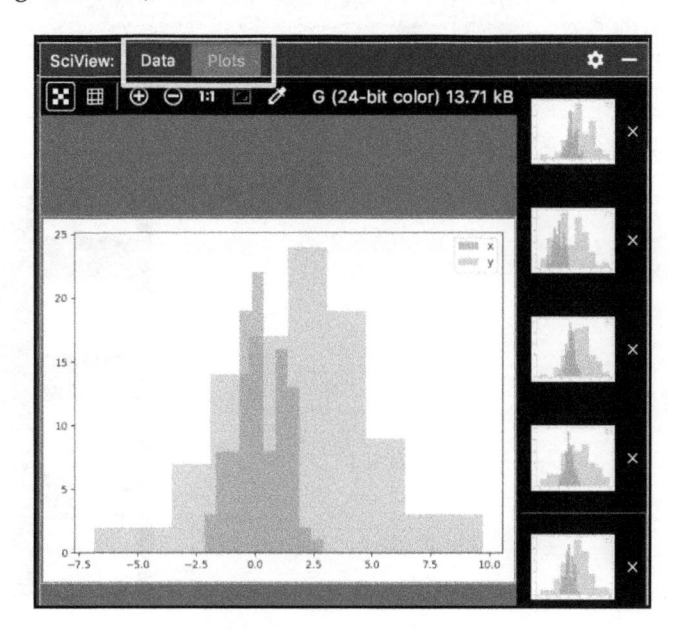

Viewing plots in PyCharm's SciView panel

Dynamic Data Viewing with SciView and Jupyter

The first thing you will notice here is that each time a plot was generated, its output was appended and shown to the **SciView** panel, and the program continued its execution. In the end, we were left with a whole array of plots, which you can navigate through by clicking on the different icons on the right-hand side of the panel.

The same program, when running via a traditional Python interpreter, would pause to display each of the generated plots and only move on after any interaction from the user (typically, when the *Q* key is pressed). This is because `plt.show()`, by default, blocks the execution of any program that contains the method call.

Here, our program ran in one go and all the generated plots were saved to the **SciView** panel. This feature is more useful than some might think. For example, when we want to generate a large number of plots that will be viewed and compared with one another, the way PyCharm handles the execution is optimal for that purpose. When using a regular Python interpreter, we would need to save the plots to files manually to achieve the same effect.

Getting back to the **SciView** panel, as you click on and display a given plot, you also have the option to zoom in and out using the toolbar at the top of the panel, remove the plot from view using the *X* button to the right of its icon, or save the plot to an image file, or remove all the plots from view by right-clicking on the plot icon, as follows:

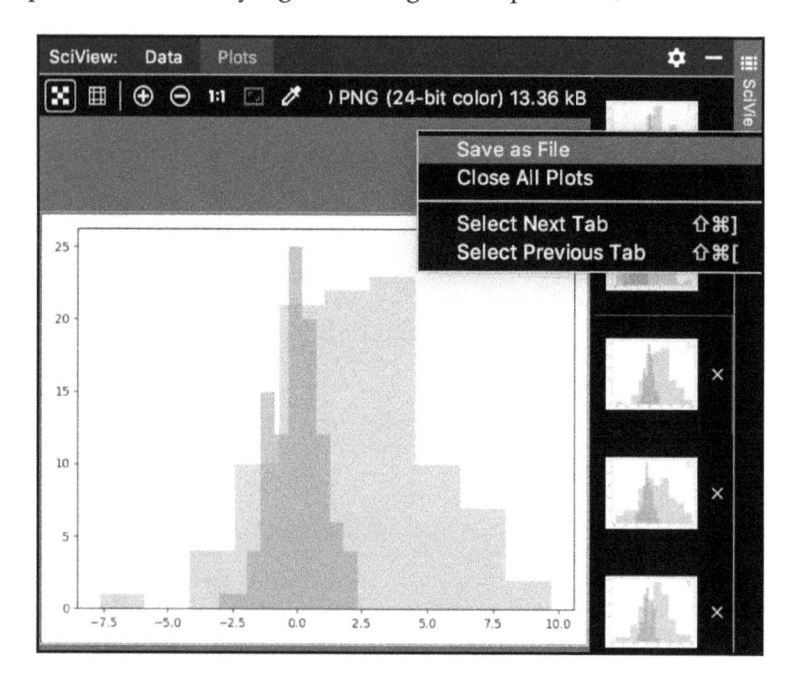

More options for working with plots in PyCharm

[334]

Chapter 12

Working with plots in PyCharm via the **SciView** panel is arguably better than interacting with a bare-bones Python interpreter, for many reasons that we have already discussed. However, this is not the only use for the **SciView** panel. We have mentioned that all the plots that are generated by our Python program are included in the **Plots** tab of the **SciView** panel. The other tab, as you might have noticed, is the **Data** tab, which we will discuss in the next subsection.

Viewing and working with data

The **Data** tab offers us a nice and clean way to inspect the values of the variables in the Python program. In the following steps, we will explore its capabilities with our example program:

1. First, let's shift our attention to the **Python Console** panel, which appeared (most likely) at the bottom of the project window when we ran our program in the console. On the right-hand side of the panel, we can see a section that lists all the variables in our program and their respective values. Our variables should look similar to the following:

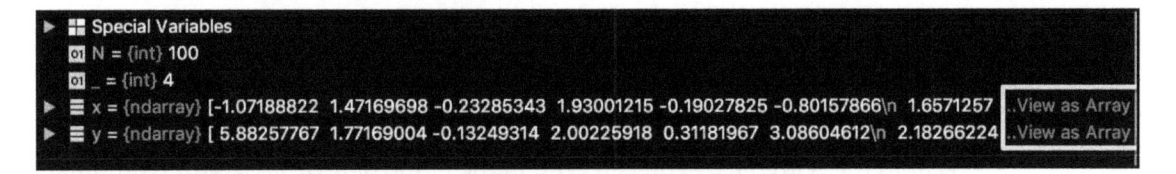

   ```
   ▶ ▦ Special Variables
     ᴏ₁ N = {int} 100
     ᴏ₁ _ = {int} 4
   ▶ ≡ x = {ndarray} [-1.07188822  1.47169698 -0.23285343  1.93001215 -0.19027825 -0.80157866\n  1.6571257   ..View as Array
   ▶ ≡ y = {ndarray} [ 5.88257767  1.77169004 -0.13249314  2.00225918  0.31181967  3.08604612\n  2.18266224  ..View as Array
   ```

   Variable viewer in the Python Console panel

2. Now, we can inspect the values of simple values such as N or the iterative index _ using this variable viewer just fine. However, for x and y—which are NumPy arrays—how their values are being represented here might not be readable enough for our purposes. Furthermore, in the context of data science projects, complex data structures such as NumPy multidimensional arrays or Pandas DataFrames need to be displayed in a better manner.

   Here is where the **SciView** panel comes into play—in the variable viewer of the **Python Console** panel, click on the **View as Array** button that corresponds to either x or y (or both), as highlighted in the preceding screenshot (you can also right-click on the variable and select the option with the same name to achieve the same effect).

Dynamic Data Viewing with SciView and Jupyter

3. This action will open a subtab in the **Data** tab of the **SciView** panel for each variable you want to inspect. The panel in your project window should look similar to the following screenshot:

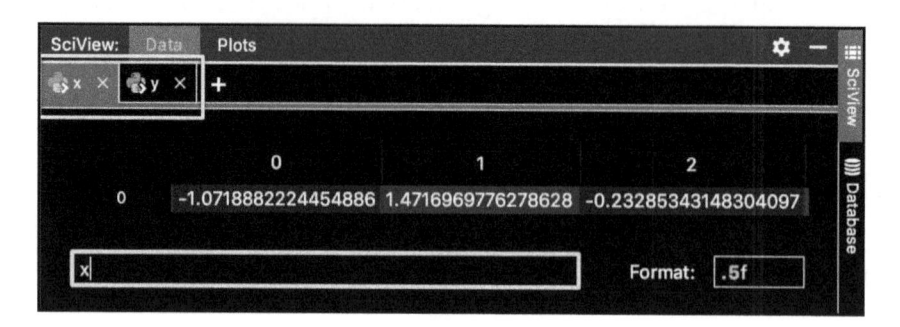

Viewing data in PyCharm's SciView panel

As you can see, the middle section of the panel displays the value of the NumPy array (x, in this case) in a table format with row and column numbers. This is evidently more graphical and thus more readable than its string representation in the viewer of the **Python Console** panel. You can also scroll left and right to go through and inspect individual values within this array.

4. The next element of note in this panel is the search bar and the formatting prompt at the bottom of the section:

   - Within the search bar, you can type in the name of a variable you would like to inspect and hit *Enter*; the current tab will then refresh and display the value of the new variable. This means that a given subtab within this **Data** tab of the **SciView** panel is not tied to the original variable it was created with—another testament to the dynamic features PyCharm offers.
   - The formatting prompt specifies how the content of the variable should be formatted. The prompt currently has .5f as its value, so 5 digits after the decimal will be displayed. As you can see, the formatting syntax is identical to that of string formatting in Python.

> You can read more about the topic in Python's official documentation: https://docs.python.org/2/library/stdtypes.html#string-formatting.

Multiple variables can be displayed at the same time in different tabs. As highlighted in the preceding screenshot, both x and y are in my **SciView** panel.

Chapter 12

> **TIP**
> You can also use the shortcuts for the **Select Previous Tab** and **Select Next Tab** actions to quickly switch between the available tabs to inspect the registered variables.

It is important to note that the data viewer of the **SciView** panel is only applicable for NumPy arrays and Pandas DataFrames. If you were to, say, enter N, which is an integer variable in our program, in the search bar, you would obtain an error message, as follows:

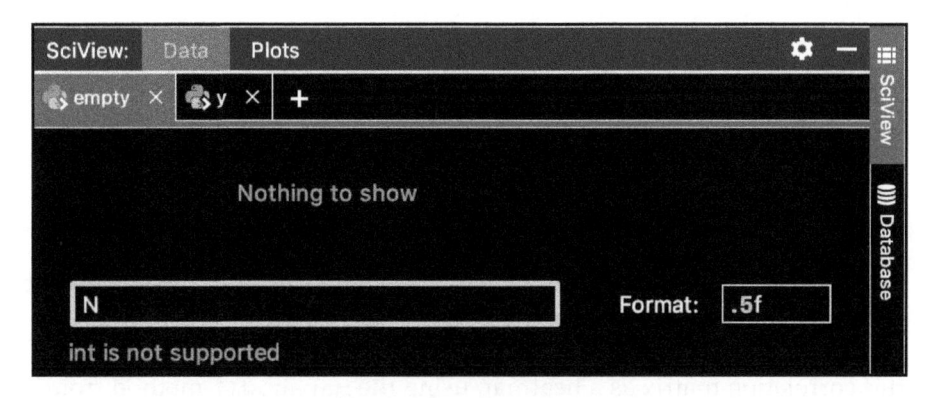

Unsupported data structures in the data viewer

However, since the arrays and DataFrames are typically the variables we need to inspect in a graphical table format, there is actually no need for the data viewer to support other, simpler data structures that can be inspected via the variable viewer of the **Python Console** panel.

5. The last feature we will discuss regarding this data viewer is the coloring of the individual cells. As you can see, in a specific variable displayed in the viewer, cells with high values are filled with warmer colors, while the ones with low values are filled with cooler colors. In the *Viewing data in PyCharm's SciView panel* screenshot, -1.072 has a deep blue color, while 1.47 has a deep red color.

6. This heatmap coloring feature is significantly useful in various scenarios in data science projects, namely while considering a correlation matrix. To see this feature in action, let's consider the corr_test.py file within our current repository folder, which contains the following code:

```
import pandas as pd
import numpy as np
import matplotlib.pyplot as plt
```

[337]

Dynamic Data Viewing with SciView and Jupyter

```
#%% generate sample data
# x and z are randomly generated
# y is loosely two times of x
x = np.random.rand(50,)
y = x * 2 + np.random.normal(0, 0.3, 50)
z = np.random.rand(50,)

df = pd.DataFrame({
    'x': x,
    'y': y,
    'z': z
})

#%% compute the correlation matrix
corr_mat = df.corr()

#%% plot the heatmap
plt.matshow(corr_mat)
plt.show()
```

In this program, we are creating a Pandas DataFrame with three different attributes (x, y, and z) that we generate ourselves. Then, we compute the correlation matrix of this dataset using the `corr()` method. Finally, we display this correlation matrix as a heatmap using the `matshow()` method from Matplotlib.

> On the theoretical side, a correlation matrix tells us how much an attribute in a given dataset is correlated to another; a higher value means a higher correlation between a pair of attributes. Generally, knowing which attributes are highly correlated to each other will offer valuable insights into the dataset of a data science project.

To demonstrate this point, we generate the y attribute to be roughly two times the size of the x attribute, thus artificially creating a correlation between these two attributes. The z attribute, on the other hand, is generated randomly and independently from x and y, so there should not be a high correlation between z and either of the other attributes.

7. Keeping all of this in mind, go ahead and run this program in the console (by right-clicking on the editor's background and choosing the corresponding option). The first output you will notice is the heatmap of the correlation matrix for our dataset in the **Plots** tab of the **SciView** panel, as shown here:

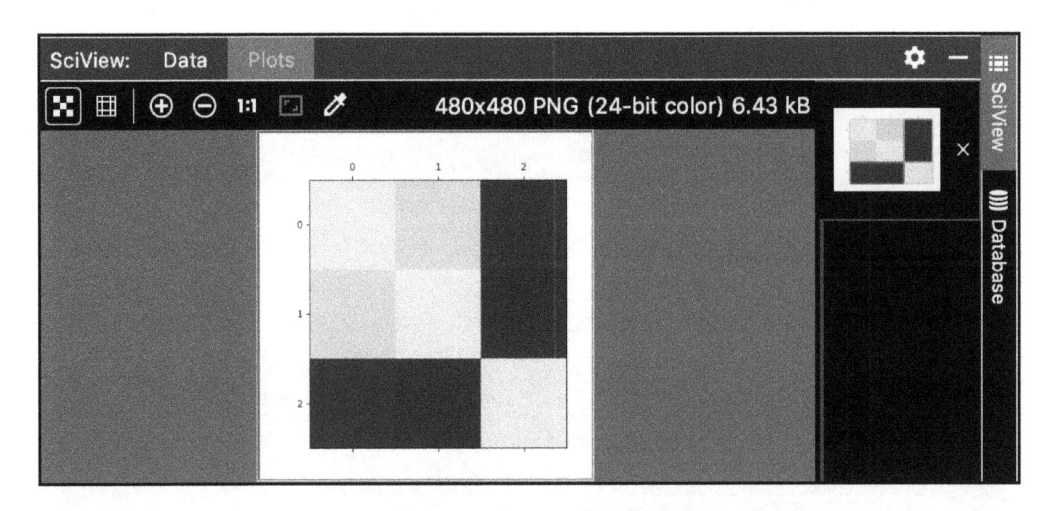

Heatmap plot in PyCharm

Note that these are the following things that we expected:

- The first and second attributes are highly correlated, so the color in the corresponding cells in the correlation matrix (row 1 column 2 and row 2 column 1) is bright
- The correlation between the third attribute with the other two is low, indicated by a dark color
- Naturally, each attribute is perfectly correlated with itself, hence the bright yellow color in the diagonal cells

Dynamic Data Viewing with SciView and Jupyter

8. To inspect the actual values within the computed correlation matrix, we can use the variable viewer of the **Python Console** panel using the following steps:

    1. Expand the `corr_mat` variable in the viewer and scroll down. You will see something similar to the highlighted section of the following screenshot:

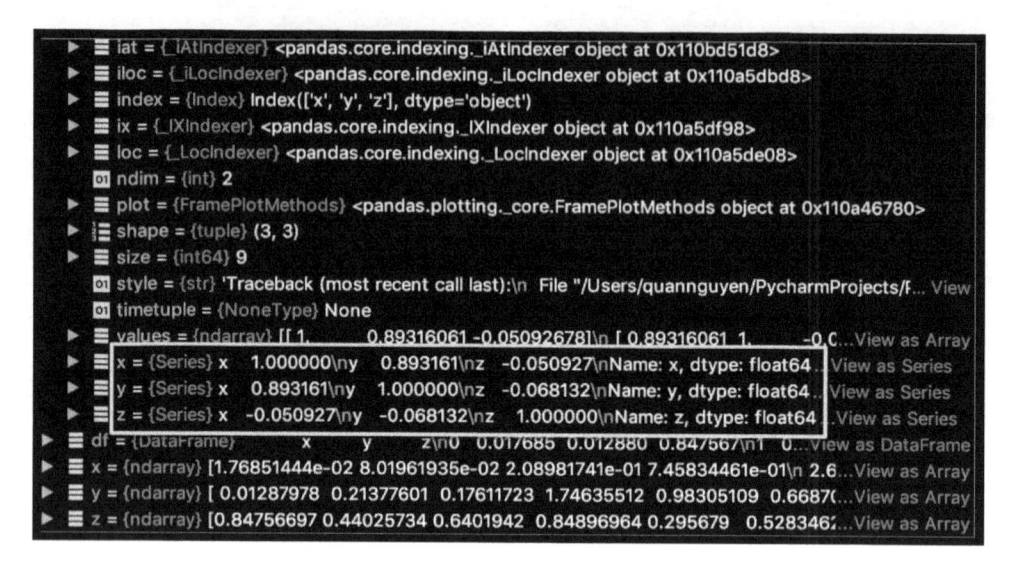

    Actual value of the correlation matrix

    2. Then, inspect the `corr_mat` variable in the data viewer of the **SciView** panel by clicking on the **View as DataFrame** button within the **Python Console** panel. You will see the following output:

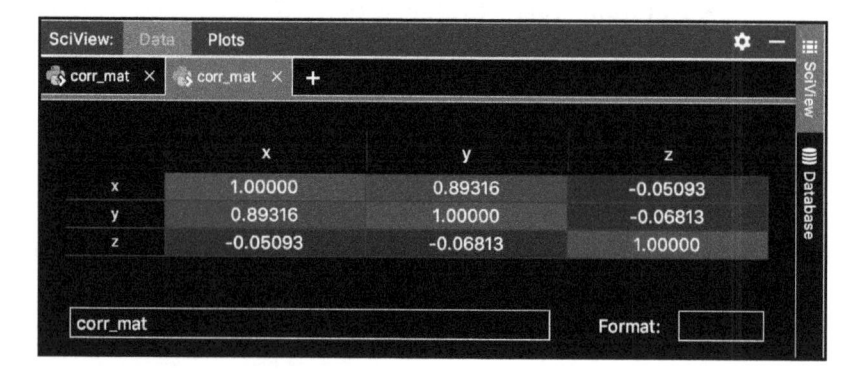

    Correlation matrix in the SciView panel

[340]

We can see that—thanks to the default coloring logic of the data viewer of the **SciView** panel—our correlation matrix is displayed as a heatmap automatically. So, by using the **SciView** panel, we do not have to even draw the correlation matrix as a plot using Matplotlib.

Furthermore, the heatmap we have here also contains the actual values of the correlation matrix, making it even more readable; implementing this in Matplotlib requires more code than what we currently have.

Overall, the data viewer in the **SciView** panel offers powerful and dynamic methods to inspect and make sense of the data we have in our data science projects. As you can imagine, this feature is also specifically useful in the context of debugging tasks, where variables and data are inspected mid-execution. Specifically, as you are stepping through a program in debug mode, you can still use the **View as Array/DataFrame** option to open a given applicable variable and inspect it in the **SciView** panel.

And that concludes our discussion on the fantastic **SciView** panel in PyCharm. In the next section, we will be introduced to another common tool in data science projects, IPython, and will learn how to use it in PyCharm.

Understanding IPython and magic commands

IPython is a variation of the **Python Console** that emphasizes the interactivity of writing code in a Python shell. As we will see later on, IPython offers some convenient options so that we can explore and manipulate Python variables. These options are more flexible than their counterparts in a regular **Python Console** and are a great help for data scientists in general.

In addition to this, we will also consider the use of magic commands in IPython, which is an interactive API that allows us to facilitate complex tasks in a quick and flexible manner. First, let's see how we can install and set up IPython.

Installing and setting up IPython

The process of installing IPython is fairly simple:

1. We can install IPython for our Python project via the familiar `pip` command:

    ```
    pip install ipython
    ```

2. Then, you can run the `ipython` command in your Terminal to start an IPython session (similar to how we can run `python` in the Terminal to evoke the **Python Console**). Alternatively, we can initiate IPython within the **Python Console** panel in PyCharm, as follows:
   1. Go to PyCharm's settings and navigate to **Build, Execution, Deployment | Console**. Make sure that the **Use IPython if available** box is checked, and finally, click **OK** to confirm the selection.
   2. Open the **Python Console** panel and click on the Rerun button in the top-left corner of the panel, which will initiate a console with a slightly different interface, which is the IPython console:

Running IPython

Specifically, we can see that the input prompt begins with `In[N]` (with N denoting the order of each command that's entered), instead of the >>> symbol in a regular **Python Console** panel. From here, you can enter in individual Python commands and use the IPython console in the same way as a **Python Console** panel.

Next, we will see what functionalities IPython has that set it apart from regular **Python Console** panels.

Introducing IPython magic commands

Magic commands in IPython denote a set of specific syntactic options that allow for considerably convenient APIs that make working with IPython seamless. Here, we will be going over some of these magic commands to get a feel of the options that IPython offers:

- `object_name?`: Say you are using an IPython console to execute a sequence of Python commands, and at one point, you'd like to inspect the value of a variable that was created earlier. You can use the variable view right next to the console, but you can also take advantage of the `object_name?` command in IPython to list detailed information about that variable.

Chapter 12

For example, as illustrated in the following screenshot, number 1 was assigned to the `a` variable, and when we type `a?` in the IPython console, we obtain an extensive explanation regarding the data type of `a`, as shown here:

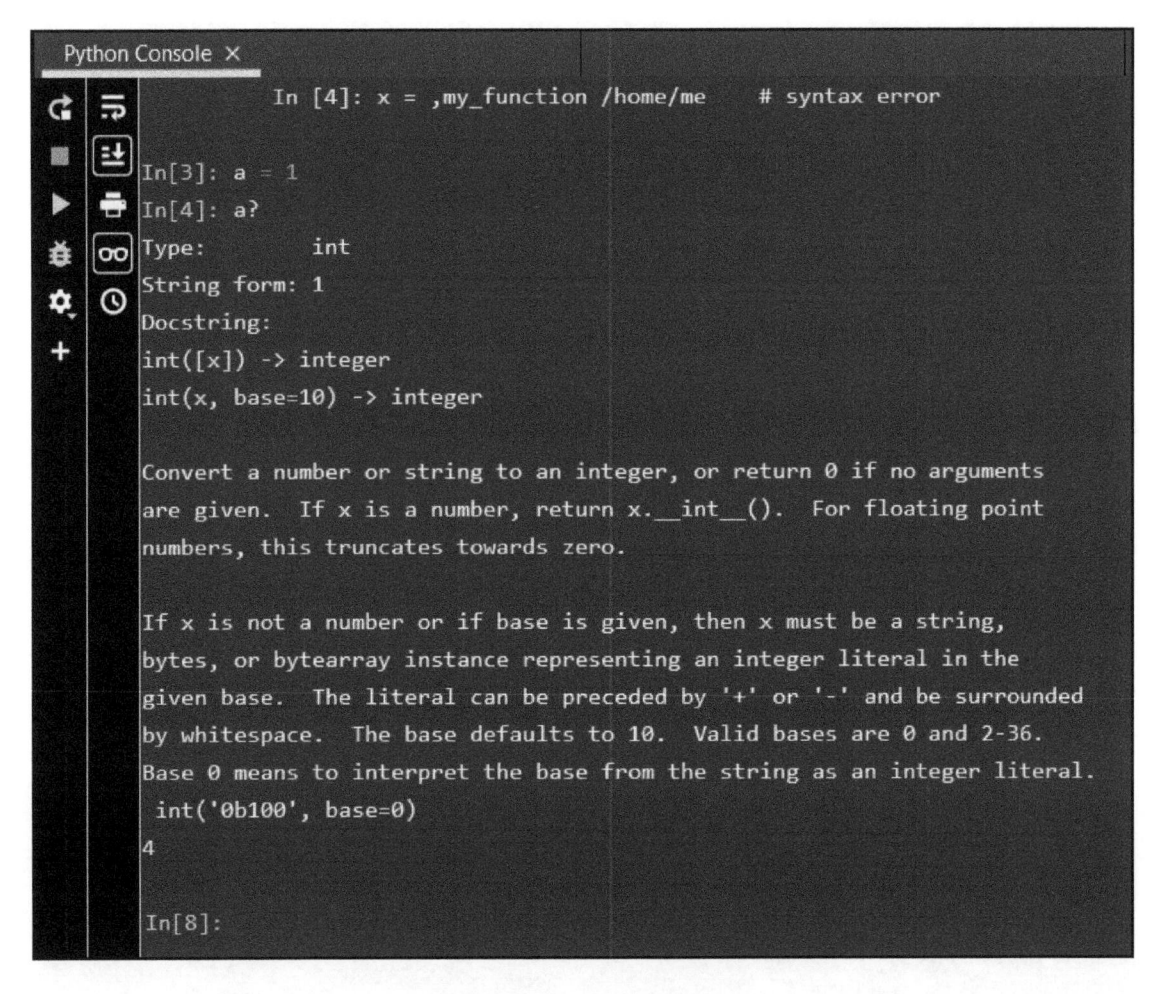

```
In [4]: x = ,my_function /home/me      # syntax error
In[3]: a = 1
In[4]: a?
Type:          int
String form: 1
Docstring:
int([x]) -> integer
int(x, base=10) -> integer

Convert a number or string to an integer, or return 0 if no arguments
are given.  If x is a number, return x.__int__().  For floating point
numbers, this truncates towards zero.

If x is not a number or if base is given, then x must be a string,
bytes, or bytearray instance representing an integer literal in the
given base.  The literal can be preceded by '+' or '-' and be surrounded
by whitespace.  The base defaults to 10.  Valid bases are 0 and 2-36.
Base 0 means to interpret the base from the string as an integer literal.
 int('0b100', base=0)
4

In[8]:
```

The object_name? command in IPython

- `%precision`: Still on the topic of inspecting the value of your variables, if you are working with numerical data that contains many decimal digits (fractional numbers), then the `%precision` magic command might come in handy. This command is used to specify how many numbers after the decimal point should be displayed in the IPython console.

Dynamic Data Viewing with SciView and Jupyter

For example, as the following screenshot illustrates, when I print out the value for e (a famous constant in math) after specifying that the precision should be 4, the printed output is formatted accordingly, as shown here:

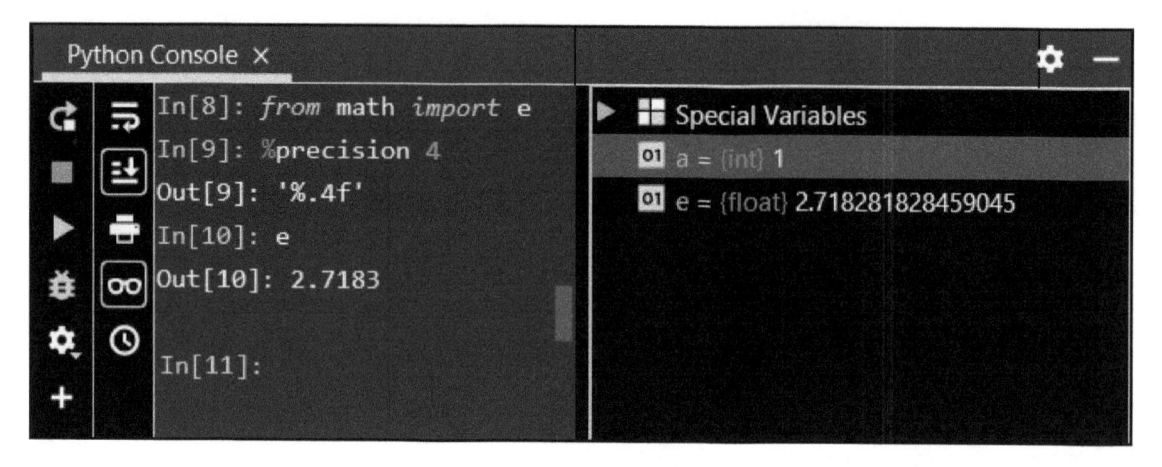

```
In[8]: from math import e
In[9]: %precision 4
Out[9]: '%.4f'
In[10]: e
Out[10]: 2.7183
In[11]:
```

Special Variables
- a = {int} 1
- e = {float} 2.718281828459045

The %precision command in IPython

- %%timeit: As we saw in Chapter 6, *Seamless Testing, Debugging, and Profiling*, keeping track of the time it takes for a specific command to run is an essential task in any profiling process. For that reason, IPython also offers a quick magic command to time the execution of any code that's entered in the IPython console—the %%timeit command.

  For example, I used the following code to profile the speed of the sort() function in Python with a completely reversed ordered list of numbers, as shown here:

```
In[2]: %%timeit
   ...: x = list(reversed(range(10)))
   ...: x.sort()
   ...:
790 ns ± 74.4 ns per loop (mean ± std. dev. of 7 runs, 1000000 loops each)
In[3]:
```

The %%timeit command in IPython

[344]

From the output, we obtain an estimation of the speed (with the mean and standard deviation) from the entered block of code to 1 million iterations of the code. Again, this feature is quite useful in profiling tasks.

Here, we have considered three of the most common magic commands in IPython. Of course, there are many other useful commands that you can take advantage of, which can be found in IPython's official documentation: https://ipython.readthedocs.io/en/stable/index.html.

With that said, the main purpose of IPython is not simply the ability to utilize convenient APIs to facilitate specific tasks such as variable inspection, formatting, or profiling—IPython actually uses those functionalities to power its underlying interactive characteristics. In the context of data science projects, IPython, when used in PyCharm, offers a great way for us to inspect and test small blocks of code before using them in a large program.

With that, let's move on to the next section, where we will consider the other notable support PyCharm offers for scientific computing—Jupyter notebooks.

Leveraging Jupyter notebooks

Jupyter notebooks are arguably the most-used tool in Python scientific computing and data science projects. In this section, we will briefly discuss the basics of Jupyter notebooks as well as the reasons why it is a great tool for data analysis purposes. Then, we will consider the way PyCharm supports the usage of these notebooks.

We will be working with the code examples from the Chapter12/JupyterNotebooks folder of this book's code repository. In its requirements.txt file, we have Pandas, NumPy, Matplotlib, and Jupyter as the external libraries that need to be installed. Whether you are creating a new project or importing the folder into your PyCharm, go ahead and install those libraries in your environment.

Even though we will be writing code in Jupyter notebooks, it is beneficial to first consider a bare-bones program in a traditional Python script so that we can fully appreciate the advantages of using a notebook later on. Let's look at the main.py file and see how we can work with it. We can see that this file contains the same program from the previous section, where we randomly generate a dataset of three attributes (x, y, and z) and consider their correlation matrix:

```
import pandas as pd
import numpy as np
import matplotlib.pyplot as plt
```

Dynamic Data Viewing with SciView and Jupyter

```
# Generate sample data
x = np.random.rand(50,)
y = x * 2 + np.random.normal(0, 0.3, 50)
z = np.random.rand(50,)

df = pd.DataFrame({
    'x': x,
    'y': y,
    'z': z
})

# Compute and show correlation matrix
corr_mat = df.corr()

plt.matshow(corr_mat)
plt.show()
```

In addition to this, we also have two extra lines of code to show a scatter plot of x and y:

```
# Plot x and y
plt.scatter(df['x'], df['y'])
plt.show()
```

Because of the way we generated these two data columns, the scatter plot will most likely produce a nice relationship. When the program is run, we would roughly obtain the following plot at the end:

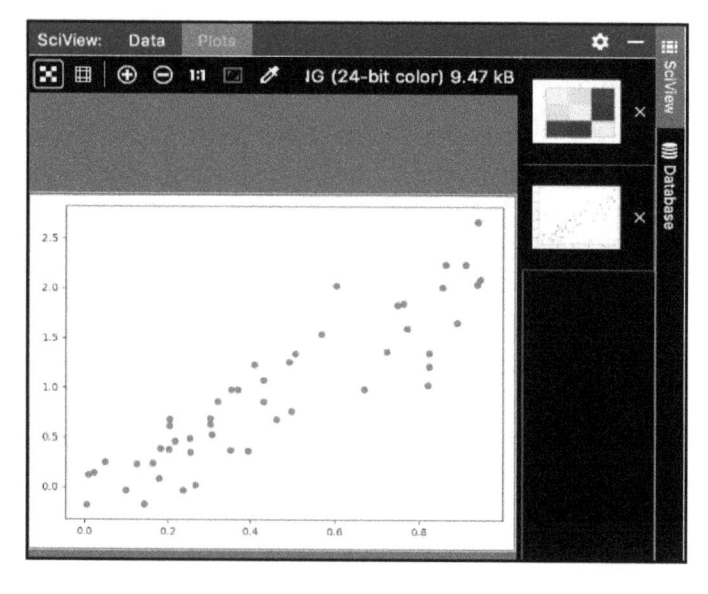

Sample scatter plot

We will come back to this program during our discussions in the following subsections.

Now, for those who are unfamiliar with Jupyter notebooks, let's move on to our first subsection, where we will be discussing the fundamentals. If, on the other hand, you are ready to learn how to integrate Jupyter into PyCharm, you can skip to the *Jupyter notebooks in PyCharm* section of this chapter.

Understanding Jupyter basics

Jupyter notebooks are built on the idea of iterative development. Specifically, by separating a given program into individual sections that can be written and run (roughly) independently from each other, programmers (in general) and data scientists (specifically) can work on the logic of their programs in an incremental way. Let's briefly talk about that in the following subsection.

The idea of iterative development

A Jupyter Notebook consists of multiple code cells, each containing only a block of code that achieves a specific goal. The output of a code cell is displayed immediately after that cell in the notebook, making the process of debugging easier than in traditional programs. We will see more examples of code cells later in this subsection.

Furthermore, this incremental characteristic of Jupyter notebooks makes them considerably popular among data scientists and enthusiasts. For example, imagine that, during a process of exploratory data analysis, you notice that a dataset you have read in the middle of the program needs to be encoded in a different way. Now, in a traditional Python program, you would have to adjust the reading function for that dataset and the whole program would need to be rerun.

In general, starting off a program you want to implement with a low number of functionalities and adding in features in an incremental and robust way later on, are good practices to have. This is the general idea of iterative development, and it can be applied to general programming as well.

Getting back to Jupyter notebooks, you would simply need to make the appropriate changes in the code cell that reads in the dataset and rerun the subsequent cells, as opposed to rerunning the code before it. As a tribute to its users, Jupyter notebooks were named after the three most common scientific programming languages: *Julia*, *Python*, and *R*.

Another integral part of Jupyter notebooks is the support for the Markdown language. As we mentioned previously, at the beginning of the previous chapter, Markdown is a markup language that's commonly used in README.md files in GitHub. Furthermore, because of its ability to work with LaTeX (which is typically used for writing mathematical equations and scientific papers in general), Markdown is heavily favored by the data science community.

Next, let's see how we can use a Jupyter Notebook in a regular Python project.

Editing Jupyter notebooks

For this task, we will be translating the program we have in the main.py file into a Jupyter Notebook so that we can see the interface that Jupyter offers compared to a traditional Python script. Again, note that we will not be using PyCharm during this process. Now, let's look at the following steps:

1. First, we will create a regular folder to follow this example without using PyCharm. Go ahead and open a Terminal at this directory as well.
2. Then, we will need to install Jupyter, which can be done via the pip package manager:

    ```
    pip install jupyter
    ```

    We will also be using the regular scientific libraries, that is, NumPy, Pandas, and Matplotlib, all of which can be installed using pip as well.

3. Next, since Jupyter is, in essence, a web application, we need to serve it via our local server by running the following command in the Terminal:

    ```
    jupyter notebook
    ```

4. This command will open a new tab in your web browser, displaying the current directory where you ran the command. For example, my Jupyter page opens at our current folder:

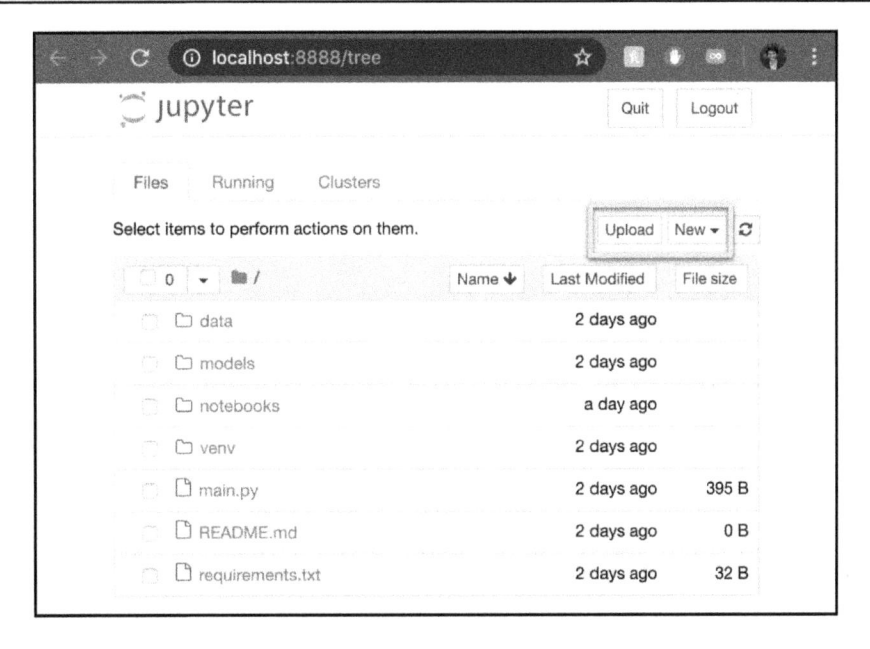

Jupyter welcome page

5. From here, you can create new notebooks or upload existing ones from your local machine using the two buttons highlighted in the preceding screenshot. For now, we will use the **New** button and choose the **Python 3** option to create a new notebook.

6. Another tab in your browser will open, displaying the newly created notebook for you to edit:

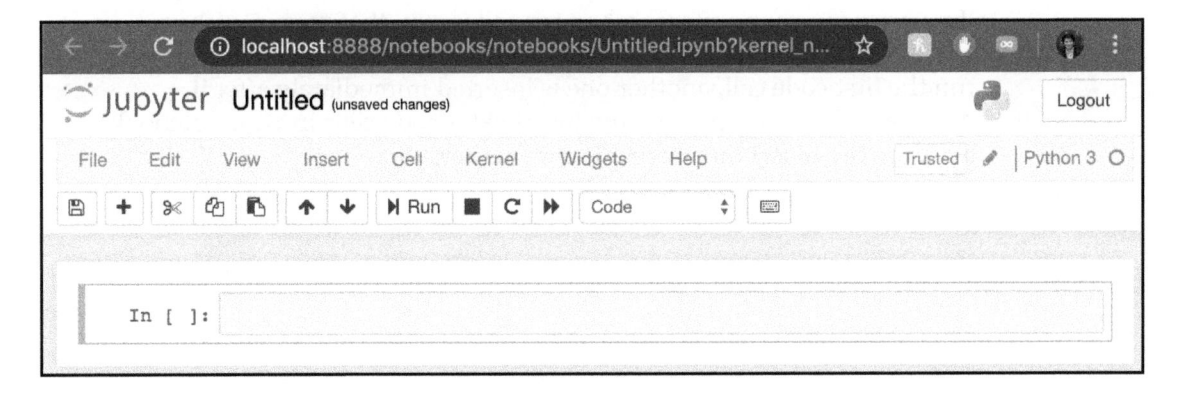

A new Jupyter notebook

7. We can edit the name of the notebook in the top-left corner of the window. Furthermore, what we currently have inside the notebook is a code cell. As we mentioned previously, we would only enter a part of our code in a cell. Each cell can also be run independently from each other. For now, we will use this code cell to import the libraries that our program will be using. Enter the following code into the cell:

   ```
   import pandas as pd
   import numpy as np
   import matplotlib.pyplot as plt
   ```

8. To run a code cell, you can click on the **Run** button, as shown here, or simply use the *Shift + Enter* shortcut:

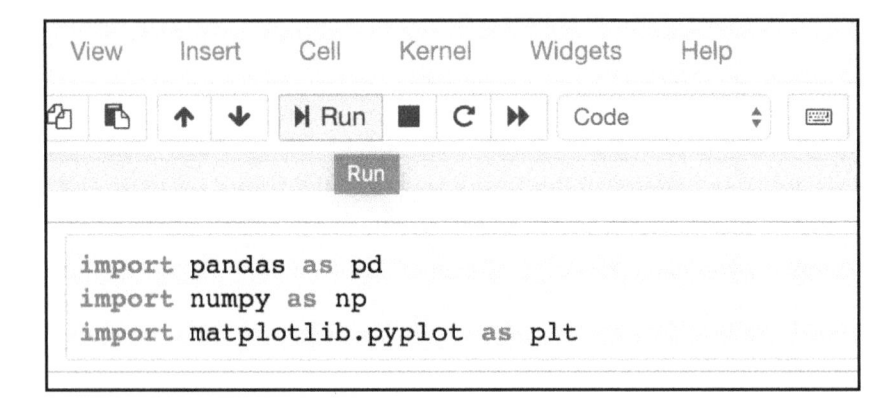

Running a code cell

> If no error message appears when the cell is run, that means we have successfully imported our libraries. You might have noticed that, as you run the first code cell, another one is inserted immediately after it. Alternatively, you can manually insert extra code cells in your notebook by using the **Insert** menu from the menu bar.

9. Next, simply type in individual parts of the program we have, into separate code cells. By the end, you should have the following notebook:

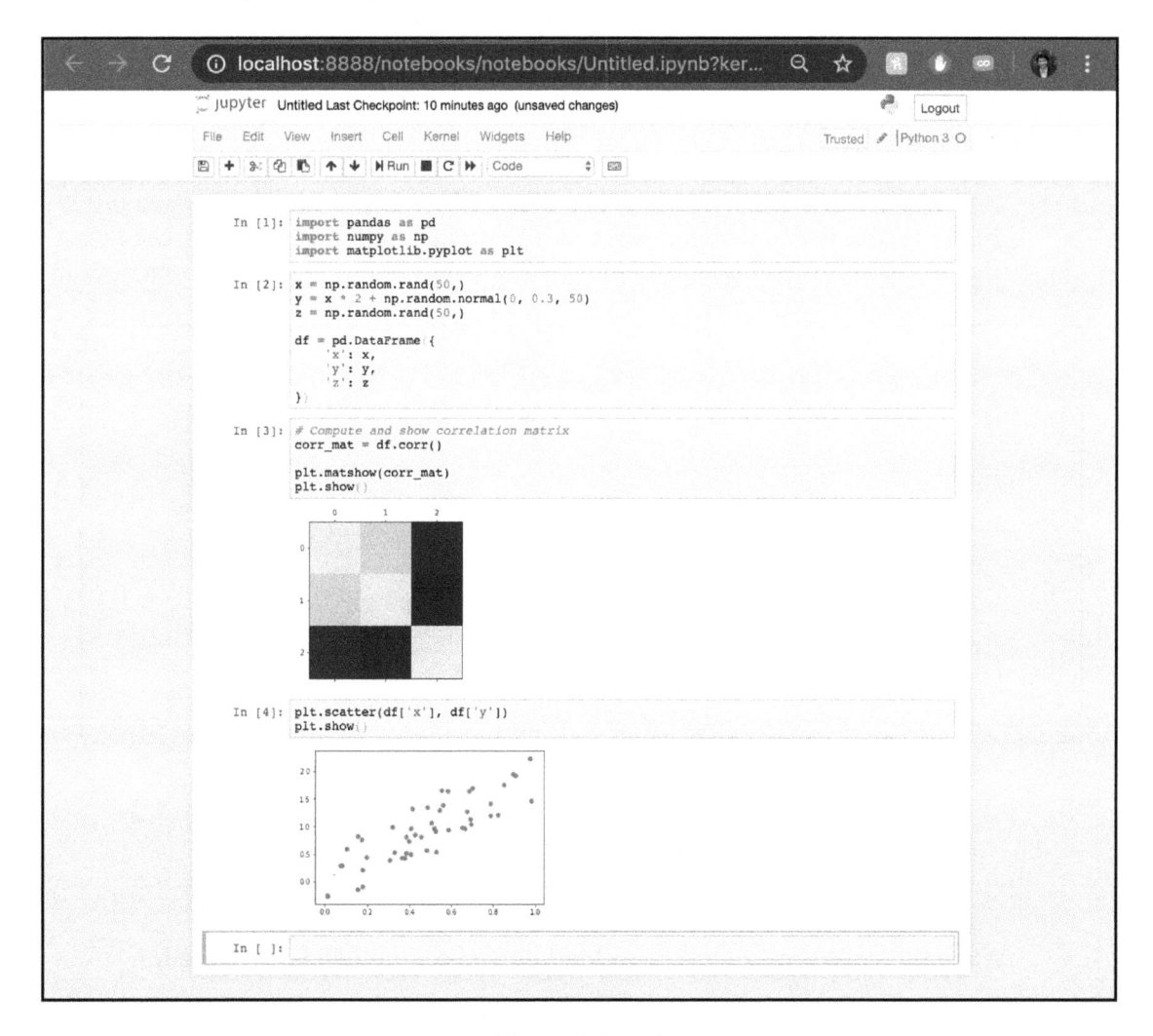

A Jupyter notebook example

Dynamic Data Viewing with SciView and Jupyter

As we can see, any code output (be it printed output or visualization) is displayed immediately following the code that produces it. This, again, allows Jupyter users to read and edit their notebooks in a sequential and incremental way.

10. To improve the readability of our notebook even further, let's add some Markdown to our code. Go ahead and insert a cell in front of our first one (using the **Insert** menu).

    A newly inserted cell is a code cell by default. We need to convert it into a text cell to be able to enter Markdown code. To do that, select the new cell, click on the drop-down menu on the menu bar like so and choose the **Markdown** option:

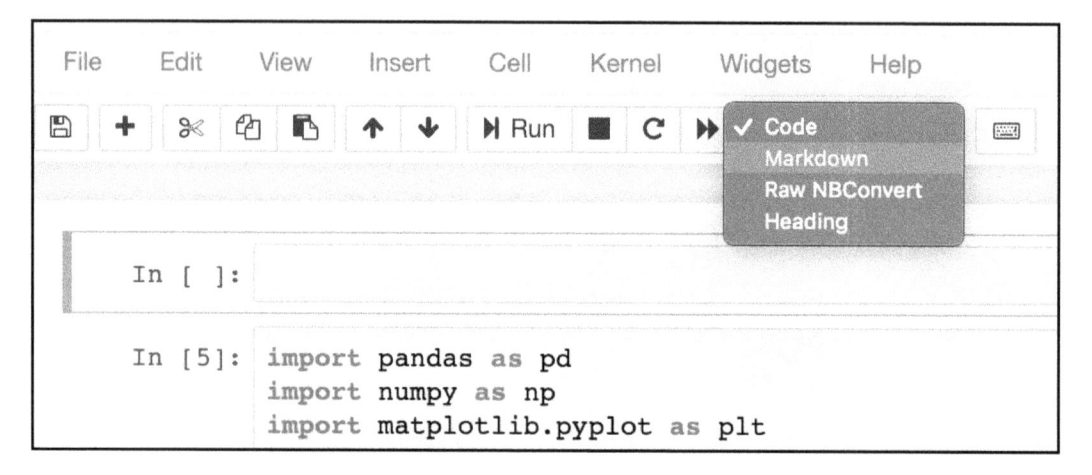

Changing the cell type in Jupyter

11. After this, enter the following Markdown code:

    ```
    ### Importing libraries
    ```

    When this code runs, a level three Markdown heading will be produced.

[352]

12. Here, we are using these headings to describe our individual code cells. In the same manner, insert a Markdown heading above each of your code cells, like so:

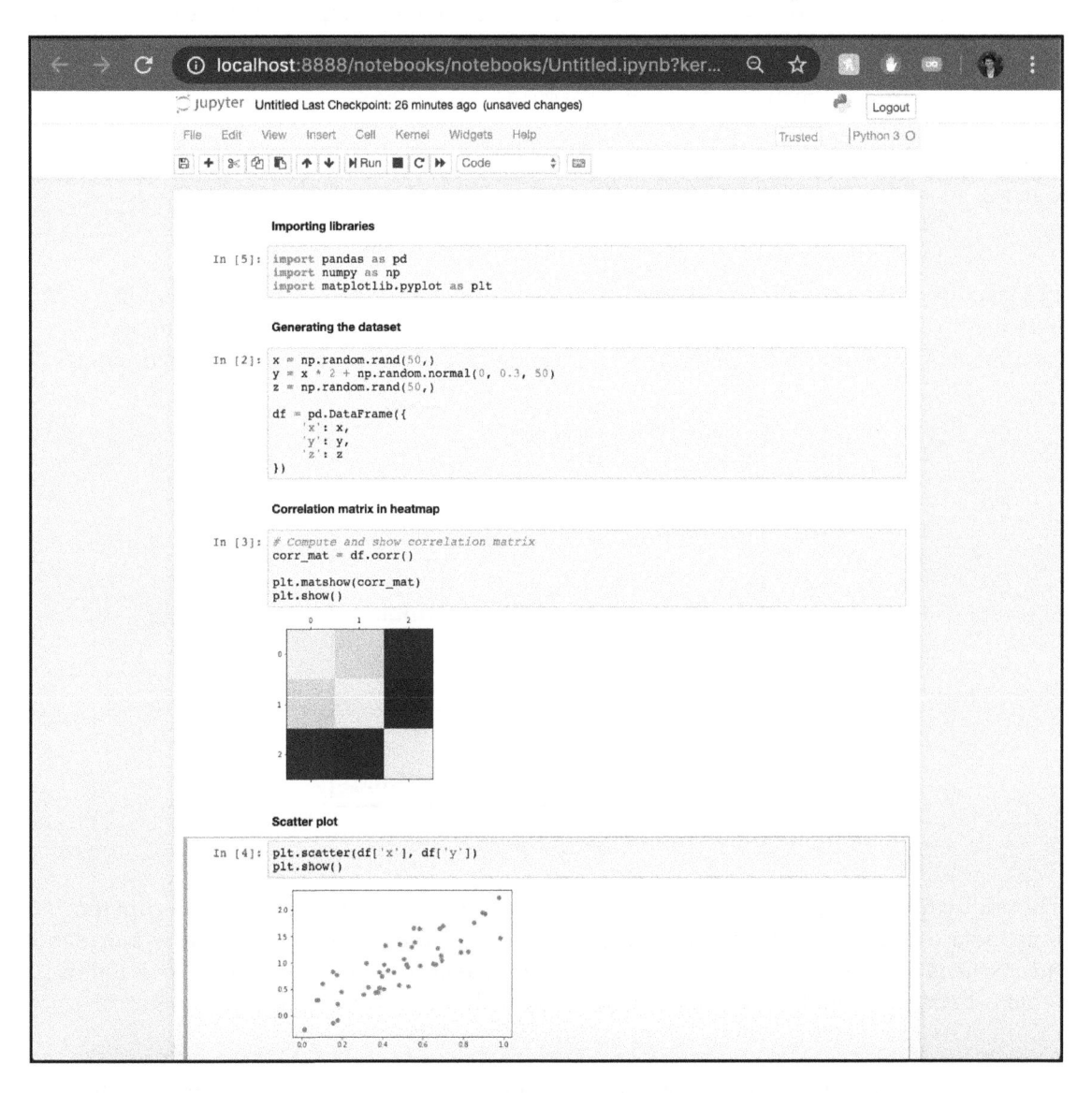

Combining Markdown headings with code in Jupyter

13. We mentioned earlier that one reason for the popularity of Markdown is its support for mathematical equations in LaTeX. Let's see how that plays out in Jupyter. Insert a Markdown cell right before the **Correlation matrix in heatmap** section and enter the following code:

    ```
    ### Pearson correlation formula

    $r_{XY}
    = \frac{\sum^n_{i=1}{(X_i - \bar{X})(Y_i - \bar{Y})}}
    {\sqrt{\sum^n_{i=1}{(X_i - \bar{X})^2}}\sqrt{\sum^n_{i=1}{(Y_i - \bar{Y})^2}}}$
    ```

In Markdown, the preceding code produces the formula for the `Pearson` correlation between two given arrays of numbers, which is what the `corr()` method in our code computes. After running the preceding code, you will obtain the following Markdown:

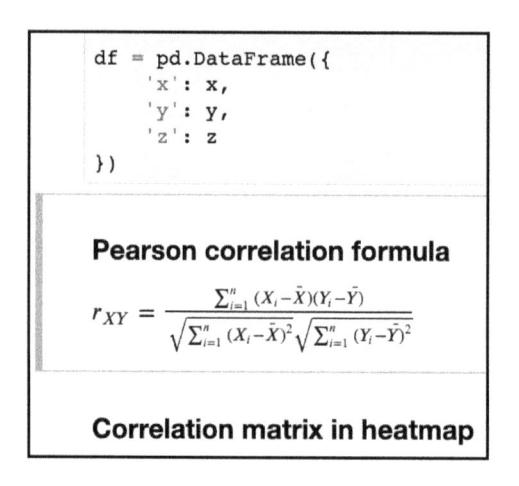

LaTeX in Jupyter Markdown

The ability to combine LaTeX and general Markdown text with live code makes Jupyter notebooks a flexible tool in data science projects. Being able to display the code in between text explanations of a data analysis process can help readers of a Jupyter Notebook follow what is being done to that data much more easily. This is why Jupyter notebooks are a common tool for making presentations and reports in data science teams.

Finally, when you finish working on your notebooks, you can come back to the Terminal and terminate the Jupyter server by using the *Ctrl* + *C* shortcut. Now, we have gone through the different basic uses of Jupyter notebooks. In the next section, we'll see how PyCharm supports this tool.

Jupyter notebooks in PyCharm

If you had the chance to work with Jupyter notebooks in PyCharm before 2019, you may remember that the features from PyCharm that supported Jupyter were subpar and left much to be desired. However, with the big update at the beginning of 2019, PyCharm has proven itself to be one of the best Python IDEs once again by completely revamping its support for Jupyter. In this section, we will go over these support features to see how integrated Jupyter is in PyCharm:

1. First, we can create a new notebook inside the PyCharm editor by right-clicking on a folder inside the directory tree and choosing the **New** option, as follows:

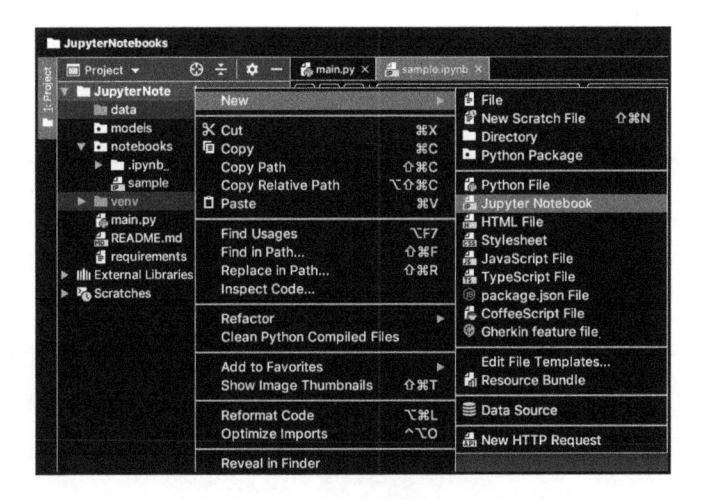

Creating a new Jupyter notebook in PyCharm

2. This will open the notebook file inside the editor, which means that you can run your notebooks from within PyCharm, as opposed to having to use a web browser as in the previous subsection. Moreover, if, at this point, you don't have Jupyter installed in your environment, PyCharm will also let you know as soon as the notebook is opened:

Installing Jupyter with PyCharm

3. With the notebook opened in the editor, we can see that editing Jupyter notebooks is similar to editing Markdown text—we can edit the code using the left panel of the editor, and the right panel will display the rendered output. The rendering of the notebook output is done in real time, so it will adjust as you enter code into your notebook.

> **TIP**
> One thing to keep in mind is that any printed output or visualization that's produced by code will only be displayed in the right-hand panel when the code cell is actually executed, which we will do in a later step.

4. The beginning of each code cell in the notebook is indicated by the `#%%` symbol (there is already one in the blank notebook we created). The code cell lasts until there is another `#%%` symbol. If you want to specify a Markdown cell, you can use `#%% md` at the beginning of a given cell.

5. Now, open the `basics.ipynb` file inside the `notebooks` folder of the current chapter's code directory in the editor in PyCharm. This file contains the Jupyter code for the notebook we considered in the previous subsection. Go ahead and copy it over the new notebook we just created. Your workspace will look similar to the following:

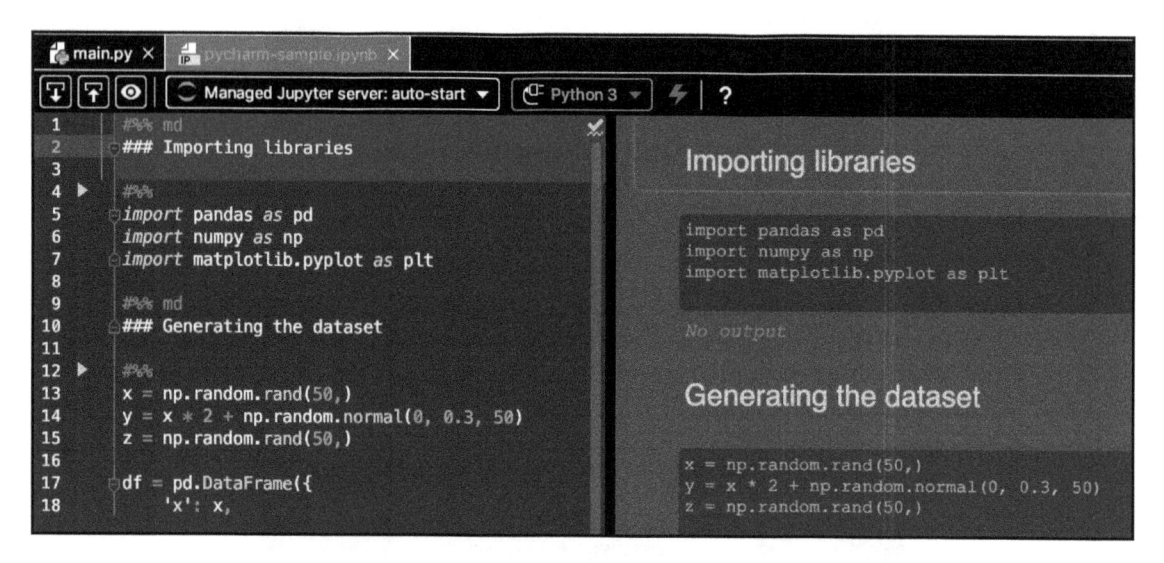

Jupyter notebooks in PyCharm

[356]

The first thing we notice is the Run buttons for the individual code cells. Markdown cells can be processed in real time, but as we mentioned earlier, code cells need to be run to produce their effects.

6. To run a code cell, simply click on its Run button and choose the **Run Cell** option.
7. This action will initiate a Jupyter server that handles the backend execution of our notebook. Additionally, a new **Jupyter** panel will appear (most likely at the bottom of your window), displaying information about the execution of the Jupyter server:

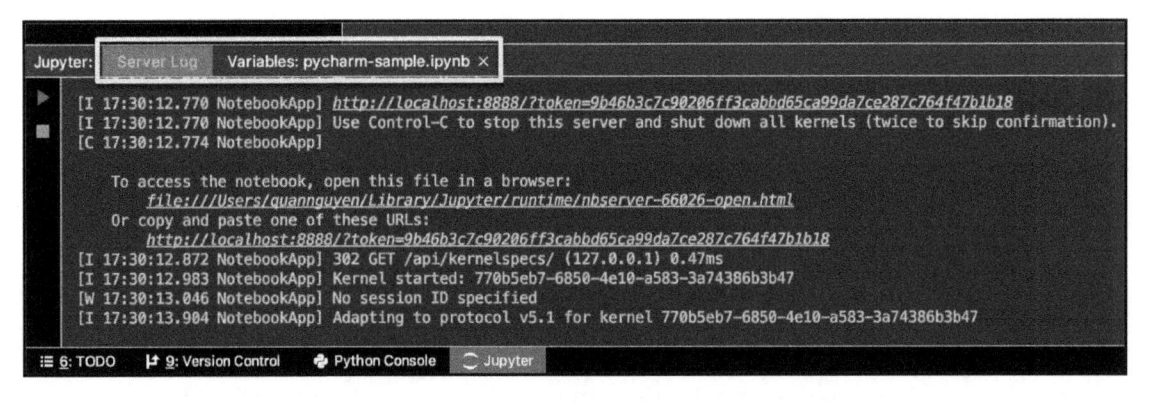

The Jupyter panel in PyCharm

There are multiple tabs in this panel that you can navigate between using the section that's highlighted in the preceding screenshot. The **Server Log** tab is basically the Terminal when we use Jupyter outside of PyCharm. In other words, you can use this tab to access the server in an actual web browser (by clicking on the link that was printed in the preceding screenshot) or close the server with the *Control + C* shortcut.

The other **Variables** tab in this panel display information about the variables that are declared in their respective notebooks. As you execute the second code cell of our current notebook, you will see that the tab is populated in the same way as a regular **Variables** panel.

8. As we execute the code cells in our notebook, the right-hand panel of the Jupyter editor in PyCharm also updates its display accordingly in real time. Specifically, we can see the visualizations inside this panel as the cells producing them are run.

We have gone through the main features of PyCharm in the context of Jupyter notebooks. In general, one of the biggest drawbacks of using traditional Jupyter notebooks is the lack of syntax formatting and code completion while writing code in individual code cells. Specifically, when we write code in Jupyter notebooks in our browser, the process is very similar to writing code in a simple text editor with limited support.

However, as we work with Jupyter notebooks directly inside the PyCharm editor, we will see that all the code-writing support features that are available to regular Python scripts are also available here. In other words, when using PyCharm to write Jupyter notebooks, we get the best of both worlds—powerful, intelligent support from PyCharm and an iterative development style from Jupyter.

Summary

A Python programmer typically works on a data science project in two ways—writing a traditional Python script or using a Jupyter Notebook, both of which are heavily supported by PyCharm. Specifically, the **SciView** panel in PyCharm is a comprehensive and dynamic way to view, manage, and inspect data within a data science project. It offers a great way for us to display visualizations that have been produced by Python scripts as well as to inspect the values within Pandas DataFrames and NumPy arrays.

On the other hand, Jupyter notebooks are a great tool for facilitating iterative development in Python, allowing users to make incremental steps toward analyzing and extracting insights from their datasets. Jupyter notebooks are also well supported by PyCharm, being able to be edited directly inside the PyCharm editor. This allows us to skip the middle step of using a web browser to run our Jupyter notebooks while being able to utilize the powerful code-writing support features that PyCharm provides.

By going in-depth into what PyCharm helps with regarding the process of viewing and working with data, either via the **SciView** panel or with Jupyter notebooks, we have learned how to use PyCharm to facilitate various data science tasks in Python. With this, we have equipped ourselves with enough knowledge and tools to tackle real-life projects using PyCharm.

In the next chapter, we will combine all the knowledge we have learned so far regarding the topic of data science and scientific computing and walk through the process of building a data science pipeline in PyCharm.

Questions

1. What two main features does the **SciView** panel contain?
2. What is the advantage of using the plot viewer in the **SciView** panel when multiple visualizations are generated by a Python program?
3. What kind of data structures does the data viewer in the **SciView** panel support?
4. What is the idea of iterative development and how do Jupyter notebooks support that?
5. What are Markdown and LaTeX? Why is it beneficial to have support for them in Jupyter notebooks?
6. How is a Jupyter code cell represented in the PyCharm editor?
7. What are the benefits of writing Jupyter notebooks in the PyCharm editor?

Further reading

More information can be found in the following articles and readings:

- *JetBrains official documentation: Scientific Mode Tutorial*, JetBrains s.r.o. (www.jetbrains.com/help/pycharm/matplotlib-tutorial.html)
- *JetBrains official documentation: Running and Debugging Jupyter Notebook Cells*, JetBrains s.r.o. (www.jetbrains.com/help/pycharm/running-jupyter-notebook-cells.html)
- *Jetbrains official documentation: SciView*, JetBrains s.r.o. (www.jetbrains.com/help/pycharm/data-view.html)
- *Jupyter home page*: (https://jupyter.org)

13 Building a Data Pipeline in PyCharm

This chapter covers a step-by-step process of building a Python data pipeline within PyCharm via a hands-on example. The term *data pipeline* generally denotes a set of actions or steps in a procedure to collect, process, and analyze data. This term is widely used in the industry to express the need for a reliable workflow of taking raw data and converting it into actionable insights.

On a smaller scale, this includes working with and maintaining data for your data science projects, pre-processing methods, and the visualization of data. In addition to the practical know-how of using PyCharm in this process, you will also be able to gain knowledge on the general workflow, as well as common practices in a complete data science project.

The following topics will be covered in this chapter:

- Working with and maintaining datasets
- Data cleaning and processing
- Data visualizations
- Machine learning

Throughout this chapter, you will be able to apply what you have learned on the topic of scientific computing so far to a real project with PyCharm. This serves as a hands-on discussion to conclude this topic of working with scientific computing and data science projects.

Technical requirements

The following is a list of prerequisites for this chapter:

- Ensure that you have both Python 3.6+ and PyCharm installed on your computer.
- Download the GitHub repository at https://github.com/PacktPublishing/Hands-on-Application-Development-with-PyCharm.

First of all, we will be using the PyCharm project inside the `Chapter13/Pipeline` folder in our code repository during our discussions. Let's now start our discussion with the central element of any data science project—the data.

Working with datasets

Datasets are the backbone of any data science project—with a good, well-structured dataset, we will have more chances to explore and discover important insights from the data; conversely, a bad dataset can lead to erroneous and harmful conclusions and decision-making. This is why we need to pay extra attention to see what kind of data we are working with, well before starting developing code to analyze it.

In this section, we will go over some things to keep in mind in terms of the data for our projects, as well as some hands-on practices of working with datasets. These practices will help us to form good habits that place us at a good starting point when working on a data-related project.

Now, the first step we need to take to start a data science pipeline is to actually determine what question and/or problem we are trying to address. After that, we will briefly discuss the different ways to collect data and facilitate version control.

Starting with a question

For this step, in total, there can be two situations—either we have a specific question in mind and we need to find an appropriate dataset to analyze to answer that question, or we already have a dataset and the content of that dataset gives rise to a question we want to answer.

Either way, we need to have a specific direction to move forward even before starting the data science project.

Needless to say, as we continue to work on and explore a dataset, new questions and insights might come up that can alter our original direction. However, it is always better to start with a clear question in mind so that the dataset can be analyzed deliberately.

As an example, we will be working with a dataset provided by Kaggle, which can be found at www.kaggle.com/valkling/tappy-keystroke-data-with-parkinsons-patients.

> Kaggle is an online data community designed for data scientists and machine learning engineers. The site provides competitions, datasets, playgrounds, and other educational activities to promote the growth of data science, both in academia and the industry. More information on the website can be found on its homepage: https://www.kaggle.com/.

As you can find out from the website, this dataset was used in a research study on the early detection of Parkinson's disease using time-based finger movement data while typing. Specifically, the dataset contains the time it takes for 200 subjects to perform normal typing activities on a custom keystroke recording application on their own computer. The data was then collected over several weeks or months. Via the analysis of this dataset, researchers hope to find a correlation between typing speed and other characteristics of finger movements and the fact that a patient has Parkinson's disease. A robust statistical or machine learning model that can learn from that correlation might help doctors to streamline the process of detecting the disease in its early stages.

> More details on the context of this dataset could be found in one of the *Further readings* sections at the end of this chapter.

In our project directory, the data files are saved in two separate folders in the data subfolder (Archived users and Tappy Data). If you started a PyCharm scientific project from scratch, instead of importing the project from our code repository, simply copy these two folders to the data folder in your own project. While we are at it, let's double-click on some of the data files in these two folders to see what kind of data we are working with.

Building a Data Pipeline in PyCharm

We can see that the individual data files in these two folders are text files with the .txt extension. This prevents us from taking advantage of our CSV plugin to inspect the files via a graphical interface. For example, the first file in the Archived users might look as follows:

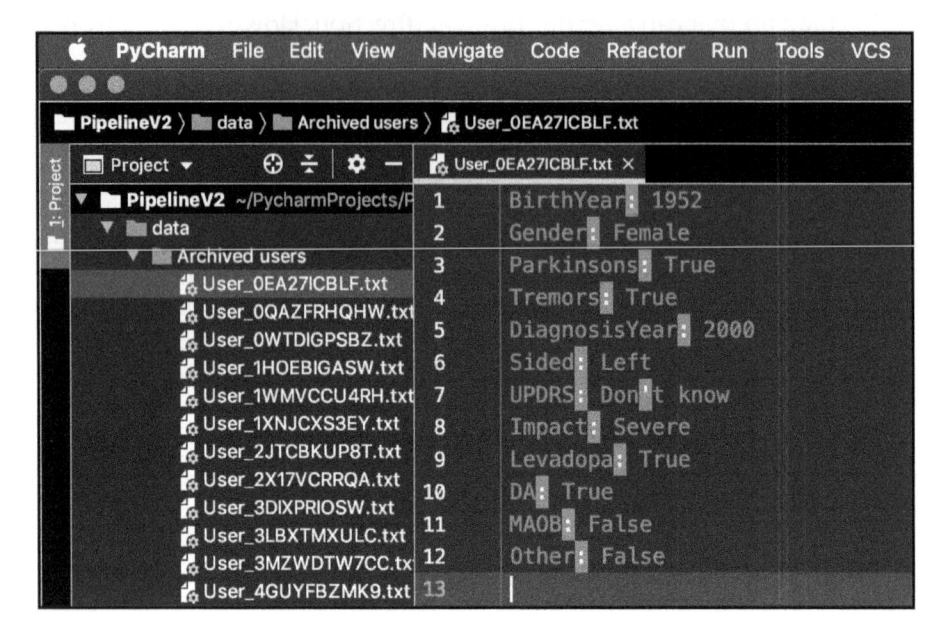

```
  PyCharm  File  Edit  View  Navigate  Code  Refactor  Run  Tools  VCS
 PipelineV2 > data > Archived users > User_0EA27ICBLF.txt
 Project ▼                           User_0EA27ICBLF.txt ×
 ▼ PipelineV2 ~/PycharmProjects/P   1   BirthYear: 1952
   ▼ data                            2   Gender: Female
     ▼ Archived users                3   Parkinsons: True
         User_0EA27ICBLF.txt         4   Tremors: True
         User_0QAZFRHQHW.txt         5   DiagnosisYear: 2000
         User_0WTDIGPSBZ.txt         6   Sided: Left
         User_1HOEBIGASW.txt         7   UPDRS: Don't know
         User_1WMVCCU4RH.txt         8   Impact: Severe
         User_1XNJCXS3EY.txt         9   Levadopa: True
         User_2JTCBKUP8T.txt        10   DA: True
         User_2X17VCRRQA.txt        11   MAOB: False
         User_3DIXPRIOSW.txt        12   Other: False
         User_3LBXTMXULC.txt        13
         User_3MZWDTW7CC.tx
         User_4GUYFBZMK9.txt
```

From this preceding data, we can speculate that the data in this Archived users folder contains administrative information about specific patients. In particular, we see that the preceding patient was born in 1952, is a female, and was indeed diagnosed with Parkinson's.

Furthermore, each patient is assigned a unique identification string that is the name of their corresponding text file. For example, the patient whose data we showed in the preceding screenshot has an ID of 0EA27ICBLF. This ID is very important as we will need to use it, later on, to combine the data from our two data folders.

Turning our attention to the second data folder, Tappy Data, we see that the names of the files in this folder are formatted as [patient ID]_[year][month], denoting the time that data was collected from a specific patient. For example, the first file, 0EA27ICBLF_1607.txt, contains data from patient 0EA27ICBLF that was collected in July 2016. For this reason, a patient can have more than one file in this folder associated with them.

Let's go ahead and open the preceding text file in our PyCharm editor to see what the data inside looks like. You will have something similar to the following:

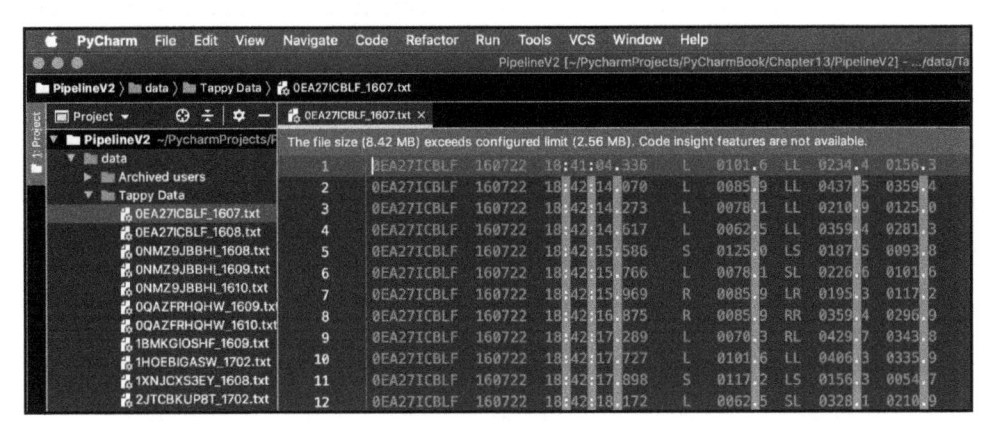

This data file is divided into different rows, each denoting information about a keystroke that the patient performed, and different columns, which contain information such as the following (respectively):

- Patient ID
- The date of data collection
- The timestamp of each keystroke
- Which hand performed the keystroke (*L* for left and *R* for right)
- Hold time (time between press and release, in milliseconds)
- The transition from the last keystroke
- Latency time (time from pressing the previous key, in milliseconds)
- Flight time (time from releasing the previous key, in milliseconds)

So, that is the general structure of the data that we will be working with. Again, our data files are currently in text format, which we will need to process, combine, and convert into some sort of tabular data as CSV files (which we will do in the next section). This is also sometimes the case for real-life data, where our raw data does not come in the format that we want.

For now, we will move on with our discussions. So, in this case, we are already provided with a dataset and a potential question to answer (that is, can we establish patterns in typing speed as an early symptom of Parkinson's disease?). In general, a data scientist might have to manually collect, scrape, or use a third-party service to generate the data they need for their project. Therefore, we will briefly discuss this topic of data collection next.

Collecting data

While the specifics of the different data collection techniques are outside of the scope of this chapter, we can still briefly consider some of them:

- **Downloading from an external source**: This is the case for our example dataset since I downloaded it from Kaggle. When using a dataset downloaded from the internet, we should always make sure to check its copyright license. Most of the time, if it is in the public domain, we can freely use and distribute it without any worry. The example dataset we are using is an instance of this. On the other hand, if the dataset is copyrighted, you might still be able to use it by asking for permission from the author/owner of the dataset. I have personally found that, after reaching out to them via email and explaining how their datasets will be used in detail, dataset owners are often willing to share their data with others.
- **Manually collecting / web scraping**: If the data we want is available online but not formatted in tables or CSV files, most of the time, we need to collect it and manually put it in a dataset ourselves. At most, we can write a web scraper that can send requests to the websites containing the target data and parse the returned HTML text. When you have to collect your data this way, it is also important to ensure that you are not doing it illegally. For example, it is against the law to have a program scrape data off some websites; sometimes, you might need to design the scraper so that only a certain number of requests are made at a given point. An example of this was when LinkedIn filed a lawsuit against many people who anonymously scraped their data in 2016. For this reason, it is always a good practice to find the terms of use for the data you are trying to collect this way.
- **Collecting data via a third party**: Students and researchers who find that the data they are looking for their study cannot be collected online often rely on third-party services to collect that data for them (for example, via crowd-sourcing). Amazon **Mechanical Turk** (**MTurk**) is one such service—you can enter any form of questions to make a survey and MTurk will introduce that survey to its users. Participants receive money for taking the survey, which is paid by the owner of the survey. This option is, again, specifically applicable when you want a representative dataset that is not available online anywhere.

- **Making queries to a database**: This is most likely the case if you are working with data from your company or organization. Luckily, PyCharm offers many useful features in terms of working with databases and their data sources. This process was discussed in `Chapter 9`, *Understanding Database Management with PyCharm*, and I highly recommend you to check it out if you haven't already. Specifically, PyCharm provides a separate tool panel for the process of connecting with a database source. Additionally, we can also use a graphical interface to view and make changes to the data inside a database table in PyCharm, as illustrated here:

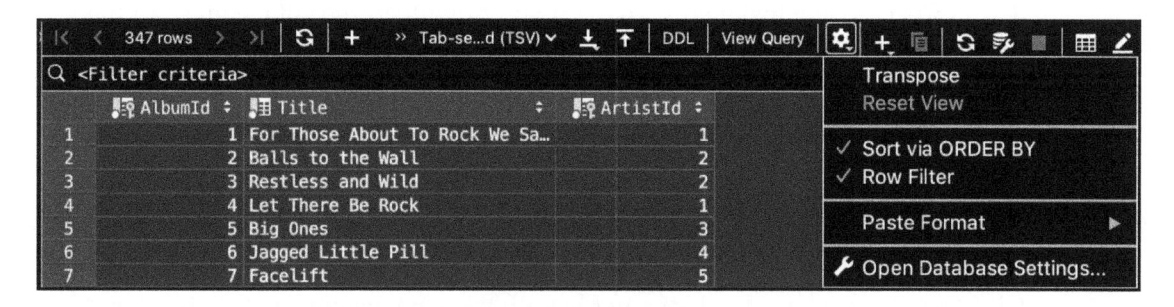

Database table viewer in PyCharm

Overall, there are multiple ways for a data scientist to collect the data for her project; each has its own pros and cons, depending on the purpose and the context of the project.

In the next section, we will talk about the process of version control for datasets.

Version control for datasets

Let's start with understanding the importance of version control in data science. Now, there is somewhat of a crisis of reproducibility in the data science and scientific computing community. This is when one data team can extract a specific insight from a dataset but others cannot, even when using the same methods. Many instances of this are because the data used across these different teams is not compatible with each other. Some might be using the same, but an outdated dataset, while other datasets might have been collected from a different source.

For this reason, version control for datasets is increasingly important. However, as we discussed in `Chapter 5`, *Version Control with Git in PyCharm*, common version control tools such as Git are not applicable for datasets, which are typically large files that are not suitable for being stored with code. In particular, we are not allowed to push any file larger than 100 MB onto our GitHub repositories.

Luckily, there is another version of Git that is specifically designed for this purpose, **Git Large File Storage** (**Git LFS**), which is also integrated nicely with traditional Git. The way it works is that, when we register a file using Git LFS, the system will replace that file with a pointer that simply references it. So, when the file is placed under version control, Git will only have a reference to the actual file, which is now stored in an external server.

In short, Git LFS allows us to apply version control to large files (in this case, datasets) with Git, without actually storing the files in Git. Now, let's go through the process of using Git LFS through the following steps:

1. Git LFS is typically installed with Git if you download the Git Client from their official website, https://git-scm.com/. Otherwise, you can run the following command to install the software:

   ```
   git lfs install
   ```

2. To have Git LFS track files of a given extension, run the following command:

   ```
   git lfs track ".[extension]"
   ```

   Git LFS will now keep track of any file with the same extension. Go ahead and run the command with the .txt extension within our current project, which will register our text data files with Git LFS.

3. We also need to add the .gitattributes file to Git. This is because this file contains the information on the file extensions we are tracking:

   ```
   git add .gitattributes
   ```

That is essentially the process of using Git LFS. Now, when a file with an extension tracked by Git LFS is added by the regular Git, Git LFS will automatically handle all of the backend referencing logic that we mentioned earlier. With this topic, we also conclude our discussion on the topic of working with our datasets in a data science project.

In the next step, we will start the exploratory process with the dataset we have.

Data cleaning and pre-processing

In this section, we will attempt to clean and pre-process the dataset in our current project. This process can also be called **exploratory data analysis**. In general, the term *exploratory data analysis* denotes the process of exploring and analyzing a dataset at the same time.

As we have said before, in an iterative development process with data, we need to take incremental steps to learn about the specifics of a dataset and, from there, know how to analyze it better.

For example, a dataset attribute that contains continuous numerical values (such as length or area) should be handled differently than a discrete attribute (such as age or number of siblings) or even categorical data (such as city, country, or gender). In this case, we will apply various cleaning and pre-processing techniques to the attributes in our dataset per their data types.

Data cleaning and pre-processing are important processes in a data pipeline. As we have seen from our dataset (and this is certainly true in real-life projects), raw data often comes in bad formats that are not fit for actual visualization or machine learning tasks. In data cleaning and pre-processing, we need to reformat and transform our data into nicely encoded attributes that can be fed to visualization functions as well as machine learning models.

For this discussion, we will be considering the code stored inside the `data_clean.py` file in the code repository. To be more specific, we will be looking at individual code cells inside this file. First, we will start by reading in our dataset and normalizing the data types for the attributes in the dataset.

Reading in dataset

First, we will import the libraries we need throughout the program and read in the data in the `Archived user` folder. The Pandas and NumPy libraries in Python will be used, as they are two of the most flexible and versatile tools in Python data analysis. Let's follow these steps to achieve this:

1. Enter and run the following code block in PyCharm:

   ```
   import pandas as pd
   import numpy as np

   import os
   import gc
   ```

   We are already familiar with Pandas and NumPy, which will be used for various data manipulation tasks. We will also need `os` to iterate through the individual data files in our data folders, as well as `gc` to perform some memory-management-related functions.

2. First, we have said that the `Archived user` folder contains files that are dedicated to patient-specific information such as year of birth and diagnosis, while the `Tappy Data` folder contains keystroke data collected from these patients.
3. Now, we would like to eventually combine these two datasets, which requires us to have a consistent set of patients. In other words, a set of patients included in the first folder must match exactly with the set from the second folder.
4. To ensure this, we first compute the intersection of these two sets, extracted from our raw data:

    ```
    #%% Read in data

    user_file_list = os.listdir('data/Archived users/')
    user_set_v1 = set(map(lambda x: x[5: 15], user_file_list)) # [5:
    15] to return just the user IDs


    tappy_file_list = os.listdir('data/Tappy Data/')
    user_set_v2 = set(map(lambda x: x[: 10], tappy_file_list)) # [: 10]
    to return just the user IDs


    user_set = user_set_v1.intersection(user_set_v2)

    print(len(user_set))
    ```

    In the preceding code, we extract the set of patient IDs from the `Archived users` folder and assign it to variable `user_set_v1` (and the same goes for the `Tappy Data` folder and `user_set_v2`). Then, we finally take the intersection of these two sets to obtain the set of patients that are present in both datasets.

5. After running this code cell, you should get **217** as the printed output (the number of matched patients), as illustrated here:

Chapter 13

```
user_set_v1 = set(map(lambda x: x[5: 15], user_file_list))   # [5: 15] to return just the user IDs

tappy_file_list = os.listdir('data/Tappy Data/')
user_set_v2 = set(map(lambda x: x[: 10], tappy_file_list))   # [: 10] to return just the user IDs

user_set = user_set_v1.intersection(user_set_v2)

print(len(user_set))
217
```

6. We will now actually read in the data from `Archived users` and convert it into a tabular format in the next code block:

```
#%% Format into a pandas dataframe

def read_user_file(file_name):
    f = open('data/Archived users/' + file_name)
    data = [line.split(': ')[1][: -1] for line in f.readlines()]
    f.close()

    return data

files = os.listdir('data/Archived users/')

columns = [
    'BirthYear', 'Gender', 'Parkinsons', 'Tremors',
    'DiagnosisYear', 'Sided', 'UPDRS', 'Impact',
    'Levadopa', 'DA', 'MAOB', 'Other'
]

user_df = pd.DataFrame(columns=columns) # empty Data Frame for now

for user_id in user_set:
    temp_file_name = 'User_' + user_id + '.txt' # tappy file names
    have the format of `User_[UserID].txt`
    if temp_file_name in files: # check to see if the user ID is in
      our valid user set
        temp_data = read_user_file(temp_file_name)
        user_df.loc[user_id] = temp_data # adding data to our
        DataFrame

print(user_df.head())
```

The `read_user_file` function takes in a filename (corresponding to a file in `Archived users`), reads in the text data from that file, and returns it in separate lines stored in a Python list.

In the `for` loop at the end of the cell, we loop through all of the patient IDs computed earlier and stored in `user_set` to pass the appropriate filename to `read_user_file`. As we obtain the returned data from the function in each iteration, we append it to the running Pandas DataFrame (`user_df`), which was initialized with the appropriate column names, using the accessor, `loc`. Basically, we are creating a new row with the appropriate patient ID and data at each iteration of the `for` loop.

At the end of the code cell, we print out the first five rows of our final DataFrame, which should look similar to the following:

```
...:         temp_data = read_user_file(temp_file_name)
...:         user_df.loc[user_id] = temp_data # adding data to our DataFrame
...:
...: print(user_df.head())
...:
            BirthYear  Gender Parkinsons Tremors  ... Levadopa     DA   MAOB  Other
ARUGT4UL2R       1955    Male       True    True  ...     True  False   True   True
UUIZH9TDXR       1958  Female       True   False  ...     True  False  False  False
JIRZDKEJQN       1985    Male       True    True  ...    False  False  False   True
XWAX2IHF3O       1970  Female       True    True  ...     True   True  False  False
2X17VCRRQA       1951    Male       True    True  ...     True  False  False  False
```

So, our current data is now in a nice tabular format as a Pandas DataFrame. In the next subsection, we will see how we can perform various data cleaning tasks.

Data cleaning

Real-life datasets often come with bad formatting schemes as well as a lot of missing data. So, data cleaning and data imputation (the processing of filling in missing data) are extremely crucial in any data science pipeline. In this subsection, we will go through some techniques that can be applied to our dataset. Doing this will give you insights on how to handle other situations in your own projects. With that said, let's get started:

1. First, we will convert columns in our dataset that contain numerical values into the correct format. These columns are `BirthYear` and `DiagnosisYear`, which should both contain integer values denoting year numbers. To do this, we use to `to_numeric` function in Pandas:

   ```
   #%% Change numeric data into appropriate format

   # force some columns to have numeric data type
   user_df['BirthYear'] = pd.to_numeric(user_df['BirthYear'],
   errors='coerce')
   user_df['DiagnosisYear'] = pd.to_numeric(user_df['DiagnosisYear'],
   errors='coerce')
   ```

   Here, we are also saying that, if there are errors in the conversion process (that is, when there are invalid values that cannot be translated into a number), then we forcibly replace those values with `NaN`, denoting that they are invalid.

2. We also see that our dataset contains a number of columns with `true`/`false` data (`Gender`, `Parkinsons`, `Tremors`, and so on), and we would like to *binarize* these columns. This is the process where we would convert a `true`/`false` dataset into one containing just zeros (denoting `false`) and ones (denoting `true`). Doing this will make the data we have much more machine-friendly for our machine learning models later on:

```
#%% "Binarize" true-false data

user_df = user_df.rename(index=str, columns={'Gender': 'Female'}) #
renaming `Gender` to `Female`
user_df['Female'] = user_df['Female'] == 'Female' # change string data to
boolean data
user_df['Female'] = user_df['Female'].astype(int) # change boolean data to
binary data

str_to_binary_columns = ['Parkinsons', 'Tremors', 'Levadopa', 'DA', 'MAOB',
'Other'] # columns to be converted to binary data

for column in str_to_binary_columns:
    user_df[column] = user_df[column] == 'True'
    user_df[column] = user_df[column].astype(int)
```

Building a Data Pipeline in PyCharm

3. At this point, we can take a look at our current `user_df` DataFrame using **SciView**. The following screenshot was what I had:

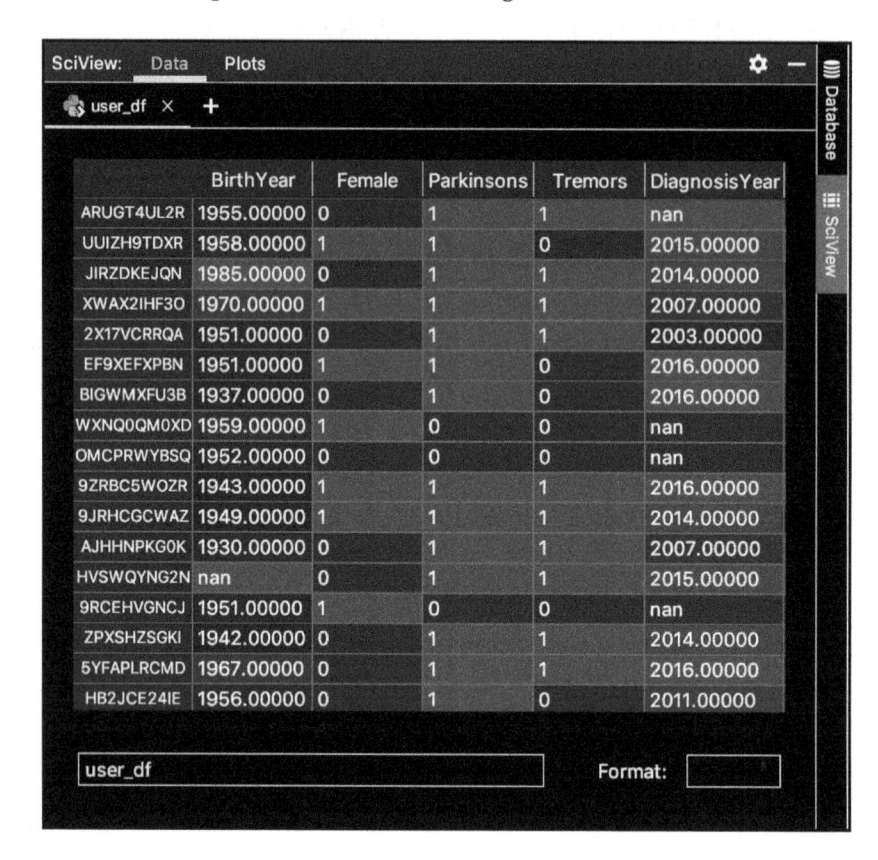

	BirthYear	Female	Parkinsons	Tremors	DiagnosisYear
ARUGT4UL2R	1955.00000	0	1	1	nan
UUIZH9TDXR	1958.00000	1	1	0	2015.00000
JIRZDKEJQN	1985.00000	0	1	1	2014.00000
XWAX2IHF3O	1970.00000	1	1	1	2007.00000
2X17VCRRQA	1951.00000	0	1	1	2003.00000
EF9XEFXPBN	1951.00000	1	1	0	2016.00000
BIGWMXFU3B	1937.00000	0	1	0	2016.00000
WXNQ0QM0XD	1959.00000	1	0	0	nan
OMCPRWYBSQ	1952.00000	0	0	0	nan
9ZRBC5WOZR	1943.00000	1	1	1	2016.00000
9JRHCGCWAZ	1949.00000	1	1	1	2014.00000
AJHHNPKG0K	1930.00000	0	1	1	2007.00000
HVSWQYNG2N	nan	0	1	1	2015.00000
9RCEHVGNCJ	1951.00000	1	0	0	nan
ZPXSHZSGKI	1942.00000	0	1	1	2014.00000
5YFAPLRCMD	1967.00000	0	1	1	2016.00000
HB2JCE24IE	1956.00000	0	1	0	2011.00000

We see that this format is much more readable than what our raw data used to look like. Additionally, **SciView,** with its highlighting feature, does a great job emphasizing different numerical values in the columns of our dataset.

Of course, in a real data pipeline, you might have to face many more problems and inconsistencies with your data, so that more extensive data cleaning tasks than data conversion might be required. The preceding process, on the other hand, introduces some of the common Pandas functions that you might find useful in your own data cleaning process.

So, we have learned how to perform various cleaning techniques on our dataset at this step in the pipeline. Next, we will discuss a specific data engineering technique called one-hot encoding.

One-hot encoding

In this context, an encoding technique is a method of converting the values of a dataset or of an attribute into a dataset so that data analysis techniques and machine learning models can process them more easily. One-hot encoding is a method that is to be used on categorical data.

Let's discuss the theory of one-hot encoding first. Say we have a simple table with the following data:

User ID	City
1	New York
2	St. Louis
3	San Francisco
4	St. Louis

Sample tabular – categorical data

Now, the string data in the **City** column is not very machine-friendly. There are, of course, a number of machine learning models that will have no problem processing this attribute (for example, random forests), but there are models that can only take in numerical data. We would like to transform this attribute so that we can still preserve the information we have, but it will be in numerical form.

A simple solution can be to create a one-to-one mapping between the values in the categorical attribute and a set of numbers. For example, we can replace every instance of **New York** with the number 1, every instance of **St. Louis** with 2, and **San Francisco** with 3. Doing this will result in the following table:

User ID	City_v1
1	1
2	2
3	3
4	2

One-to-one encoding

However, there is a potential problem to this approach—by replacing the categorical data with numerical values, we are unintentionally creating an ordered relation between these new values. For example, machine learning models might interpret that, in the **City_v1** attribute, number 1 is somehow less than numbers 2 and 3 or number 3 comes after number 2, which, in turn, comes after number 1. Obviously, there is no such relation in the original data with the actual city names, but, by using numerical values as we did, a number-related connection between the encoded data might be made.

One-hot encoding addresses this problem for us. Specifically, via a one-hot encoding process, each unique value inside the categorical attribute being considered will be used to create a new attribute. These new attributes all contain binary data, indicating whether a specific attribute is applicable for a given entry or not. For example, our original table, with one-hot encoding, will be transformed into the following:

User ID	City_New_York	City_St_Louis	City_San_Francisco
1	1	0	0
2	0	1	0
3	0	0	1
4	0	1	0

One-hot encoding

Since the **City** attribute of the first user is **New York**, the **New York** entry is set to **1** (indicating yes), while the rest of the entries are set to **0** (indicating no), and the same goes for the other rows. We see that this method successfully avoids the problem of creating a false ordering between our new numerical data since now we have separate attributes containing independent data. We don't lose any information from our original categorical attribute either.

A big drawback of using one-hot encoding is the fact that we are creating additional attributes, one for each unique value in the set of the categorical attribute we'd like to encode. So, if we have a categorical attribute that contains, say, 1,000 unique values, that one-hot encoding will generate 1,000 additional new attributes—this is clearly not desirable.

Chapter 13

In other words, one-hot encoding is quite a powerful tool, but it is only applicable for categorical data that have a low number of unique values.

Now, let's see how to apply one-hot encoding in Python. Getting back to our example, in Python, this process can be implemented using the `get_dummies()` method, callable from a Pandas DataFrame. Here is one of the next code cells in our script; we have the following code:

```
#%% Dummy variable (one-hot encoding)
# prior processing for `Impact` column
user_df.loc[
    (user_df['Impact'] != 'Medium') &
    (user_df['Impact'] != 'Mild') &
    (user_df['Impact'] != 'Severe'), 'Impact'] = 'None'


to_dummy_column_indices = ['Sided', 'UPDRS', 'Impact'] # columns to be one-hot encoded

for column in to_dummy_column_indices:
    user_df = pd.concat([
        user_df.iloc[:, : user_df.columns.get_loc(column)],
        pd.get_dummies(user_df[column], prefix=str(column)),
        user_df.iloc[:, user_df.columns.get_loc(column) + 1 :]
    ], axis=1)

print(user_df.head())
```

Here, we are applying one-hot encoding to three attributes: `Sided`, `UPDRS`, and `Impact`. Basically, the `get_dummies()` method takes in a categorical column and returns encoded data with the newly created attributes. This is why we need to insert back these new attributes to our dataset (using `concat()`).

[377]

Go ahead and run the code cells up until this point. When you inspect the current dataset, you should see the following new attributes:

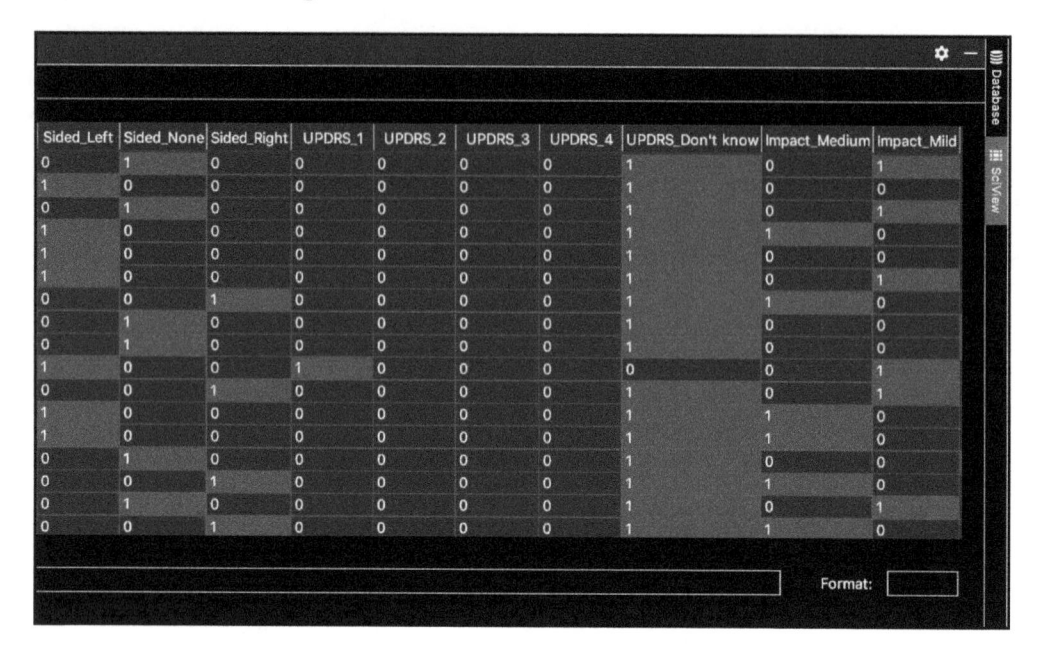

One-hot encoding in PyCharm

So, we have discussed the idea behind one-hot encoding, a popular data pre-processing technique in data science, and how to implement it in Python. Next, we will bring in our second dataset, explore its characteristics, and extend our discussion on data cleaning further in the next subsection.

Problem-specific techniques

As the term suggests, problem-specific techniques are applied when we take into account the particular characteristics of our current dataset and proceed to process it accordingly. In general, there is no way to tell what particularities your dataset contains; the only approach is to, again, extensively explore the dataset and address any problems as they arise.

In the following steps, we will go over some more pre-processing techniques that are specific to our datasets, so that you will have more experience dealing with badly formatted data. Note that, while the gist of each section of our code will be discussed, if you have trouble understanding the effect of any specific command, you can examine it further in the documentation of Pandas, included in the *Further reading* section of this chapter:

1. First, let's read a sample file from the `Tappy Data` folder:

   ```
   #%% Explore the second dataset
   file_name = '0EA27ICBLF_1607.txt' # an arbitrary file to explore

   df = pd.read_csv(
       'data/Tappy Data/' + file_name,
       delimiter = '\t',
       index_col = False,
       names = ['UserKey', 'Date', 'Timestamp', 'Hand', 'Hold time',
       'Direction', 'Latency time', 'Flight time']
   )

   df = df.drop('UserKey', axis=1)

   print(df.head())
   ```

2. Now, use the **SciView** to inspect this `df` variable:

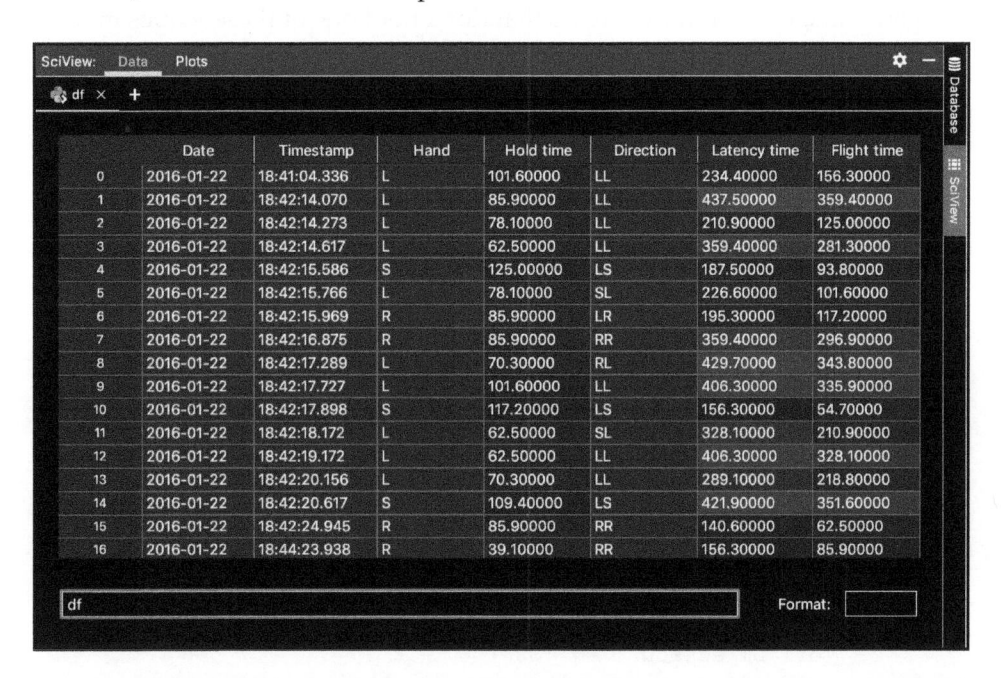

	Date	Timestamp	Hand	Hold time	Direction	Latency time	Flight time
0	2016-01-22	18:41:04.336	L	101.60000	LL	234.40000	156.30000
1	2016-01-22	18:42:14.070	L	85.90000	LL	437.50000	359.40000
2	2016-01-22	18:42:14.273	L	78.10000	LL	210.90000	125.00000
3	2016-01-22	18:42:14.617	L	62.50000	LL	359.40000	281.30000
4	2016-01-22	18:42:15.586	S	125.00000	LS	187.50000	93.80000
5	2016-01-22	18:42:15.766	L	78.10000	SL	226.60000	101.60000
6	2016-01-22	18:42:15.969	R	85.90000	LR	195.30000	117.20000
7	2016-01-22	18:42:16.875	R	85.90000	RR	359.40000	296.90000
8	2016-01-22	18:42:17.289	L	70.30000	RL	429.70000	343.80000
9	2016-01-22	18:42:17.727	L	101.60000	LL	406.30000	335.90000
10	2016-01-22	18:42:17.898	S	117.20000	LS	156.30000	54.70000
11	2016-01-22	18:42:18.172	L	62.50000	SL	328.10000	210.90000
12	2016-01-22	18:42:19.172	L	62.50000	LL	406.30000	328.10000
13	2016-01-22	18:42:20.156	L	70.30000	LL	289.10000	218.80000
14	2016-01-22	18:42:20.617	S	109.40000	LS	421.90000	351.60000
15	2016-01-22	18:42:24.945	R	85.90000	RR	140.60000	62.50000
16	2016-01-22	18:44:23.938	R	39.10000	RR	156.30000	85.90000

We see that this is the same data that we saw in the *Working with datasets* section of this chapter, now formatted as a Pandas DataFrame. Next, we will need to perform various preprocessing techniques on this dataset.

Building a Data Pipeline in PyCharm

3. From here, we can also see that we need to convert the `datetime` columns into their appropriate data types:

    ```
    #%% Format datetime data

    df['Date'] = pd.to_datetime(df['Date'], errors='coerce',
    format='%y%M%d').dt.date
    # converting time data to numeric
    for column in ['Hold time', 'Latency time', 'Flight time']:
        df[column] = pd.to_numeric(df[column], errors='coerce')

    df = df.dropna(axis=0)

    print(df.head())
    ```

4. Now, each of the `Hand` and `Direction` columns have a fixed set of valid values. In particular, each cell in `Hand` should hold the value of L (left), R (right), or S (spacebar) and the data in `Direction` is one of the nine possibilities going from one of the three values to another (LL, LR, LS, and so on). For this reason, we would like to filter out the rows that don't hold one of these values in the two columns, using the code in the next block:

    ```
    #%% Remove incorrect data

    # cleaning data in Hand
    df = df[
        (df['Hand'] == 'L') |
        (df['Hand'] == 'R') |
        (df['Hand'] == 'S')
    ]

    # cleaning data in Direction
    df = df[
        (df['Direction'] == 'LL') |
        (df['Direction'] == 'LR') |
        (df['Direction'] == 'LS') |
        (df['Direction'] == 'RL') |
        (df['Direction'] == 'RR') |
        (df['Direction'] == 'RS') |
        (df['Direction'] == 'SL') |
        (df['Direction'] == 'SR') |
        (df['Direction'] == 'SS')
    ]

    print(df.head())
    ```

Note that our current data might not contain any of the invalid values as of now, but it is good practice to have this filtering logic in our code in case our data is changed or updated in the future, ensuring that our pipeline stays consistent.

5. Next, recall that what we have been working with so far is typing speed data for a specific patient at a given time. A patient is simply a single data point within our first dataset, and we would like to combine the two datasets together somehow, so we need a way to aggregate our current data into a single data point.

   Since we are working with numerical data (typing time), we can take the average (mean) of the time data across different columns as a way to summarize the data of a given user. We can achieve this with the `groupby()` function from Pandas in the next code cell:

   ```
   #%% Group by direction (hand transition)
   direction_group_df = df.groupby('Direction').mean()
   print(direction_group_df)
   ```

6. Let's now inspect this `direction_group_df` DataFrame in **SciView**:

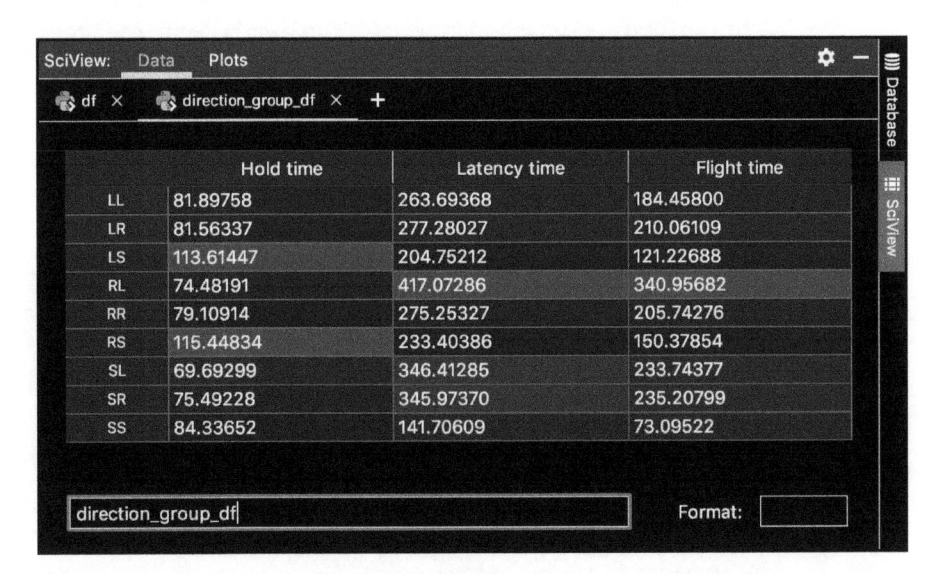

	Hold time	Latency time	Flight time
LL	81.89758	263.69368	184.45800
LR	81.56337	277.28027	210.06109
LS	113.61447	204.75212	121.22688
RL	74.48191	417.07286	340.95682
RR	79.10914	275.25327	205.74276
RS	115.44834	233.40386	150.37854
SL	69.69299	346.41285	233.74377
SR	75.49228	345.97370	235.20799
SS	84.33652	141.70609	73.09522

   As we can see, this DataFrame is divided into rows of different `Direction` data (`LL`, `LR`, `LS`, and so on), and its columns are the different time-based attributes. This is what we want as a single data point that can be appended to our first dataset.

Building a Data Pipeline in PyCharm

7. Now, remember that this dataset was computed with a single file in the `Tappy Data` folder. However, we need to iterate through all of the files in that folder. To do that, we first refactor all of the data-manipulation logic so far into a function in the next code cell:

```python
#%% Combine into one function

def read_tappy(file_name):
    df = pd.read_csv(
        'data/Tappy Data/' + file_name,
        delimiter='\t',
        index_col=False,
        names=['UserKey', 'Date', 'Timestamp', 'Hand', 'Hold time',
               'Direction', 'Latency time', 'Flight time']
    )

    df = df.drop('UserKey', axis=1)

    df['Date'] = pd.to_datetime(df['Date'], errors='coerce', format='%y%M%d').dt.date

    # Convert time data to numeric
    for column in ['Hold time', 'Latency time', 'Flight time']:
        df[column] = pd.to_numeric(df[column], errors='coerce')
    df = df.dropna(axis=0)

    # Clean data in `Hand`
    df = df[
        (df['Hand'] == 'L') |
        (df['Hand'] == 'R') |
        (df['Hand'] == 'S')
    ]

    # Clean data in `Direction`
    df = df[
        (df['Direction'] == 'LL') |
        (df['Direction'] == 'LR') |
        (df['Direction'] == 'LS') |
        (df['Direction'] == 'RL') |
        (df['Direction'] == 'RR') |
        (df['Direction'] == 'RS') |
        (df['Direction'] == 'SL') |
        (df['Direction'] == 'SR') |
        (df['Direction'] == 'SS')
    ]

    direction_group_df = df.groupby('Direction').mean()
```

```
        del df
        gc.collect()

        direction_group_df = direction_group_df.reindex(
            ['LL', 'LR', 'LS', 'RL', 'RR', 'RS', 'SL', 'SR', 'SS'])
        direction_group_df = direction_group_df.sort_index() # to
            ensure correct order of data

        return direction_group_df.values.flatten() # returning a
            numpy array
```

Specifically, this `read_tappy()` function takes in a filename in the `Tappy Data` folder and performs the same processing that we discussed in the previous steps. This function will return the aggregated averaged time data that we saw as a flattened (1-dimensional) NumPy array. This is necessary for us to be able to append it to our first dataset.

8. Then, we have another function, `process_user()`, that iterates through all of the files associated with a common patient and calls `read_tappy()` to process those files:

```
    def process_user(user_id, filenames):
        running_user_data = np.array([])

        for filename in filenames:
            if user_id in filename:
                running_user_data = np.append(running_user_data,
                    read_tappy(filename))

        running_user_data = np.reshape(running_user_data, (-1, 27)) #
            flatten time data

        return np.nanmean(running_user_data, axis=0) # ignoring NaNs
            while calculating the mean
```

In the end, this function returns a summary of all of the time-related data of a specific patient.

9. In the next code cell, we finally iterate through all of the valid patient IDs and call `process_user()` using a `for` loop:

```
    #%% Run through all available data

    import warnings; warnings.filterwarnings("ignore")

    filenames = os.listdir('data/Tappy Data/')
```

Building a Data Pipeline in PyCharm

```
                column_names = [first_hand + second_hand + '_' + time
                                for first_hand in ['L', 'R', 'S']
                                for second_hand in ['L', 'R', 'S']
                                for time in ['Hold time', 'Latency time', 'Flight
            time']]

                user_tappy_df = pd.DataFrame(columns=column_names)

                for user_id in user_df.index:
                    user_tappy_data = process_user(str(user_id), filenames)
                    user_tappy_df.loc[user_id] = user_tappy_data

                # Some preliminary data cleaning
                user_tappy_df = user_tappy_df.fillna(0)
                user_tappy_df[user_tappy_df < 0] = 0

                print(user_tappy_df.head())
```

As we iterate through the `for` loop, we call `process_user()` to obtain the aggregated data and append it to a running DataFrame stored in `user_tappy_df`.

10. When the code block finishes executing, let's open it in our **SciView**:

As you can see, our current DataFrame is indexed by the unique patient IDs and, at the same time, contains data on their typing speed as individual columns. This is the exact format that we want our data to be in.

That technique also concludes our discussion on data cleaning and pre-processing methods that are specific to our example dataset. Next, we finally combine our two datasets and write them to file.

Saving and viewing processed data

As the last step of our process, let's combine our two datasets and write our processed dataset to file so that we can start working on this cleaned version in the future, which is achieved using the code in the next cell:

```
combined_user_df = pd.concat([user_df, user_tappy_df], axis=1)
print(combined_user_df.head())

combined_user_df.to_csv('data/combined_user.csv')
```

This is generally a good practice in a given data pipeline. Saving the processed, cleaned version of a dataset can save data engineers a lot of effort if something goes wrong along the way. It also offers flexibility, if and when we want to change or extend our pipeline further.

One interesting note about this cleaned version of our data is that, when we open the CSV file in the PyCharm editor, it can actually be displayed in the table viewer:

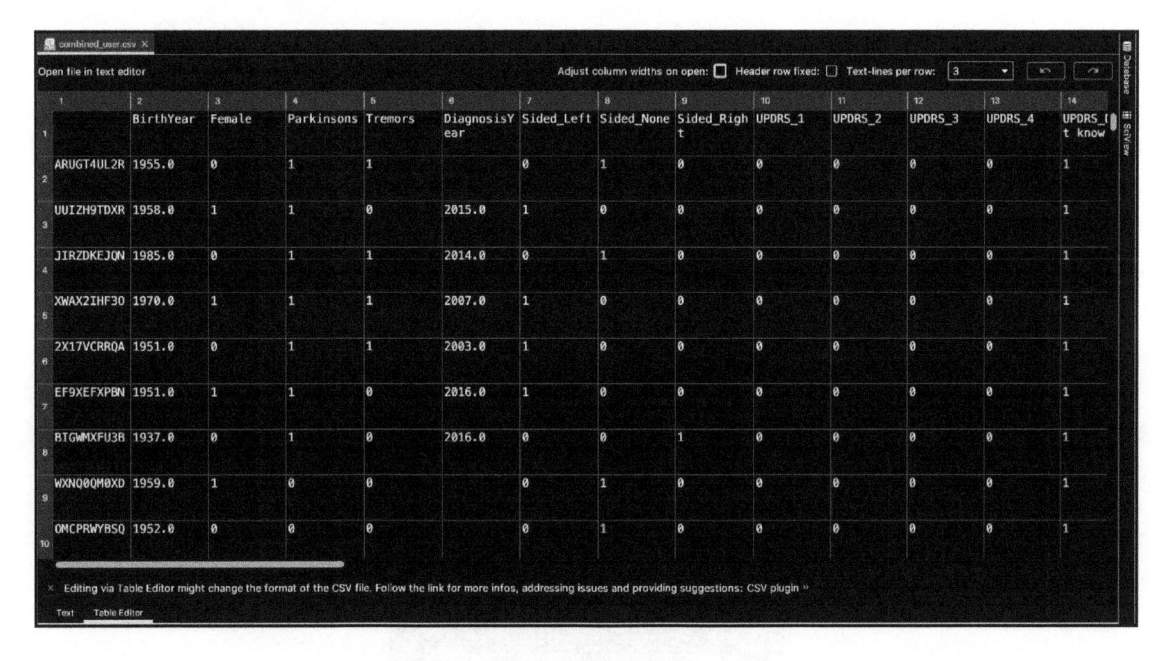

Cleaned data in the table viewer

Recall that this option was not available for the raw version of the dataset. However, during the cleaning process, we actually removed a large number of bad formatting and inconsistencies from our dataset. After this combination of cleaning techniques, our dataset can now be interpreted even by the PyCharm table viewer, again highlighting the crucial roles data cleaning and pre-processing play in a data science pipeline.

With that, we are ready to start exploring our dataset and search for insights in the next section of this chapter.

Data analysis and insights

Remember what we said about the importance of having a question in mind when starting to work on a data science project? This is especially true during this phase where we explore our dataset and extract insights, which should revolve around our initial question—the connection between typing speed and whether a patient has Parkinson's or not.

Throughout this section, we will be working with the EDA.ipynb file, located in the notebooks folder of our current project. In the following subsections, we will be looking at the code included in this notebooks folder. Go ahead and open this Jupyter notebook in your PyCharm editor, or, if you are following our discussions and entering your own code, create a new Jupyter notebook.

Starting the notebook and reading in data

As mentioned in the previous chapter, a Jupyter notebook being opened in the PyCharm editor does not mean that it is active. This is indicated by the fact that the output panel (on the right) does not contain any output from the code just yet. To start running Jupyter, use the **Run** button for the first code cell in our notebook:

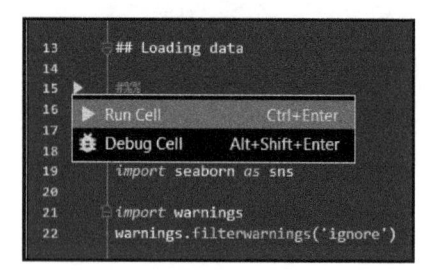

Running a Jupyter code cell in PyCharm

Doing this will both initialize a Jupyter server in the backend and run the first code cell, which imports the necessary libraries and reads in our cleaned dataset:

```
import pandas as pd
import numpy as np

import matplotlib.pyplot as plt
import seaborn as sns

combined_user_df = pd.read_csv('../data/combined_user.csv', index_col=0)
combined_user_df.head()
```

Since we are specifying (in the last line of code) that we would like to print out the first five rows of our dataset, that output is displayed in the right-hand-side panel. Note that you can use the scrollbar at the bottom of the printed table (as indicated here) to scroll through the different columns in our current dataset:

Navigating a big printed DataFrame in PyCharm

With our dataset being read in and organized this way, let's move on with our analysis, starting from the next subsection, with various visualization techniques that will be applied to our current dataset.

Using charts and graphs

One of the most common ways to visualize a dataset is through bar charts. The idea is that, if we have an attribute that could only contain a specific set of values, seeing the distribution of the counts of those unique values could give us an insight into which factor could affect the dependent variable we are interested in (in this case, it is whether a person has Parkinson's or not).

Building a Data Pipeline in PyCharm

But first, we will use bar charts to visualize the amount of missing data we have in our current dataset:

```
#%%

missing_data = combined_user_df.isnull().sum()

g = sns.barplot(missing_data.index, missing_data)
g.set_xticklabels(labels=missing_data.index, rotation=90)

plt.show()
```

Running this code cell should produce the following visualization:

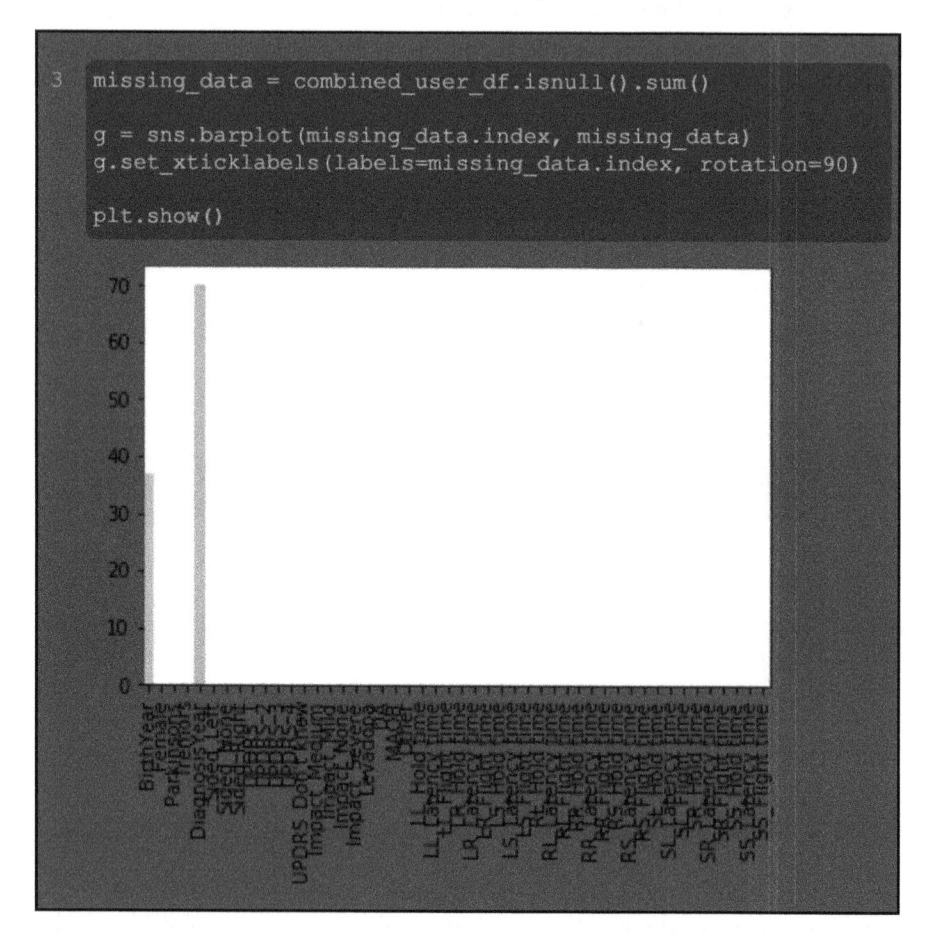

From here, we see that besides the columns, `BirthYear` and `DiagnosisYear`, our dataset does not contain a significant amount of missing data. The analysis of missing values is an important one, and we will come back to the process of filling in these values later on. For now, let's move on with our discussion on visualizations.

A great feature in Matplotlib is subplots, which allows us to generate multiple visualizations side by side. In the next code cell, we will create multiple visualizations with this feature, to highlight potential differences between patients with and without Parkinson's:

```
#%%

f, ax = plt.subplots(2, 2, figsize=(20, 10))

sns.distplot(
    combined_user_df.loc[combined_user_df['Parkinsons'] == 0,
    'BirthYear'].dropna(axis=0),
    kde_kws = {'label': "Without Parkinson's"},
    ax = ax[0][0]
)
sns.distplot(
    combined_user_df.loc[combined_user_df['Parkinsons'] == 1,
    'BirthYear'].dropna(axis=0),
    kde_kws = {'label': "With Parkinson's"},
    ax = ax[0][1]
)

sns.countplot(x='Female', hue='Parkinsons', data=combined_user_df,
ax=ax[1][0])
sns.countplot(x='Tremors', hue='Parkinsons', data=combined_user_df,
ax=ax[1][1])

plt.show()
```

Building a Data Pipeline in PyCharm

After running the code cell, you will generate a visualization similar to the following:

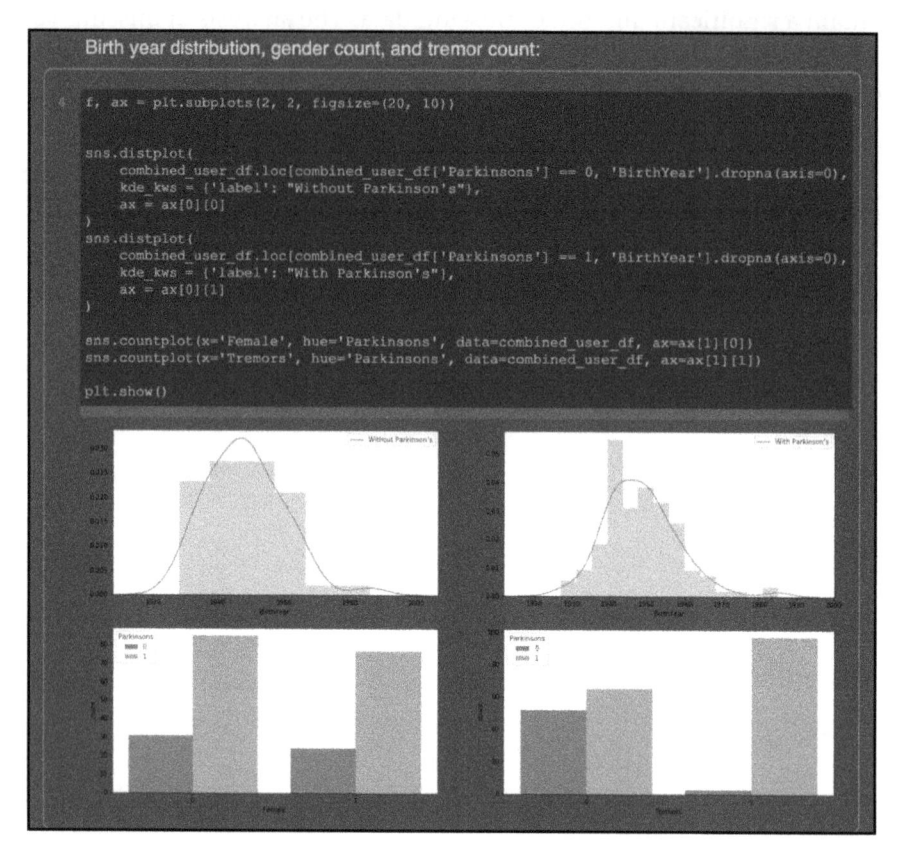

```
Birth year distribution, gender count, and tremor count:
f, ax = plt.subplots(2, 2, figsize=(20, 10))

sns.distplot(
    combined_user_df.loc[combined_user_df['Parkinsons'] == 0, 'BirthYear'].dropna(axis=0),
    kde_kws = {'label': "Without Parkinson's"},
    ax = ax[0][0]
)
sns.distplot(
    combined_user_df.loc[combined_user_df['Parkinsons'] == 1, 'BirthYear'].dropna(axis=0),
    kde_kws = {'label': "With Parkinson's"},
    ax = ax[0][1]
)

sns.countplot(x='Female', hue='Parkinsons', data=combined_user_df, ax=ax[1][0])
sns.countplot(x='Tremors', hue='Parkinsons', data=combined_user_df, ax=ax[1][1])

plt.show()
```

Now, let's take a moment to break down what we have:

- The top two visualizations represent the distribution in the year of birth of people with (top-right) and without (top-left) Parkinson's. We see that these distributions roughly follow the normal bell curve. In other instances and projects, if you encounter a distribution that is skewed or in a strange shape, it might be worthwhile to dig into that data further. Note that we can also apply the same visualization for the `DiagnosisYear` column.
- In the bottom-left visualization, we have a bar chart representing the count of male patients (two bars on the left) and female patients (two bars on the right). Patients with Parkinson's are counted with the orange bars, and patients without are counted with the blue bars. In this visualization, we see that while there are more patients with the disease than the ones without, the breakdown across the two genders is roughly the same.

- The bottom-right visualization, on the other hand, illustrates the breakdown between patients with tremors (two bars on the right) and without tremors (two bars on the left). From this visualization, we can see that tremors are significantly more common with patients with Parkinson's, which is quite intuitive and can serve as a sanity check for our analyses so far.

Next, we will move on to box plots. Specifically, we will use box plots to visualize the distributions of different time data (Hold time, Latency time, and Flight time) among patients with and without Parkinson's. We will again use the subplots feature to generate multiple visualizations at the same time:

```
#%%

column_names = [first_hand + second_hand + '_' + time
                for first_hand in ['L', 'R', 'S']
                for second_hand in ['L', 'R', 'S']
                for time in ['Hold time', 'Latency time', 'Flight time']]

f, ax = plt.subplots(3, 3, figsize=(10, 5))

plt.subplots_adjust(
    right = 3,
    top = 3
)

for i in range(9):
    temp_columns = column_names[3 * i : 3 * i + 3]
    stacked_df = combined_user_df[temp_columns].stack().reset_index()
    stacked_df = stacked_df.rename(
        columns={'level_0': 'index', 'level_1': 'Type', 0: 'Time'})
    stacked_df = stacked_df.set_index('index')
    
    for index in stacked_df.index:
        stacked_df.loc[index, 'Parkinsons'] = combined_user_df.loc[index,
            'Parkinsons']
    sns.boxplot(x='Type', y='Time',
                hue='Parkinsons',
                data=stacked_df,
                ax=ax[i // 3][i % 3]
                ).set_title(column_names[i * 3][: 2], fontsize=20)
plt.show()
```

In this code cell, each subplot will visualize data of a specific direction type (LL, LR, LS, and so on) and will contain different splits denoting patients with and without the disease. You should obtain the following visualization:

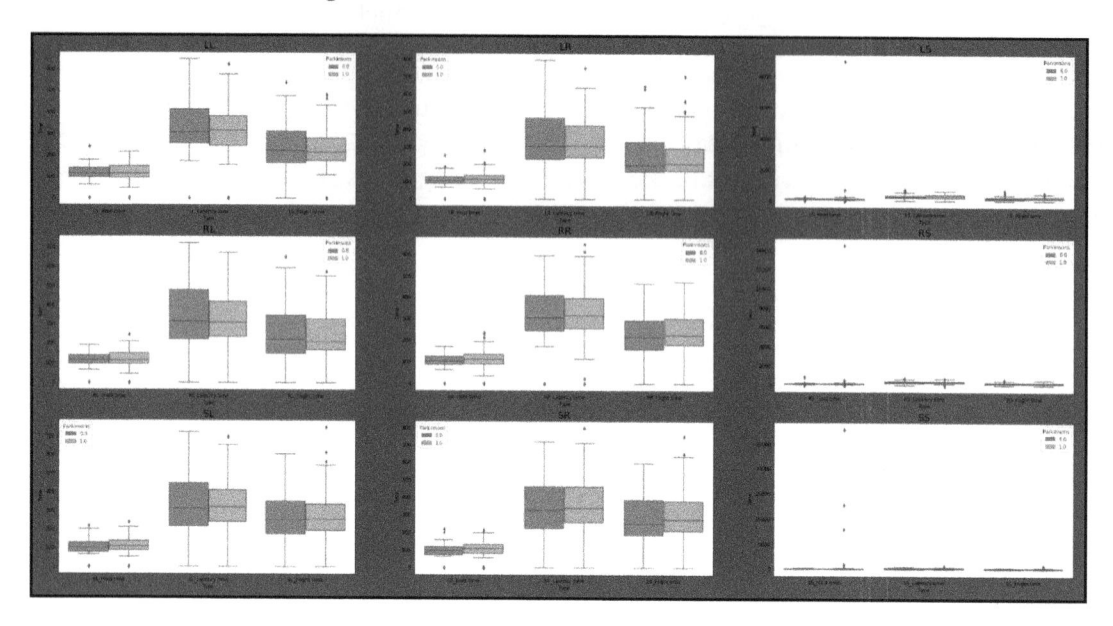

What we can gather from this visualization is that, surprisingly, the distribution of typing speed among patients without Parkinson's can span across higher values and have more variance than that among patients with Parkinson's, which might contradict the intuition some might have that patients with Parkinson's take more time to press keystrokes.

Overall, bar charts, distribution plots, and box plots are some of the most common visualization techniques in data science tasks, mostly because they are both simple to understand and powerful enough to highlight important patterns in our datasets. In the next and final subsection on the topic of data analysis, we will consider more advanced techniques, namely, the correlation matrix between attributes and leveraging machine learning models.

Machine-learning-based insights

Unlike the previous analysis methods, the methods discussed in this subsection and others similar are based on more complex mathematical models and machine learning algorithms. Given the scope of this book, we will not be going into the specific theoretical details for these models, but it's still worth seeing some of them in action by applying them to our dataset:

1. First, let's consider the feature correlation matrix for our dataset. As the name suggests, this model is a matrix (a 2D table) that contains the correlation between each pair of numerical attributes (or features) within our dataset. A correlation between two features is a real number between -1 and 1, indicating the magnitude and direction of the correlation. The higher the value is, the more correlated the two features are.

   To obtain the feature correlation matrix from a Pandas DataFrame, we call the `corr()` method, like in our next code cell:

   ```
   corr_matrix = combined_user_df.corr()
   ```

2. We usually visualize a correlation matrix using a heat map, as implemented in the same code cell:

   ```
   f, ax = plt.subplots(1, 1, figsize=(15, 10))
   sns.heatmap(corr_matrix)

   plt.show()
   ```

   This code will produce the following visualization:

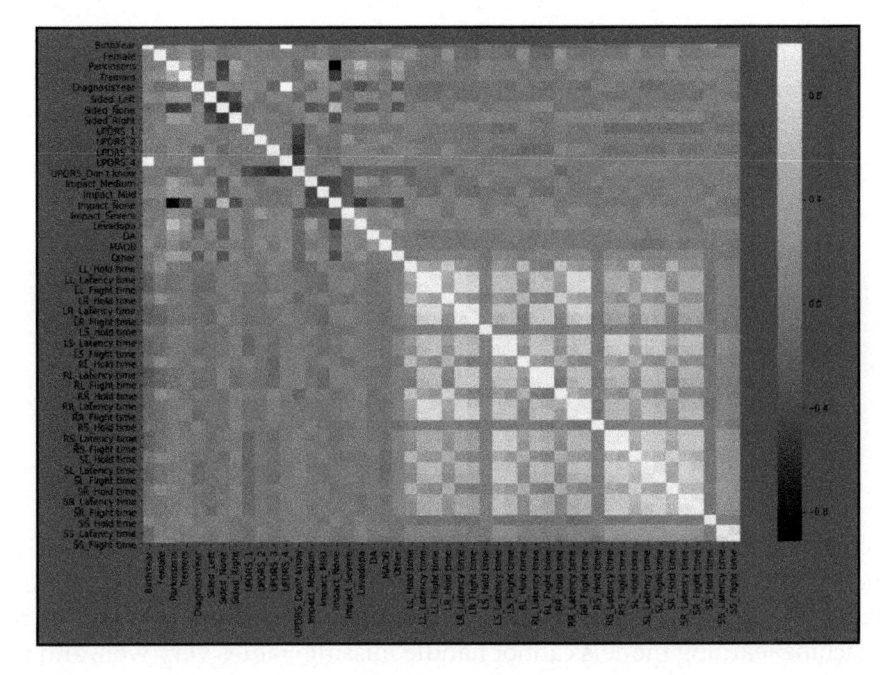

   A feature correlation matrix heat map

3. From this heat map, we can focus on the cells that are especially bright (which indicates a strong positive correlation), as well as the ones that are especially dark (which indicates a strong negative correlation). For example, we see high correlations between the time-based attributes in the lower-right corner of the heat map. This is reasonable as they all describe some statistics about a patient's typing speed.

4. Next, we will try applying a machine learning model for our dataset. Contrary to popular belief, in many data science projects, we don't take advantage of machine learning models for predictive tasks, where we train our models to be able to predict future data. Instead, we feed our dataset to a specific model so we can extract more insights from that current dataset.

   Here, we are using the linear **Support Vector Classifier** (**SVC**) model from scikit-learn to analyze the data we have and return the feature importance list:

   ```
   #%%
   
   from sklearn.svm import LinearSVC
   
   
   combined_user_df['BirthYear'].fillna(combined_user_df['BirthYear'].mode(dropna=True)[0], inplace=True)
   combined_user_df['DiagnosisYear'].fillna(combined_user_df['DiagnosisYear'].mode(dropna=True)[0], inplace=True)
   
   X_train = combined_user_df.drop(['Parkinsons'], axis=1)
   y_train = combined_user_df['Parkinsons']
   
   clf = LinearSVC()
   clf.fit(X_train, y_train)
   
   
   nfeatures = 10
   
   coef = clf.coef_.ravel()
   top_positive_coefs = np.argsort(coef)[-nfeatures :]
   top_negative_coefs = np.argsort(coef)[: nfeatures]
   top_coefs = np.hstack([top_negative_coefs, top_positive_coefs])
   ```

   Note that, before we feed the data we have to the machine learning model, we need to fill in the missing values we have in the two columns we identified earlier—`BirthYear` and `DiagnosisYear`. This is because some (if not most) machine learning models cannot handle missing values very well, and it is up to the data engineers to choose how these values should be filled.

Here, we are using the mode (the most commonly occurring data point) of these two columns to fill in the missing values. This is because the mode is one of the statistics that tend to represent the range of different kinds of data well, especially for discrete/nominal attributes (which is what we have here). If you are working with numerical and continuous data such as length or area, it is also common practice to use the mean of a given attribute. Finally, getting back to our current process, this code trains the model on our dataset and obtains the `coef_` attribute of the model afterward.

5. This attribute contains the feature importance list, which is visualized by the last section of the code:

```
plt.figure(figsize=(15, 5))
colors = ['red' if c < 0 else 'blue' for c in coef[top_coefs]]
plt.bar(np.arange(2 * nfeatures), coef[top_coefs], color = colors)
feature_names = np.array(X_train.columns)
plt.xticks(np.arange(0, 1 + 2 * nfeatures),
feature_names[top_coefs], rotation=60, ha='right')

plt.show()
```

This code produces the following graph:

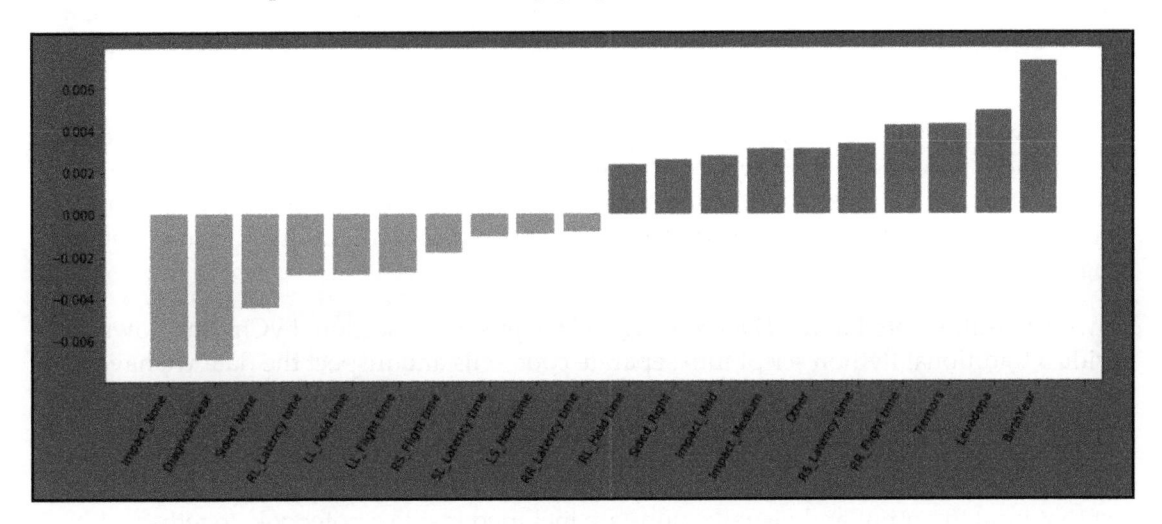

Feature importance from SVC

6. From the feature importance list, we can identify any features that were used extensively by the machine learning model while training. A feature with a very high importance value could be correlated with the target attribute (whether someone has Parkinson's or not) in some interesting way. For example, we see that `Tremors` (which we know are quite correlated to our target attribute) is the third most important feature for our current machine learning model.

That's our last discussion point regarding the analysis of our dataset. In the last section of our chapter, we will have a brief discussion on deciding how to write a script in a Python data science project.

Scripts versus notebooks in data science

So, in the preceding data science pipeline we just went through, there are two main sections—data cleaning (where we remove inconsistent data, fill in missing data, and appropriately encode the attributes) and data analysis (where we generate visualizations and insights from our cleaned dataset).

The data cleaning process was implemented by a Python script while the data analysis process was done with a Jupyter notebook. In general, deciding whether a Python program should be done in a script or in a notebook is quite an important, yet often overlooked aspect, while working on a data science project.

As we have discussed in the previous chapter, Jupyter notebooks are perfect for iterative development processes, where we can transform and manipulate our data as we go. A Python script, on the other hand, offers no such dynamism—with a traditional Python script, we need to enter all of the code necessary in the script and run it as a complete program.

However, as illustrated in the *Data cleaning and pre-processing* section, PyCharm allows us to divide a traditional Python script into separate code cells and inspect the data we have as we go using the **SciView** panel. In other words, the dynamism in programming offered by Jupyter notebook can also be found with PyCharm.

Now, another core difference between regular Python scripts and Jupyter notebooks is the fact that printed output and visualizations are included inside a notebook, together with the code cells that generated them. While looking at this from the perspective of data scientists, we see that this feature is considerably useful when making reports and presentations.

Specifically, say you are tasked with finding actionable insights from a dataset in a company project, and you need to present your final findings, as well as how you came across them with your team. Here, a Jupyter notebook can serve as the main platform for your presentation quite effectively—not only will people be able to see which specific commands were used to process and manipulate the original data, you will also be able to include Markdown texts to further explain any subtle discussion points.

Compared to that, regular Python scripts can simply be used for low-level tasks where the general workflow has already been agreed upon, and you will not need to present it with anyone else. In our current example, I chose to clean the dataset using a Python script, as most of the cleaning and formatting changes we applied to the dataset don't generate any actionable insights that can address our initial question. I only used a notebook for data analysis tasks, where there are many visualizations and insights worthy of further discussion.

Overall, the decision to use either a traditional Python script or a Jupyter notebook solely depends on your tasks and purposes. We simply need to remember that, for whichever tool we would like to use, PyCharm offers incredible support that can streamline our workflow.

Summary

In this chapter, we have walked through the hands-on process of working on a data science pipeline. First, we discussed the importance of having version control for not just our code and project-related files but also our datasets; we then learned how to use Git LFS to apply version control to large files and datasets.

Next, we looked at various data cleaning and pre-processing techniques that are specific to the example dataset. Using the **SciView** panel in PyCharm, we can dynamically inspect the current state of our data and variables and see how they change after each command.

Finally, we considered several techniques to generate visualizations and extract insights from our dataset. Using the Jupyter editor in PyCharm, we were able to avoid working with a Jupyter server and work on our notebook entirely within PyCharm. Having walked through this process, you are now ready to tackle real-life data science problems and projects using the same tools and functionalities that we have discussed so far.

So, we have finished our discussion on using PyCharm in the context of scientific computing and data science. In the next chapter, we will finally consider a topic that we have mentioned multiple times through our previous chapters—PyCharm plugins.

Questions

1. What are some of the main ways of collecting datasets for a data science project?
2. Can Git LFS be used with Git? If so, what is the overall process?
3. Which type of attribute can have their missing values filled out with the mean? What about the mode?
4. What problem does one-hot encoding address? What problem can arise from using one-hot encoding?
5. Which type of attribute can benefit from bar charts? What about distribution plots?
6. Why is it important to consider the feature correlation matrix for a dataset?
7. Aside from predictive tasks, what can we use machine learning models for (like we did in this chapter)?

Further reading

More information can be found in the following articles and readings:

- The *Tappy Keystroke Data with Parkinson's Patients* data, uploaded by Patrick DeKelly: (https://www.kaggle.com/valkling/tappy-keystroke-data-with-parkinsons-patients)
- *Building a Data Pipeline from Scratch*, by Alan Marazzi: (https://medium.com/the-data-experience/building-a-data-pipeline-from-scratch-32b712cfb1db)
- *A Business Perspective to Designing an Enterprise-Level Data Science Pipeline*, by Vikram Reddy: (https://www.datascience.com/blog/designing-an-enterprise-level-data-science-pipeline)
- *Data Science for Startups: Data Pipelines*, by Ben Weber: (https://towardsdatascience.com/data-science-for-startups-data-pipelines-786f6746a59a)
- Documentation for the Pandas library: (https://pandas.pydata.org/pandas-docs/stable/)

Section 5: Plugins and Conclusion

This section starts with Chapter 14, *More Possibilities with PyCharm Plugins*. Consisting of the final two chapters of this book, this section provides some parting thoughts regarding the use of PyCharm and how to make the best of it while developing your Python projects. Firstly, we will discuss the wide range of options when it comes to additional plugins that you can add to your PyCharm software. These are further extensions of PyCharm you can download and install that can help to improve your productivity even further.

In the final chapter, we will go through a compiled version of important topics and features discussed throughout this book. We will then bring this book to a close with a few general suggestions on how to effectively use PyCharm and a list of potential further reading.

This section includes the following chapters:

- Chapter 14, *More Possibilities with PyCharm Plugins*
- Chapter 15, *Future Developments*

14
More Possibilities with PyCharm Plugins

This chapter will introduce you to the concept of PyCharm plugins and walk you through the process of downloading plugins and adding them to the PyCharm environment. In general, plugins are add-ons to PyCharm's core functionalities that can help improve your productivity in specific tasks. We have seen examples of these plugins with database management, when writing Markdown code, and when working with CSV data.

In this chapter, we will look in detail at the most popular PyCharm plugins and how they can optimize our productivity. These discussions will help you to familiarize yourself further with the concept of plugins, as well as learn more about the plugins that other PyCharm users have found useful.

The following topics will be covered in this chapter:

- Downloading and installing PyCharm plugins
- Working with plugins
- Using popular plugins for your projects

By considering the collection of PyCharm plugins available online, we will again emphasize the point of how extendable PyCharm is and that PyCharm users can always find new and better ways to facilitate the development process. By the end of the chapter, you will be ready to explore all the available plugins that can help you with your own projects.

Technical requirements

Please ensure that you have both Python 3.6+ and PyCharm installed on your computer.

Exploring PyCharm plugins

The level of customization PyCharm offers does not stop at what users can use from the software upon installation. In fact, PyCharm users have the option of adding customized plugins that can further improve productivity in many topics.

Let's start by checking out the plugin window.

Opening the plugin window

To open the main window from which we can work with PyCharm plugins, we go to the settings in PyCharm and go to the **Plugins** tab. Or, if we are currently at the welcome window, we can use the **Configure** menu, as illustrated here:

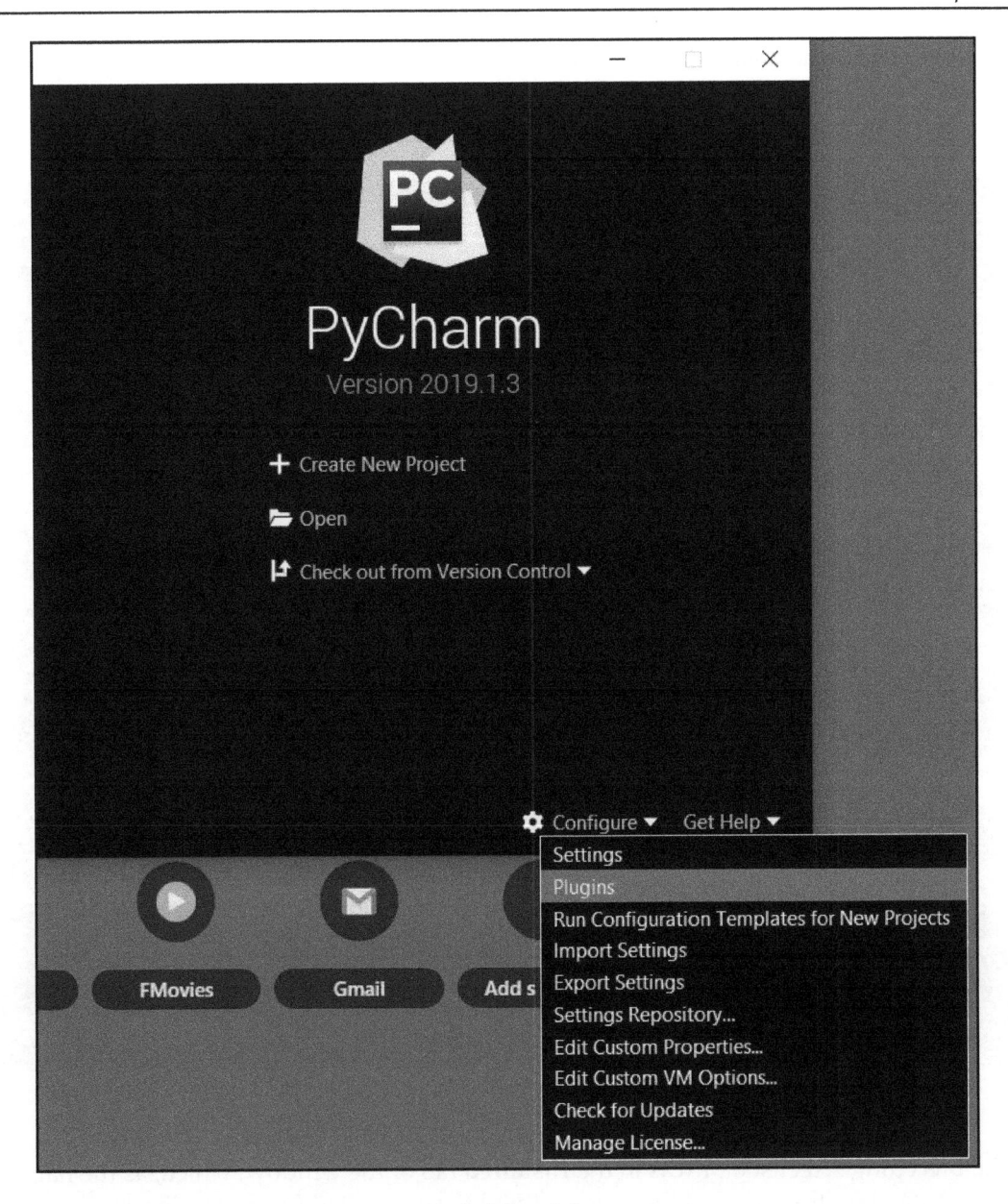

Opening PyCharm plugins

More Possibilities with PyCharm Plugins

This will open up the main window, where we can manage our PyCharm plugins. There are three tabs in this window (**Marketplace**, **Installed**, and **Updates**), as illustrated here:

Managing your PyCharm plugins

In the preceding screenshot, I was in the **Installed** tab of the window, which, as the name suggests, displays the list of all the plugins that I have installed for my PyCharm. We are already familiar with some of these plugins such as the **CSV Plugin** or **PyCharm cell mode**. On the other hand, the last tab on the right lists all the updates available for the installed plugins.

From the **Marketplace** tab, we can browse through different plugins that are available for download, which we will discuss in the next subsection.

Downloading and installing a plugin

In addition to browsing through the plugins in the **Marketplace** tab, you can also use the search bar at the top of the window to find specific plugins. For example, if I'd like to search for more themes for my PyCharm, I type in `theme` in the search bar and hit *Enter*, which return the following results:

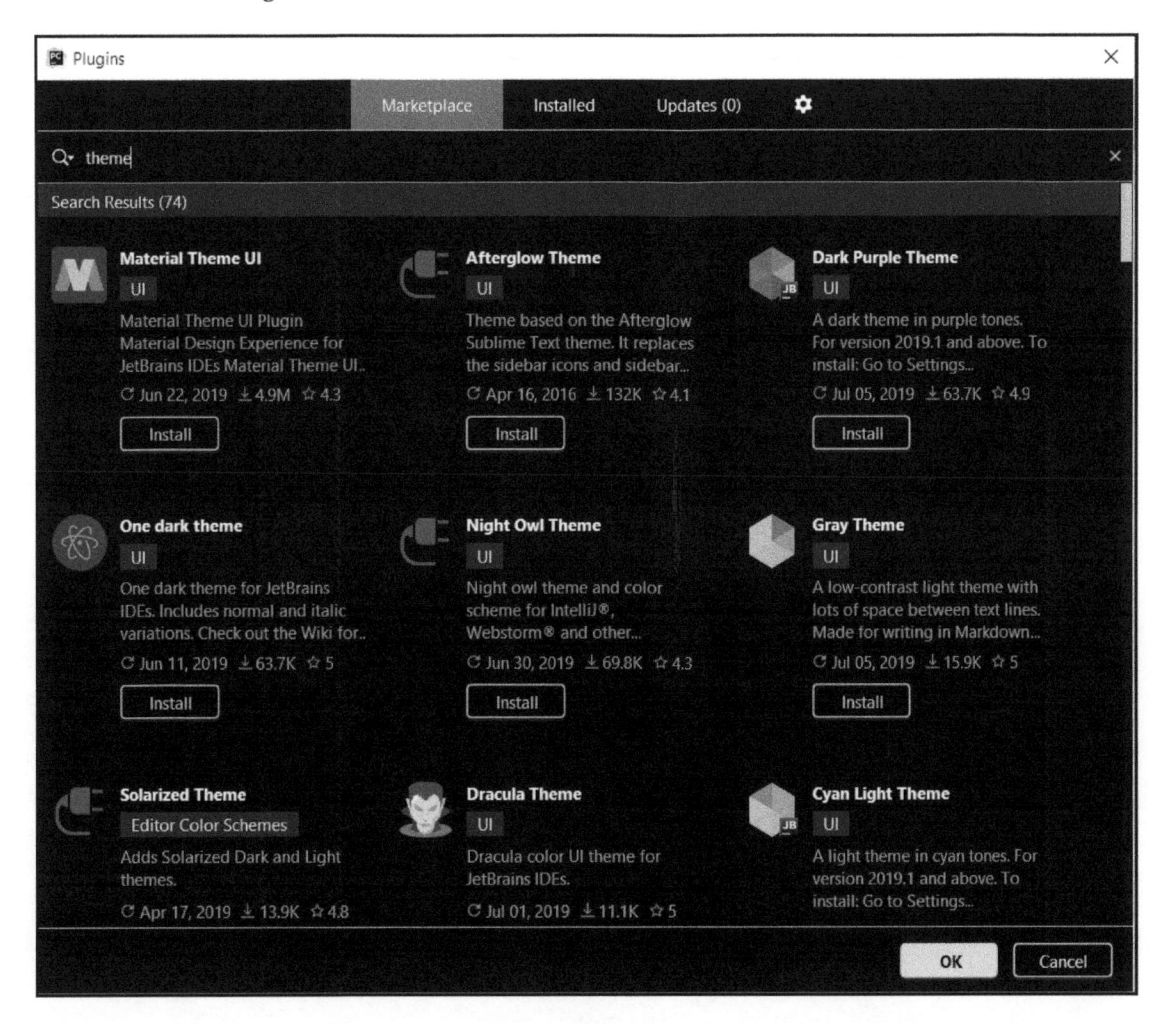

Searching for specific plugins

More Possibilities with PyCharm Plugins

By the way, to be able to search for the plugins in a more extensive and exhaustive way, we can head to `plugins.jetbrains.com/pycharm`, which contains more categories and searching capabilities for PyCharm plugins. Specifically, we can browse through the list of plugins on the website in a web browser, and once we have decided on which plugin we would like to install, we can go back to PyCharm and start the process.

Now, let's try installing one of these plugins. Here, I'm choosing to install the first and most popular plugin theme in PyCharm: **Material Theme UI**. After clicking on the **Install** button, the downloading process will start. Once the source code for a plugin has been downloaded, we in most cases need to restart PyCharm so that the plugin can be used upon the reboot. The **Restart IDE** button is typically included next to the plugin as follows:

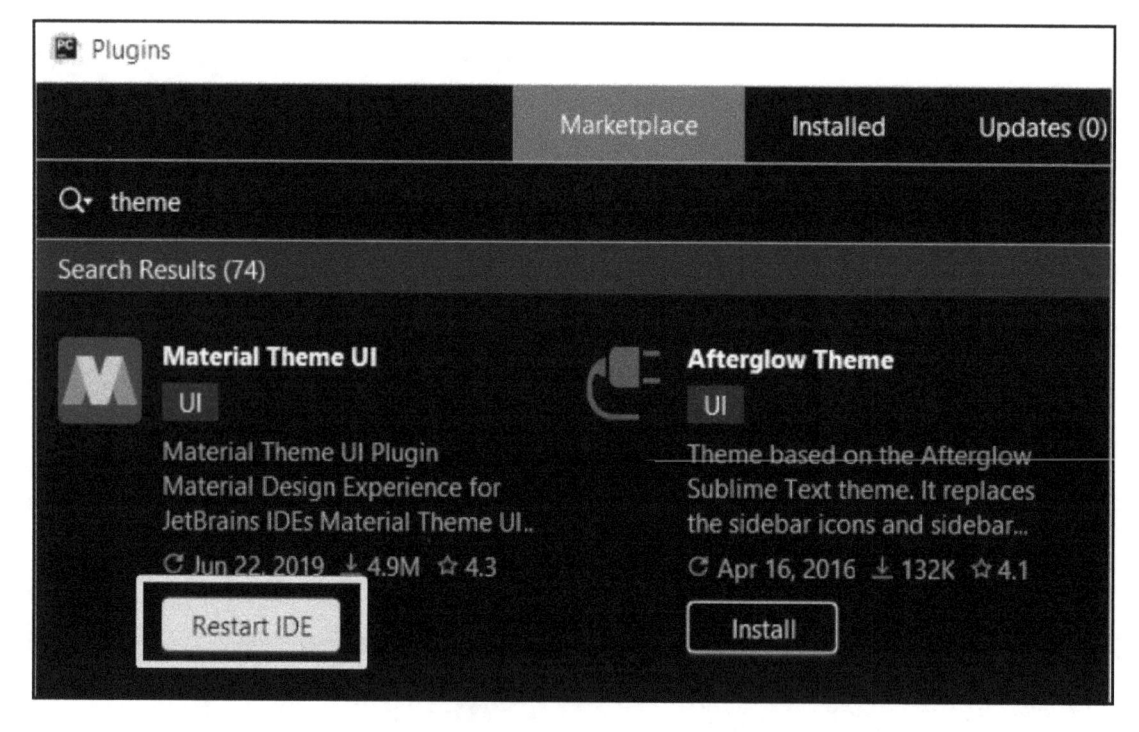

Restarting PyCharm after installing a plugin

If you are following my example and installing the theme for yourself, once PyCharm relaunches itself, we will have to go through a couple of steps and options to set up the theme. Once this process finishes, we can see that the theme starts taking effect in PyCharm.

For example, the following is a screenshot from my PyCharm workspace after this Material Theme has taken effect, which has an entirely different feel from the regular theme:

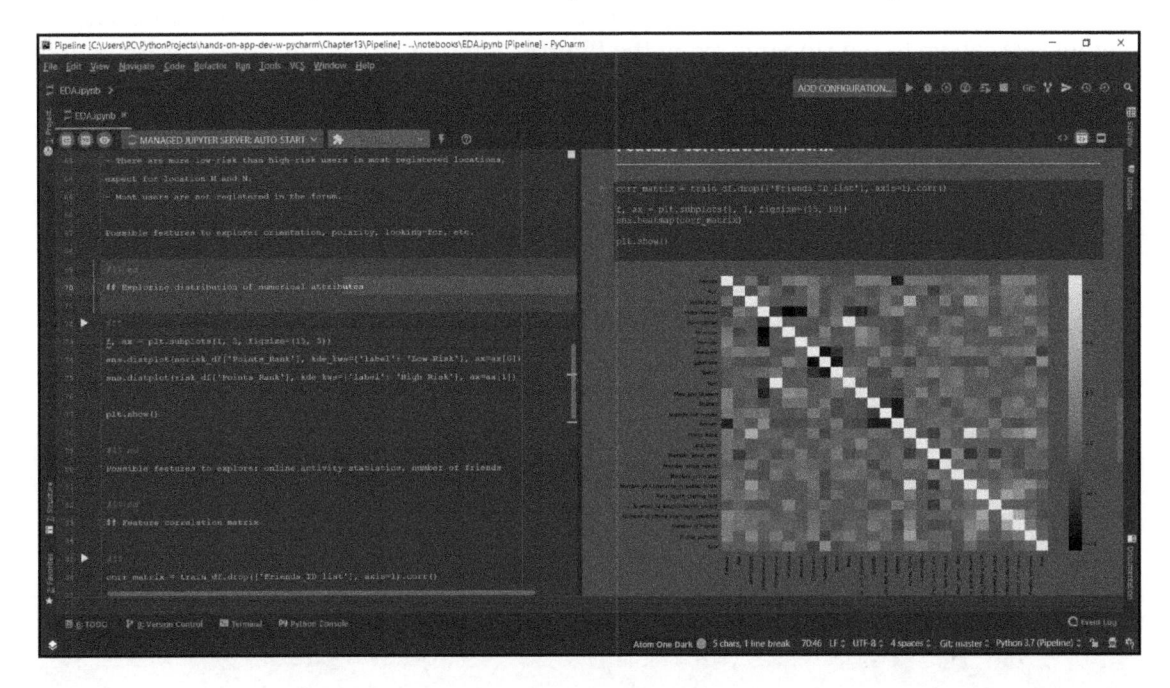

Material Theme in PyCharm

For most of the other plugins, we can simply start using them upon restarting PyCharm. This is the case for the various plugins we have seen throughout this book, such as the CSV viewer and PyCharm code cell plugins.

Finally, as the last topic of this section, we will see how we can update or uninstall a plugin in PyCharm.

More Possibilities with PyCharm Plugins

Updating and removing plugins

As we have seen before, to check whether there are any updates available for our installed plugins, we can go to the **Updates** tab of the **Plugins** window in PyCharm. As for removing a plugin, from the list of plugins in the **Installed** tab, you can right-click on the plugin you would like to remove and choose either of the following options:

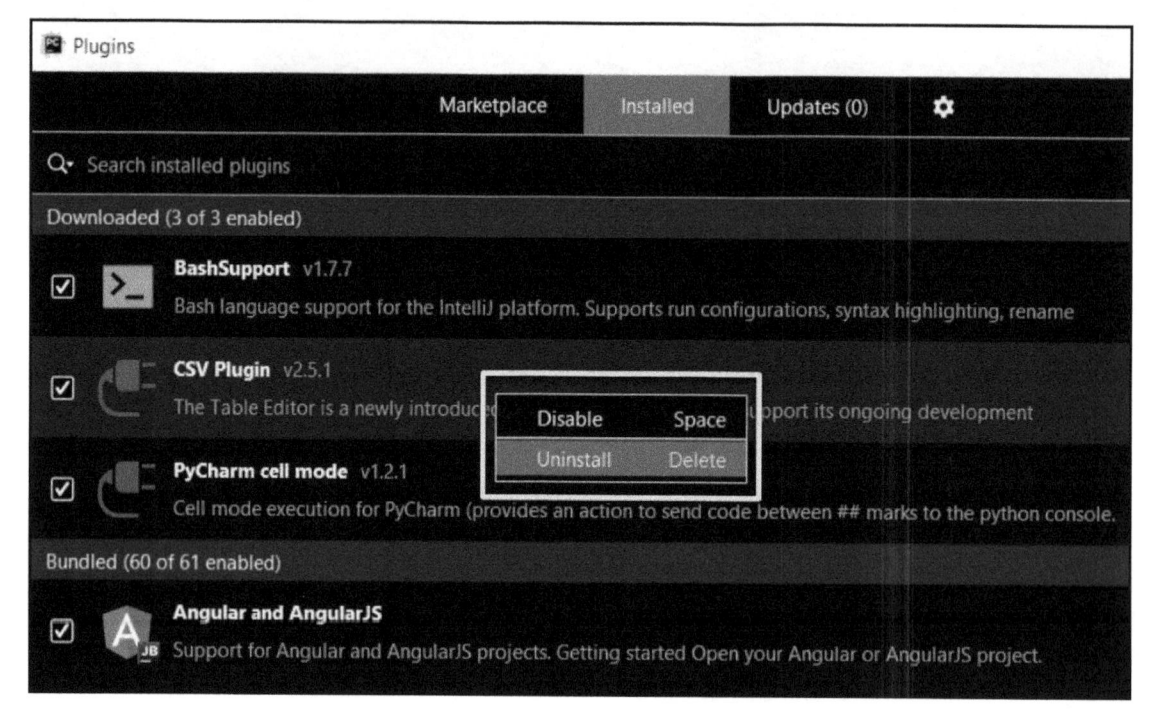

Removing a plugin in PyCharm

Disabling a plugin will simply deactivate its effect in your PyCharm work environment, while uninstalling it will completely remove its source code from PyCharm.

So we have gone through the basic workflow of working with PyCharm plugins. Most of the time, the effect a plugin has on your PyCharm will vary, depending on the purpose of the plugin. However, the preceding steps we discussed should apply to all PyCharm plugins. In the next section, we will go through some of the plugins that I think are the most useful in Python projects.

Best plugins to use for your PyCharm projects

With the basic idea of how to install a PyCharm plugin in mind, let's go through a list of some of the most popular PyCharm plugins and see the support they can provide for our projects. Some of the plugins we are discussing might have already been mentioned in previous chapters, so feel free to skip this section.

> **TIP**: Note that for each of the plugins to be discussed, I will be including a URL to the home page of the plugin on the official website of JetBrains, where more information about these plugins as well as ratings and comments can be found.

First, let's start with a plugin for database management.

Using Database Navigator

We saw some level of database support in PyCharm in `Chapter 9`, *Understanding Database Management with PyCharm*, using the **Database** panel and the database viewer. This PyCharm plugin takes working with databases to another level by providing more extensive and powerful options to integrate databases into PyCharm. The plugin's interface includes extensive navigations and features for viewing and manipulating data in database tables.

As we have discussed, working with databases is a common task in web development and even data science projects. Aside from having great support to view and make edits to the data within a database table (as illustrated previously), the Database Navigator plugin also offers options such as SQL editing, database connection management, database compiler operations, and many more.

More details regarding this plugin can be found at `plugins.jetbrains.com/plugin/1800-database-navigator`. Next, we will look at another plugin that is commonly used in web development projects.

Using LiveEdit

The specifics of this plugin were briefly discussed in `Chapter 7`, *Web Development with JavaScript, HTML, and CSS*. In general, this plugin allows us to view the output of a rendered web page in real time as we make edits to the source code in HTML and CSS.

This behavior normally can only be achieved by manually refreshing the output page, so LiveEdit helps us skip that process, which can save a lot of time. If you are working on a Node.js application, LiveEdit can also reset the application automatically when a new change is applied.

The following setting window highlights some of these options that LiveEdit offers:

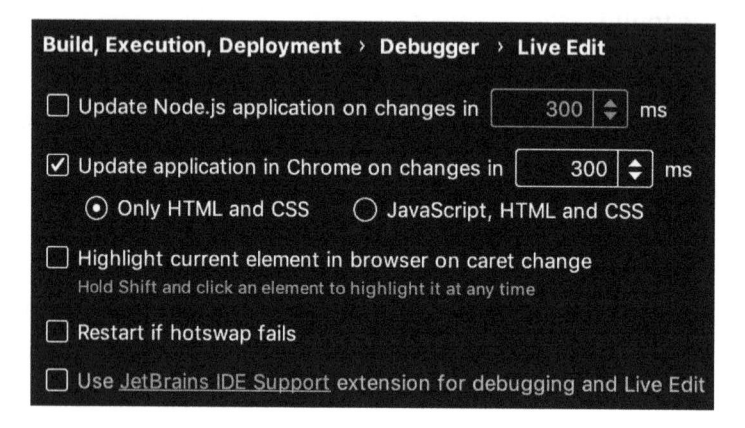

LiveEdit behavior customizations

Overall, this plugin can prove to be useful in the development process as well as debugging sessions. It is a must-have feature if you are a Python web developer. For more information about this tool, you can visit `https://plugins.jetbrains.com/plugin/7007-liveedit`.

Moving along, the third plugin we will be discussing is the one we have mentioned many times before: the CSV Plugin.

Using the CSV Plugin

As discussed in the *Advanced features in PyCharm's scientific projects* section of `Chapter 11`, *Turning On Scientific Mode*, this plugin offers a great way to work with CSV files in PyCharm. The CSV Plugin allows us to view data using the same environment used for code editing, while also providing a tabular interface that displays the data in a more user-friendly manner, as shown here:

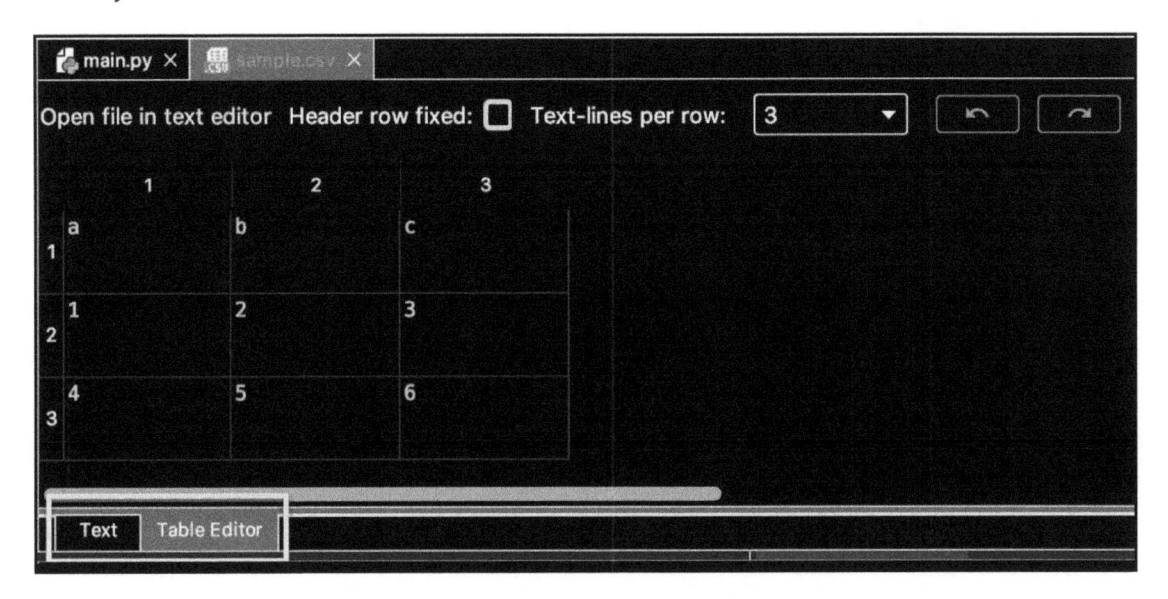

The table viewer from the CSV Plugin

Similar to the Database Navigator, this plugin also allows us to view and edit the data in a CSV file in PyCharm as we go. In addition to CSV files, this plugin can also handle tabs, commas, semicolons, or pipe characters (|) as the separators. As we have seen from the previous chapter, there is a limit to the size of a file this plugin can handle; most of the time, it can work just fine.

This plugin is a must-have for data scientists, specifically any Python developers that work with CSV. More details on this plugin can be found at plugins.jetbrains.com/plugin/7793-markdown.

Next, we will look at another plugin that we used in the book: Markdown.

Using Markdown

In Chapter 11, *Turning On Scientific Mode*, we were introduced to the Markdown plugin. In general, Markdown is a markup language that is often used to generate introductory GitHub documents as well as texts in Jupyter notebook. The Markdown plugin, integrated with the PyCharm editor, streamlines the process of writing standalone Markdown documents.

For example, as shown in the following screenshot, this plugin allows us to write Markdown code and see what the final rendered output will look like in real time so that we can make changes to the code in a dynamic manner:

The Markdown editor in PyCharm

As illustrated here, the editor is split into two sections when a Markdown file is being opened:

- The editing section on the left
- The rendered output section on the right

The output section is rendered in real time with respect to the code in the editing section, so we will be able to see the Markdown code in the end in a dynamic way. More details on the plugin can be found at plugins.jetbrains.com/plugin/7793-markdown.

In the next subsection, we will look at the last most popular PyCharm plugin: String Manipulation.

Using String Manipulation

This plugin offers powerful options in terms of editing and manipulating text, even in large amounts. This includes toggling between different text styles, such as `camelCase`, `snake_case`, `dot.case`, `Words Capitalized`, and so on.

As you know, programming languages have a set of standards in terms of naming for variables, functions, and classes. For example, in Python, the variable and function names should be in `snake_case` (for example, `my_var` and `get_num()`), while class names should be in Pascal case (for example, `MyClass` and `DataFrame`). Variables in Java, on the other hand, should be in `camelCase` (`myVar` and `userAccount`).

To have a string switch between these cases, we simply need to right-click on a selected block of text, go to the **String Manipulation** section, and choose whatever editing option we'd like to apply, as illustrated here:

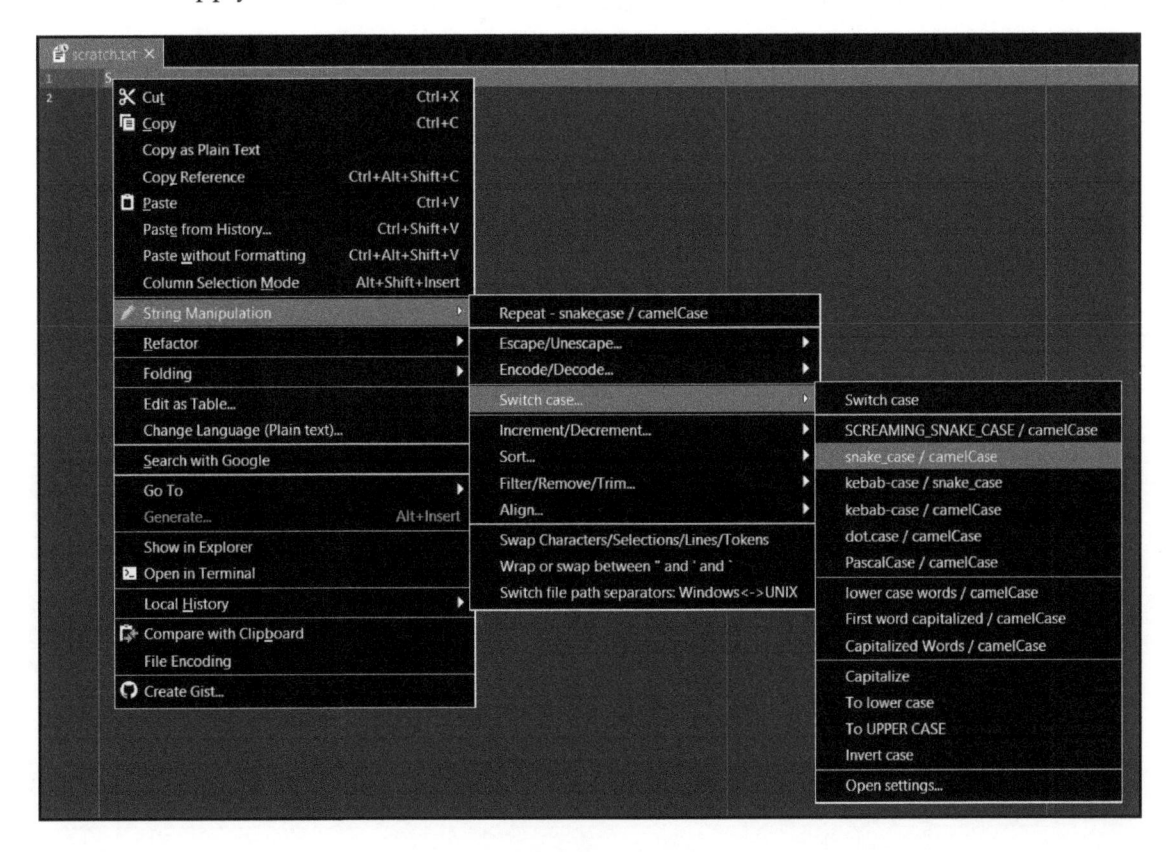

String Manipulation in PyCharm

The plugin can also handle more complex text-editing functionalities, such as sorting lines of text alphabetically or randomly shuffling different lines of text, and incrementing and decrementing all numbers in a block of text. Other editing options include trimming/filtering out specific special characters, text alignment, and formatting as tables.

And that is a list of some of the most popular PyCharm plugins that you can use for your projects. Of course, this list is entirely subjective and was compiled from my own experience and research, and there are definitely other good plugins out there that you can explore yourself.

In the next and last section of the chapter, we will briefly consider some advanced tasks while working with plugins.

Advanced plugin-related options

Aside from installing, updating, and removing plugins in your PyCharm software, there are more advanced options that we should keep in mind in terms of working with PyCharm plugins. First, we can specify a particular plugin as a requirement of a PyCharm project.

Required plugins

Similar to how we have a `requirements.txt` text file to list the names and versions of the packages necessary for a Python project, we can specify given plugins as requirements for a PyCharm project. This is because some PyCharm plugins not only assist programmers with various tasks in their projects, but also can play a crucial role in the development of that project:

1. Within a project, you can specify the required plugins by going to the **Build, Execution, Deployment** option in the settings and selecting **Required Plugins**, as illustrated here:

Chapter 14

Adding a required plugin to a project

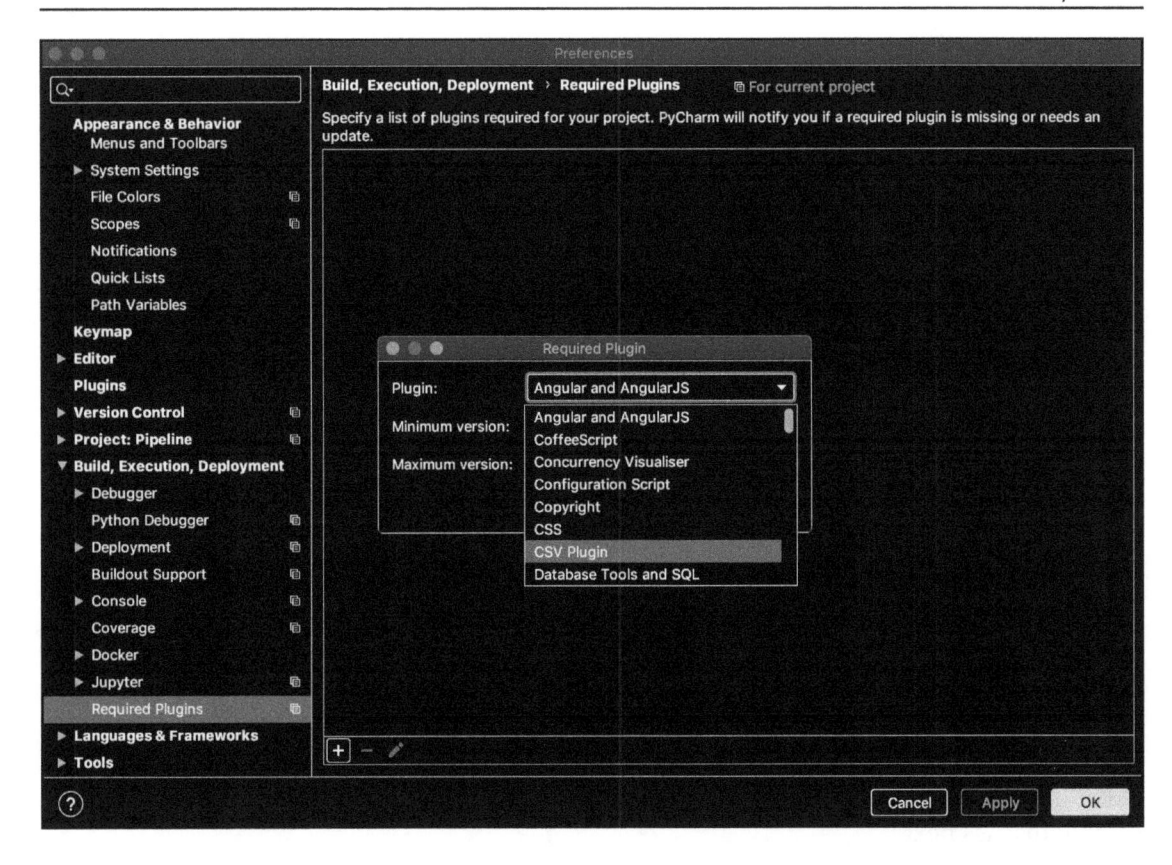

2. From this window, we can add items to the list of required plugins for our current project by clicking on the plus sign in the top-right corner:

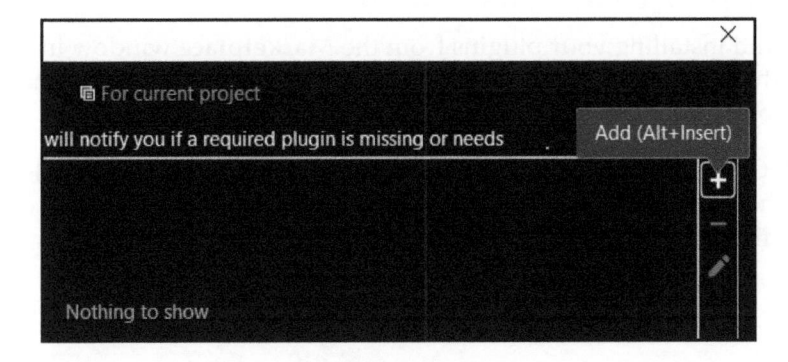

Adding a required plugin to a project

[415]

3. From there, we can specify which particular plugin we have that should be made into a requirement for our project, as well as the actual version number of the plugin, as illustrated here:

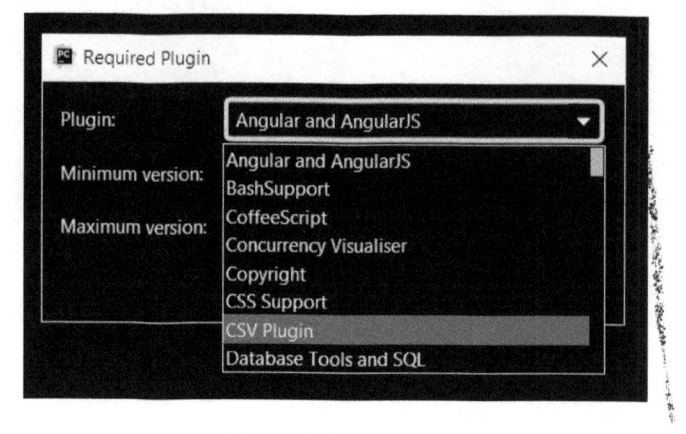

Adding a required plugin to a project

4. After confirming the selection, whenever the current project is opened in PyCharm, we will be notified if and when a required plugin has somehow not been installed, is disabled, or has an update pending.

Other advanced options to work with plugins are the ability to install one from disk, which we will discuss next.

Installing plugins from disk

Downloading and installing your plugins from the **Marketplace** window in PyCharm via the internet is the most common way to add a plugin to your work environment. However, there is a less common method of installing a PyCharm plugin: from disk.

Specifically, PyCharm plugins can be saved as local archive files (for example, JAR or ZIP files), and PyCharm can use the very source code to install those plugins. In order to install a plugin from disk, follow these steps:

1. From the **Plugins** window, click on the ✿ icon and choose the appropriate option, as illustrated here:

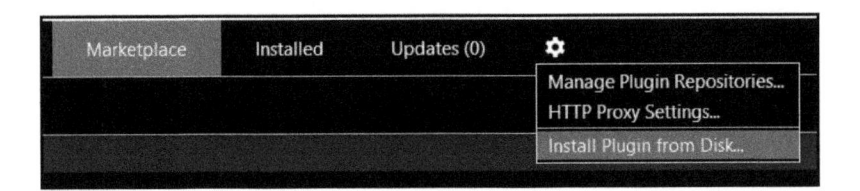

Installing a PyCharm plugin from disk

2. From there, navigate the file browser to the local file that contains the source code of the plugin you would like to install.

The rest of the process is very similar to installing a plugin from the internet. Moreover, we can simply drag the archive file into PyCharm's welcome window, and the same installation process will begin.

Finally, as the last topic in this chapter, we will very briefly discuss the process of developing your own PyCharm plugins.

Developing custom plugins

Since PyCharm is written for the most part in Java, its plugins will actually need to be developed with Java as well. For this reason, I will only go over very high-level points regarding this process, as it does not actually pertain to Python programming, in the following steps:

1. To start working on a PyCharm plugin, you will need to download the IntelliJ IDEA software (the popular IDE for Java, also developed by JetBrains). You can download either the Community or the Ultimate edition of this software.
2. While using this software to create a new project, choose **Gradle** as the project type, **Java 8** as the project SDK (basically the main language used in the project), and select **Java** and **IntelliJ Platform Plugin** in the **Additional Libraries and Frameworks** section.
3. From here, we can enter the Java code that implements the backend logic as well as the frontend appearance of the plugin. Again, this process is entirely done with Java, so I will not be going into it any further.
4. Before being able to publish your application as an official PyCharm plugin, you will need to have your credentials for a JetBrains account ready.

[417]

More Possibilities with PyCharm Plugins

5. Then log into the portal for JetBrains plugin authors, which can be found at `plugins.jetbrains.com/author/me`.
6. From your profile, click on the drop-down menu in the top-right corner of the window and choose the **Upload plugin** option, as indicated here:

Uploading a custom plugin to JetBrains

7. With that (and maybe after a reviewing process as well), your very own PyCharm plugin can be shared and used among many PyCharm users.

This also marks the end of our discussions on PyCharm plugins and their usage.

Summary

PyCharm plugins are customized add-ons that can further add to the list of features and functionalities one can take advantage of while using PyCharm. We have seen how to browse through, download, and manage different plugins in the PyCharm environment. By taking advantage of these plugins, we can further customize our workspace and improve our own productivity. Plugin management in PyCharm can be done in the **Plugins** tab in the settings.

We also learned about a number of popular and commonly used plugins in PyCharm that you can consider installing for your projects, namely Database Navigator, LiveEdit, Markdown, CSV Plugin, and String Manipulation. Each of these plugins has a specific usage and purpose, and all can further streamline your Python development process.

This topic of Pycharm plugins also concludes our general discussions on PyCharm's main features and functionalities. In the next and final chapter of this book, we will take a step back and look at the topics we have discussed so far from a high-level perspective, while also considering some miscellaneous topics regarding the use of PyCharm.

Questions

1. What is a PyCharm plugin?
2. How can one install or update a plugin in PyCharm?
3. Which options are available for removing a specific plugin from your personal work environment?
4. Briefly describe the usage of some common PyCharm plugins discussed in this chapter, namely, Database Navigator, LiveEdit, Markdown, CSV Plugin, and String Manipulation.
5. How can you specify having a plugin as a requirement for a PyCharm project?

Further reading

More information can be found in the following articles and readings:

- *PyCharm Professional Plugins*, the JetBrains official website (`https://plugins.jetbrains.com/pycharm`)
- JetBrains official documentation, *Managing plugins* (`www.jetbrains.com/help/pycharm/managing-plugins.html`)
- JetBrains official documentation, *Creating Your First Plugin* (`www.jetbrains.org/intellij/sdk/docs/basics/getting_started.html`)

15
Future Developments

This chapter will gloss over the important topics discussed in the previous chapters of the book and offer a comprehensive view of PyCharm's most popular feature. First, we will discuss a number of miscellaneous topics, such as automation using macros or file watchers. We will then conclude the book with a few general suggestions on how to effectively use PyCharm, including keeping up to date with future updates and the Educational Edition of PyCharm.

The following topics will be covered in this chapter:

- Miscellaneous usage of PyCharm
- Reviewing important information covered in previous chapters of the book
- Concluding thoughts on how to use PyCharm

These discussions will tie up our book by offering you a general view on your whole journey, and prepare you for your next steps in using PyCharm for your projects.

Technical requirements

As in previous chapters, ensure that you have both Python 3.6+ and PyCharm installed on your computer.

Miscellaneous topics in PyCharm

Given the sheer number of features and functionalities that PyCharm software provides, it goes without saying that we could not fit all of them into our structured discussions so far. So in this section, I'd like to go over a number of topics that we haven't covered, but are still important for us to know. First, let's start by looking at using a remote interpreter in PyCharm.

Future Developments

Using remote Python interpreters

The general term *remote* is used to denote anything that is not physically connected to your computer but can be connected and operated on. You might be familiar with the process of logging in to a remote server via the `ssh` command.

In PyCharm, it is possible to connect the work environment with a Python interpreter in a remote server. There might be many reasons why we would want to do this. For example, using the remote interpreter means that our local computer does not need to execute any command, thus saving us some computing resources. Moreover, since the interpreter is on a remote server, other programmers might have access to it as well. In other words, many people have the ability to share the same Python interpreter, which helps with ensuring reproducibility.

Obviously, in order to take advantage of this feature, you will need to have access to a remote server first. This can be your online computing server, such as AWS, from your school or company's server, or from a free remote server service. If your access is password protected, you will need to have your credentials ready as well.

Now, let's see how we can configure a remote Python interpreter within a specific PyCharm project:

1. Go to **Project** | **Project Interpreter** from the settings. Here, we will then customize the Python interpreter to be used by clicking on the ✱ icon in the top-right corner of the window and choosing **Add**, as indicated here:

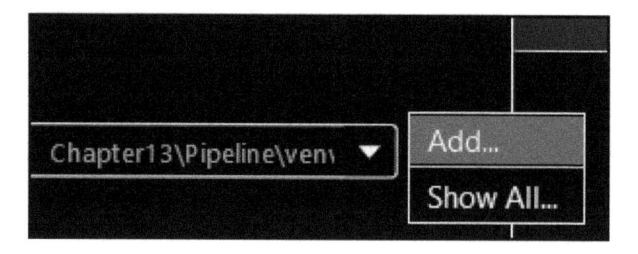

Adding a new interpreter to your project

Chapter 15

2. Within the new window, select the **SSH Interpreter** option in the left-hand panel, enter the host address and your username in the main section, and hit **Next**:

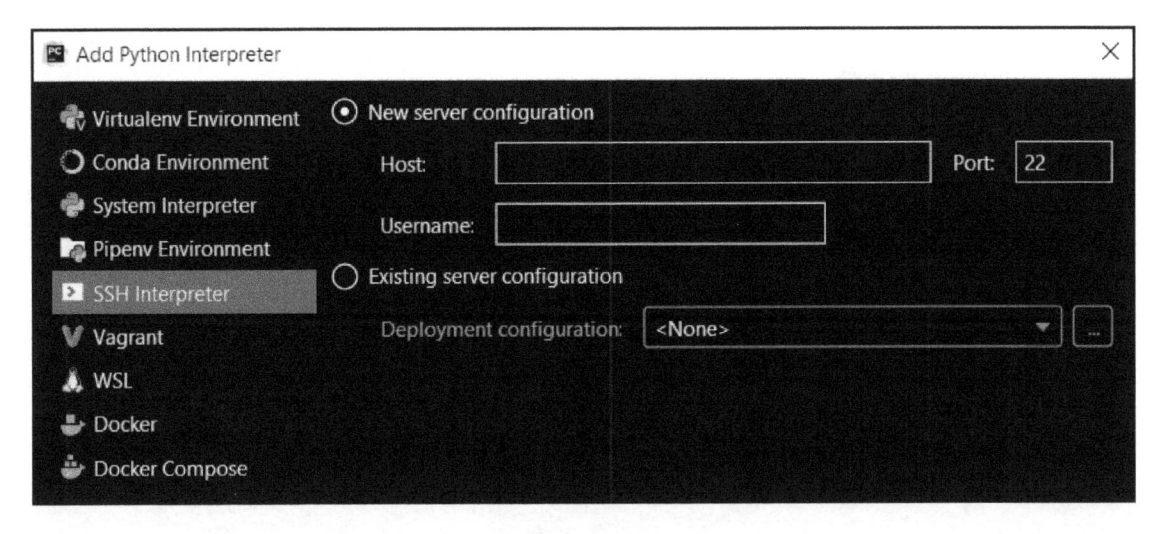

Adding a remote interpreter

3. In the next window, you might be prompted to enter your password for the remote server:

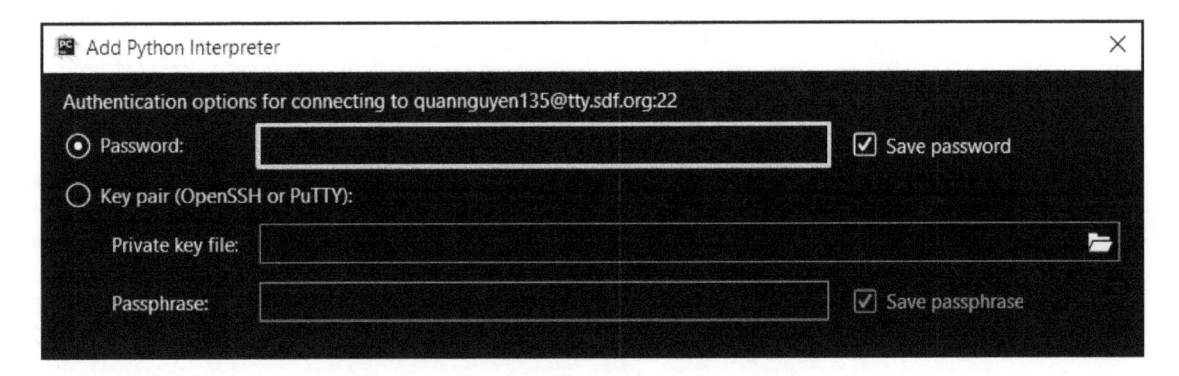

Logging in to a remote server

Future Developments

Alternatively, you can use your credentials in other tools, such as **OpenSSH or PuTTY**, to log in. After entering the password, click **Next**.

4. Finally, in the next window, enter in the path to the Python interpreter on the remote server:

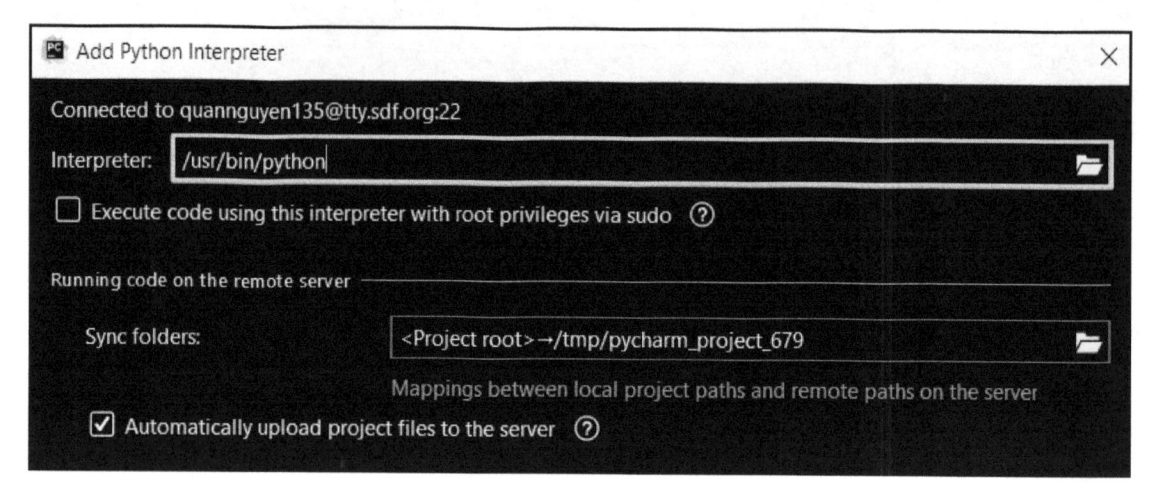

Locating the remote Python interpreter

You can also enable the checkbox below the prompt to run the interpreter using root privileges. Click **Finish** to finalize the process.

Chapter 15

5. Next, we need to set up a deployment process to automatically copy the code we have in our local project to the remote server. Normally, programmers have to facilitate this manually, but PyCharm allows us to streamline this process. From the settings, navigate to **Build, Execution, Deployment | Deployment | Options**, and check the **Create empty directories** box, illustrated as follows. This option ensures synchronization between our local and remote directories:

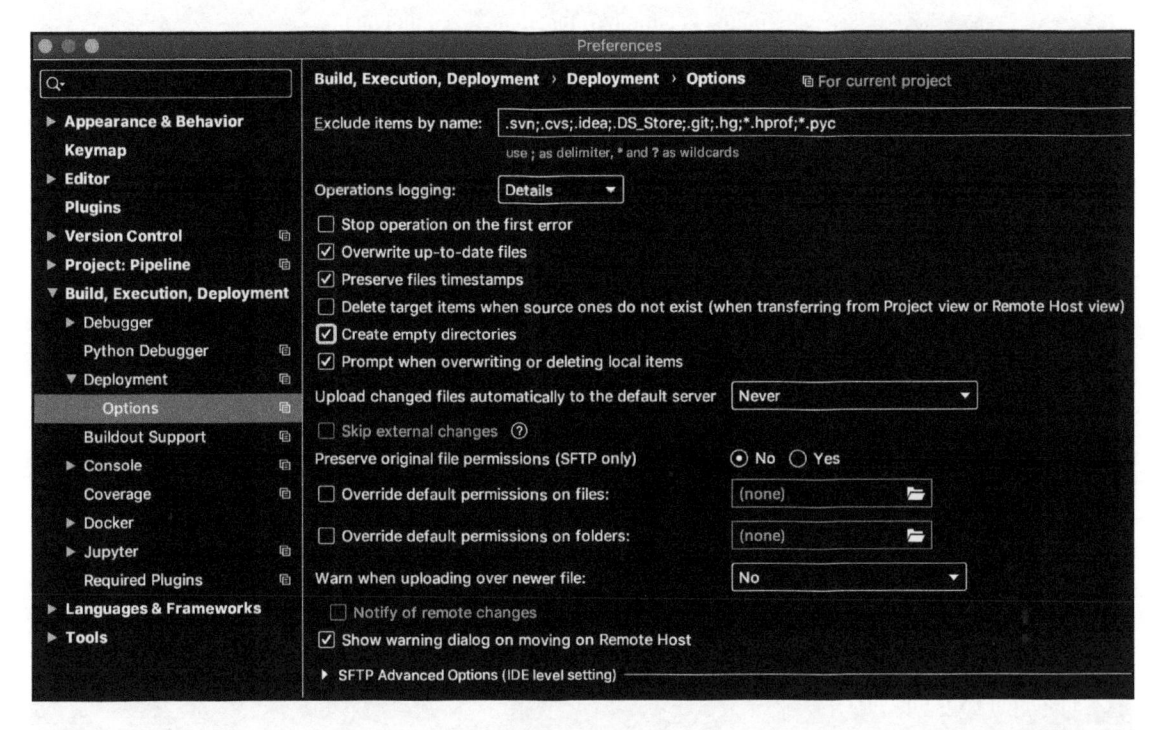

Setting up options

Future Developments

6. Go back to **Build, Execution, Deployment | Deployment** in the settings. You will see in the window that we don't have a configured development for our remote server yet. To do that, click on the + button in the top-left corner and choose the **SFTP** option to add in a new server as follows:

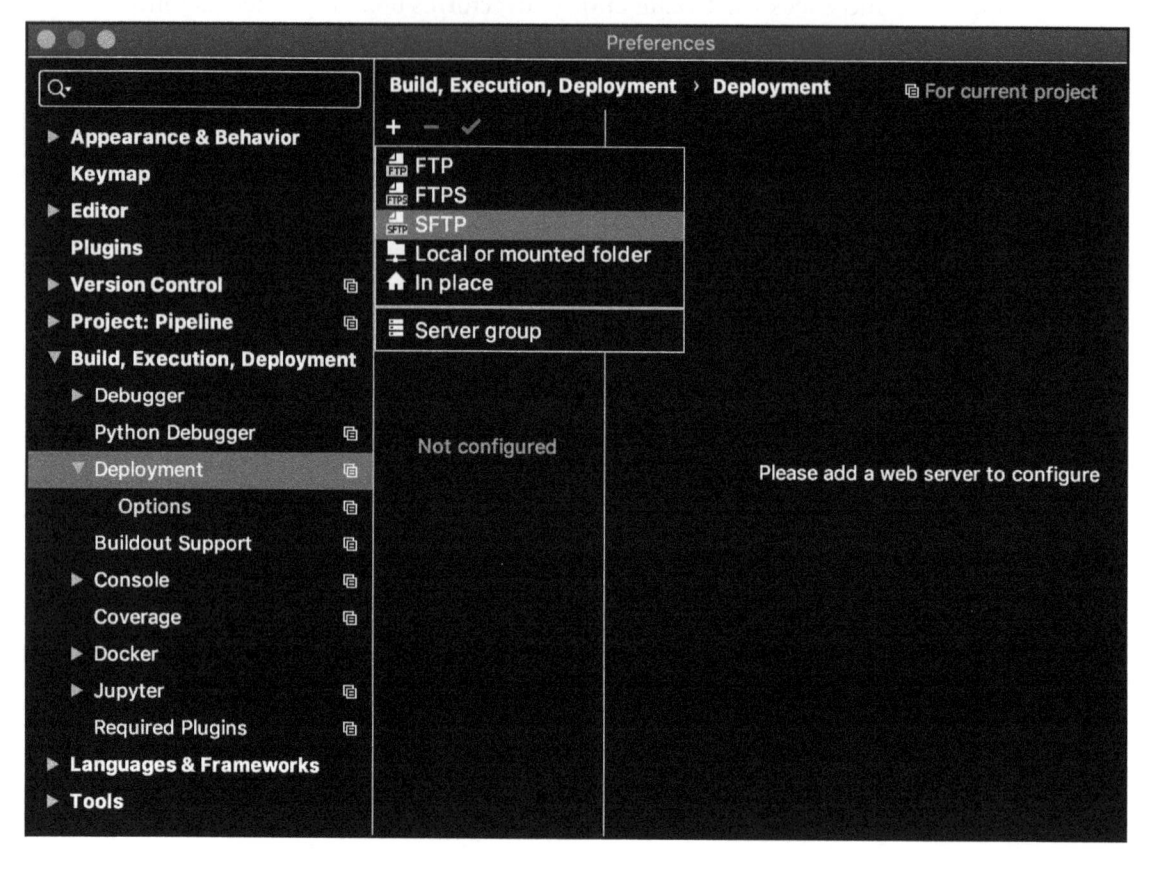

Selecting file source type

7. Next, enter a name you like for this server. We will also need to input our credentials for this connection in the following prompt:

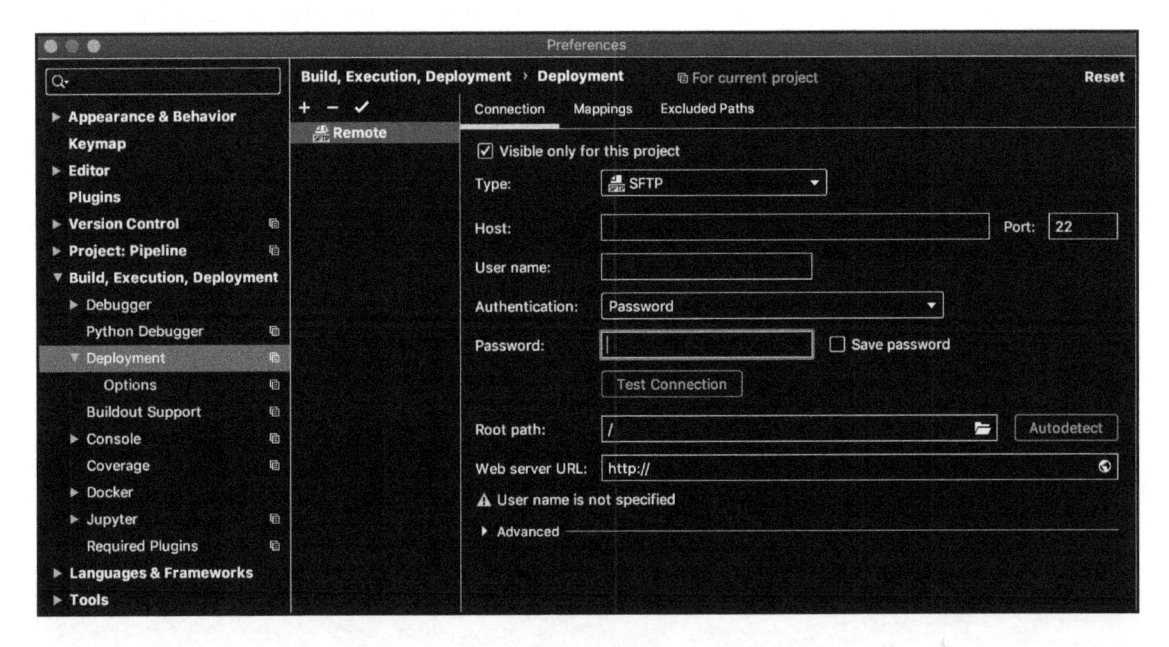

Entering connection details

Note that most of the time, the option in the **Authentication** prompt should be either of the following:

- **Key pair (OpenSSH or PuTTY)**, in which case you will need to locate your private key path. Depending on your operating system and the SSH client you use, the path could be `/Users/<your username>/.ssh/id_rsa` (for macOS) or `%APPDATA%\SSH\UserKeys` (for Windows users).
- **OpenSSH config and authentication agent**, in which case PyCharm itself will look for the appropriate authentication method.

Future Developments

8. Another important aspect we need to consider is the **Root path** prompt in the preceding window, which is used to specify the home directory of our remote server. You can also use the corresponding **Autodetect** button to have PyCharm look for a suitable directory.
9. Still in the same configuration window, click on the **Mappings** tab (highlighted here), which is used to specify the deployment path of our remote server:

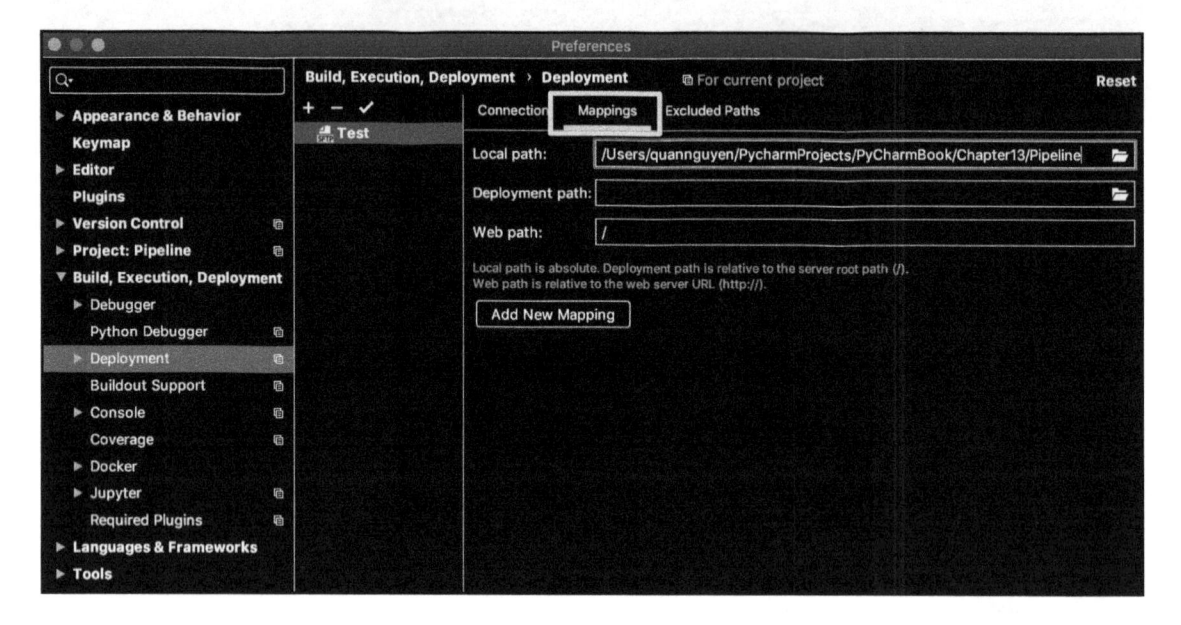

Enter mappings

In particular, in the **Deployment path** prompt, enter the path to the directory that you want PyCharm to copy the files of your current project to (whose root directory can be configured with the **Local path** prompt). Note that this path will be relative to the remote root path we specified in the last step.

10. Finally, confirm all of your configurations by clicking **OK** or **Apply**. Our last step in terms of setting things up for the remote server is to enable automatic uploads of our local files to the remote server in **Tools | Deployment | Automatic Upload**:

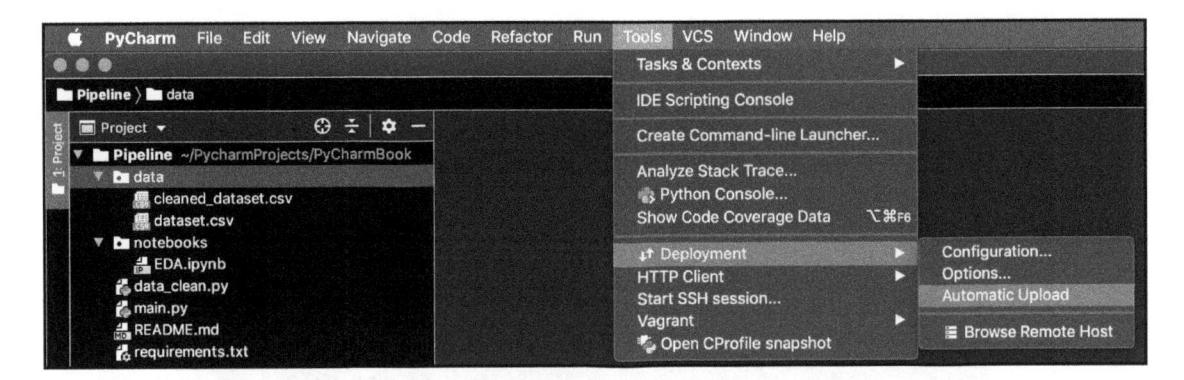

Setting automatic upload

11. To have a graphical directory explorer for your remote server, go to **Tools | Deployment | Browse Remote Host**, which will open the **Remote Host** panel that you can use to inspect the structure of your remote server.

So that is the complete procedure of adding a Python interpreter from a remote server to our PyCharm workspace. As mentioned, this ability can prove useful in many situations, especially in group settings. PyCharm also offers a number of automation-related features, including working with macros, which we will discuss next.

Using macros

You might already be familiar with this term from other software, such as Microsoft Excel. In essence, a macro is a sequence of instructions to be executed in order. If you have a specific action that consists of multiple steps, a macro is a way to automate that sequence of steps.

Future Developments

For example, we would like to create a macro to profile a selected block of code within a Python file currently opened in the editor, and finally open the Terminal in the directory that contains the Python file. We will go through the following steps:

1. Open any Python file in the editor and select any block of code as an example.
2. From the **Edit** menu, go to **Macros** | **Start Macro Recording**:

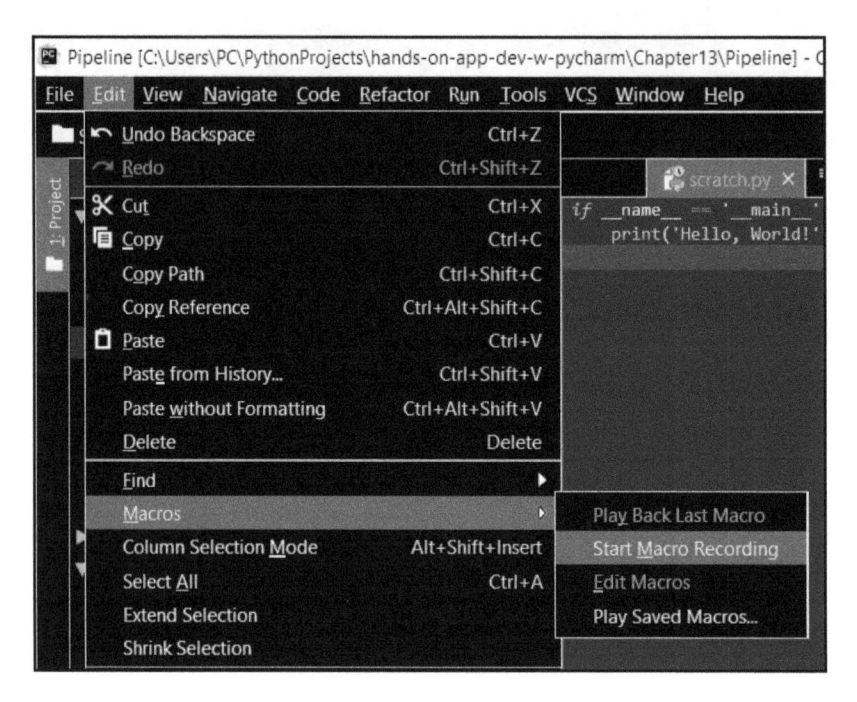

Recording a macro in PyCharm

This will start the macro recorder, which means every action that we will take from now on will be recorded.

3. Right-click on the selected block of code in the editor and choose **Profile [name of file]**. This is the first action in the sequence we would like to record in our macro. If successful, you will notice a message in the bottom-right corner of your window, indicating that the action has been recorded, as shown here:

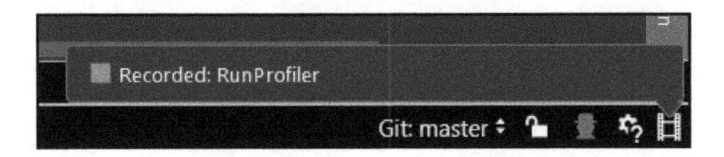

Running a profiler, recorded by the macro recorder

4. Navigate back to the Python file in the editor, right-click on the selected code, and choose **Open in Terminal**. This action should also be recorded as part of the macro, indicated by a similar message in the corner.
5. Since our macro is finished, from the **Edit** menu, go to **Macros | Stop Macro Recording**.
6. Here, a pop-up window will appear, asking us for the macro name. Enter a name that you want for the macro or simply leave it blank (if the macro is intended for temporary use).

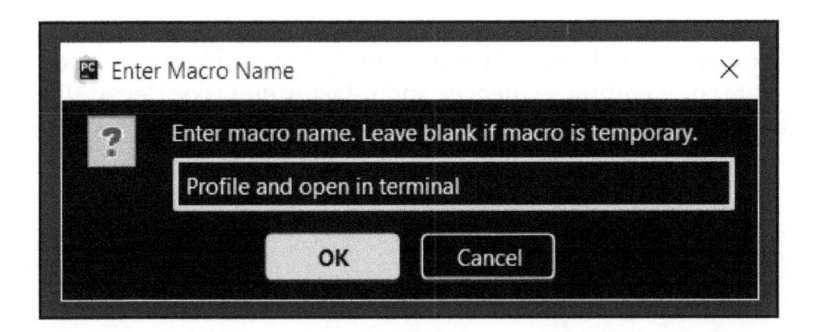

Naming a macro

4. From now on, we can invoke the macro by going to **Edit | Macros | [Name of macro]**.
5. Even more conveniently, we can assign a specific keyboard shortcut to a given macro. Open the settings and go to the **Keymap** section.

Future Developments

6. Expand the **Macros** item in the main section of the window and right-click on the macro that you want to assign a keyboard shortcut to, as indicated here:

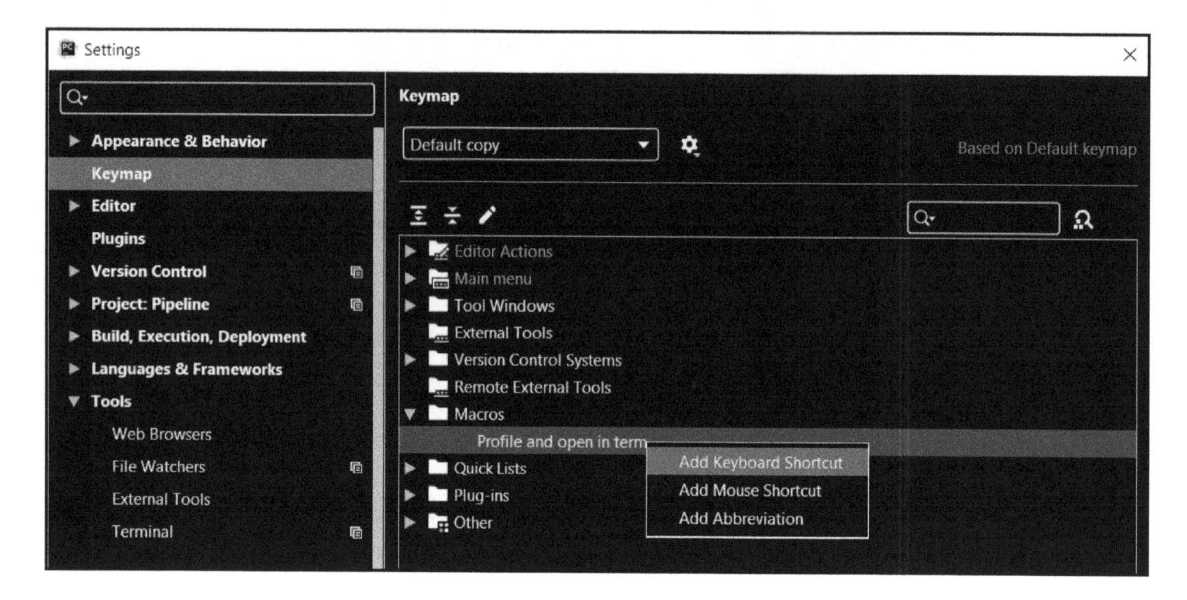

Assigning a shortcut to a macro

And that is the process of working with macros in PyCharm. In practice, you can create macros to automate code-editing sequences and refactoring tasks, depending on your own work and needs. In the next subsection, we will discuss another method of automation in Pycharm: file watchers.

File watchers

File watchers, in general, are tools that allow us to monitor the changes taking place in a given file and apply a specific action to the file when a change does take place. As an example, let's say even though PyCharm is a great IDE, there are files where we only want to use Atom (the text editor) to write code, and YAML files are one of them. So anytime there is a change taking place in a YAML file within PyCharm, we would like to open it in Atom instead.

To set up such a file watcher, we will go through the following:

1. From the settings, go to **Tools** | **File Watchers**. This will take you to the main window to manage file watchers.
2. Click on the **+** button in the top-right corner of the window to add in a new file watcher and choose to create a new custom file-watcher template:

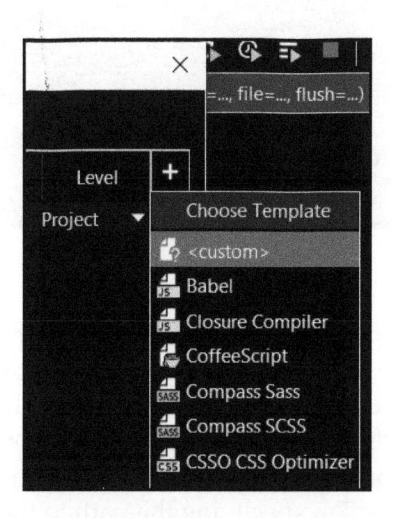

Creating a file-watcher template

Future Developments

3. Now, enter the following information in the new pop-up window to specify our file watcher:

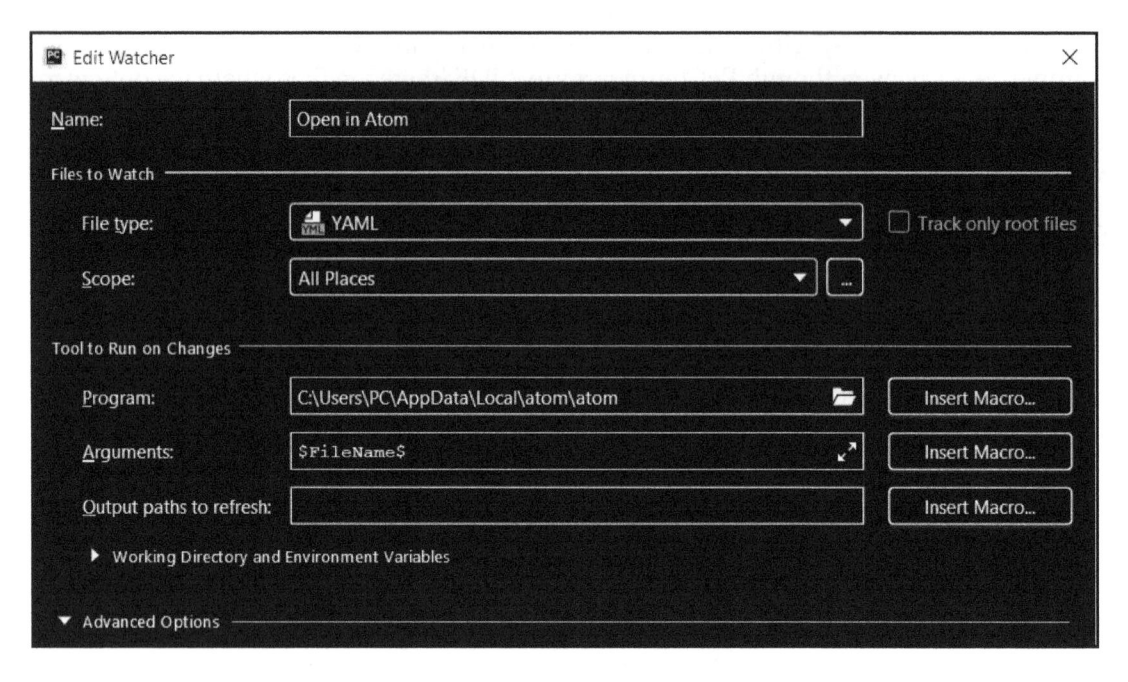

Creating a file watcher in PyCharm

4. The name for the file watcher can be anything you like. The **File type** prompt specifies the file extension that will be monitored by this file watcher (in our case, it is YAML files). The **Scope** prompt, on the other hand, defines where this file watcher is to take effect; here, I'm specifying it to be in all places in PyCharm.
5. The **Program** prompt should be the path to the program that we'd like to use in the file watcher. Here, I'm specifying the path to the executable for Atom. In the **Arguments** prompt, we use a macro (`$FileName$`) to dynamically specify the name of a given YAML file.

> **TIP**
> To open a file in Atom, we run the `atom [file name]` command, so that's why we specify the command as previously. You need to customize the **Program** and **Arguments** prompts so that when combined, the command can successfully achieve your goal.

6. Finalize your customization by clicking **OK**.

Chapter 15

To see if this file watcher is working as intended, simply create a new YAML file within PyCharm and attempt to edit it. You will see that the file will be opened in Atom as well. As you can imagine, this feature is quite useful for automating tasks that run every time a specific type of file is edited. For example, common files that you can apply file watchers to are LESS files (which can be compiled into CSS) or CoffeeScript files (which can be converted into JavaScript).

This discussion also concludes the miscellaneous topics in PyCharm that I wanted to cover. In the next section, we will walk through the other topics that we have looked at throughout this book.

Taking a step back

After a long journey, it is always important to look back and see what we have achieved. This is especially true for this book, which consists of many different topics and discussions on the various features and functionalities in PyCharm. Doing this will help us review and solidify what we have learned so far.

The first few chapters introduced the software and the idea of using an IDE to write Python code. Regarding the differences between PyCharm and other development tools, PyCharm tends to come out on top in many respects. However, not everyone is ready to take full advantage of the software; in other words, PyCharm is only applicable for a specific group of users who have familiarized themselves with the main workflow of Python programming. This is to say that you should make sure that PyCharm is indeed the most suitable tool for your purposes, before fully committing to using the software.

In this section, we also talked about the differences between the Community edition and the Professional edition of PyCharm. While the Community edition does retain a good deal of features that will undoubtedly help you improve your productivity as a Python programmer, the Professional edition is by far the better tool for extensive and fully supported development. There is actually another, less-known edition of PyCharm – Educational Edition, which we will discuss later in this chapter.

Finally, we walked through the process of downloading and installing PyCharm on our local computer; this process is fairly straightforward. It was at this point that we also saw the flexibility and customizability in PyCharm's keymap and keyboard shortcuts. Overall, the software is designed to provide programmers with the best options and usability. After this, we moved on to the topics of productivity-related features in PyCharm.

Improving your productivity

Here we got into the specific features in PyCharm that streamline various tasks and processes in Python programming. From creating and managing virtual environments to version control, testing, and debugging, PyCharm handles all the low-level, backend tasks, leaving its users on a high level so that they can focus on the development side of things.

During these discussions, we saw that PyCharm can work well with external software and tools such as Conda and Git/GitHub that are common elements of a Python project. On another note, the testing and debugging options even extend to other non-traditional Python scripts, such as PyCharm code cells and Jupyter notebooks. This feature allows PyCharm users to combine the unique advantages of working with different tools in one environment.

The point about PyCharm handling low-level repetitive tasks is also illustrated by the wide range of different project types that PyCharm offers (simply Python projects, web development such as Django or Flask, scientific computing, Angular, or even React projects), as illustrated here:

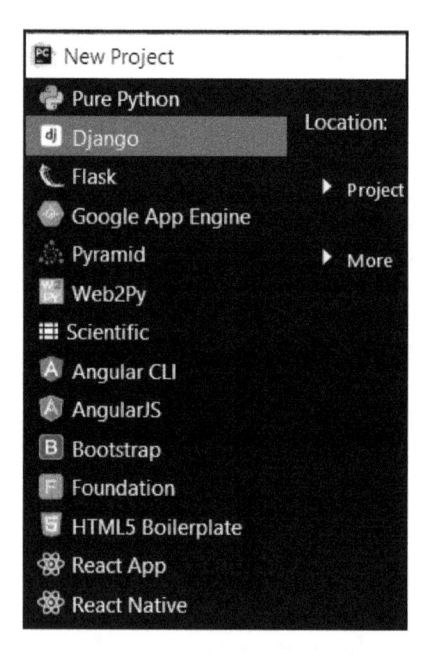

PyCharm project types

Each type of project is created with various boilerplate files and folders automatically generated so that the programmer can immediately start working.

One of the best supports that PyCharm offers must be its intelligent coding support engine. Having the ability to adjust its scope, the code-completion engine in PyCharm allows users to find the most relevant suggestions with respect to other files in the same project. The quality of this coding support engine ensures that the code written in PyCharm is compatible with all conventions and standards of the Python community.

Having learned about the various features and functionalities PyCharm offers to improve our productivity, we thus move onto to the specific usage of PyCharm in web development projects.

Web development with PyCharm

Web development has always been a big topic in general programming, and it has also been growing in popularity in the Python community specifically. A direct result of this is the wide range of support that PyCharm offers for web development projects and tasks. In these chapters, we first saw that as a Python IDE PyCharm can also handle the development of JavaScript, HTML, and CSS, which are the main web programming tools.

In this section, we also discussed the integration of the web framework Django into PyCharm. Django is a heavy and batteries-included framework with numerous setting-up tasks, so having PyCharm handle all the boilerplate code can save us a lot of time. The model-view-template relationship that Django operates on is embedded in the logic of the coding support engine from PyCharm, which ensures that the code we put in ourselves is consistent with that relationship.

For example, when we create a view that does not have a corresponding template yet, PyCharm will alert us with a message and offer a convenient interface to address the problem. As you can see in the following screenshot, where we are creating a template for a view we have just written:

Creating a template for a view

Future Developments

Another great feature in PyCharm to support web development projects (as well as others) is its interface when working with data sources and databases. Specifically, when a database connection has been established in PyCharm, the editor can be used to write and submit SQL commands to that database. Even more impressively, the actual data in the database can be opened within the editor, from which we can view and edit the data in real-time.

So in this section, we saw the extensiveness of PyCharm's support for web development projects. Other types of projects that can be optimized by PyCharm in terms of workflow are scientific computing and data science projects.

Data science with PyCharm

Data science is undoubtedly one of the biggest reasons for the sudden growth in popularity of the Python language, and for good reasons. With Python, data analysis models and algorithms can be easily implemented; the community also already possesses a large number of tools and support libraries, ready to be used. However, there are still ways to improve your productivity in data science projects.

Specifically, the IDE offers a dedicated setting called *Scientific Mode*, which is highly optimized for data analysis and scientific tasks. An element of this *Scientific Mode* is the **SciView** panel, which allows PyCharm users to inspect common data structures in scientific computing/data science projects such as Pandas DataFrames and NumPy arrays.

Much like the normal variable viewer in other PyCharm projects but more powerful, the **SciView** panel is a great way to dig deep into the values within a specific variable, as illustrated here:

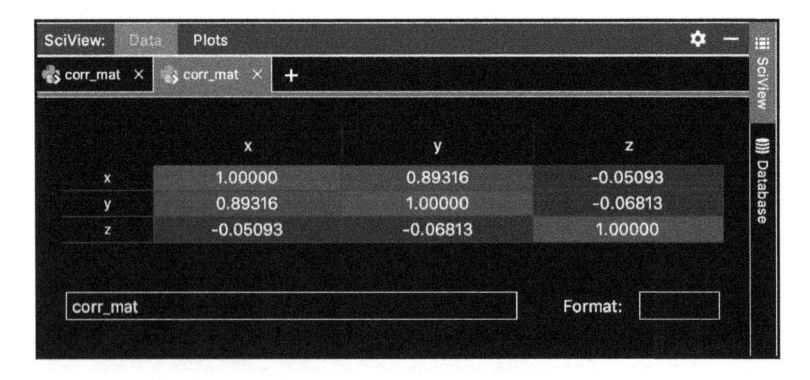

Variable viewer in the SciView panel

[438]

Something that has to be discussed in terms of PyCharm supporting scientific computing projects is how it handles Jupyter notebooks. The technology itself is already a great tool for scientific computing and data science projects, and PyCharm takes it to the next level. The support for iterative development—one of the best features of Jupyter notebook—is entirely preserved in the PyCharm interface, with powerful code-completion and formatting options added in.

Finally, in the previous chapter and this one, we looked at other additional features in PyCharm that can assist with your projects, specifically plugins and other miscellaneous topics.

So we have reminded ourselves of what was discussed throughout the book. Hopefully doing this has given you a complete overview of the book and solidifies the knowledge you have gained. In the next and final section of this book, we will consider some of the high-level aspects of using PyCharm.

Moving forward with PyCharm

So far, we have considered specific features in PyCharm and how they can help you write your Python applications. Now we will briefly go over a number of more general discussion points on how to use the software at a high level. First, let's talk about a resource for learning how to use PyCharm that I have included in further reading lists—the official documentation from JetBrains.

Using official documentation

As with any great software out there, PyCharm comes with detailed and extensive official documentation, which lays out the individual features and functionalities available in PyCharm as well as how to use them. All of these resources can be found at `www.jetbrains.com/pycharm/documentation/`.

For example, this link shows how to use the Python web framework Flask in PyCharm: `https://www.jetbrains.com/help/pycharm/creating-web-application-with-flask.html`.

Future Developments

In general, here you can find tutorials, walk-throughs, forum discussions, and even hands-on demonstration videos on how to use PyCharm. Other resources that you can find include webinars, developers' blogs, keyboard shortcut reference cards, release notes for different editions of PyCharm, and the early access program. Overall, it contains everything and anything that you want to know about the PyCharm software.

It is important to note that the difference between a book on software such as this and the official documentation is that while the documentation might contain very extensive information regarding the usage of the software, it is not structured in a way that is narration-based and beginner-friendly.

In other words, you need to know exactly what you are looking for when using the official documentation. It is the same difference when you take an online course on a programming language and reading through the documentation of that language.

That is to say that the official documentation, while a very useful reference, should be used in conjunction with other resources. Another element that is included in the PyCharm home page is the information on future updates and releases.

Future updates and releases

You might recall when we said in `Chapter 4`, *Editing and Formatting with Ease in PyCharm*, that you have the option to send your data on runtime types in PyCharm to JetBrains, and this data will then be used to design and implement other bug fixes and features. This is to say that JetBrains constantly looks for new ways to improve the PyCharm software, and as a result updates and new releases of PyCharm come out regularly.

It is therefore beneficial to keep yourself up to date with future releases for your PyCharm distribution. These releases might address a bug that you have been working with for a while, or they can come with a new feature that might accelerate your work even more.

For example, the new PyCharm update 2019.2 (as shown in the following screenshot) that came out at the time of writing this book contains an inline debugger for Jupyter notebooks, which gives us the ability to dynamically debug Jupyter code cells separately. This greatly adds to the flexibility that we already have with Jupyter notebooks in PyCharm.

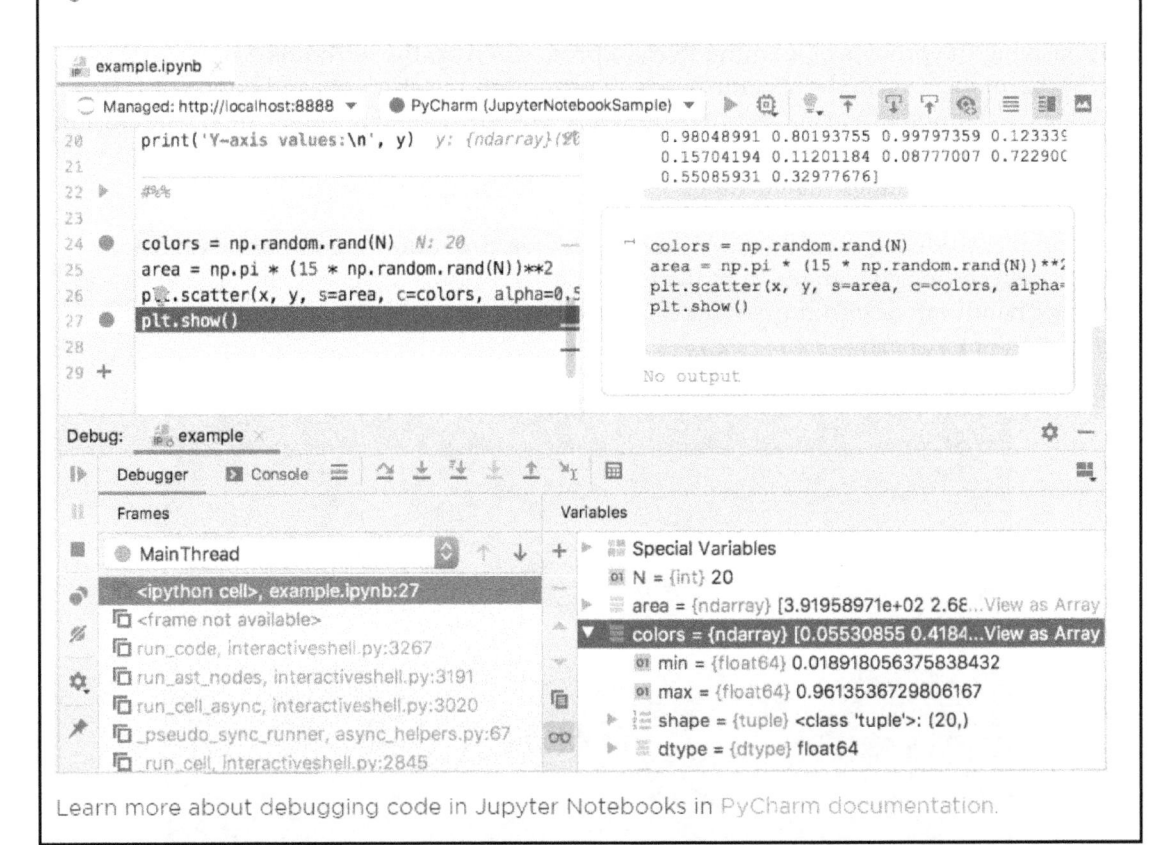

A new release for PyCharm from JetBrains

Overall, it is generally beneficial to keep yourself informed about the happenings of the software and technology that you use. The easiest way to do that with PyCharm and its new updates is to follow the development team on the JetBrains official website or on Twitter.

Future Developments

So, throughout this book, we have mentioned multiple times that there are two main editions of PyCharm—the free Community edition and the paid Professional edition. However, there is another edition of PyCharm that is less well known, the Educational Edition, which we will take a look at in the next subsection.

PyCharm – the Educational Edition

Emphasizing the process of learning Python programming, the JetBrains educational tool for PyCharm focuses on the specific needs of programming students and educators. The Educational Edition of PyCharm is a completely free software that offers a flexible learning platform. This edition includes most of the best features in PyCharm, while also including additional functionalities that facilitate interactive learning processes.

For example, students can follow tutorials on Python programming and receive instant feedback on coding challenges from the Educational Edition. Teachers and educators, on the other hand, can design courses (as illustrated here), tests, and assignments, all within this edition of PyCharm:

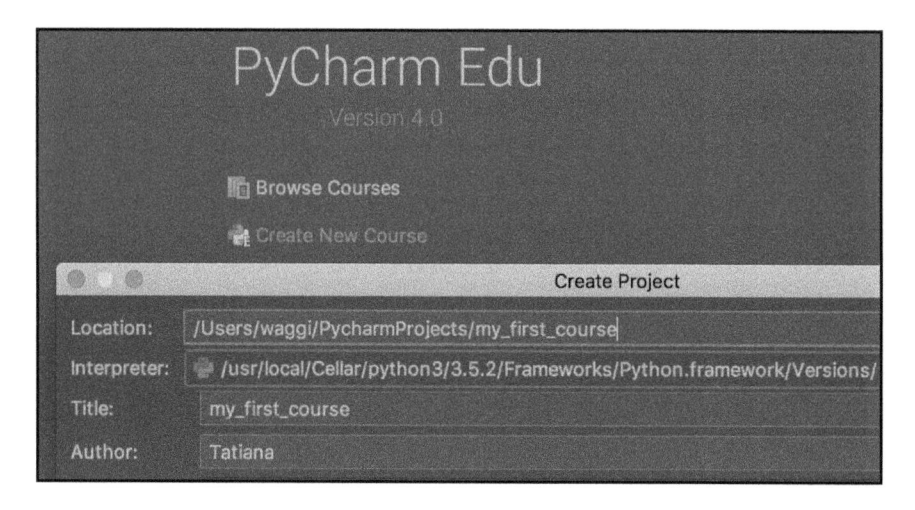

Creating a course in PyCharm Edu. Source: JetBrains

In short, the Educational Edition of PyCharm turns the IDE and its great functionalities into a learning environment, providing an interactive platform for students and teachers alike. Knowing how to use the main edition of PyCharm allows you to be more than equipped to work with this edition to create your own learning platform. More details on the software can be found at `www.jetbrains.com/pycharm-edu/`.

So, we have been talking about the great things in PyCharm and how it can significantly improve your productivity as a programmer. However, there will be times when a feature fails to do its job, or there is a bug within a specific element in PyCharm, causing frustration. In the next subsection, we will discuss some ways to deal with these problems when they occur.

Troubleshooting at a high level

We have already briefly discussed the topic of troubleshooting in PyCharm in `Chapter 4`, *Editing and Formatting with Ease in PyCharm*, but we only talked about various troubleshooting methods to try with your PyCharm software if something goes wrong. In this subsection, we will briefly cover some other ways to take advantage of the community when a problem you are encountering cannot be solved with regular troubleshooting.

In general, if you are experiencing a bug in PyCharm, the chances are someone has already or is currently experiencing the same problem. Searching for discussions online about the bug in the JetBrains support forums or Stack Overflow will typically help you identify the cause and address the root problem.

Future Developments

On the off-chance that there is no discussion regarding a problem or no solution is available, we can turn to technical support from JetBrains itself. Typically, you can chat with the support team or send them an email explaining the problem. More options to troubleshoot can be found at `https://intellij-support.jetbrains.com/hc/en-us/?pycharm`.

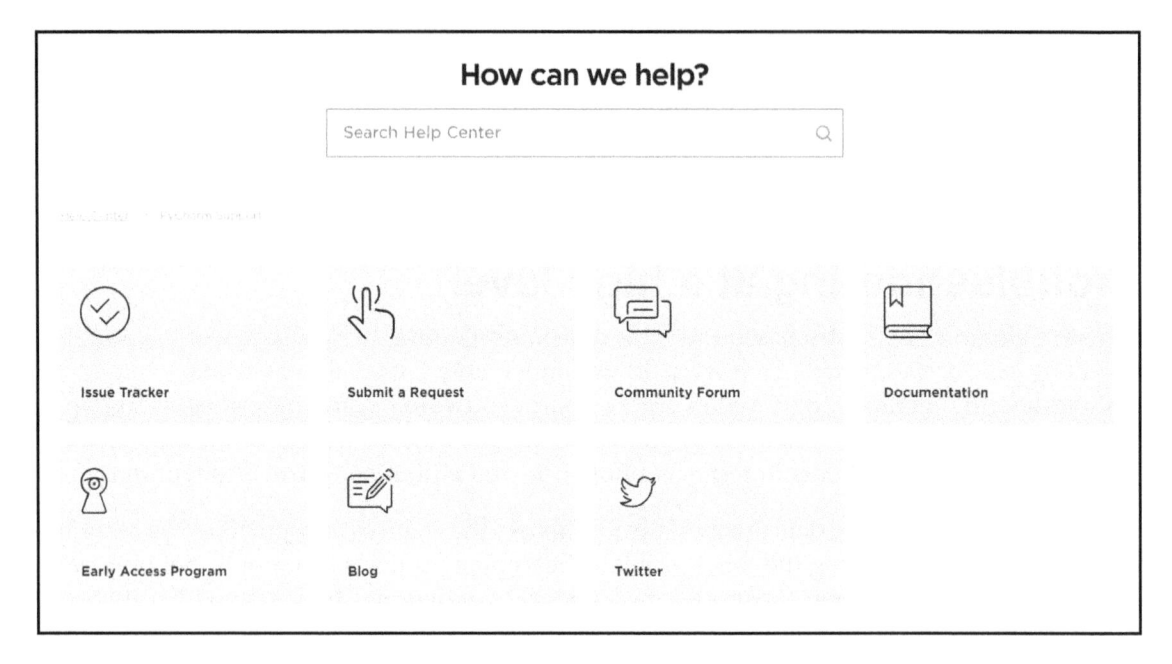

Technical support for PyCharm

Specifically, we can submit a request to report the bug we are experiencing, which will create an issue tracker that we can monitor later on.

Summary

In this chapter, we have covered various topics to conclude our book. First, we looked at various miscellaneous topics in PyCharm, such as using remote PyCharm interpreters and automation with PyCharm macros and file watchers. These features nicely add to the topics that we discussed in previous chapters, and the combination of these features allows you to further improve your productivity.

Then we reminded ourselves of the big ideas and discussions throughout this book. These include an introduction to PyCharm, general options when it comes to using the software, and specific usage in web development and scientific computing—two of the most common project types in Python programming. This walk-through offers a high-level perspective on the discussions included in this book, thus helping us, again, solidify the knowledge we have gained.

Finally, we went over various topics you should keep in mind when moving forward with PyCharm, such as how to take advantage of the official documentation and the Educational Edition, or how to get help if and when you encounter a bug while using the software.

And that is the end of *Hands-on Application Development with PyCharm*. Congratulations on making it to the end, and I hope that this book has helped you learn.

Questions

1. What is the advantage of using a remote Python interpreter in PyCharm?
2. What is the purpose of PyCharm macros?
3. What can we use file watchers in PyCharm for?
4. What is the idea behind the Educational Edition of PyCharm?

Further reading

More information can be found in the following articles and readings:

- *JetBrains official documentation: Configure a remote interpreter using SSH* (www.jetbrains.com/help/pycharm/configuring-remote-interpreters-via-ssh.html)
- *JetBrains official documentation: Macros* (www.jetbrains.com/help/pycharm/using-macros-in-the-editor.html)
- *JetBrains official documentation: Using File Watchers* (www.jetbrains.com/help/pycharm/using-file-watchers.html)
- *PyCharm: the Educational Edition* (www.jetbrains.com/pycharm-edu/)

Assessments

Chapter 1

1. An editor is a simple, minimal platform for editing text without any additional highlighting or aligning functionalities. An example of an editor is Notepad. On the other hand, an **Integrated Development Environment** (**IDE**) is a special piece of software that has various features integrated within it; these typically include syntax highlighting, automatic indention, debugging tools, and much more.
2. Development in Python does not require significant boilerplate code, which is one of the aspects of programming that an IDE sets out to solve. Some have argued that relying on an IDE too much can make programmers forget—or altogether prevent them from learning—the core principles and syntax of a given programming language.
3. A good strategy is to start off by using a simple editor to familiarize yourself with the language and its core syntax structure; once a good understanding of the language has been gained, you can then explore advanced functionalities that an IDE provides to see whether they will be able to make you more productive. Being familiar with a text editor can also help you learn how to use an IDE faster, so that is one more reason to employ this strategy.
4. PyCharm operates on two main principles: improving the productivity of the user and developing a good real-time coding assisting feature. PyCharm looks set to incorporate several features that set itself above the rest of the Python editors and IDEs: streamlined, graphical support for testing/debugging; integrated web development tools; and support for scientific computing options.
5. PyCharm offers two versions: the free Community version and the paid Professional version. The Professional version includes all the functionalities of the Community version while having other exclusive features such as web development tools and scientific computing support.
6. While there are some important features that are only included in the paid Professional version, any Python programmer can still benefit from the free Community version. However, if you are working with large, complex projects with many moving parts (including database management, web development languages, and viewability in scientific reports), then you will most likely benefit from using the Professional version.

Assessments

Chapter 2

1. You can download either the free Community version, which has fewer functionalities but is still convenient, or the paid Professional version, with fully supported features. You can also qualify for a free license for the Professional version if you're a student or teacher, or if you are working on an open source project.
2. There are three ways to activate your license:

    - Using your JetBrains account information, which is used to simply log you into the JetBrains server and verify your license.
    - Using your activation code, which was generated during your purchase. For your information, at the time of writing, a PyCharm license ID (also known as an activation code) is a string of 10 characters, each character being either a digit or capital letter.
    - Using a JetBrains license server, which is used to manage licenses for JetBrains products within a company. Most of the time, one of the two aforementioned methods will be used to activate your license, so I will not be discussing this method here.

3. In the **Preferences** window, you can change various aspects of the general theme of PyCharm in the **Appearance & Behavior > Appearance** tab. The same can be achieved for the PyCharm editor in the **Editor** tab.
4. A keymap, in the most general sense, is the way a computer system defines the mappings of keys—this includes both keyboard keys and buttons from additional external hardware such as the mouse.

    As a programmer works with a specific development environment for a long time, he or she will become accustomed to its keymap. This can potentially cause problems when the programmer transitions to another environment with different keymaps and shortcuts. PyCharm allows you to revert back to your favorite keymap (in Eclipse, Emacs, NetBeans, and Visual Studio).
5. In the **Keymap** tab of the **Preferences** window, you can use the search bar to search for specific actions by name. The result includes not only the actions whose names match with the search terms but also their respective shortcuts (if applicable).
    Next to that search bar is a button called **Find Actions by Shortcut**, which can be used to search for a particular action via its shortcut combination.

Assessments

6. From the starting welcome window of PyCharm, you can choose the **Create New Project** option (choose the **Pure Python** option in the left panel if you're using the Professional version, choose to use an existing Python interpreter for the project, and click **Create**.

   In a project window, you can right-click on the project name in the left panel and choose **New > Python File** to add a new Python file to the current project. To run a Python file, go to **Run > Run** (the second **Run** option). You can also take advantage of the shortcut for the **Run context configuration** action to run the file.

Chapter 3

1. There are a number of panels/window tools that can be displayed and utilized in PyCharm: project directory tree (**Project**), to-do items (**TODO**), version control statistics (**Version Control**), database information (**Database**), the **Python Console**, Terminal, and so on.
   You can drag and drop a panel tag that corresponds to a specific panel along the left, right, and bottom edges of the project window.
2. The bar denotes the indexing process where PyCharm scans through most files and documents in your current project to support important functionalities such as searching, syntax highlighting, and code completion. When this indexing process is still running, some features might not be functional, which would confuse new, unfamiliar users. Most of the time, the features will function as normal as soon as the indexing process completes.
3. There is a number of different project types available to choose from when a PyCharm project is being created: a **Pure Python** project, a Django project, a Google App Engine project, a Flask project, a Web2Py project, and so on. These options, however, are not available in the Community version. With that said, everything achieved through the selection of a project type in Professional PyCharm can be accomplished manually in Community PyCharm.
4. In the different types of PyCharm project (referenced in the previous question), boilerplate code that is conventionally appropriate for a project type is generated by PyCharm when that project is created. For example, a new Django project will have a `templates` folder and a `manage.py` file, while a scientific computing project will have commonly used folders such as `data`, `models`, and `notebooks`.

Assessments

5. A Python interpreter is a program that can take in Python code, then interpret and translate that code into lower-level machine language, thus executing the Python program. A Python virtual environment, on the other hand, is an independent, isolated environment that manages its own libraries and packages.

   Interpreters and virtual environments are independent of each other in Python. This means multiple virtual environments can share the same Python interpreter, and one environment can switch among and utilize multiple interpreters.

6. You can choose to create a virtual environment using Virtualenv, Pipenv, or Conda. PyCharm takes care of the details regarding creating and managing the source of the virtual environment, so whichever tool you use to create your virtual environments, the subsequent details of managing the environments remain consistent.

   This means there is no preferred way to create and manage your virtual environments in PyCharm out of the three options (Virtualenv, Pipenv, or Conda). Therefore, you should keep using your go-to virtual environment tool, as you yourself know best about the specifics of that tool.

7. You can go to **Preferences** (in macOS) or **Settings** (in Windows) and select **Project Interpreter** to customize the interpreter for the current PyCharm project. This ability is especially useful for testing and porting purposes, where the working of libraries and packages might depend on which Python interpreter is being used. These situations are fairly common in large group projects that have been maintained for a long time.

8. To import an external project in PyCharm, you can simply go to **Open** and navigate to the specific project to be imported. In this process, it is important to make sure that the destination project has all the libraries and packages that are required to execute the code included in the project. Reading data from `requirements.txt`, PyCharm is able to suggest what unmet requirements (if any) are still present, and even offers a way to download and install those requirements in a streamlined way.

Chapter 4

1. There are, in total, three possible levels of severity indicated in the top-right corner of the editor: errors (●), warnings ( ), and nothing detected (✓). It is generally good practice to address any problems in your code if the severity is either error or warning before using it or committing it to GitHub.

2. Some of the most common problems in Python code detected by PyCharm are dead code, unused declarations, unresolved references, and PEP 8 style suggestions. Each of these problems can be addressed with various simple and convenient commands in PyCharm.
3. The approach of code completion support from JetBrains' products in general, and not just PyCharm, is smart code completion, which only looks for the most applicable and most likely APIs to suggest in the pop-up list. Additionally, the logic that's used by code completion in PyCharm can be customized by users so that they have particular behaviors that fit individual needs.

   Finally, JetBrains always looks to improve its code completion logic by collecting data regarding runtime types, if allowed by users. This allows PyCharm's code completion to be always evolving and accommodate the changing needs of Python programmers.
4. The following are common code completion options in PyCharm that can prove useful for Python programmers:

   - **Smart code completion**: Suggests the most applicable APIs in the pop-up list.
   - **Postfix code completion**: Helps programmers correctly format various expressions without having to move their caret back and forth.
   - **Hippie completion**: Suggests the items that are in the visible scope and context.
   - **Intention**: Allows complex transformations after code has already been written. This feature can also be used outside the context of code completion.

5. Common cases in which code completion support from PyCharm does not work are listed here:

   - **Running indexing**: Wait until the indexing process is complete before using any code completion features.
   - **Power-save mode**: Go to **File > Power Save Mode** to turn it off if your PyCharm is in power-save mode, which prevents code completion from working.
   - **Out-of-scope files**: Move external files and scripts into the current project to have them scanned by PyCharm, or include external libraries in `requirements.txt`.

Assessments

6. In PyCharm, programmers can perform the following refactoring tasks via convenient shortcuts:

    - **Renaming**: This includes variables, functions, classes, methods, and even files. PyCharm takes care of the renaming in all locations where the name to be changed is used.
    - **Extracting methods**: This is used to move a specific block of code outside the current scope and convert it into a function or method. All of the parameters and return types for the function/method are automatically generated by PyCharm.
    - **Converting between methods and functions**: This allows users to change a class method into a function outside the scope of the class, and vice versa. All calls to the new function are handled and converted accordingly as well.

7. Three main aspects of working with Python documentation in PyCharm are listed here:

    - **Creating documentation**: This is done when a pair of triple-double quotes are expanded into multiple lines. A Python docstring template is used to generate specific formats for documentation created in this way.
    - **Customizing docstring format**: To change the way the default docstring is generated in the aforementioned process, you can go to **Tools > Python Integrated Tools** in PyCharm's general settings.
    - **Viewing documentation**: Quick Documentation and Quick Definition can be used to dynamically view the documentation and definition of a specific API in PyCharm. This can be applied to built-in functions, external packages and libraries, as well as self-written functions, classes, and methods.

Chapter 5

1. Version control denotes the process of using a specific system to record and save changes and overall progress in directories and files so that a programmer can come back to it later. If multiple separate changes have been applied to a project that is under version control, you can even switch between these different changes (versions) in the development process.

2. Version control can offer the following benefits to programmers:

    - Being able to revert projects back to previous versions when a change is not desirable (without having to manually change the project code)

- Having backups on the cloud, which allows us to avoid losing code when local systems are damaged
- Being able to collaborate with others in a systematic way

3. When you are using version control with Git, there is a specific workflow that you need to follow: creating a GitHub repository, initializing a local Git repository and linking it to the one created on GitHub remotely, adding files to be version controlled to Git, committing any changes that have been made to the local repository, and finally pushing the committed changes to GitHub.

   While working with other people, you need to fork the original GitHub repository to your own account. Any changes to be made to that original repository would need to go through the forked one and be done via pull requests.

4. The **Version Control** panel in PyCharm offers the same common Git commands (setting up a local repository, `add`, `commit`, and `push`) in an accessible user interface. It also displays a list of files at various stages in the version control process (specifically, unversioned and added, but not yet committed) so that developers can easily keep track of the changes they have made.

5. The ability to create a UML diagram for local changes in a PyCharm project provides you with a unique method to visualize the progress you have made, which can also be utilized in documentation and reporting processes.

Chapter 6

1. Testing in software development is looking for inconsistencies and errors in our programs and code. There are several different testing methods with varying levels of abstraction:

   - **Unit testing**: Looking at the individual unit components of a given program
   - **Integration testing**: Looking at groups of unit components while they're working together
   - **System testing**: Looking at the complete software as a whole

2. PyCharm offers convenient commands to generate test skeletons/boilerplate code that usually take time for developers to manually write.

3. Debugging is, in essence, narrowing down and identifying the causes for bugs and errors that have been detected during testing.

4. With a graphical interface combined with various options to track the values of variables throughout a program (inline debugging, watchers, evaluating expressions on the fly, and more), PyCharm allows us to debug our programs in a dynamic way with considerable freedom. The various stepping functions also provide a flexible way for you to step through the program you are trying to debug.
5. Profiling is analyzing the performance of our program and finding ways to further improve it. This can be looking for faster ways to compute a value and identifying a performance bottleneck in the program.
6. With the ability to generate a comprehensive set of statistics on the running time of each function that's executed, as well as a call graph that corresponds to the program, PyCharm helps developers navigate through the different components of a profiled program with ease.
7. Run arrows are essentially a convenient interface for PyCharm users to initiate testing, debugging, and even profiling sessions. Run arrows are distributed among different code blocks in a specific program, so you can utilize the corresponding run arrow to analyze an individual set of commands instead of having to execute the whole program.

Chapter 7

1. HTML is responsible for specifying the actual content and the general structure of a web page. In an HTML file, individual elements are included inside tags, which are a way to specify the type of content each element contains. For example, HTML tags can be `<p></p>` for paragraphs, `<table></table>` for tables, or `<li></li>` for lists.
2. CSS is used to customize the visual aspects of the content of a given web page. A typically CSS file, similar to HTML, contains separate sections, each specifying how an HTML element should be styled.
3. JavaScript is typically used to process and manipulate data and feed it to the HTML code that is responsible for displaying that data. Being a programming language, JavaScript allows web developers to implement object-oriented development ideas, specifically classes.

   JavaScript is extremely popular among web projects due to its ability to integrate and work with HTML/CSS, as well as other web development tools, so well.

4. There are two methods we can use to include a stylesheet or a script within an HTML file while using PyCharm:
    - Manually create a corresponding HTML tag and point it to the stylesheet or the script in question. This method is supported by the code completion features of PyCharm.
    - Drag and drop the stylesheet or the script from the directory tree (in the **Project** panel) directly into the HTML file in the editor. PyCharm will automatically create an appropriate tag pointing to the dropped file.
5. With Emmet, web developers can enter shorthand for HTML and CSS code and it will be converted into actual code. This allows for faster writing and editing. Emmet is not a part of the Python web development process or the PyCharm IDE. It is simply a general toolkit that can be installed and utilized in web projects.

    However, since Emmet is such as powerful and widely used tool, PyCharm offers full support in its web development projects. Additionally, you can configure the behavior of Emmet within PyCharm by going to the general settings and navigating to **Editor > Emmet**.
6. A Python-native debugging session with all of its features (which were discussed in `Chapter 6`, *Seamless Testing, Debugging, and Profiling*) can also be applied to a JavaScript application. This includes breakpoints, stepping functions, and watchers.
    Furthermore, PyCharm creates a local server to execute the web application so that developers can debug their applications in an appropriate environment.
7. LiveEdit is a PyCharm feature that updates the web page for you automatically every time there is a change in the source code. This is quite a useful feature as it will save web developers significant time from having to manually reload a web page. The feature is nicely integrated into PyCharm's debugging functionalities.

Chapter 8

1. Some notable components of the Django framework are as follows:

    - Models, which offer the ability to implement database objects in an object-oriented way. Django also handles the implementation of the corresponding database table for a model in the backend automatically.
    - The admin interface, which is generated solely by Django to have a straightforward yet extensive set of functionalities.

- Templates, which can be viewed as placeholder HTML code. Django views can render a given template while sending information to it so that placeholders within the template will be populated by that information dynamically.

Overall, Django offers extensive support for Python web applications; you can build a complex, fully functional website using Django, even with limited effort. On the other hand, Flask is a lightweight web framework that consists of simple, intuitive APIs that can help web developers quickly implement their ideas in the context of a real web application. However, to incorporate complex features into your Flask web application, you would have to spend significantly more effort than in Django.

2. PyCharm's **manage.py** panel, similar to the **Terminal** panel, is a built-in interface for the functionalities that are typically achieved via calling on the **manage.py** file. By having the **manage.py** panel inside your project window, you can run the server, make migrations, or execute any **manage.py**-specific task without having to switch to another window.
To open the **manage.py** panel, go to **Tools > Run manage.py Task** or use the corresponding keyboard shortcut.
3. Django's admin interface implements administrative privileges for superusers. An example of an action requiring admin access may be to add, change, or delete content in an online blog. Django's mindset is that since most of the work that has to be done to set up admin privileges (and the corresponding interface) is somewhat tedious and repetitive, it should be automated.

After registering and logging in as a superuser, to add an instance of an implemented model within the admin interface, you can simply use the **Add** button within the interface. An important thing to note is that the model will need to be registered with the admin application in the `mysite/admin.py` file (where `mysite` is the name of our Django project).

If the model references another model, the new instance can only be created with respect to either an existing instance or a new one of the referenced model.
4. PyCharm's run/debug configuration feature is used to specify various elements of the execution of a given Python program. With a Django project, we can specify the default page that will be opened up when the server is launched.
5. PyCharm's intelligent code completion engine supports Python, HTML, and Jinja, as well as other Django-specific syntax.

6. Django views and templates are heavily connected to each other due to the foundational design model of Django. For this reason, Django developers usually work on a view and its corresponding template at the same time. PyCharm offers us the ability to switch between views, and their respective templates can significantly speed up this process.

Chapter 9

1. The term **data source** indicates a given method of accessing a database from a server. You can connect to a data source in PyCharm by adding it via the **Database** panel, downloading any missing driver files, and selecting an appropriate schema.
2. Within the **Database** panel, you can manage different data sources for a project (viewing, adding ,and/or removing), configure the underlying database system and driver files, examine the structure of a given database, and open the database console.
3. **Structured Query Language**, or **SQL**, is the most common tool developers and data engineers use to interact with databases, as well as being the standard language for relational database management systems. With SQL queries, you can retrieve data from and submit changes to a database table.
4. PyCharm allows us to write, edit, and run SQL commands within a console. In addition to being able to work with the console as a simple text file, PyCharm users also have the added bonus of code completion and syntax checking when using this console.
5. The table view offers the same options in terms of retrieving and changing data from database tables. As opposed to writing and executing queries in the console, the table view provides a graphical interface that is more intuitive and straightforward.
6. Firstly, we can create diagrams for database objects and any potential relationships between them. These include one-to-one, many-to-one, and many-to-many relationships. Secondly, it is possible to visualize the underlying logic of a query using a diagram, which makes working with SQL commands significantly more intuitive.

Chapter 10

1. Database objects in a Django project can also be accessed and modified in a Python script using various Django APIs. For example, the `Table.objects.get()` method (with `Table` being the name of a database table) will return all the saved database records in a given table, while the `Table.objects.create()` method, along with the appropriate arguments, can be used to create a new record in a database table.

2. Double underscores (__) are used to look up the specific fields of an attribute of a database record. In our example, we use `__year`, `__month`, and `__day` with the `publish_date` attribute to look up the year, month, and day of that attribute, respectively.

3. The `{% csrf_token %}` tag is a way to generate a token that counters **cross-site request forgery** (**CSRF**) attacks. This tag is required in a Django application in any given form element.

4. To set up an SMTP email server, you would need to specify the following variables in the main `settings.py` file:

    - `EMAIL_HOST`: This variable specifies your SMTP host server.
    - `EMAIL_PORT`: This variable specifies your SMTP port.
    - `EMAIL_HOST_USER` and `EMAIL_HOST_PASSWORD`: This pair of variables specifies the credentials for the SMTP server.
    - `EMAIL_USE_TLS`: This variable specifies whether a **Transport Layer Security** (**TLS**) protocol should be used.

   The specific values of these variables will depend on our own SMTP server, be it a custom one or one from an email provider such as Gmail.

5. The Django deployment checklist includes settings and configurations that you need to implement before deploying a Django project to production. This is to avoid unsecured communication and leaked information within our Django applications. Items in this checklist include hiding keys and passwords, disabling debugging mode, listing valid hosts that are allowed to serve the site, implementing logging, and making views for potential errors.

Chapter 11

1. Markdown is a markup language that is most commonly used in README.md files in repositories on GitHub (and other version control platforms). The README.md file that is stored at the root of a repository is displayed on the main page of the repository. It is generally used to introduce other developers to that repository.
2. The data folder is excluded from version control tasks by default. This is because this folder is likely to contain significantly large files that are unsuitable for a typical version control workflow with Git and GitHub. It is common practice to exclude data folders from Git and GitHub.
3. Scientific Mode is on by default in a scientific project. To toggle this mode, you can use the **View > Scientific Mode** option from PyCharm's menu bar. After turning Scientific Mode off in our current project, you will see that the **SciView** panel becomes a floating element instead of a pinned section within our project window. The **Documentation** panel is also hidden away when Scientific Mode is off. Turning it on again will restore these panels.
4. The **Documentation** panel displays real-time documentation data in a dynamic way. Specifically, as you move your caret to a particular method or function call in the editor, the panel will show the official documentation corresponding to that method/function. This functionality is also applicable mid-editing.
5. PyCharm's code cells are a way to separate and execute different portions of a large Python program sequentially. This ability is valuable in scientific computing projects when different sections of a program are run in order, allowing programmers to follow the logic of the program better in an incremental way.

    Code cells in PyCharm are defined by lines of code that start with the following characters: #%%. These lines are treated as standard comments in the low-level execution of Python, but PyCharm will recognize them as code cell separators in its editor.
6. The CSV plugin can display CSV files in two separate formats: raw data (which is typically done by text editors) and in table format (which is typically done by heavy-duty software such as Microsoft Excel). This combined feature allows users to inspect and edit CSV data in a graphical manner within the same software that they use to develop their code.

Chapter 12

1. The **SciView** panel contains the **Plots** tab, which displays all the visualizations that have been generated by a Python program, and the **Data** tab, which can be used to inspect the values of data-related variables.
2. All of the visualizations that are generated by a Python program are included in the **Plot** viewer of the **SciView** panel, where a user can navigate through them with a straightforward graphical interface. Since all of the visualizations are temporarily saved to the panel, the whole program can run in one go. This also allows us to avoid clicking through the Matplotlib plots in order to proceed with the execution, which is the case when executing a Python program from, say, the Terminal.
3. The data viewer of the **SciView** panel supports pandas DataFrames and NumPy arrays.
4. Iterative development is done when a given program is split into different sections so that the logic and execution of that program can be considered in an incremental way. This idea is specifically appropriate for data science and scientific computing tasks, where you need to consider the characteristics of a dataset before applying different processing methods and algorithms.

    Jupyter notebooks consist of multiple code cells, each containing only a block of code that achieves a specific goal. The output of a code cell is displayed immediately after that code cell when it is executed, making the process of debugging easier than in traditional programs.
5. Markdown is a markup language that's typically used for writing README files in GitHub repositories. LaTeX is a word processing system that is popular among members of the academic community, who use LaTeX to write scientific research papers.

    The ability to combine LaTeX and general Markdown text with live code makes Jupyter notebooks a flexible tool in data science projects. Being able to display the code between text explanations of a data analysis process can help readers follow what is being done to that data much more easily.
6. The beginning of a code cell is marked with the `#%%` symbol, while that of a Markdown cell is marked with `#%% md`.

7. Writing Jupyter notebooks in the PyCharm editor addresses the lack of code-writing support in traditional, web-based Jupyter notebooks. In other words, when using PyCharm to write Jupyter notebooks, we get the best of both worlds: powerful, intelligent support from PyCharm and iterative development style from Jupyter.

Chapter 13

1. To collect a dataset, you can do any of the following:

    - Download it from an external source
    - Manually collect it or use web scraping
    - Collect it via a third party
    - Work with a database

2. Git LFS can work seamlessly with Git. Specifically, we can use Git LFS to track the extensions of large files that we want to have version control on, and Git will work with Git LFS to delegate those files when we want to push our projects to GitHub. Afterward, we simply need to use Git in the usual way.
3. An attribute that contains continuous, numerical data often has its missing values filled out with the mean. On the other hand, attributes with discrete numerical data as well as categorical data can use the mode to fill out their missing values.
4. In a naive encoding scheme, you may inadvertently apply some sort of an ordered relation to the data when the original data is replaced with numerical values. With one-hot encoding, we can avoid this problem by creating new binary attributes that contain the same data as the original attribute. However, in an attribute with a large number of unique values, one-hot encoding might greatly increase the dimensionality of our dataset, which is undesirable in many cases.
5. Bar charts can be applied to categorical attributes while distribution plots can visualize numerical attributes, both discrete and continuous.
6. The feature correlation matrix of a dataset can identify any attribute that is highly correlated with the target attribute we are interested in, which can help us obtain valuable insights regarding the dataset.

7. Sometimes, we use specific machine learning models to analyze a dataset and compute the feature importance of each dataset attribute. This feature importance value denotes how important that attribute was during the learning process of the mode, thus indicating some sort of correlation between that attribute and our target attribute.

Chapter 14

1. PyCharm plugins are customized add-ons that can further add to the list of features and functionalities you can take advantage of while using PyCharm. A PyCharm plugin is much the same as a Google Chrome add-on, for example.
2. From the general settings in PyCharm, navigate to the **Plugins** section. Here, you can choose to search for and install specific plugins in the **Marketplace** tab or apply any pending updates to the plugins you already have installed. Then, a complete reboot of PyCharm is required for the installation or the update to take effect.
3. In the same **Plugins** section from the general settings, you can right-click on a specific item in the **Installed** tab. Here, you can choose to either disable the plugin or completely uninstall it from PyCharm.
4. The answers are listed here:
    1. Database Navigator offers a more advanced interface for us to work with databases in PyCharm. This includes data viewing and editing, SQL editing, database connection management, and database compiler operations.
    2. LiveEdit allows for changes that were made to HTML and CSS files in a web development project to automatically take effect in the rendered output web page. This behavior can normally only be achieved by manually refreshing the output page.
    3. CSV Plugin combines the ease of viewing data using the same development environment that our code is in and the graphical interface that can only be found in dedicated applications. In short, it provides a convenient way for us to work with CSV files with a graphical interface.
    4. Markdown is used for editing Markdown code in PyCharm. It renders the output produced by Markdown in real time so that users can adjust their code in a dynamic way.
    5. Finally, string manipulation offers powerful options in terms of editing and manipulating text. This includes toggling between different text styles such as camel case, snake case, dot case, and more.

5. Within a project, you can specify its required plugins by going to the **Build, Execution, Deployment** option in the general settings and selecting the required plugins. From this window, we can add items to the list of required plugins for our current project by clicking on the plus sign in the top-right corner.

    From there, we can specify which particular plugin we have that should be made into a requirement for our project, as well as the actual version number of the plugin. After confirming the selection, whenever the current project is opened in PyCharm, we will be notified if and when a required plugin is somehow not installed, disabled, or has an update pending.

Chapter 15

1. Using the remote interpreter means that our local computer does not need to execute any command, thus saving us some computing resources. Moreover, since the interpreter is on a remote server, other programmers might have access to it as well. In other words, many people have the ability to share the same Python interpreter, which would help with ensuring reproducibility.
2. A macro is a sequence of instructions that are to be executed in order. If you have a specific action that consists of multiple steps, a macro is a way to automate that sequence of steps. In practice, you can create macros to automate code-editing sequences and refactoring tasks, depending on your own work and needs.
3. File watchers, in general, are tools that allow us to monitor the changes that are taking place in a given file and apply a specific action to that file when a change does take place. They are quite useful for automating tasks that are run every time a specific type of file is edited. For example, common files that you can apply file watchers to are LESS files (which can be compiled into CSS) or CoffeeScript files (which can be converted into JavaScript).
4. The Educational Edition of PyCharm is a completely free piece of software that offers a flexible learning platform. This version includes most of the best features of PyCharm, while also including additional functionalities that facilitate interactive learning processes.

Other Books You May Enjoy

If you enjoyed this book, you may be interested in these other books by Packt:

Learn Python by Building Data Science Applications
Philipp Kats & David Katz

ISBN: 978-1-78953-536-5

- Code in Python using Jupyter and VS Code
- Explore the basics of coding – loops, variables, functions, and classes
- Deploy continuous integration with Git, Bash, and DVC
- Get to grips with Pandas, NumPy, and scikit-learn
- Perform data visualization with Matplotlib, Altair, and Datashader
- Create a package out of your code using poetry and test it with PyTest
- Make your machine learning model accessible to anyone with the web API

Other Books You May Enjoy

Mastering Object-oriented Python
Steven F. Lott

ISBN: 978-1-78328-097-1

- Understand the different design patterns for the __init__() method
- Discover the essential features of Python 3's abstract base classes and how you can use them for your own applications
- Design callable objects and context managers that leverage the with statement
- Perform object serialization in formats such as JSON, YAML, Pickle, CSV, and XML
- Employ the Shelve module as a sophisticated local database
- Map Python objects to a SQL database using the built-in SQLite module
- Transmit Python objects via RESTful web services
- Devise strategies for automated unit testing, including how to use the doctest and the unittest.mock module
- Parse command-line arguments and integrate this with configuration files and environment variables

Leave a review - let other readers know what you think

Please share your thoughts on this book with others by leaving a review on the site that you bought it from. If you purchased the book from Amazon, please leave us an honest review on this book's Amazon page. This is vital so that other potential readers can see and use your unbiased opinion to make purchasing decisions, we can understand what our customers think about our products, and our authors can see your feedback on the title that they have worked with Packt to create. It will only take a few minutes of your time, but is valuable to other potential customers, our authors, and Packt. Thank you!

Index

A
add command 148
adding remotes process 147
admin interface
  about 238
  connecting, to models 240, 241, 242, 243, 244
  logging in 239, 240
  superuser, creating 239, 240
  using 280, 281, 282, 283
advanced plugin-related options
  about 414
  custom plugins, developing 417, 418
  plugins, installing from disk 416
  required plugins 414, 416
Amazon Web Services (AWS) 304
American National Standards Institute (ANSI) 260

B
basic code completion
  versus smart code completion 102, 103, 104, 105
blog application
  admin interface, using 280, 281, 282, 283
  building, in PyCharm 276
  Database panel, working with 284, 285, 286
  Django application, creating 278, 280
  Django model, creating 278, 280
  Django project, creating 276, 277, 278
  Django's detail views, creating 294, 295, 296, 297
  Django's list views, creating 287, 288, 289, 290, 291, 292, 293, 294
  queries, creating via Python code 286, 287
branching process 151

C
Cascading Style Sheets (CSS)
  about 200
  code, writing with 202, 203
  need for 200
  using, in PyCharm 205
code analyzer
  specifications 94
code completion engine
  customizing 111, 113
  intentions 115, 116
  item documentation, displaying 114
  Match case options 113
  parameter information 114
  suggestions, sorting in alphabetical order 113
code completion issues, in PyCharm
  about 118
  indexing process 118
  out-of-scope files 119
  power save mode 118
code completion support, in PyCharm
  about 102
  basic code completion, versus smart code completion 102, 103, 104, 105
  customizing 99
  hippie completion 107, 108
  intentions 109, 110, 111
  postfix code completion 105, 106, 107
  use case 100, 101, 102
code inspection 94
code refactoring 120
commit command 148
Community edition
  reference link 19
Community PyCharm
  considerations 76

Counter class
  about 172
  tests 175
cProfile profiling tool 190
CSRF (cross-site request forgery) 300
CSV data
  working with 327
CSV plugin
  URL 411
  using 328, 329, 411

D

data science
  scripts, versus notebooks 396, 397
data source
  connecting to 254, 255, 256, 257, 258, 259
data
  cleaning 368
  collecting, techniques 366, 367
  pre-processing 368
  viewing 335, 336, 337, 339, 340, 341
  viewing, with plots 333, 334, 335
  viewing, with PyCharm's SciView 332, 333
  working with 335, 336, 337, 339, 340, 341
  working, with plots 333, 334, 335
Database Navigator
  reference link 409
  using 409
database objects
  diagrams for 269, 270, 271
Database panel
  working with 284, 285, 286
database
  diagrams 268
  working with, in PyCharm 260
datasets
  about 362, 364, 365, 386, 387
  charts, using 387, 389, 390, 392
  cleaning techniques 372, 374
  exploring 386
  graphs, using 387, 389, 390, 392
  insights, extracting 386
  one-hot encoding technique 375, 376, 377, 378
  problem-specific techniques 378, 379, 381, 383, 384

reading 369, 370, 372
  version control 367, 368
  working with 362
debugger 177
debugging method
  debugger, using 177
  logging 176
  print debugging 176
  tracing 177
debugging, in PyCharm
  about 177, 178
  breakpoints, placing 181, 182, 183, 184
  Debug panel 178, 179, 180, 181
  debugging session, initiating 178, 179, 180, 181
  expressions, evaluating 188
  functionalities, stepping 184, 185, 186
  watches 186, 187, 188
debugging
  about 176
  fundamentals 176, 177
diagrams
  for database objects 269, 270, 271
  for databases 268
  for queries 272
DigitalOcean 305
distributed version control 145
Django application
  creating 278, 280
Django deployment checklist
  debugging, disabling 306
  errors views, creating 306
  keys and passwords, hiding 306
  logging implementation 306
  valid hosts, listing 306
Django model
  creating 278, 280
Django project
  creating 276, 277, 278
  creating, in PyCharm 74, 75
Django projects, in PyCharm
  about 228
  admin interface 238
  creating 228, 229, 230
  debug configuration, customizing 246, 247
  Django models, creating 234, 235, 236

initial configurations 231, 232
manage.py, running 232, 233, 234
migrations, creating 236, 237, 238
run configuration, customizing 246, 247
server, launching 232, 233, 234
structure 230, 231
templates, creating 247, 248, 249
views, creating 244, 245
Django web project
deploying 304
hosting services 304
production-specific settings 306, 307
Django's detail views
creating 294, 295, 296, 297
Django's list views
creating 287, 288, 289, 290, 291, 292, 293, 294
Django
about 222, 223
administrative access, implementing 224, 225
emails, configuring 302, 303
Jinja, using 225, 226
models, using 223, 224
overview 222
templates 225
versus web frameworks 223
vesus Flask 227
docstrings 134
documentation viewer 322, 323
documentation, for Python
docstrings 134
documentation
creating 134, 135, 136, 137
dynamic approach 134
Quick Definition 139
Quick Documentation 138
viewing 138, 208, 209
double-under (dunder) 122

E

emails 297
Emmet 209, 210
exploratory data analysis 369

F

factoring 120
Fetch 150
file watchers 433, 434, 435
files
ignoring 151, 152, 159
Flask
versus Django 227
foreign key 269
fork 148
forking process
reference link 149
Frames section 180

G

Git essentials 144
Git Large File Storage (Git LFS) 368
Git tools
setting up 146
Git
about 146
download link 146
downloading 146
repository, setting up 147
GitHub tools
setting up 146
GitHub
about 146
account, reference link 146
add command 147, 148
branching process 151
commit command 147, 148
files, ignoring 151, 152
merging process 151
pull requests, creating 148, 149, 150
push command 147, 148
registering 146
repository, cloning 148, 149, 150
repository, forking 148, 149, 150
source code, download link 52
source code, obtaining from 51, 52
gitignore
reference link 152
Google Cloud 304

gutter 182

H

Heroku 305
hippie completion 107, 108
horizontal toolbar 181
hosting services
  about 304
  Amazon Web Services (AWS) 304
  DigitalOcean 305
  Google Cloud 304
  Heroku 305
HTML code
  external files, including 207, 208
HTML files
  creating 206
HTML output
  viewing, in browsers 210, 211
HTML source code
  extracting, in PyCharm 211, 212
Hypertext Markup Language (HTML)
  about 200
  code, writing with 200, 201
  need for 200
  using, in PyCharm 205

I

IMAP, setup
  reference link 302
inlining variables 128
integrated development environments (IDEs)
  about 40
  comparison, reference link 19
  philosophy 13, 14
Interactive Python (IPython)
  about 341
  installing 341, 342
  reference link 345
  setting up 341, 342
interface
  creating, for share feature 297, 298, 299, 300, 301
IPython magic commands 341, 342, 343, 344, 345

J

Java Runtime Environment (JRE) 31
JavaScript, using in PyCharm
  about 212
  code, debugging 214, 215
  framework, specifying for applications 218, 219
  live editing 216, 217, 218
  parameters, hints 213, 214
  version, selecting 213
JavaScript
  about 200
  need for 203, 204, 205
JetBrains
  reference link 444
Jinja
  using 225
Jupyter notebooks
  about 386, 387
  basics 347
  editing 348, 349, 350, 351, 352, 353, 354
  in PyCharm 355, 356, 357, 358
  iterative development concept 347
  leveraging 345, 346, 347
  versus scripts, in data science 396, 397

K

Kaggle
  reference link 363

L

LiveEdit
  reference link 410
  using 410
local repository
  setting up 153
logging 176

M

machine learning models 392, 393, 394, 395, 396
macros
  using 429, 430, 431, 432
markdown language, syntax
  reference link 318
Markdown

URL 412
  using 412
merging process 151
Monokai 37
Mozilla Developer Network (MDN) 209

O

one-hot encoding technique 375, 376, 377, 378
open source licenses
  reference link 20

P

packages
  installing, with PyCharm 67, 69
PEP 8 style suggestions
  reference link 98
plots
  data, viewing with 333, 334, 335
  data, working with 333, 334, 335
Post 278
postfix code completion 105, 106, 107
print debugging 176
processed dataset
  saving 385, 386
  viewing 385, 386
production-specific settings 306, 307
profiling
  about 189
  fundamentals 189, 190
  in PyCharm 190, 191, 192, 193
push command 148
PyCharm code cells
  debugging 323
  implementing 323, 324, 325, 326, 327
PyCharm plugins
  CSV plugin, using 411
  Database Navigator, using 409
  downloading 405, 406, 407
  exploring 402
  installing 405, 406, 407
  LiveEdit, using 410
  Markdown, using 412
  removing 408
  String Manipulation, using 413, 414
  updating 408

  using 409
  window, opening 402, 404
PyCharm project window
  about 58, 60, 61, 62
  panels, moving 69, 70, 71
PyCharm projects
  available interpreters, viewing 85, 86
  creating 46, 47, 48, 72
  interacting with 48, 49, 51
  navigating, to windows 62, 63
  project-specific boilerplate code 74, 75
  Python interpreter, configuring for 83, 84
  Python interpreters 76, 77
  Python virtual environment 76, 77, 78
  type, selecting 72, 73, 74
  virtual environments, with interpreters 78, 79
  working with 45, 46
PyCharm scientific project
  advanced features 322
  code, executing 318, 320
  creating 314, 315, 316
  CSV data, working with 327
  CSV plugin, using 328, 329
  documentation viewer 322, 323
  PyCharm code cells, debugging 323
  Python packages, installing 318
  README.md file 316, 317, 318
  Scientific Mode, toggling 320, 321
  setting up 316
PyCharm tool windows 63, 64, 65, 66, 67
PyCharm workspace
  customizing 58
PyCharm's code analyzer
  about 94, 95, 96
  dead code 96
  PEP 8 style suggestions 98, 99
  unresolved references 97
  unused declarations 96
PyCharm's SciView
  used, for viewing data 332, 333
PyCharm, core principles
  intelligent coding assistance 15
  productivity, improving 14
  real-time assistance 15
  scientific computing support 16

streamlined programmer tools 15
visual debugging 16
web development options 15
PyCharm, editor
  about 36
  font settings 38
  line wrapping 39
  options 37
PyCharm, educational edition
  URL 443
PyCharm, general preferences
  about 34
  settings 35, 36
PyCharm, keymap
  about 39, 40
  selecting 40, 41
PyCharm
  about 10, 17, 439
  as Python IDE 14
  blog application, building 276
  Cascading Style Sheets (CSS), using 205
  Community Edition 19
  comparison, reference link 19
  data science with 438, 439
  database, working with 260
  debugging, using 177, 178
  differentiating, with editors 17, 18, 19
  differentiating, with IDEs 17, 18, 19
  Django project, creating 74, 75
  downloading 28, 30
  edition comparison, reference link 22
  edition, selecting for profession 22, 23
  educational edition 442, 443
  external project, importing into 86, 88, 89
  file watchers 433, 434, 435
  future updates 440, 441
  high level, troubleshooting 443, 444
  HTML source code, extracting 211, 212
  Hypertext Markup Language (HTML), using 205
  IDEs, philosophy 13, 14
  installing 28, 30, 31
  Jupyter notebooks 355, 356, 357, 358
  license activation 31, 33
  macros, using 429, 430, 431, 432
  miscellaneous topics 421
  official documentation, using 439, 440
  prices and licensing 19, 20
  productivity, improving 436, 437
  Professional Edition 19
  Professional Edition, support 21, 22
  Python 10, 11, 12
  Python interpreters, managing 80, 81, 83
  Python virtual environments, managing 80, 81, 83
  registering 28
  releases 440, 442
  remote Python interpreters, using 422, 423, 424, 425, 426, 427, 428, 429
  scientific project, initiating 314
  setting up 33
  shortcut customizations 41, 42, 43, 44, 45
  SQL, using 261, 262, 263
  system requirements 28
  table view 264, 265, 266
  unit testing, using 167
  used, for creating unit testing 172, 173, 174
  used, for installing packages 67, 68, 69
  version control 152
  web development with 437, 438
  web pages, implementing 205
Python code
  queries, creating via 286, 287
Python Developers Survey
  reference link 17
Python IDE 14
Python packages
  installing 318
Python Tools for Visual Studio (PTVS) 18
Python web framework Flask
  using, reference link 439
Python
  about 10, 11, 12
  reference link 11
  unit testing, using 165, 166, 167

Q

queries
  creating, via Python code 286, 287
  diagrams for 272
query output

comparing, in PyCharm 266, 267, 268
exporting, in PyCharm 266, 267, 268

R

race condition 175
README.md file 316, 318
refactoring 119, 120, 121, 122, 123
refactoring, in PyCharm
  about 123
  function, exporting to file 132, 133
  inline variable 127, 128
  method, converting to function 131, 132
  methods, extracting 129, 130
  renaming 124, 125, 126, 127
relational database 268, 269
remote Python interpreters
  using 422, 423, 424, 425, 426, 428, 429
repository
  about 147
  setting up 147
runtime types
  obtaining 116, 117

S

Scientific Mode
  toggling 321
Scientific Python Development Environment (Spyder) 18
SciView 16
share feature
  interface, creating 297, 298, 299, 300, 301
Simple Mail Transfer Protocol (SMTP) 302
smart code completion
  versus basic code completion 102, 103, 104, 105
source code
  obtaining, from GitHub 51, 52
String Manipulation
  using 413, 414
Structured Query Language (SQL)
  fundamentals 260, 261
  using, in PyCharm 261, 262, 263
  working with 260

T

tab-separated values (TSV) 268, 329
table view
  in PyCharm 264, 265, 266
tracing 177
Transport Layer Security (TLS) 302

U

unit testing, in PyCharm
  about 167
  Counter class, tests 175
  creating 172, 173, 174
  run arrows 167, 168, 169
  Run panel, used for execution 169, 170, 171
unit testing
  about 164
  fundamentals 164, 165
  in Python 165, 166, 167

V

Variable explorer
  reference link 18
Variables section 180
version control diagrams 159, 160, 161
Version Control panel 153, 154
version control, in PyCharm
  about 152
  add command 154, 156, 157
  branching 158
  commit command 154, 155, 156, 157
  diagrams 159, 160, 161
  files, ignoring 159
  local repository, setting up 153
  merging 158
  push command 154, 155, 156, 157
  Version Control panel 153, 154
version control
  about 144, 145
  scenarios 145
vertical toolbar 181
VMProf profiling tool 190

W

watches 186
web frameworks
 idea 222, 223
 versus Django 223

web pages
 implementing, in PyCharm 205

Y

yappi profiling tool 190

Lightning Source UK Ltd.
Milton Keynes UK
UKHW031419060720
366107UK00010B/2393